Understanding Race, Class, Gender, and Sexuality

A Conceptual Framework

SECOND EDITION

LYNN WEBER

University of South Carolina

New York   Oxford

OXFORD UNIVERSITY PRESS

2010

Oxford University Press, Inc., publishes works that further Oxford University's
objective of excellence in research, scholarship, and education.

Oxford   New York
Auckland   Cape Town   Dar es Salaam   Hong Kong   Karachi
Kuala Lumpur   Madrid   Melbourne   Mexico City   Nairobi
New Delhi   Shanghai   Taipei   Toronto

With offices in
Argentina   Austria   Brazil   Chile   Czech Republic   France   Greece
Guatemala   Hungary   Italy   Japan   Poland   Portugal   Singapore
South Korea   Switzerland   Thailand   Turkey   Ukraine   Vietnam

Published by Oxford University Press, Inc.
198 Madison Avenue, New York, New York 10016
http://www.oup.com

Oxford is a registered trademark of Oxford University Press

Library of Congress Cataloging-in-Publication Data
Weber, Lynn.
   Understanding race, class, gender, and sexuality : a conceptual framework /
Lynn Weber.—2nd ed.
      p.   cm.
   Includes bibliographical references and index.
   ISBN 978-0-19-538024-8 (pbk. : alk. paper)   978-0-19-539641-6 (hardback : alk. paper)
   1. Social stratification.   2. Race dicrimination.   3. Sex discrimination.   I. Title.
   HM821.W44 2010 305—dc22   2009021439

Printing number: 9 8 7 6 5 4 3 2 1

Printed in the United States of America
on acid-free paper

Contents

Preface

FIRST EDITION

In writing the first edition of this book, I was addressing the need for a conceptual framework for evaluating the scholarship on and for teaching about the nature of race, class, gender, and sexuality as systems of oppression—what has come to be called intersectional scholarship. Those of us who had been teaching about the intersections of race, class, gender, and sexuality relied on anthologies[1] or course packets of articles and books to demonstrate that because these systems of social inequality operate simultaneously and are inextricably intertwined, they must be examined together. But even though the anthologies clearly illustrate how truly interconnected these systems are—especially in our individual lives—they fail to provide us with a framework for conducting such analyses ourselves or for assessing the studies we read for their effectiveness and quality in revealing the intersecting dynamics and fundamental character of race, class, gender, and sexuality.

As I began the project, I had doubts that it should be done. The study of race, class, gender, and sexuality had arisen primarily from women of color, from working-class and lesbian scholars who critiqued feminist scholarship for its unstated and unproblematized White, middle-class, Eurocentric, and heterosexual bent. In their critiques, these scholars contended that, to be inclusive, feminist scholarship should be historically and geographically situated—in time and place—and clear about the social locations or standpoints of the groups studied and the scholars themselves. Furthermore, the critiques implied that to claim to have uncovered universal or at least pervasive truths about women and gender from analyses that were based only on dominant-culture women's lives was as problematic as the universal claims of male-centered scholarship that White feminists had so vehemently and correctly contradicted.[2]

---

[1]For a list of some of these anthologies, see Lynn Weber and Heather Dillaway (2000), *Understanding Race, Class, Gender, and Sexuality: Case Studies*. New York: McGraw-Hill.

[2]For an example of these debates in which I participated, see Baca Zinn et al. (1986).

I had to ask myself if it would be possible to construct a conceptual framework for understanding race, class, gender, and sexuality that would not be abstract and ahistorical, would not be a replication of the very model it would be designed to replace. But as more scholarship employed what had started to become a mantra of race, class, and gender but that lacked the fundamental themes and focus of the foundational research, I felt compelled to write a text to clarify those themes.

The first edition was in many ways a collaborative effort that included the feedback and understandings about curriculum transformation that I gained from faculty from across the nation in workshops beginning in the early 1980s at the Center for Research on Women. It reflects the perspective I developed from years of working with Bonnie Thornton Dill and Elizabeth Higginbotham. More directly, in the early stages of work on the book, I benefited from brainstorming sessions and the critical pedagogical, empirical, and theoretical insights of two good colleagues—Elizabeth Higginbotham and Tina Hancock.

But the first edition was primarily developed in the classroom. From 1994, when I began the project, until the spring of 2000, I incorporated the framework and the latest iteration of the text into my classes. My students, graduate and undergraduate, came from a wide array of disciplinary backgrounds. They pushed me to strive for greater clarity and to make my analysis better—to make it consistent with the ideals I claimed to be striving for and to make it useful for the purposes of social justice. Because there were no similar books to serve as models, I tried a number of different formats. My students helped me decide what worked and what didn't. And they always encouraged me to pursue the project.

CHANGES AND ADDITIONS

As the more than two hundred new citations in the second edition of the book attest, information and data throughout the book have been extensively updated.

New Scholarship

The second edition of the book incorporates and references the extensive new scholarship on intersectionality that has been produced in the past nine years.

New Data

Data on social issues and inequality and the time lines have all been updated. The citations include websites so that readers will have access to the latest data as these sites update their information.

New and Extended Discussions of Current Social Issues

These discussions include the 2008 U.S. presidential election, challenges to affirmative action, growing economic inequalities, increasing globalization, multiracial identification, effects of welfare reform, and gay, lesbian, bisexual, and transgender

(GLBT) issues. Also included are discussions of emergent issues in education in the United States: the No Child Left Behind Act, accountability, school funding formulas, de facto tracking, resegregation, single-sex kindergarten through twelfth grade (K-12) education, and GLBT organizations in schools.

Websites

The second edition contains a list of useful websites for researching inequalities, particularly in the domain of education.

Case Studies

For the first edition, the case studies with references and questions for analysis were published separately. For the second edition, the case studies are integrated into the book. Still containing references and questions, the four case studies include two from the first edition, one on men and feminism and one on Mexican immigration, and two new ones, one on Hurricane Katrina and one on the 2008 U.S. presidential election.

SECOND EDITION

Even though I grew up in the tumultuous 1960s and 1970s, no decade in my lifetime has been of greater consequence to Americans than the past one. In the nine years since I finished the first edition of this book, our nation suffered an attack on our own soil, became embroiled in two wars, watched as our government allowed a hurricane to destroy one of America's finest cities and abandoned poor and working-class people across the Gulf Coast, and is now facing an economic crisis not seen since the Great Depression. In this decade, the rich got richer than ever in American history, and the wealth gap between the wealthiest Americans and the rest of the nation grew to unprecedented proportions. Although American workers' productivity rose to its greatest heights, wages remained stagnant, and two-earner households became the norm. By the decade's end, the United States elected its first African American president, who received the largest number of votes in U.S. history and won by the largest margin ever for a nonincumbent president.

As I began to write this second edition, I was overwhelmed and daunted by the task in front of me. How could so much of such consequence happen in such a short period of time? And how could I hope to capture the significance of these shifts for our deeply embedded systems of social inequality? As I weighed these questions, the answer came to me—*I* couldn't, but *we* could. Just as the first edition was the product of my interactions with many students, colleagues, and friends, so too is this second edition.

Maxine Baca Zinn encouraged me from the beginning to write the second edition, mentored me in the process of working on a revised edition, and made important suggestions for improving the text itself. The comments of reviewers, almost all of whom had used the first edition in their teaching, have immensely improved this edition. They are Laurie J. Kendall, University of Maryland, Baltimore County; Laura Gillman, Virginia Tech University; A. Lynn Bolles, University of Maryland; Joshua C. Woodfork, Skidmore College; Loren Redwood, Washington State University; Gust A. Yep, San Francisco State University; Melissa Bronstead-Bruns, University of Wisconsin—Eau Claire; Elizabeth Higginbotham, University of Delaware; Dennis Malaret, Grand Valley State University.

As a graduate student in history and women's studies at the University of South Carolina, Rebecca Shrum helped to create the historical time line for the first edition and has used the book in her own teaching. Now as a faculty member at the University of Wisconsin at Whitewater, she made important contributions to the case studies and brought the time lines up to date. These time lines are invaluable to students, many of whom keep the text as a reference because of the time lines. Just as with the first edition, my friend and colleague Craig Kridel helped me to comprehend the unprecedented changes in education over the past decade, including the accountability movement and the No Child Left Behind Act of 2001. Sharon Hanshaw, the executive director of Coastal Women for Change, whom I met in my research on the Mississippi Gulf Coast, has been generous with her time and her story, the subject of one of the case studies.

Several graduate students made critical contributions to the book. Beth Fadeley combed the literature on every aspect of educational inequality and reform. Her attention to detail combined with an ability to grasp the big picture were invaluable in updating the education section of the book. Christina Griffin and Joanne Stevenson, who work with me researching inequalities in the aftermath of Katrina, created tables and graphs, examined interviews for the Katrina case study, and took on the tedious task of getting copyright permissions. And I owe a debt of gratitude to the many students who have continued to provide feedback on the text as I used it in my classes over the past nine years.

After eleven years as director of the women's studies program at the University of South Carolina, in 2007 I was able to turn my full attention once again to my research and writing when I moved to new homes in Women's and Gender Studies and in the Department of Psychology. The staff in both places, especially Weldon Horne, Paulette Jimenez, and Vicki Lewter, has made the process of writing this edition immensely easier, always ensuring that I had what I needed to get the job done. Likewise, both Sherith Pankratz and Whitney Laemmli at Oxford University Press were enthusiastic and supportive throughout, models of good editorship.

Finally, and most important, the book would never have been done—neither the first edition nor this one—without the support and encouragement of Jean Astolfi Bohner. She sees the value in this work even when I lose sight of it, she guides me through stuck places, she fine-tunes the final product, and she continues to live her life as a model of social justice.

About the Author

Lynn Weber is a professor of women's and gender studies and psychology at the University of South Carolina, where she directed the women's studies program from 1996 to 2007. Her early work on social class, resulting in *The American Perception of Class* (with Reeve Vanneman, 1987), and her work for fourteen years as cofounder and later director of the Center for Research on Women at the University of Memphis marked her as a pioneer in the emerging field of intersectionality.

Founded in 1982 by Weber, Bonnie Thornton Dill, and Elizabeth Higginbotham, the Center for Research on Women was the first in the nation to focus on women of color and on the intersections of race, class, and gender. Over the years, Weber—in conjunction with many scholars associated with the Center—produced pioneering scholarship on intersectionality and served as a leader in innovative teaching and curriculum change. Many of today's leading intersectional scholars were deeply involved with the work of the Center, serving on the faculty and the advisory board and as visiting scholars and curriculum workshop leaders and participants: Maxine Baca Zinn, Bernice Barnett, Patricia Hill Collins, Esther Chow, Cheryl Gilkes, Evelyn Nakano Glenn, Kenneth Goings, Sharon Harley, Elaine Bell Kaplan, Sandra Morgen, Leith Mullings, Judith Rollins, Mary Romero, Sheryl Ruzek, Denise Segura, Kathy Ward, Ruth Zambrana, and many others. For the pioneering research of the center, the American Sociological Association awarded Weber, Dill, and Higginbotham both the Jessie Bernard Award for contributions to scholarship on women and the Distinguished Contributions to Teaching Award for innovative pedagogical work—a dual honor never bestowed before or since.

For over twenty-five years, Weber's research and teaching have explored the ways in which the intersections of race, class, gender, and sexuality operate in individual lives, in communities, and in the broader social order. And she has consulted with many higher education institutions on ways to integrate race, class, gender, and sexuality into the curriculum. One of Weber's focuses has been on classroom dynamics and ways to convey difficult and potentially volatile material so that learning is enhanced. Her current research brings the insights of intersectional scholarship to the problem of persistent inequalities in health, to inequalities in the recovery from Hurricane Katrina among communities on the Mississippi Gulf Coast, and to people displaced by Katrina to Columbia, South Carolina.

Introduction

When I published the first edition of this text in 2000, the new millennium had just begun. I opened the book with a few key indicators of social inequality and a set of predictions about what the millennium would bring:

> As we begin the next millennium in the United States, several trends foreshadow what we can expect in our social, political, and economic future as a nation:
>
> - Both the power of economic elites and the concentration of the nation's wealth in the hands of fewer people will continue to increase, while poverty persists.
> - The racial and ethnic diversity of the population will increase, as people of color become one-half of the population within the next fifty years.
> - Gender relations will become more complex, and diverse family forms (e.g., single parents, gay and lesbian parents, older parents) will become more prevalent as women and men increasingly challenge restrictions on their work, family, and personal lives.
> - Sexual politics will continue to generate controversy as the marketing of sexuality and individuals' desires for exploration and free expression of sexuality confront the reassertion of traditional heterosexual norms.
> - International government and business relations will increasingly shape political, economic, and social processes in the United States.
>
> It does not take a crystal ball or psychic powers to make these predictions and to be fairly confident that they will hold for the foreseeable future. These trends have characterized at least the last fifty years in the United States, and they represent some of the most significant processes for understanding what life will be like for most Americans in the twenty-first century (Weber 2001: 2).

In making these predictions, I did, indeed, not need a crystal ball. Current data suggest that these trends—the concentration of wealth and increase in poverty, the growing complexity of global networks, and population diversity—all persist well into the twenty-first century.

ECONOMIC CHANGES SINCE 2000

- **THEN**: *The seven richest people in the world were U.S. heterosexual White men worth a total of $208 billion dollars.*
- **NOW**: Only Warren Buffett and Bill Gates are in the top seven; the remaining five—all men—are from Mexico, the United Kingdom, India (two), and Switzerland. Together the seven are worth a total of $341 billion, *64% more than in 2000.*

   Of the next eighteen richest people in the world's top twenty-five, two are American, and only one (Liliane Bettencourt of France) is a woman. The remaining fifteen hail from Sweden, India, Russia (seven), Germany (two), Hong Kong (two), Spain, and Saudi Arabia.[1]

- **THEN**: *An average full-time, year-round employed male college graduate over the age of twenty-five earned $72,665, and his female counterpart earned $49,835.*
   NOW: In 2007, he earned $70,401, and his female counterpart earned $50,398. In short, real wages (after inflation) remained stagnant for women and slightly dropped for men.[2]
- **THEN**: *For every dollar earned by full-time, year-round employed White men, Black men earned 73¢, White women earned 72¢, Black women earned 61¢, Hispanic men earned 58¢, and Hispanic women earned 50¢.*
   NOW: In 2007, Black men earned 72¢, White women earned 73¢, Black women earned 62¢, Hispanic men earned 60¢, and Hispanic women earned 53¢. The differences in earnings by people working full time, year round— not including part-time and seasonal workers who are lower paid and more likely to be women and minorities—improved slightly for Hispanics but overall changed little.[3]
- **THEN**: *The U.S. minimum wage was $5.15 an hour, or $10,712 a year for a full-time worker, and 10 million workers earned at, below, or near that wage.*
   NOW: In 2007, the minimum wage was raised for the first time since 1997, to $5.85 an hour. It rose in 2008 to $6.55 and is due to rise in 2009 to $7.25, or to $15,080 for a full-time year-round worker. This change is expected to affect 14.9 million workers, or 11 percent of the labor force, the majority of whom are either White women or people of color, and these workers are highly concentrated in the retail and hospitality industries.[4]

---

[1]Luisa Kroll,, ed. "The World's Billionaires," *Forbes*, March 5, 2008. Available online from http://www.forbes.com/2008/03/05/buffett-worlds-richest-cx_mm_0229buffetrichest.html.

[2]U.S. Census Bureau, *Historical Income Tables—People.* Available online from http://www.census.gov/hhes/www/income/histinc/p24.html, accessed January 2, 2009.

[3]U.S. Census Bureau, *Historical Income Tables—People.* Available online from http://www.census.gov/hhes/www/income/histinc/p38AR.html, accessed January 2, 2009.

[4]Lawrence Mishel, Jared Bernstein, and Sylvia Allegretto, *The State of Working America 2006/2007* (Ithaca, NY: ILR Press, 2007), 190–196.

- **THEN**: *In 1980, the chief executive officers (CEOs) of Standard and Poor's top 500 companies averaged thirty-five times an average American worker's pay per year.*

  NOW: In 2007, CEOs of the Standard and Poor's top 500 companies averaged *344 times* an average American worker's pay per year. The top hedge fund and private equity fund managers averaged more than *19,000 times* the earnings of an average American worker per year.[5]

SOCIAL CHANGES SINCE 2000

- *The total U.S. population increased* by 7.2 percent from 281 million to 301 million. Racial and ethnic diversity also increased, as all non-White groups grew more than did White groups at 5.7 percent. Asians and Hispanics increased by more than 25 percent, and people who identify as mixed race increased by about one million, or 24.5 percent. Projections are now that the United States will be over 50 percent non-White by 2050.[6]

- *An international economic crisis*—the worst since the Great Depression in the United States—has intensified inequalities of race, ethnicity, gender, and class and has shattered the American Dream for millions of Americans, even shaping the outcome of the 2008 presidential election, when the country elected its first African American president, Barack Obama.

- *Accessibility to higher education decreased dramatically.* College tuition and fees more than doubled, and medical care costs increased by 66 percent. But median family incomes remained relatively stable. At public four-year colleges, the net costs of college (tuition, room, and board, minus financial aid) for low-income families increased by 16 percent and for highest income families, by 3 percent. Student borrowing has more than doubled.

- High school graduation rates dropped for all groups. But race, ethnic, and income gaps in college enrollment and graduation rates did not drop.[7]

---

[5]Arthur B. Kennickell, "Currents and Undercurrents: Changes in the Distribution of Wealth, 1989–2004" (Washington, DC: Federal Reserve Board, 2006). Available online from http://www.federalreserve.gov/pubs/oss/oss2/scfindex.html ; Sarah Anderson, John Cavanagh, Chuck Collins, Sam Pizzigati, "Executive Excess 2008: How Average Taxpayers Subsidize Runaway Pay, 15th Annual CEO Compensation Survey" (Washington, DC: Institute for Policy Studies and United for a Fair Economy, 2008). Available online from www.ips-dc.org. Accessed January 2, 2009; see also *Forbes* Magazine and www.demos.org/inequality/numbers.cfm.

[6]U.S. Census Bureau, *Statistical Abstract of the United States: 2009.* Available online from www.census.gov/prod/2008pubs/09statab/pop.pdf. Accessed January 2, 2009. U.S. Census Bureau, *National Population Projections: Table 6. Percent of the Projected Population by Race and Hispanic Origin for the United States: 2010 to 2050* (2008e). Available online from http://www.census.gov/population/www/projections/summarytables.html. Accessed January 7, 2009.

[7]National Center for Public Policy and Higher Education, *Measuring up 2008: The National Report Card on Higher Education* (San Jose, CA: National Center for Public Policy and Higher Education, 2008). Available online from www.highereducation.org.

• *Sexual politics remained contested.* Even as public approval of gay rights measures (marriage, civil unions, adoption) has increased, especially among the young, opposition has intensified as well. In 2008, California voted to outlaw gay marriage after previously ruling it constitutional and marrying more than eighteen thousand couples. At the same time, Arkansas joined Florida by voting in 2008 to ban gay adoptions under any circumstance (single, joint, second-parent); in many states the law remains unclear, especially in the case of second-parent adoption.[8]

These social inequalities in our lives have shaped our past and are increasingly implicated in our present and our future. The unprecedented economic crisis gripping the United States in 2009 deepened the divides between the powerful and the rest of the nation and further increased public awareness of the disparity, which had last been at the forefront of our national discourse in the wake of Hurricane Katrina (cf. Tyson 2005).

The time has never been more critical for understanding how the powerful social systems of race, class, gender, and sexuality operate and for deploying that knowledge to mobilize ourselves, our communities, and our nation toward socially just outcomes for all people. These systems structure both our individual lives and our society. Without examining how they play out in our lives, we cannot fully understand our world or even our own identities. Our race, class, gender, and sexuality are deeply interconnected and shape what we see and what we do not see—in every area of our lives, even the seemingly least important and insignificant areas.

Take tennis, for example. I first began to learn about my own "place" in race, class, gender, and sexuality hierarchies when I entered the world of competitive tennis forty-some years ago. In the early 1960s and 1970s, tennis was a "country club sport," played almost solely at racially, socially, and economically exclusive country clubs by White upper-middle and upper-class men and by growing numbers of women. In 1961, at the age of eleven, I enrolled in free tennis lessons in the public parks in Nashville, Tennessee. Soon I began to enter local tournaments and to win. Over the next twelve summers, I became city and state champion and traveled across the South and to other regions playing—and ultimately also teaching—tennis. I was the first person ever in Nashville who had learned to play in the public parks—the first working-class person—to become a city or state champion, to become the fifth-ranked woman in the South.

What those years afforded me was the opportunity to see things that many White working-class people never see. I frequently stayed with upper-class families

[8]J. Simpson, "CA Supreme Court Hears Prop 8 Challenge" (New York: Lambda Legal, 2009). Available online from http://www.lambdalegal.org/publications/articles/proposition-8-challenged. html. Accessed January 17, 2009; Ramon Johnson, "Where is gay adoption legal?" Available online from http://gaylife.about.com/od/gayparentingadoption/a/gaycoupleadopt.htm?p=1 Accessed January 17, 2009.

who had agreed to house tournament participants. I was in the world of competitive tennis, but it was always clear to me in subtle and not so subtle ways that I was not of it. It was not my world. My clothes were homemade, not designer made. My socks were cheaper, thinner. I had no personal coach. My parents never traveled with me to tournaments. In the country clubs, I could play in the tournaments but not eat in the restaurants—as did most of the participants who were either members of the clubs or of similar clubs with reciprocal agreements. I could not afford to travel to all of the important tournaments needed to attain regional and national rankings.

✳ Yet I was young, and I was determined. I also believed that tennis was a game, where the rules are known, where talent, skill, and effort pay off more than in any other place. Class doesn't matter. Race doesn't matter. Your clothes don't matter. The rules are in place. The ball is either in or out. You win or you lose.

✳ But I came to see that it's not that simple. The better I got, the higher I was ranked, the farther I traveled, the clearer the differences became. Over a period of several years, for example, I played the same player more than ten times in the finals of city, state, and regional tournaments. I won all but the last time we played. But every time we traveled to the next tournament, she and her parents would arrive a day or two ahead so that they could meet tournament officials and influence their decisions about seedings (rankings that determine whom you play). And every time, she would be seeded first—so she played easier matches on the way to the finals. She had lessons, she had coaches, and somehow she had a power that I didn't. It was as if what I did didn't matter. When she finally beat me, I felt as if I had held off the inevitable for a very long time.

I also came to see myself associated with other people who were "outsiders" within the world of competitive tennis. The most elite state tournament was called—not ironically—the "closed" tournament. Regions of the state sent teams—by invitation only—to compete at the most exclusive country club in Nashville, Belle Meade. The year that Chattanooga sent a Black woman on its team, I was slated to play her. And after much ado and a two-hour delay, we were sent to play at another club in the city—alone, the two of us. In 1970 Black people were not allowed to belong to Belle Meade, nor even to play on the courts. Every servant in the club, however, was Black—allowed only in servants', not tennis, whites. Although I had faced great obstacles to success and certainly felt that I was an outsider, I had never been banished. Class and gender circumscribed my presence in the tennis world, but my racial privilege had protected me from the most insurmountable obstacle—complete exclusion.

I was aware of the obstacles that I faced in tennis because of my social class location and because of my gender: At that time, girls and women received smaller rewards for winning, got less press, played at less desirable times, and had fewer options to continue in tennis as a career, either as a playing or a teaching pro. I was also aware of how heterosexual norms and homophobia shaped my and other girls' presence in tennis. Leaders in the sport have always promoted it as a more genteel (upper-class) but also more feminine sport for women—one that leaves players less vulnerable to homophobic accusations of being manly, dykes, or lesbians—as basketball or softball often do. But I had been unaware of the ways that my race was simultaneously benefiting me—by allowing me on the court to begin with. And that is the nature of privilege: It obscures rather than illuminates the unequal power relationships on which the systems of race, class, gender, and sexuality are built. In contrast, to lack power and to experience oppression draws attention to those same relationships.

I began to understand how these complex, pervasive, and persistent systems operate in the same way that most people do. Although I was for many years unaware of the benefits of my racial privilege, I was aware of the negative and limiting effects of gender and social class in my life, because I occupied a social location—a "place" in social life—that tended to illuminate rather than to obscure the impact of my gender and social class. Patricia Hill Collins (1991b, 1998) has described this position as "outsiders within"; others have called it "border crossing" or "migrating." "Outsiders within" occupy social positions in which they gain knowledge of a dominant group without gaining the full power accorded members of the group, as I had done in the elite world of competitive tennis.

I use the tennis example from my life to explain the roots of my interest in race, class, gender, and sexuality and to illustrate several points—that the systems of race, class, gender, and sexuality are pervasive in every aspect of our lives (such as whether or not we win a tennis match), that all the systems are operating at all times and in all places, that they are interrelated and complex.

For a long time I have tried to find the right image to help people understand the fundamental qualities that characterize these systems. Until recently, the best image I could come up with was that of a disco ball—where light doesn't reflect out but in—and where each glass surface represents a different social hierarchy: Beams of light would intersect and represent, say, White women who live in rural areas in the United States, have a high school education, and work full time in retail sales. Or another set of beams of light might intersect and represent married college-educated African American men in the South.

This image has some resonance because the term that most scholars today use to refer to the study of these complexities of social life is *intersectionality,* a term first highlighted by Kimberle Crenshaw to convey how patriarchy, racism, and post-colonialism converge in Black women's lives like roads meeting at an intersection (Crenshaw 1989, 1991). Other scholars have also used images to convey the complex dynamics of multiple identities and systems of inequality. Some have imagined more traditional, even mathematical images of concentric, overlapping circles (Carbado and Gulati 2001) or of a matrix of domination (Collins 1991a, 2000).

But I have never been completely happy with the image of the disco ball: Light doesn't cut through a disco ball; it reflects out. And the image of discrete beams of light intersecting in totally different places does not capture the complexity of the ways that these structures intertwine in our society and in our individual lives. So I continued to search—until one of my women's studies colleagues, a biologist in the medical school, confirmed that a fly might be a much more precise image.

A fly is not only annoying but also easily missed in our much larger world. People say, "if I could be a fly on the wall," when they want to convey the notion that they would like to be somewhere they are not allowed or able to be otherwise, where they would not be seen but where they could see and hear everything that was going on—where they could spy on people. The fly can take in the whole scene from a hidden place without changing in any way the dynamic it is observing.

The fly is in the room, just not a powerful player in the dynamic. In the study of how social inequalities are created and maintained in our world, the fly is the classic outsider-within.

Collins (1986) argues that outsider-within intellectual communities, such as those of Black women scholars, have unique advantages when they choose to use their location to investigate social life:

- A kind of "objectivity" that is a peculiar combination of nearness and remoteness, concern and indifference
- A tendency for people to confide in a stranger in ways they would not with each other
- The creativity that is spurred by being on the margins

Our fly has much the same advantage: It is both near and remote; an observer, not a player; marginal.

The last advantage of outsiders-within that Collins discusses is the ability of a stranger to see patterns that those immersed in a situation cannot see. And it was this notion of seeing things differently that first led me to think about looking for an image of something that sees the world in a more complex way. Flies and other insects have compound eyes made up of many different units, with each unit functioning as a separate visual receptor that forms a portion of an image. The compound eye takes input from all its units to make up the entire visual image. If only one unit's perceptual information is transmitted, the insect perceives only part of the image. But the fly's tiny 1-milligram brain assembles all the transmissions into a single coherent image that is more remarkably detailed, although more softly focused, than the human eye can see (see Berardelli 2006 for an approximation of the fly's vision).

Especially powerful is the fly's ability to spot movement in shadows, to see moving objects when the background is filled with interference and when the level of light in a scene varies greatly. If you take a photo of a person whose back is to the sun, the background is washed out, and the person appears quite dark. This distortion happens because cameras rely on a single level of brightness for their images. But relying on its multiple receptors, the fly can piece together a complete image, can see things in a scene that are partially obscured, that are in the shadows.

In the same way, if we try to make sense of our world without incorporating the input of the many different images produced by the intersections of race, class, gender, and sexuality, we allow ourselves only a distorted glimpse of the larger picture. When we do get the full image, we get a much more complex picture: We can see the ways that the intersections of these social structures shape our lives and our understandings of the world. But the picture is also never clearly and sharply cut. Like the fly's image, there is always a "softness" or fuzziness around the edges because no pattern of social inequality is always one way or the other. Patterns change in different circumstances and in different times. And no aspect of social life is as clear and simple—black or white, race or gender, man or woman, gay or straight—as our popular discourse would often have us believe.

Indeed, race, class, gender, and sexuality are powerful social systems that have structured individual private lives and collective social existence for the entire history of the United States. In this country, founded on the ideal that "all men are created equal," power and privilege are distributed not only along individual but also along group lines so that some groups are privileged—Whites, heterosexuals, upper classes, men—whereas others are oppressed—people of color; gays, lesbians, bisexuals, and transgender people; the working classes; the poor; and women. This tension—between the ideal of individual equality and the reality of systematic group inequality—is a long-standing source of controversy and contest in U.S. society. Yet group inequality persists because the privilege and power of some is directly tied to the oppression of others: Powerful groups gain and maintain power by exploiting the labor and lives of others.

Bill Gates, Warren Buffett, and the Walton family, for example, can amass billions of dollars in wealth *because* millions of people—in the United States and across the globe—earn the minimum wage or less. Exorbitant wealth is available to the few *only* because there are millions of workers whose low-wage labor makes, distributes, and sells products and services worth much more. And the political, economic, and social system in the United States supports the acceptance of this exploitation as a basis for the social order—through tax, inheritance, minimum-wage, welfare, and other business- and labor-related state policies and practices.

Yet the United States is also a nation in which groups that face exploitation because of their race, class, gender, sexuality, ethnicity, and other dimensions of inequality have always challenged oppression in myriad ways. As a consequence of those challenges, significant shifts in power and privilege across group lines have taken place:

- African Americans, initially brought to this country as slaves—one of the most extreme forms of exploitation known to our nation—have struggled and gained full citizenship rights, significant entry into middle- and upper-class social and economic positions, and a major political voice.
- Chinese Americans, initially denied families and citizenship and exploited as low-wage laborers in the building of railroads, have built communities, attained high levels of education, and gained considerable political and economic power, especially on the West Coast and in the Northeast.
- Native Americans, suffering conquest and removal from their own lands, have struggled successfully to gain political rights, to regain stolen lands, to raise their economic status—the lowest of all racially oppressed groups in the United States—and to assert principles of dignity and respect for all peoples and the lands on which they live.

- Mexican Americans and other Latino/as, both immigrants and native born, have maintained culture and family life despite the strains of low wages, often in seasonal and part-time work. Amidst growing antagonism, they have become such a strong political force in American life that Anglo candidates often speak Spanish and target policies (e.g., on bilingualism in schools and immigration reform) to attract the rapidly growing Latino/a vote, which played a decisive role in the 2008 presidential election.
- Gays and lesbians, not long ago, had no legal protection against hate and harassment on the job or in their personal lives. Now twenty states, many municipalities, and the District of Columbia prohibit employment discrimination on the basis of sexual orientation, and thirteen of those also prohibit it on the basis of gender identity (Badgett, Ramos, and Sears 2008). By 2009, gay marriage was recognized in five states and civil unions in eleven. Through the campaign for rights, gays and lesbians have become a greater political, social, and economic force in the United States today.

The interplay of exploitation and the struggle against it have always characterized the relations of dominant and subordinate groups in this country. Yet despite major changes in these social relations over time, the same groups who seized power and established this nation state in 1776—married (heterosexual), upper-class, White men—continue to dominate it politically, economically, and socially.

Despite significant resistance, how do such unequal and unfair power relationships as those between billionaire White men and impoverished women and children of color persist in a democracy founded on principles of equality? How do people view and deal with social and economic injustice in their own lives? What knowledge would empower oppressed groups to challenge injustice in effective ways, so that group membership no longer determines life's options and outcomes?

These are the types of questions that have concerned me in one form or another for most of my adult life and that have driven me to write this book. I began to see these inequalities not only as a working-class girl playing tennis but also as I experienced the desegregation of my all-White Catholic girls' high school in 1964. I pursued answers to these questions over thirty years: as a student in the tumultuous 1960s, as a professor of sociology from the middle 1970s, as cofounder in the early 1980s of a center for research on women that focused on women of color and Southern women, as the director of a women's studies program into the new century, and now as a researcher investigating inequalities in the aftermath of Hurricane Katrina.

What I have learned has led me to join others in seeking ways to analyze social life that

- Are complex, not superficial and simplistic, and that incorporate multiple dimensions of inequality in the same analysis
- Do not seek to rank the dimensions of inequality according to which one represents the greatest oppression or which group has suffered the most

✸ • Empower; further the cause of social and economic justice by providing understanding and insights that lead to effective challenges to injustice

Many scholars have looked at social life by focusing attention on a single dimension of inequality, but increasingly I and others have become dissatisfied with the resulting analyses that were not complex enough to capture the major social relations involved and consequently were not particularly effective when used as a basis for challenging social and economic injustice. When analyses have a singular focus in a world that is far more complex, the conclusions generated and the resulting change strategies are incomplete—much like the incomplete image in only one receptor of a fly's eye.

Often such one-dimensional analyses have the unintended consequence of making one form of oppression (e.g., race or class, gender or ethnicity, sexuality or nation) seem to be the most important, most serious or of making one group seem most victimized. When one group is singled out in this way, the focus of attention moves away from relations of power among dominant and multiply oppressed groups. And oppressed groups often end up vying with each other for attention and for the status of "most victimized" so that they can be seen as most deserving of whatever resources might get shifted to redress inequality. Instead, studying multiple dimensions simultaneously, intersectional scholars generate complex analyses that empower people to challenge and overcome injustice centered in race, class, gender, and sexuality.

In this book, I aim to present a conceptual framework for an intersectional analysis of race, class, gender, and sexuality that helps to improve our understanding of the workings of these systems and to further the cause of social and economic justice. By identifying the common themes in the growing scholarship, I derived a framework that takes account of all four dimensions in a complex way, that does not give primacy to a single dimension, and that provides insights likely to move us toward greater social and economic justice because it deals with broad power relations among groups.

In thinking about the most effective way to communicate the framework, I made several decisions about the style, form, and structure of this book.

STYLE, FORM, AND STRUCTURE OF THE BOOK

Style—Direct But Not Simplistic

To reach the widest possible audience—not only scholars in the academic community but also students and people outside it, including those working for social justice—I have tried to make the writing accessible by eliminating or defining, when necessary, disciplinary language, which often makes information inaccessible. Using straightforward and clear language to convey the subject clearly makes the work more powerful, enabling it to reach a larger audience. Ideas are no less complex and difficult to comprehend when written in clear and concise language than when written in the more opaque language specific to academic disciplines. Clear, direct, and concrete writing is more useful in the struggle for justice. As

Patricia Hill Collins (1998, p. xxiii) states, "Privatizing and hoarding ideas upholds inequality. Sharing ideas through translation and teaching supports democracy."

Form

Liberal Use of Examples and Case Studies I have used numerous examples to illustrate the ideas in the work. Because race, class, gender, and sexuality must be understood within a social context, examples help to convey the meanings of these systems in the contexts within which they actually take their meanings. I use examples from my own life to foreground the way that my understanding of these systems is shaped by my own location in these hierarchies and by my own history. Throughout the text, I use case studies to enable the reader to follow an analysis of the race, class, gender, and sexuality dynamics in particular situated cases. And at the end of the text, I provide case studies so that readers can pursue their own analyses in different arenas from those in the text.

Emphasis on Micro and Macro Systems The examples and the case studies emphasize the simultaneous expression of race, class, gender, and sexuality in individual lives and in broad social patterns. To see these often hidden broader patterns, it is sometimes helpful to start from individual lives—from stories of people's personal, face-to-face micro experiences. But because race, class, gender, and sexuality are fundamentally systems of group relationships, we must learn to investigate and understand larger group patterns of relations—the macro systems—to comprehend even our own individual experiences.

Research by Faye Crosby and others, for example, has demonstrated that only when members of powerful groups see the overall, systemwide patterns of discrimination against race and gender groups in an organization are they likely to believe that discrimination actually exists. In the absence of systemwide data (e.g., about the average salaries or distribution in upper ranks of women and men and of people of color and Whites), individuals' stories of discrimination tend to be seen by those in power as problems stemming from individual traits, such as personality, and not from problems facing the group as a whole (Crosby and Stockdale 2007).

Emphasis on Both Dominant/Privileged and Subordinate/Oppressed Group Experiences Because race, class, gender, and sexuality are interrelated systems of inequality based in social relationships of power and control, I use examples and case studies that focus on the lives of people in dominant, as well as in subordinate, groups. Because the privilege—advantages, benefits, options—of one group is dependent on the oppression—disadvantages, harm, restrictions—of others, privilege and oppression cannot be understood in isolation from one another. Everyone is situated in race, class, gender, and sexuality hierarchies—not just people of color, working-class and poor people, women, and gays, lesbians, bisexuals, and transgender people. The lives of Whites, the middle and upper classes, men, and heterosexuals are equally shaped by their social location along these dimensions. My experiences in tennis, for example, were shaped as much by the fact that I was White and playing a "feminine" sport—and thus was allowed on the courts to play and was not subjected to homophobic attacks—as by the fact that I was working class and female, realities that posed obstacles to my success.

The fact that dominant groups are often ignored in public discussions of race, class, gender, and sexuality has to do with the processes of dominance itself. One way that dominant groups justify their existence and privilege is by promoting beliefs that race, class, gender, and sexuality are not important in determining group location and should not be taken into account when attempting to understand events or processes. This denial is represented in the familiar notions of society as "gender blind" or "race blind" or as postracial or postgender, meaning that the nation has moved beyond the point at which race and gender are relevant. And parallel belief systems exist about class and sexuality.

Women, people of color, working-class and poor people, gays, lesbians, bisexuals, and transgender people all have a special role to play in alerting *everyone* to the workings and consequences of these harmful systems of inequality. So although the experiences of dominant groups are included, those of oppressed groups appear more frequently and more centrally in the text.

Organization

The book is organized into four sections:

- Section I introduces key concepts, identifies and defines the domains and structures of oppression, and provides historical and contemporary evidence of the contests over and consequences of oppression.
- Section II presents a conceptual framework for the analysis of race, class, gender, and sexuality systems.
- Section III provides a detailed example of the application of this framework to the institution of education.
- Section IV includes four case studies to provide opportunities to apply the framework in other race, class, gender, and sexuality contexts.

Education As an Example

Although the conceptual framework is intended to facilitate a race, class, gender, and sexuality analysis in any societal domain, I chose to focus the detailed application of the framework on the institution of education for several reasons.[9]

---

[9]Although I use United States education as an example of how to apply the framework presented in the book, the focus of the book is to illuminate the framework, not to cover all the scholarship that has addressed race, class, gender, and sexuality in education. Many educators have provided theoretical treatments and in-depth analyses of the workings of educational inequality in particular locales, time periods, and types of schools and with various race, class, gender, and sexuality groups. I hope this analysis will encourage you to explore the works of James Anderson, Jean Anyon, Michael Apple, William Ayers, James Banks, Samuel Bowles, Dennis Carlson, Elizabeth Ellsworth, Michelle Fine, Michelle Foster, Paulo Friere, Herbert Gintis, Henry Giroux, Gloria Ladsen-Billings, Cameron McCarthy, Jeannie Oakes, Mike Rose, and many others.

Characteristics of the Educational System

- Education is the first major social institution that most people encounter fully outside of the family.
- Through processes that include ability group tracking, school ranking, standardized testing, and different curricula, education plays a major role in sorting and preparing people for different social locations as adults—their occupations, social classes, earnings, political power.
- Education is the formal institution whose central purpose is to promote dominant culture beliefs about how and why the society is the way that it is, including the rationale for our systems of race, class, gender, and sexuality. The American Dream ideology—the belief that hard work and talent are rewarded and that anyone can succeed—is perhaps the primary rationale employed in the United States to explain and justify our system of inequality. The presence of educational opportunity for all is the cornerstone on which the American Dream rests.
- Education has been a central site of conflict over the gap between its egalitarian mission and its unequal structure, process, and outcomes. It is also a primary institution in which groups seeking to challenge race, class, gender, and sexuality hierarchies have focused their efforts.

Researching, Teaching, and Learning in the Educational Environment

- Despite its central role in promoting and preserving race, class, gender, and sexuality systems, education—particularly kindergarten through grade 12—has received less attention in scholarship that addresses the intersections of all four of these dimensions than have other areas, including family, work, economics, politics, social movements, health, and identity development.[10]
- It is important that those of us teaching and learning in the educational system develop a critical vision of the ways that race, class, gender, and sexuality shape our place and our interactions in this system. Teachers, for example, have power over students because of our location in the social class system, and yet race, class, gender, and sexual orientation affect the extent of the power and the ways that power is played out in classroom environments.
- From an early age, almost everyone has extensive firsthand experiences in educational institutions. Except for the family, people experience most other institutions—work and the economy, politics, law and criminal justice,

---

[10]Extensive literature addresses race, class, gender, and, increasingly, sexuality as they separately manifest in the institution of education. Some combinations, particularly race and class, have also received extensive attention, but less literature explores gender and/or sexuality in combination with race and class than in some other areas.

health care—more intensively as adults. So education is relevant to the largest number of people.

- Education is currently a major site of struggle over race, class, gender, and sexuality equity in multicultural curricula, affirmative action in admissions, bias in standardized tests, performance-based funding, single-gender schools, school desegregation, bi- or multilingual instruction, sex education curricula, and teacher evaluation and compensation.

WHAT'S IN IT FOR YOU? THE PERSONAL BENEFITS OF DEVELOPING A RACE, CLASS, GENDER, AND SEXUALITY ANALYSIS

Race, class, gender, and sexuality scholars study these social systems to further the cause of social justice. But everyone can contribute to the cause of social justice and gain personally from pursuing knowledge about these systems.

The study of race, class, gender, and sexuality systems is not simply about dichotomies such as good and bad, winners and losers, abusers and victims. These systems encompass a vast and complex array of human interactions and human responses that defy simple dichotomies. Awareness of these complexities is critical to understanding the ramifications of race, class, gender, and sexuality in our lives.

Recognizing Limiting Views of Others

Through our participation in a social system that devalues and denies resources and privileges to some people while elevating and rewarding others, all of us in great likelihood have contributed to the oppression of others—whether we are in dominant or subordinate groups or whether we occupy dominant and subordinate group locations simultaneously, as do, for example, working-class, heterosexual, White males and middle-class, Asian American, heterosexual women. When we accept stereotypes—images that are meant to limit and control the lives of a group of people—we contribute to a system that in fact restricts the lives of others. If we accept stereotypes of Latinas, for example, as highly sexual and promiscuous, are we likely to oppose immigration reforms that might end up deporting them and in the process separating them from their children?

Even if our own lives have been restricted by controlling images, we can unwittingly contribute to the oppression of others through the same process. Heterosexual working-class people, women, and people of color, for example, contribute to the social environment that oppresses others when they accept controlling images of homosexual, bisexual, and transgender people as pedophiles or sexual predators or as mentally ill.

When we challenge and reject these stereotypes, however, we confront the "oppressor within" ourselves. In 2007, for example, on the fortieth anniversary of the Supreme Court's historic 1967 *Loving v. State of Virginia* decision ruling miscegenation laws unconstitutional, Mildred Loving, the African American woman whose interracial marriage was the subject of the suit, was approached in her Virginia home by a gay rights group and asked to make a statement in support of gay marriage. For forty years she had lived a quiet life as a devout Christian, never publicly becoming involved in politics. At first, unsure of her position, she studied the issue carefully, spoke with many people, and decided that she could not understand why two people who loved each other could not be married and express their love publicly. One year before her death, at the age of sixty-six, she broke her many years of silence on political issues and endorsed the proposal with a simple statement: "I understand it and I believe it" (Dominus 2008). If Loving had allowed controlling images to shape her thinking and behavior, she would have contributed to the oppression not only of others but also, ultimately, of herself. In confronting and resisting destructive images, we liberate ourselves.

Recognizing the Oppressor Within: Internalized Oppression

Another benefit of studying these social structures is our increased ability to recognize negative or limiting views of ourselves associated with our own multiple social locations. These negative or limiting self-definitions—internalized oppression—come from subtle and not so subtle societal messages about what groups of people are like, what they should be like, and what material rewards and psychosocial resources, such as respect and admiration or devaluation, they should receive. The forces of internalized oppression are most often played out unwittingly in a person's life and may take the shape of many kinds of limitations. A person may deny his or her membership in a subordinate group; for example, a gay's refusing to acknowledge even to himself his same-sex preference or a working-class person's pretending to have a middle-class upbringing. At the least, these compromises of identity and self-definition may lead to a self-image defined by the views of others and therefore may obstruct the process of valuing oneself and one's roots. In the extreme, internalized oppression may lead to severe identity and self-esteem problems and to self-destructive behaviors such as substance abuse or risky sexual practices.

Recognizing the Costs of Dominance

People in dominant groups reap many benefits but also pay a price to maintain their position of power and control. Growing attention is being given, for example, to the consequences that men—particularly White, middle-class, heterosexual men—may pay for a socialization process aimed at maintaining their dominance in our society:

- In part because strength is associated with dominant masculinity and illness with weakness and femininity, men have a tendency to ignore their health and their need for medical attention. Both White men and men of color have shorter life expectancies than women: In 2005 the life expectancy of men at birth was 75.2 years, whereas women's expectancy was 80.4 years (National Center for Health Statistics 2007).

- Because expressing emotions and needs such as fear and sadness, nurturing, empathy, receptivity, and compassion are associated with femininity, weakness, dominant-culture men are socialized to bury or deny their own emotions and needs, as well as those of others. Emotional numbness makes being expressive or intimate difficult and restricts the full experience of life, even though it also enables heterosexual, middle-class, White men to remain emotionally distant from those whose lives their economic, political, and ideological privilege restricts: people of color, the working class, women, gay men, and transgender people (Brod and Kaufman 1994; Kimmel 2009).
- White men commit suicide four times as often as White women (19.7 vs. 5.0 per 100,000 deaths), more than twice as often as Black men (8.7), and ten times as often as Black women (1.8; Kung et al. 2008). Of suicides committed in the workplace between 1993 and 2001, 94 percent were male, 79 percent were White, and the majority were in managerial and professional occupations (Pegula 2004). Since the recession began in 2007, a series of high-profile multimillionaire and billionaire White men who lost vast amounts of money have committed suicide.[11]

Because manhood, particularly for White men, is so tied to expectations for success in the world of work, psychiatrist Gaylin explains that suicide occurs often because of perceived social humiliation tied to failure in business:

> Men become depressed because of loss of status and power in the world of men. It is not the loss of money, or the material advantages that money could buy, which produces the despair that leads to self-destruction. It is the "shame," the humiliation, the sense of personal failure....A man despairs when he has ceased being a man among men. (Gaylin 1992, 32)

Gaining a Realistic Assessment of Our Environment

Another benefit that comes from understanding the forces of social location in our own lives is the opportunity to examine unrealistic personal expectations that may accompany our social location. These expectations distort reality and serve to maintain personal oppression. People in subordinate groups, for example, may come to believe that socially unjust outcomes are an unchangeable reality and may withdraw from efforts to protest injustices through avenues that have at times

---

[11]They include men in the United States such as Thierry Magon de la Villehuchet, an investment fund manager who lost $1.4 billion with Bernard Madoff, who pled guilty to orchestrating a $50 billion fraud (see http://www.cnbc.com/id/28368184), as well as wealthy capitalists in England and Germany (e.g., Kirk Stephenson; see "Credit Crunch Suicide," http://www.thesun.co.uk/sol/homepage/news/article1743349.ece; Christopher Foster; see "Millionaire killed family and himself, police say," http://www.guardian.co.uk/uk/2008/sep/02/ukcrime3; and Adolf Merckle (see "Billionaire kills himself over financial crisis," http://www.msnbc.msn.com/id/28522036).

worked, such as public demonstration. This withdrawal in turn serves to reinforce the political, ideological, and economic status quo. In this way, oppressed group members contribute to the reproduction of the oppressive system and of the limits on their own lives by internalizing—believing and acting on—the negative and restricted views of their lives.

People in dominant groups, on the other hand, may expect a disproportionate share of material rewards, or they may believe that their location in a dominant group will protect them from events such as unemployment that many subordinate groups have historically had to contend with. When these expectations are not realized, anger, bitterness, depression, guilt, and an overwhelming sense of abandonment may result. Unmet expectations for job security in an environment of corporate downsizing, shrinking wages, and mortgage foreclosures, for example, may help to explain why some White, middle- and working-class men have scapegoated—blamed—relatively powerless women, people of color, and immigrants; have opposed affirmative action programs; and, in extreme cases, have targeted people of color for violence (Ferber 1998).

More realistic expectations serve to reduce negative behavior or attempts to scapegoat subordinate groups during times of economic insecurity. Realistic expectations also foster our ability to interact with a diverse range of people, to see their economic and social needs as being as legitimate as our own, and to work together to redress the injustices we face.

Achieving Good Mental Health

Studying race, class, gender, and sexuality also helps us understand how important it is to individual and group mental health that we resist negative images resulting from our locations in these social structures. Gay Pride marches, for example, resist condemning images by affirming and valuing self and asserting a positive group definition.

These public displays of pride are especially critical because they counter the feeling that people are alone in their struggle to value themselves. Isolation renders people vulnerable to the powerful forces of negative controlling structures and images that pervade every institution of society, from families to schools to workplaces. Individuals and groups also affirm themselves every day in less public ways. When people speak up against negative treatment of themselves or of others on the job, they resist internalizing oppression and work toward positive mental health.

WHAT'S IN IT FOR ALL OF US?

The African American phrase "lifting as we climb" refers to the belief that no individual can be truly free in a system that oppresses others. Individual liberation requires that we lift everyone as we seek to improve our own lives. When prosperity is not the result of restrictions on and harm to others, society becomes a more humane place for all. It is difficult to imagine, for example, how anyone can be free in a system in which one's health and welfare depend on limiting and restricting the health of others. And yet our current system does just that. The United

States, for example, has among the highest infant mortality rates and the lowest life expectancies of any industrialized country in the world yet spends 134 percent more money per capita for health care than other industrialized nations (Kawachi 2005; MacDorman and Mathews 2008; Sered and Fernandopulle 2007). Why? In part because we spend our health care money in grossly unequal ways: We have more highly paid medical specialists and more expensive technologies than any other country.

If the wealthy are sick here, they can receive the best treatment in the world. But because our nation treats health care as a privilege and not as a basic human right, as a commodity to be bought and sold for profit, as a benefit of and tied to employment, forty million people in the United States today have no access to health care for many conditions and diseases. Nor are they covered for routine life events such as pregnancy and childbirth, and many infants die unnecessarily as a consequence (MacDorman and Mathews 2008; Seccombe and Hoffman 2007).

In addition, many more people with chronic conditions cannot afford the drugs they need to maintain their health, in part because prescription drugs are also a for-profit enterprise. Consequently, pharmaceutical companies spend two to three times as much on marketing as they do on research (Edwards 2005) and focus their marketing efforts on promoting a relatively small number of highly profitable drugs. These drugs are the newest and most likely to be used over a life-time for chronic conditions such as high cholesterol, asthma, and stomach acid, a side effect of the drugs taken for other diseases, such as AIDS. Out of ten thousand drugs available in the U.S. pharmaceutical market, the fifty top-selling drugs are the focus of over one-half of the advertising (Ma et al. 2003; Fugh-Berman 2008). So drugs that are less profitable because they are needed by only a small number of people or because they are now available in generic form (i.e., the initial patent has run out) are not promoted (Fugh-Berman 2008). And Americans pay close to twice as much for prescription drugs as people in any other country (Anderson et al. 2004).

It is well known that many poor, near poor, and working-class families, often families of color, with little or no access to basic preventive health care are more likely to use expensive emergency room services for routine problems (Jacobs 2005; Seccombe and Hoffman 2007; Sered and Fernandopulle 2007). Hospitals then pass the costs of that care along to those who have coverage, significantly raising the costs for all.

Industrialized countries with guaranteed health care for all have better overall health indicators than the United States. And because access to health care is not tied to employment, recessions in those countries do not make their people less healthy, people are less likely to stay in undesirable jobs just to keep health care benefits, and employers do not have the burden of health costs nor the ability to eliminate them without consequence, especially in times of economic down-turn. In short, health care inequalities provide a clear example of how policies and practices that seek to provide health for all benefit everyone much more than systems like that in the United States today, which pit groups against each other in a competition for money and the health it can buy.

But even money, lots of it, in such a system does not guarantee freedom from constraints. Even the wealthiest and most successful Americans are not free to live and be as they please. Bill Gates, for example, is certainly financially capable of buying anything he desires, including some small countries. His house, however, is a fortress with many of the same characteristics as a prison. He has tried to create an entire social world that is completely self-contained so that he can be "free" to live in comfort and happiness without fear of physical harm or loss of property. What does he have to fear? In part, it may be the wrath of the desperate populations—the poor, the uneducated, the disenfranchised—whose exclusion from the system of opportunity made his excessive wealth possible. He may also fear other business people—professionals, owners, and executives—who may seek even greater wealth by stealing his products, ideas, and plans. It may not have been fear but a growing recognition of the gross inequality between him and most of the world that fueled Gates and others among the super rich to increase charitable giving (largely in stocks but also in cash) since 2000 to amounts exceeding the tax breaks they would receive (Johnston 2004). But we can ask, "Is he free?"

By referring to the constraints on Bill Gates's life, I do not intend to equate them with the restricted options and life chances of, for example, a poor Puerto Rican family struggling to pay the rent and feed and educate their children in New York City. Instead, I wish to point out that the unfairness of the system that privileges Bill Gates and others by impoverishing Puerto Rican and other families will always produce some kinds of constraints—even in the lives of the privileged—because their place of dominance will always be threatened by those unfairly treated.

More important, when all members of society—particularly of a society as diverse as the United States—have the opportunity to contribute to their fullest potential, more efficient, more effective, more creative solutions to problems can be found. When people have an excellent education, basic health care, quality housing, and rewarding work for decent wages, they are prepared to contribute to society. Then multiple cultures can bring diverse knowledge and perspectives to bear effectively on the complex issues facing modern societies in an increasingly interdependent world system.

Understanding the ways in which the systems of race, class, gender, and sexuality operate in both our lives and our society offers many benefits. When we are involved in the pursuit of social justice, we gain a sense of purpose that makes our lives more fulfilling, more satisfying. Our work, in turn, makes society more humane and further enhances our sense of purpose.

SECTION I

◂◯

Laying the Foundation

One of the greatest obstacles to understanding the system of race, class, gender, and sexuality oppression is that its continuation *depends* on ensuring that it is not clearly seen or understood. Just as cable TV companies could not continue to sell access to specific channels for movies or sports unless they could scramble and make the signal incomprehensible to those homes that did not subscribe, so systems of oppression, which benefit some at the expense of others, could not possibly survive unless they were able to scramble and obscure the ways that they accomplish creating and perpetuating that oppression.

Were it not for the success of processes that obscure the existence of the systems of race, class, gender, and sexuality, we would all be clear about how they work, in part because so many current and historical indicators document the privilege of some groups and the harsh treatment and difficult existence of others. Consequently, a first step toward understanding oppression is to make visible the processes that obscure and deny its existence—the signal scramblers—so that the underlying processes can be seen, the signal can be clearly received.

In Chapter 1 of this section, I define key concepts, including race, class, gender, sexuality, oppression, and social location and describe in detail some of the processes that make seeing and comprehending—even defining—race, class, gender, and sexuality oppression difficult. Because these processes of oppression manifest differently in different social arenas, I also discuss the major social domains—ideological, political, and economic—in which race, class, gender, and sexuality systems are generated and maintained.

To give some general markers that signal the extent of oppression for specific groups, Chapter 2 includes (1) a historical time line marking points in which basic rights were secured, gains made, and setbacks experienced by groups and (2) recent data indicating the current status of groups on wealth, poverty, education, and political representation.

CHAPTER 1

✦◯

Defining Contested Concepts

To analyze race, class, gender, and sexuality, it is necessary to characterize what we mean by the terms. But because their meanings are in fact contested and often obscured, defining these social systems is not a simple task. This chapter offers working definitions of key terms, discusses some of the processes that operate to obscure these systems, and describes social arenas in which they are manifested differently—in political, economic, and ideological institutions.

RACE, CLASS, GENDER, AND SEXUALITY AS COMPLEX SOCIAL SYSTEMS

Race, class, gender, and sexuality are social systems, patterns of social relationships among people that are

- *Complex*   Intricate and interconnected
- *Pervasive*   Widespread throughout all societal domains—for example, in families and communities, religion, education, the economy, government, the law and criminal justice, the media
- *Variable*   changing, always transforming
- *Persistent*   prevailing over time and across places
- *Severe*   serious in their consequences for social life
- *Power Based*   hierarchical, stratified (ranked), centered in power— benefiting and providing options and resources for some by harming and restricting options and resources for others

Stated otherwise, race, class, gender, and sexuality are systems of oppression. *Oppression* exists when one group has historically gained power and control over valued assets of a society (e.g., wealth, information, and political power) by exploiting the labor and lives of other groups and then by using those assets to secure its position of power into the future. In exploitative relationships, the welfare of one group of people—the exploiters, the dominant group—*depends* on the poverty and efforts of another—the exploited, the subordinate group. Exploitation is thus a *power relationship* resulting from and reinforcing the unequal distribution of productive assets in society (Wright 2008). The unequal distribution of society's valued opportunities and resources is repeatedly reinforced in daily life, and its fundamental unfairness is masked in a pervasive belief system—an ideology, a set of stereotypes—that interprets the inequalities as a "natural" outcome of each group's presumed superior or inferior traits.

When we first meet people, we often try to get an idea of who they are by asking questions that situate them in time and place, as well as in meaningful social categories. We ask "Where are you from?" often meaning geographic location, and "What do you do?" often meaning work or occupation. But we actually use these questions as indicators of more important social and cultural experiences and background that we associate with time, place, and work. When we meet people, we also situate them in other critical social locations—race, class, gender, and sexuality—that are powerfully embedded in all our institutions, that touch every aspect of life, and that suggest other commonalities of experience and background. *Social location* refers to an individual's or a group's social "place" in the race, class, gender, and sexuality hierarchies, as well as in other critical social hierarchies such as age, ethnicity, and nation.

Although the meaning and experience of race, class, gender, and sexuality change over time and place, they also have a persistence and resilience that leads people to believe that they will always be with us. Perhaps the central principle undergirding these hierarchies and the primary reason they persist over time is that they are intersecting systems of *power relationships.* One way of defining power is the capacity to achieve one's aims despite resistance. Groups remain dominant in a system over time because their position enables them to continue no matter what the will or aims of others might be: They have power. Lani Guinier and Gerald Torres (2002) describe the ways these systems operate, much like a zero-sum game. Games have winners and losers, and the powerful are those who have the advantage on three fronts, the three faces of power:

- The power to design or manipulate the rules
- The power to win the game through force or competition
- The power that winners have to name the game, to tell the story about the game, its significance, and why they won—in modern slang, to spin the story

Who makes the rules that give some groups privilege? Those with power in our political, economic, and ideological systems. Who wins the game? Those whom the rules have advantaged. Who gets to put the spin on the game–who names the game and interprets its outcome? The winners.

Heterosexism: An Example

Heterosexism, like racism, classism, and sexism, is a system of power relations. Heterosexuals set the laws and acceptable practices governing adult intimate life ("the rules"), the advantages that go to those who follow the rules ("the winners"), and the rationale for the hierarchy that justifies the unequal treatment ("the spin"). In our culture, heterosexual marriage was long ago established as the standard and legally privileged status against which all other ways of conducting adult intimate life are measured ("the rules"). Advantages accrue to those who conform ("the winners"): the right to marry, to adopt children, to receive survivor benefits from Social Security, to file taxes as married couples, to receive health insurance from a spouse's employer, to inherit from one's partner, and to claim a legal family connection in medical emergencies. To be sure, significant changes have taken place in the legal status of gay people (e.g., twenty states, the District of Columbia, and many municipalities now prohibit employment discrimination on the basis of sexual orientation) and in public attitudes about alternative sexualities, especially among the young (Arthur Levitt Public Affairs Center 2006; Badgett et al. 2008). Still, most people who depart from the sexual standards set by those in power are denied full citizenship rights, making it difficult for them to create and to maintain families at all.

These restrictions, however, do not affect all gay, lesbian, bisexual, or transgender people in the same way. Some middle- and upper-class White men and women, for example, have more political, economic, and social resources to construct families in spite of legal obstacles and social disapproval. Class and race privilege give White upper-middle-class, educated gay men and women the options of suing if employers discriminate; of living without spousal insurance; of establishing estates with the help of estate attorneys who can find other tax shields for their monies; of traveling to other cities, states, or countries that may allow adoption or marriage and paying the costs incurred; of living well without a partner's Social Security.

The rationale for the unequal treatment of gay, lesbian, bisexual, and transgender people is provided in the interpretation that the powerful place on them by defining them variously as "other," "deviant," "sexual predators," "sinners," as less than fully human—not deserving of full citizenship status ("the spin"). And because they are defined as not "normal," gay, lesbian, bisexual, and transgender people have only recently begun to appear in popular culture texts—books, videos, films, television shows, advertisements—in ways that are less stereotypical, as was the case in such popular TV shows as *Will and Grace* or *Ugly Betty* (Gay and Lesbian Alliance Against Defamation [GLAAD] 2009). The advertising industry has even coined a term, *gay vague*, for ads constructed to appeal to gay consumers—a market estimated to have had $690 billion in buying power in 2007—without overtly challenging heterosexual dominance (HarrisInteractive 2009; Wilke and Applebaum 2001).

This third arena of power, "the spin," is carried out in the world of ideas through the media, the knowledge experts, and the image makers. These sources provide us with explanations and interpretations intended to help us make sense of our everyday lives, including hierarchies of power and privilege, and thereby either help to create and reinforce or to challenge and transform the systems of race, class, gender, and sexuality. They can encourage us to feel comfortable with harsh treatment of some people by presenting a pervasive belief system—an ideology, a set of stereotypes— that interprets the treatment as a "natural" outcome of a group's presumed inferior traits.

WHY RACE, CLASS, GENDER, AND SEXUALITY?

When we examine these four systems of social inequality—race, class, gender, and sexuality—and recognize their interrelationships as the previous example of heterosexism's interaction with race, class, and gender suggests, you might ask which of the four is most important. And what of other forms of oppression? By focusing on these four dimensions, I do not intend to suggest that these are the only hierarchical dimensions of inequality that matter in social life. People face oppression along many other dimensions—disability, region, nation, ethnicity—and those patterns of relationships are also hierarchical and intersect with race, class, gender, and sexuality. In different times and places, and with regard to particular issues, they may carry more significance than the four dimensions examined here.[1]

But race, class, gender, and sexuality are given priority for several reasons:

- This book focuses on inequalities in the context of the United States. And in the United States, race, class, gender, and sexuality each have such a significant history as powerful organizers of social hierarchy that they are deeply embedded in our most important institutions: law and justice, education, religion, family, economy.
- Subordinate groups have struggled in large-scale social movements of resistance against these oppressions in legal, educational, religious, family, economic, and other institutions for many years. As a consequence, each of these inequalities is quite visible in the public consciousness now in the United States. In recent years, for example, the persistent and rapidly growing social movements of gays, lesbians, bisexuals, and transgender people for social power and self-determination has precipitated significant social change and enhanced attention from the political, religious, and other realms, including a vastly expansive scholarship on the topics (cf. Bernardi 2009 D'Emilio 2002; Freedman 2006; Gamson and Moon 2004).

---

[1]Some consider age to be a dimension of structured inequality that rivals the four mentioned here. Although it is certainly true that rights and responsibilities, options and opportunities are structured differently for different age groups, unlike other dimensions of inequality, the power and the oppression that accompany different ages can be overcome simply by living long enough (e.g., in the case of youth). A more fruitful way to consider age is as a birth cohort or generation (e.g., baby boomers, generation Xers), as people who share the major events and structures of inequality throughout a lifetime because they were born and raised at the same time. Events like the Great Depression, the recent economic collapse, wars, and technological advances, shape the world views of people of the same age as they live through them. And race, class, gender, sexuality, ethnicity, and nation, for example, structure the power relations that characterize how each of those broad social events are experienced. It is important, therefore to consider age, birth cohort, time period—generation—to identify the context within which inequalities of race, class, gender, and sexuality are played out.

- Given the visibility and the fundamental importance of these dimensions at this time in the United States, this analysis of race, class, gender, and sexuality and its extended application to education in the United States should give you the tools—the conceptual framework and the questions to ask—to analyze other dimensions of inequality, as well.

The primary purpose of this book is to deepen our understanding of the intersections of race, class, gender, and sexuality and to demonstrate how to analyze those intersections in specific times and places. But the framework should encourage you to look beyond the most clearly visible dimensions of inequality in any arena, to look for more subtle expressions of power dynamics, and to seek out the structures and mechanisms that undergird oppression in all areas of society.

PROCESSES THAT OBSCURE RACE, CLASS, GENDER, AND SEXUALITY

Race, class, gender, and sexuality shape everyone's life every day. Yet these systems are often hard to see, to understand, even to define. In U. S. society, these constructs are typically defined by referring to social groups selected for unequal treatment and ranked according to

- Race: Ancestry and selected physical characteristics, such as skin color, hair texture, and eye shape[2]
- Class: Position in the economy: in the distribution of wealth, income, and poverty; in the distribution of power and authority in the workforce
- Sex/Gender: Biological and anatomical characteristics attributed to males and females (sex); culturally and socially structured relationships between women and men (gender)
- Sexual Orientation: Sex of partners in emotional-sexual relationships

Yet these definitions tend to reify the categories, to make them seem universal, seem tied to a presumably stable biology, rigid and unchanging—characteristics quite the opposite of the way the framework in this book presents them. One of the challenges of this book is to present a more complex picture of these systems and their intersections so that we can see their persistence and significance in shaping social life and their shifting nature over time and space.

In fact, the reasons that these intersecting systems of oppression are so difficult to understand and to define are contained in the very nature of the systems themselves:

---

[2]Ethnicity, a concept closely related to race, is conceived as shared culture based on nationality/national origin, language, religion, and, by some definitions, also race. I address ethnicity in the context of race because the Black-White divide in the United States has most powerfully shaped the terrain on which ethnic groups—people of color (Asians, Latinos, Arabs, Natives) and Whites (Irish, Italians, Jews, Poles)—have historically been viewed and treated (cf., Brodkin 2004; Ignatiev 1995; Perlman 2005).

Every social situation is affected by societywide historical patterns of race, class, gender, and sexuality that are not necessarily apparent to the participants and that are experienced differently depending on the race, class, gender, and sexuality of the people involved.

Typically, the beneficiaries of long-standing patently unfair practices that routinely reinforce social injustice, such as giving special preference in college and law school admissions to the sons and daughters of wealthy alumni, do not come away viewing the practices as unfair, do not associate them with affirmative action, and may in fact view them as fair and even desirable practices (Crosby and Stockdale 2007; Karabel 2005; Sturm and Guinier 1996). To those who occupy positions of privilege, that is, who benefit from the existing social arrangements, the fact that their privilege is dependent on the unfair exclusion of or direct harm to others is obscured, unimportant, practically invisible.

Although I remember, for example, when my all-White girls' high school desegregated in the 1960s, the event meant very little to me at the time. I had never even seen the segregated African American schools whose inferior conditions had made school desegregation such an important goal in the African American community. But for my new African American schoolmates, the unfairness of racial segregation was painfully apparent, and being the first African Americans to attend my school was most certainly a critical life event for them.

Systemic patterns of inequality can also be obscure to those disadvantaged by them because they lack access to information and resources that dominant groups control. So, at the same time that I experienced my high school's integration as a nonevent because of my racial privilege, I became aware of the significant restrictions on my life imposed by my gender.

I rode to school on a bus with other students from my end of town who had gone to elementary school with me. The bus stopped at the three small Catholic girls' high schools and the single large Catholic boys' high school. Every day on the bus, my good friend Mickey O'Hara and I, who had competed with each other academically in elementary school, compared notes about what we were learning in high school. As the days, weeks, and years went on, it became clear that Mickey was being taught much more than I. The boys in college prep courses went further in math, read more in English, had more science. They scored better on standardized tests. They had better facilities, books, and teachers. Why? In large part because each parish was required to contribute money to the boys' high school for each boy in the parish who attended the school. And for the girls? Nothing. So the girls' schools ran on tuition alone; the boys' ran on subsidies from the parishes—a fact I didn't learn until years later. My brother's education cost my parents far less and provided him much more, a discrepancy that few saw as troublesome because the school system was organized to prepare boys to provide materially for their families and to prepare girls to have children and to raise them in two-parent, heterosexual nuclear families.

These assumptions about the fundamental aims of our education—to learn to enact gender-specific roles in heterosexual marriages and in the labor market—were profound. They shaped every aspect of our lives–from proms to course content, from sports to labs. The girls' schools provided the homecoming queens and the cheerleaders; the boys' school, the athletes. The girls' schools provided the home economics and typing labs; the boys' school, the physics course.

So in my position as a girl in a gender-stratified school system, I had been aware of many of the differences in education between the boys' and the girls' schools but was unaware of the funding practices that supported them and would have been unable to do much about the practices even if I had known. Likewise, law school applicants who lack class and family privilege may never know or may be unable to change the fact that their chances for admission were reduced by the preferences given to the children of alumni. People often come away from a discriminatory practice not knowing whether or how the discrimination took place—even when they are the victims of the injustice. Even though those who suffer the unfairness are more likely to see it, we all participate in discriminatory systems *with and without* knowing that or how we have done so.

The dominant ideologies of a "color-blind," "gender-blind," "classless," and "sexually restrained" society obscure oppression and its history.

The dominant ideology (belief system), particularly about race and gender but also about social class and sexuality, that pervades the media and dominates public policy is that the United States is or should be a "gender-blind," "race-blind," "classless," and "sexually restrained" society. These ideologies are presented as "neutral" perspectives suggesting that a "gender-blind" or "postgender" or "race-blind" or "postracial" society is the preferred outcome of any social policy that seeks to address pervasive inequalities—the goal to strive for—as well as the way that policies designed to achieve equity should operate. Although on their surface these ideologies sound much like the arguments made by antiracists in the civil rights movement of the 1960s, they are currently aimed at obscuring the privilege that accompanies Whiteness and maleness rather than at seeking to transform them from an identity of social superiority to one of social responsibility (Bonilla-Silva 2003; McDermott and Samson 2005).

We do not hear the term *class-blind* used in public discourse because the dominant ideology of class differs from race and gender ideology. The classless ideology does not assert that even though classes are biologically determined, we should strive not to attend to them—as it does with race and gender. Although it recognizes great differences in income, wealth, and other valuable resources, it asserts that classes—either as biological groups or as social groups in a relation of oppression and conflict with one another—simply do not exist (for a review see Lareau 2008). Instead, economic positions in the United States are presumed to be earned in a free and open "meritocratic" society in which hard work and talent pay off—the land of the American Dream. And it is those differences in hard work and talent—not oppression—that are offered as the core causes of the obvious, extreme economic differences present in the population.

The dominant ideology of sexuality is one of restraint, with the alleged sexual practices of the heterosexual majority taken as the moral norm against which the sexual orientation and practices of people who are gay, lesbian, bisexual, and transgender[3] are seen as deviant and dangerous. The dominant ideology of sexuality is not that we should be blind to differences, that they should not matter or do not exist, but rather that they should be denied, contained, or ignored—neither discussed in public nor condoned. The military's policy toward homosexuals of "don't ask, don't tell," implemented since 1994, captures the dominant ideology of sexual restraint well: "We won't ask and you shouldn't tell, because if you tell you will be punished."

Think about these ideologies. Why would we use *denial* and *blindness* as bases for social policy and the assessment of moral rightness? To do so implies that we seek not to see and therefore not to know. It suggests that ignorance is a preferred foundation for social policy—an anti-intellectual stance that has no valid place in the modern academy, where we seek knowledge, truth, and wisdom.

Yet these stances on race, class, gender, and sexuality prevail for at least two basic reasons:

- Because members of privileged groups are not disadvantaged and, in fact, benefit from these systems, people in these groups find dismissing the claims of oppressed groups as unreal relatively easy.
- In our education and in mass media, we do not systematically learn about the totality of the experiences of subordinate groups.

The experiences of oppressed groups are either excluded or distorted in our society by being presented in limited and stereotyped ways: gays, lesbians, bisexuals, and transgender people solely as people who engage in particular sexual acts or wear sex-inappropriate clothes; African Americans as slaves or protesters in the civil rights movement in the 1960s, as sports heroes and music stars, and as welfare moms and criminals; Latino/as as illegal aliens swelling the schools and welfare rolls; Native Americans as unassimilable, alcoholic reservation dwellers benefiting from gambling-driven windfalls; hard-working Asian Americans as clannishly living in Chinatowns and overcoming all obstacles to rise to educational and employment heights, especially in math and science. In short, we typically learn of these groups only as they can be seen to present "problems" or threats to the dominant group or as exceptions to the "normal" way of life.

We rarely learn of the common ground in our experiences or of the ways that the lives and struggles of oppressed groups can and have benefited the entire society. The Civil Rights Act of 1964, for example, although fought for and won primarily by African Americans, expanded protections against discrimination to

---

[3]*Transgender* is a term increasingly used by people whose gender expression (e.g., masculine, feminine) is deemed inappropriate for their biological sex (e.g., male, female). As Leslie Feinberg (1996, xi) states, "Because it is our entire spirit—the essence of who we are—that doesn't conform to narrow gender stereotypes many people who in the past have been referred to as cross-dressers, transvestites, drag queens, and drag kings today define themselves as trans*gender*."

women, religious minorities, and all racial groups. In a similar vein, Lani Guinier and Gerald Torres (2002) compare the experiences of women and people of color to the miner's canary. Miners used to take a canary into the mines with them to signal whether or not the air was safe to breathe. If the canary thrived, the atmosphere was safe. If the canary became sick or died, the atmosphere was toxic.

Members of oppressed groups—people of color, poor and working classes, women, gays, lesbians, bisexuals, and transgender people—are like the canary: They signal when the atmosphere is not healthy. When oppressed groups experience high death rates from lack of access to medical care; high infant mortality rates; increasing high school dropout rates; declining college, graduate, and professional school attendance rates; high unemployment and poverty rates; and declining standardized test scores, something is wrong with the atmosphere—not with the canary. Trying to "fix" the canary or blaming the toxic atmosphere on the canary makes the atmosphere no less toxic to everyone in it. Learning about the atmosphere through the experience of the canary, we can develop a broader and healthier assessment of societal processes that affect us all—international relations, family life, and the workings of the economy, of education, of religion.

These systems are never perfectly patterned; some people have experiences that defy the overall patterns.

In my high school, some students in the college preparatory track never went to college; some home economics students did. But rags-to-riches stories, popular in America, are always more complex than we are often led to believe. For example, in "A Darker Shade of Crimson: Odyssey of a Harvard Chicano," Ruben Navarrette, Jr., a twenty-four-year-old Mexican American man, tells of how he went from valedictorian of his class in a school system with a 50 percent dropout rate for Hispanics to Harvard University and then to the University of California Los Angeles graduate school in education. He describes the guilt, pain, and isolation he felt in graduate school:

> White student colleagues smile at me as they tell me, implicitly, that people like my parents, like my old friends, like the new girlfriend back home whose immeasurable love is sustaining me, are incompetent and unintelligent and unmotivated and hopeless. They wink and nod at me, perhaps taking comfort that I am different from the cultural caricature that they envision when they hear the word "Chicano." (Navarrette 1997, 278)

Or, to take another example: President Barack Obama, rising above barriers of race and class. His is certainly the most profound upward-mobility story of the twenty-first century. Raised by a single parent, his mother, and then after her death by his maternal grandmother, he became the first Black editor of the *Harvard Law Review* and the first African American president—the top leadership position in the United States, arguably in the world. As he moved from relative obscurity on the national scene to become the Democratic nominee and then the president, many hailed his candidacy as "postracial," suggesting that the United States had moved beyond race as a determining factor in political if not economic life because he appealed to Whites as well as to people of color. But as the controversy over the incendiary statements about America made by his former pastor, Reverend Jeremiah Wright, revealed, his candidacy was anything but "postracial." Largely stoked by the millions of showings of a single brief segment on YouTube and television news shows, a sermon by Wright presenting a stereotypical image of an angry Black man—one that has stoked White fears for centuries—became the association intended to derail Obama's candidacy (http://abcnews.go.com/blotter/story?id=4443788).

Obama responded in a manner that disarmed many of his critics because he employed his unique perspective as a mixed-race American with extensive experience abroad—his intersectional perspective—to present a major speech on race in America that identified with the struggles of both Whites and African Americans, not diminishing the struggles of most White people in America while asserting the ongoing structural and personal injuries of racism (Obama 2008). His speech was praised by people and commentators from many backgrounds and political orientations, in no small part because he projected a message that he had honed—as a boy and as he moved into ever more powerful circles—in his mixed-race, multicultural, woman-centered, and cross-class life. The message was one of understanding and empathy for others projected in a demeanor of calm reserve, not of anger or threat.

His biography and campaign—for those willing to take a close look—show that neither his political stance nor his many achievements came because we are in a postracial America. One has only to consider Obama's own struggles for identity in his sometimes troubled youth as a mixed-race White/African American in Hawaii and Indonesia, and at Harvard and as a community organizer on the south side of Chicago to see that his position in America today did not come because racism had been overcome but because it had not (Obama 1995, 2006). And making sense of the world through his "outsider-within" location has helped him negotiate the increasingly diverse and globally interconnected relationships that define our world today.

So even though a pervasive pattern of oppression exists, individual exceptions also exist. And these exceptions tend to reinforce the views of dominant groups that the system is not oppressive but is indeed open and fair, because those who have benefited from the current arrangements have difficulty seeing the ways in which the exclusion of others has made their inclusion in the successful mainstream possible.

These systems are not immutable; they change over time and vary across different regional locations and different cultural milieus.

Race, class, gender, and sexuality are not fixed systems or traits of individuals. Because they are negotiated and contested every day in social relationships, they change over time and in different places. Many of the working-class White girls who were my high school classmates, for example, did not attend college immediately after high school but attended college later, in the 1970s and 1980s, after marrying and having children. Changing economic conditions no longer allowed their husbands to be the sole support of the family; changing family conditions meant that many of their marriages ended in divorce; and changing education and labor market conditions meant that there were significantly increased opportunities for women. Thus what race, class, gender, and sexuality meant for the lives of White, heterosexual, working-class women had changed considerably from the 1960s to the 1980s.

Because of the pervasive, persistent, and severe nature of oppressive systems, people resist subordination and in their resistance can develop positive skills, talents, and abilities. These skills fortify them to survive and to challenge more effectively the very system designed to limit their opportunities to use their skills, talents, and abilities.

The fact that no parish resources were sent to the all-girls schools in my community meant, for example, that the parishes could funnel all their resources into the education of their boys—to fortify their ability to succeed and to bolster the economic base of the patriarchal nuclear family. Yet because we were segregated, I was able to play leadership roles and participate in activities that girls in coeducational schools mostly could not play. In much the same way, segregated African American schools, Native American reservation schools, and barrio schools—typically inferior in resources, per-pupil expenditures, physical facilities, and teacher preparation—have become fertile ground for the development of future leaders and activists who effectively challenge the systems themselves.

Because members of oppressed groups can withstand oppression and may even succeed while facing it, dominant group members often take that success to mean that the oppression either does not exist or is not severe. But it is not the oppression itself that creates the success that some people experience: It is the human will to resist oppression and overcome obstacles that makes this success possible. Resistance in individual and collective forms pressures the dominant system to change and transform over time. If anything, because so many people are willing to resist, President Obama was able to connect powerfully to a wide cross-section of America. He asked people to believe that their resistance could bring about fundamental change, and his many new strategies of reaching people (employing the Internet, text messaging, organizer training, etc.) engaged a decisive segment of the United States in resistance to the status quo.

DOMAINS, INSTITUTIONS, AND LEVELS OF OPPRESSION

Domains and Associated Institutions

Relationships of dominance and subordination along race, class, gender, and sexuality lines are produced, reinforced, challenged, and changed in many arenas or social domains. Although historically employed to characterize the domains of class oppression (cf. Poulantzas 1974; Vanneman and Weber Cannon 1987), three broad domains—the ideological, the political, and the economic—also represent useful ways of seeing the societal context for other forms of oppression. Each domain has associated with it certain *social institutions*—patterns of social relationships that are intended to accomplish the goals of the particular domain. And relations of dominance and subordination are structured within the institutions associated with each of the three major domains of society:

- *Ideological Domain.* The media, arts, religion, and education represent institutions whose primary purpose is *ideological*—producing and distributing ideas and knowledge about society and its people, why society is organized the way it is, what people need to know in order to function in society. Control over ideological institutions enables dominant groups to shape public images and cultural beliefs about both dominant and subordinate groups. Some refer to negative group images, for example, of "welfare queens," as *controlling images* to highlight their intended purpose of restricting the lives and options of subordinate groups, in this case poor African American women (Collins 2000; Hancock 2004).

- *Political Domain.* The government, law, civil and criminal justice, the police, and the military represent institutions whose primary purpose is *political*—creating and enforcing the laws and government structures that define citizens' and non-citizens' rights, responsibilities, and privileges. Through control over these institutions, dominant groups exert direct control over the behavior of others.

- *Economic Domain.* The major industries (e.g., finance, health care, manufacturing, housing, transportation, and communication) and work represent institutions whose primary emphasis is *economic*—producing and distributing society's valued goods and services. Control over material goods and resources such as wealth, jobs, wages and benefits, health care, day care, and education makes dominant groups more competitive in the workplace and in community life.

Each of these domains and the institutions associated with them are organized to reinforce and reproduce the prevailing social hierarchies of race, class, gender, and sexuality—by producing and disseminating ideas that justify these inequalities, by concentrating government power and social control mechanisms among dominant groups, and by unequally distributing society's valued material and social resources to Whites, the middle and upper classes, men, heterosexuals, and U.S. citizens.

Although most institutions have a primary purpose, none of the major social institutions relates solely to a single domain of oppression—ideological, political, or economic. Just as race, class, gender, and sexuality are interconnected dimensions of oppression, so are social institutions intertwined with one another. If we think again about the realm of sports, for example, sports are:

- *Ideological*: Ideas about "winners and losers," fair play, and a "level playing field" often serve as a basis for defining how groups should be treated, punished, and rewarded.

- *Political:* Many connections between the powerful in society—especially among men—are first forged in sports teams in kindergarten through twelfth grade (K-12) and in college (Messner 1992). Sports also become overtly political arenas, as when, for example, the International Olympic Committee tied its decision to allow Beijing to host the Olympics in 2008 to demands for greater human rights in China (Human Rights Watch 2008; Kine 2008).
- *Economic:* Over the past forty years, as manufacturing has declined, many municipalities around the country have turned to tourism and recreation, including professional sports teams, to improve the economies of urban areas. Large colleges and universities commit millions of dollars to sports promotion to increase revenues, to satisfy alumni, and to increase donations. And some of the richest people in America are sports professionals (e.g., Tiger Woods, Phil Mickelson, LeBron James) and team owners.

Education, too, although primarily an ideological institution, is deeply implicated in the economic and political domains because it certifies people for different social locations within them.

Society's expenditures on schooling are justified on economic grounds as preparing and sorting people for different positions in the capitalist economic system as owners, managers, professionals, laborers, and—for those who drop out or otherwise fail—as society's underclass. As the costs of higher education have risen dramatically in recent years, students are increasingly viewed as consumers who must be "sold" on the "product" that any given institution offers and who must be "satisfied" in order to keep their "business." Some have even sued schools for failure to educate them. Advocates for rural and inner-city K-12 schools are challenging school funding formulas that most often rely on local property taxes and heavily advantage affluent suburban areas. For example, when its supreme court ruled that the state's constitution merely obligated it to provide students a "minimally adequate" education, a South Carolina citizens' coalition proposed a constitutional amendment to require the state to level out the gross inequities in funding across its districts in order to provide all students with a high-quality education (see www.GoodbyeMinimallyAdequate.com).

And because of the ideological and economic importance of education, the state is deeply involved in legislating the structure of education. Social movements seeking to challenge the fundamental basis of the social order often begin with and emanate from schools. Take, for example, the historical equity movements surrounding school desegregation, students with disabilities, gender equity (Title IX), and affirmative action.

Cross-Cutting Institutions

Some institutions have no single focus and uniformly cross cut all dimensions—for example, the *family*. The family is a social institution whose purpose is to meet people's basic psychological, emotional, and physical needs. And even though emotional support, love, and nurturance take place in families, families also serve as sites where inequality is reproduced in the ideological, political, and economic realms:

- *Ideological*: Families are places where the ideas that bolster and justify the dominant power structure are reinforced daily in an intimate setting. Conservative politicians and political interest groups, for example, have used the term *family values* to refer to the political values that serve the interests of nuclear, heterosexual, White, middle- and upper-class Christian families: values that serve to reinforce the dominant power structure.
- *Political*: Families are places where the public authority and power of middle- and upper-class White male heterosexuals is reinforced daily in a variety of ways. When a man rapes or otherwise sexually assaults the child of a neighbor, for example, the violation is typically seen as a crime and is often pursued in the criminal justice system. When, however, the same man, particularly if he is middle or upper class, rapes or otherwise sexually assaults his own daughter, the rape is more often not challenged at all, is treated as an issue for social services, or is dealt with in therapy. The public power of men (including their greater economic power) gives them power in the family, making it especially difficult for women and children to successfully challenge the abuse of that power either in the family or in the criminal justice system (cf. Websdale 2001).
- *Economic*: Families are places where goods and services are distributed to reinforce the economic power of dominant groups. The family wage, a wage large enough to enable a man to provide for his entire family, was extended at the beginning of industrialization to White men to lure them away from family farms and into factory work but was never extended to men of color. It also served as a mechanism for exerting control over women both by denying them access to wage work and by justifying lower wages to women (Hartmann 1997). Current tax laws determining what part of income earned by individual workers will be retained by the state is set by their family status—married, heterosexual couples pay one rate, unmarried individuals pay another rate, and deductions and tax credits accrue to parents with dependent children.

Levels of Social Relations

One way of thinking about these domains—ideological, political, and economic—is as contexts that "set the stage" on which social relations of dominance and subordination will be enacted. Theater, for example, may focus on different content—from Shakespearean dramas about star-crossed lovers (*Romeo and Juliet*, *A Midsummer's Night's Dream*) and power struggles (*Macbeth*, *King Lear*) to modern musicals singing about animals (*Cats*, *Lion King*), teen life (*Grease*), apartment life in inner cities (*Rent*), or boys who want to dance ballet (*Billy Elliott*). But in each of these theatrical contexts—just as with any institutional arena and social

DOMAINS OF OPPRESSION	IDEOLOGY		POLITY		ECONOMY	
Associated Institutions	Education Media Religion		The State (all levels of government) Law (civil and criminal justice, police, military)		Industry (agriculture, communication, finance, health care, manufacturing, mining, transportation, etc.) Work	
Power Base	Control of Ideas and Knowledge		Legitimized Direct Control Over Others		Control of Material Goods and Resources	
Structures of Oppression: R, C, G, & S	Dominant[1] Group Activity	Subordinate Group Activity	Dominant Group Activity	Subordinate Group Activity	Dominant Group Activity	Subordinate Group Activity
Macro Social Structure / Society / Community	Production and → control of ideology that justifies, supports, and rationalizes interests of dominant group—e.g., • Negative stereotypes/controlling images of subordinate groups • Positive/"normal" images of dominant group	← Collective affirmation of group value, self-definition, positive identity: • GLBT, race/ethnic pride • Women's "consciousness raising" • Alternative ideologies—e.g., multicultural education, liberation theologies	Production and→ control of laws, policies over participation as citizens—e.g., • Biased treatment in criminal justice system • Biased social policies—e.g., welfare policy • Denial of full participation in political system—e.g., high cost of participating	← Resistance through—e.g., • Equal rights movements • Alternative organizations—e.g., grassroots organizations, Welfare Rights Organization • Demonstrations, riots, block voting • Communications Technologies—e.g., internet, facebook, twitter	Production and → control over good jobs, income, wealth, health care, housing, education, e.g.: • Passage of favorable tax legislation • Exploitation of subordinate group members in labor market	←Movements for—e.g., affirmative action, antidiscrimination measures, economic self-sufficiency—e.g., • Worker-owned companies • Minority businesses • Women's businesses • Strikes, slowdowns
Micro Social Psychology / Small Groups / Individual	Ideological power→ brings sense of privilege, superiority	← Empowered:[2] Self definition, self valuation, personal empowerment Not empowered: Internalized oppression, self hatred, self destructive behaviors	Legal authority → brings control over others in everyday life and reinforces personal power	←Empowered: Assertion of political/collective consciousness and identity Not empowered: Lack of political power, no sense of control over environment	Economic power → reinforces personal power of group in family and in everyday life	← Empowered: Many forms of resistance—e.g., union organizing, extended kin networks for sharing economic resources Not empowered: job absenteeism, quitting, theft

[1]The activities listed here are not intended to be an exhaustive list but rather suggestive of the kinds of activities that take place in each domain.

[2]Some actions of subordinated groups reinforce the negative impact of oppression, while other actions are more effective in challenging the oppression and reflect a more empowered stance. While the difference will certainly depend on the context, history, and other social conditions such as the relative power of the groups, the examples here are intended to remind us that not all activities have the same effect.

domain—ideologies of dominance and subordination can be enacted and challenged at different levels:

- *Societal:* At the societal level, the writers and producers conceptualize and fund theatrical productions and the ideas they promote. Those ideologies can serve to reproduce or to challenge dominant ideologies about various groups and associated behavioral expectations.
- *Community:* At the community level, theater promotes particular dominant values and sensibilities, as well as alternative values through "alternative or independent theater." Theater provides opportunities for discussion, engagement, and conflict about what values would and should hold sway in a community.
- *Small Group/Individual:* The actors in a play, the director, and the stagehands all develop closer, face-to-face relationships with the audience as they bring the ideas to life in the enactment of a play.

Table 1.1 is organized to highlight the major societal domains, (ideology, polity, economy), the structures of oppression (race, ethnicity, gender, class, sexuality), and the levels of interaction (society, community, individual) and to provide some examples of relationships of dominance and subordination—power relations—that occur within each combination of domains and levels. Specific institutions are more or less dominant in each domain: ideology (e.g., media, education), polity (e.g., the state, criminal justice), and economy (e.g., industry, transportation, communications). And specific types of social relations of dominance and subordination are more or less centered at different societal levels—society, community, small group, and individual.

SOCIAL RELATIONS OF CONTROL

Maintaining their position of control over subordinate groups is a primary task for dominant groups. To do so, they must structure:

- Ideology so that exploitation is explained, justified, and rationalized and comes to be seen as a natural, normal, and acceptable part of social life
- The polity so that the state supports and enforces the exploitative relations
- The economy so that the exploitative relations continue, so that the poverty and labor of the exploited enhances the welfare of the exploiters

Internalized Oppression

The very fact that society continues without major disruption every day serves as a testimony not only to the power of dominant groups to effectively control the ideological, political, and material resources that subordinate groups need to shift the balance of power but also to the persuasive power of dominant ideologies to convince subordinate group members that the current social hierarchies are acceptable and cannot be changed (cf. Mullings 1994). Two processes of *internalized oppression* are at work:

- *Self-Negation*: Subordinate group members sometimes restrict their own lives because they believe the negative views and limits imposed on their group by the dominant ideology. When subordinate group members internalize oppression, they do not challenge the social order and may even exhibit self-destructive patterns such as drug abuse, family violence, or depression. In more subtle ways, for example, a woman who fails to put herself up for consideration for a promotion at work because she believes that she is less capable or less suited for management than her male counterparts has internalized the socially constructed, controlling images of women.
- *Negation of Others*: Subordinate group members sometimes restrict the lives of other members of oppressed groups or of their own group because they believe the negative views of and limits imposed on another subordinate group or their own group. When working-class Latinos, for example, accept negative images of Latinas as sexually promiscuous and treat them as sexual objects, the Latinos reinforce the larger structural patterns of race, class, gender, and sexuality dominance. When women managers fail to promote other women because they believe that women are less capable than men, they also reinforce structures of race, class, gender, and sexuality dominance, the same structures that have restricted their own lives.

Resistance

But people also resist oppression. Even though each of these social institutions is organized to reproduce the current social hierarchy and is thus a structure of oppression, strong forces of resistance occur within each. The resistance occurs at both the *macro social level of community and society* and at the *micro level of the individual and the family*. Ever since the beginning of our public education system, for example, various groups have established alternative schools—religious schools, other private schools, single-sex schools, African American schools, bilingual schools, and home schools, to name a few—to resist the dominant culture's organization of education and to produce students who have different ideas about the social order. And because education is a primary institution charged with the socialization of the young, it holds a key to the future stability of the social order. Education is thus a critical site for resistance to all forms of oppression: racism, sexism, classism, and heterosexism, as well as oppression resulting from religious, ethnic, national, political, age, and disability status.

A major focus of the civil rights, women's rights, gay and lesbian rights, and poor peoples' movements has been educational system reform—for example, through school desegregation; through battles over the gender, race, and sexuality content of school texts and curricula; through struggles for access for students with disabilities; through bilingual education; and through poor (mostly rural and inner city) school districts' challenges to school funding formulas based on property values.

Resistance also occurs at the micro level of the individual and the family when individuals develop an alternative consciousness, insist on self-definition and self-valuation, and refuse to incorporate negative images of their groups. An alternative consciousness is often nurtured in a community of resistance, such as a racial ethnic community, a community of workers, a gay and lesbian community, a religious community, or a women's community. And increasingly today, those communities of resistance are created and sustained through the use of advanced technologies such as the Internet and cell phones, which facilitate communication across vast reaches of time and space.

When groups publicly resist oppression, individuals within them can participate in the development of a positive definition of self in the face of dominant culture oppression. When, for example, gay, lesbian, bisexual, and transgender people acknowledge their sexual orientation at work, they often face ostracism, hostility, lost opportunities for promotions, and even loss of their jobs. At the same time, however, by living their lives openly—something heterosexuals take for granted—they also contradict the denial and silence that enables dominant culture distortions about their lives to persist and to operate against them. In valuing themselves in this way, gays, lesbians, bisexuals, and transgender people contribute to an environment in which others are better able to do the same. This process is one of *empowerment*, "a process aimed at consolidating, maintaining, or changing the nature and distribution of power in a particular social context" (Morgen and Bookman 1988, 4). Processes of oppression and resistance and empowerment exist in dynamic relation to one another: Each is in a continuous process of changing to adapt to the shifts in the other.

Nike in Asia: An Example

For many years Cynthia Enloe (1997, 2007) has carefully tracked the process of globalization by observing corporate strategies and actions in the athletic shoe market. In moving production to countries with "corporate-friendly" governments, companies maximize profits by employing "cheap labor," which is largely women's labor. And repressive governments make it difficult if not impossible for women to advocate for better working conditions and wages.

To show the processes of change, Enloe tracks Nike, a U.S.-based and owned company that produced its first Nike shoes in 1972. By the early 1990s, the mostly women workers in the U.S. athletic shoe industry had been successful in attaining wages approximately 1½ times the minimum wage. As Enloe (1998) reports, the response of Nike and its parallel producer, Reebok, was careful and profound. Subcontracting production so that they would no longer have to provide the wages, benefits, and health and safety protections that U.S. workers expect, the companies moved production overseas, first to South Korea and then, after South Korean women successfully organized for higher wages, to China and Thailand (Kim 1997). Hourly wages in athletic footwear factories in 1993 told the story:

- China $0.10–0.14
- Indonesia $0.16–0.20
- Thailand $0.65–0.74
- South Korea $2.02–2 .27
- United States $7.38–7.94

At the time, the retail price of a $70 pair of Nike Pegasus was divided up this way:

- Labor (total for all forty-five workers) $1.66
- Materials $9.18
- Subcontractor's profit $1.19
- Administration/overhead $2.82
- Nike markup (costs/profits) $22.95
- Shoe sold to retailer for $37.80

Nike's profits nearly tripled to $298 million in the five-year period ending in 1993, and Reebok experienced similarly large profits. Nevertheless, because oppression invites resistance, women in each of these countries began to wage successful campaigns against their exploitation. Allied through networks such as the Hong Kong–based Committee for Asian Women, women across Asia began developing their own foreign policy to address women's needs:

> how to convince fathers and husbands that a woman going out to organizing meetings at night is not sexually promiscuous; how to develop workplace agendas that respond to family needs; how to work with male unionists who push women's demands to the bottom of their lists; how to build a global movement. (Enloe 1998, 205)

But ever since 1993 the company has continued its dramatic growth and expansion. By 2007, Nike reported $15 billion in revenue, and its branded products were made by more than eight hundred thousand workers in more than seven hundred contract factories in fifty-two countries around the world. By October 2008, in the midst of the global stock and financial crisis, Nike was listed as one of the top five Global High Performer Corporations in the category of household and personal products, averaging a 10.9 percent yearly increase in sales and a 19.2 percent increase in net income for the previous five years (Zajac 2008).

Now only forty-nine (7 percent) of Nike's footwear production factories are in the United States, and Asian contractors run most of its factories: China (35 percent), Vietnam (29 percent), Indonesia (21 percent), and Thailand (13 percent) (Oxfam Australia 2008). If you wonder about the extent of outsourcing in the athletic shoe and apparel industry, try the following exercise, which Enloe recommends. The next time you are in a group of friends or family or in a class, have people check the labels in the necks of their shirts or dresses, or go to your closet and check the labels on the athletic shoes you have, old and new. You will surely see a wide array of nations and may even note changes over time in who is producing the shoes if you own both old and new ones.

Enloe (2007) argues that it is not only the poverty of the people in these Asian nations that has made them attractive sites for U.S. companies' factories but also the repressive authoritarian regimes that control them. Both China and Vietnam are governed by authoritarian one-party regimes, and the Thailand multiparty civilian government was taken over by the military in 2006, ostensibly to end the rule of a corrupt and authoritarian civilian-elected administration. All three governments "have attracted foreign investors by offering to mobilize millions of young women from rural villages to work miles away from home in new export factories" (Enloe 2007, 34). These regimes typically stifle dissent of any sort, including unionization and worker advocacy activities and, in the name of public order and national security, often employ the military and strong police forces against resisters.

During this period of dramatic growth, Nike and other large athletic apparel companies such as Adidas and Reebok have consistently come under attack by independent fair labor organizations, by new companies employing fair labor practices, by fair trade organizations, and by activist labor and women's groups. These groups have built a global movement to end the exploitation of workers, not only in the athletic shoe industry but also in textiles and clothing and many other industries. And they have had some success.

The Fair Labor Association (FLA), an international labor advocacy and watchdog group, has raised awareness of worker abuse in Nike's and other companies' subcontracted plants and has successfully negotiated concessions and changes in company practices. For example, Nike instituted a corporate responsibility compliance program that exceeds the standards of the Fair Labor Association. FLA participating companies must comply with fair labor practices, including:

- Adopting and communicating the Workplace Code of Conduct to workers and management at applicable facilities
- Conducting internal monitoring of facilities and submitting to independent external monitoring of health and safety, wages and benefits, overtime compensation, freedom of association and collective bargaining, and harassment or abuse
- Preventing persistent forms of noncompliance and remediating instances of noncompliance in a timely manner (Fair Labor Association, 2007)

In recent years, college students across the United States have joined the international movement to stop the exploitation of workers in the athletic shoe and apparel industry by protesting on campuses and pressing their administrations to cancel contracts for campus athletic wear with companies that would not stop their exploitative labor practices abroad. The movement has been successful in pressuring many companies to become engaged in improving life for workers in these factories in Asia and now across the globe and to sign on as participating companies with the Fair Labor Association. In addition to Nike and Adidas, participating companies now include such major multinationals as ASICS, GFSI (Champion, Gear for Sports), and New Era Cap company (Fair Labor Association, 2007).

Others have taken a different approach to the problem by starting their own companies that produce apparel only in factories that go beyond the dictates of FLA and that include union representation for their workers. A company called No Sweat was founded in 2004 by Jeff Ballinger, a labor rights monitor who had previously published a short newspaper, *Nike in Indonesia*, which exposed unfair labor practices. When Garry Trudeau publicized the issues raised in *Nike in Indonesia* in his Doonesbury comic strip, he increased the exposure for the issues and the newspaper, and many consumers put pressure on high-profile athlete endorsers and asked why they supported the exploitative labor practices of their sponsoring companies (Enloe 2007).

After Suharto's military regime in Indonesia was toppled in 1998 by a prodemocracy movement, Ballinger and his associates saw the opportunity to become more assertive on behalf of workers and to launch No Sweat in the new, less militarized government. Searching for a factory with the most proworker environment, they selected one owned by Bata, one of the world's biggest shoe manufacturers, to produce No Sweat's now signature low-top black-and-white and red-and-white sneakers. They worked with Bata to establish a factory that is unionized and that provides a living wage and benefits such as health care, maternity leave and pay, two sets of work clothes, a rice allowance, a 10 percent pension, and a shift allowance. But despite these improved conditions, women still face problems in male-dominated unions, and the women's bureau within the union was created by activist women to advocate for them (Enloe 2007).

As the preceding example illustrates, it is not just Americans—both consumers such as college students and men and women workers and their organizations—who are increasingly coming to connect their own plights and actions with the oppression of women and men in other countries. A Fair Trade movement operates globally and has a significant and growing presence in the United States, not only through brands such as No Sweat but also through outlets such as 10,000 Villages and many others (Global Exchange 2008; Wilkinson 2007). We are thus increasingly reminded that even though the focus of this book is on the United States, oppression, resistance, and empowerment take place in a global context.

SUMMARY

The meaning of race, class, gender, and sexuality is contested in struggles for ideological, political, and economic power and is constructed simultaneously at the macro social-structural (society and community) and micro social-psychological (family and individual) levels. Each of these domains of oppression, although primarily reflecting different societal functions and institutions, is integrally interdependent with the others, just as race, class, gender, and sexuality are interdependent.

CHAPTER 2

+○

A Historical Time Line of Indicators of Oppression

Co-authored by Rebecca Shrum

The past isn't dead. It isn't even past.
—WILLIAM FAULKNER

Race, class, gender, and sexuality are systems of oppression that have been con-
tinuously contested since the inception of this nation and that have severe
and unequal impacts on different groups. To highlight the struggles of subordinate groups to secure the basic rights, privileges, and opportunities that dominant
groups take for granted, the following time line presents a sample of significant
stages and events in these struggles. Because social changes that represent significant shifts in the relations between dominant and subordinate groups do not take
place overnight, a time line that allows us to scan a broad sweep of history can help
us see patterns in the ways that dominant and subordinate group struggles have
been waged, especially in the public arena.

LIMITS OF THE TIME LINE

As we read them and think about them, time lines also require caution. They are
superficial—they do not represent a comprehensive history of U.S. oppression and
resistance, and they cannot convey the vast and complex social processes undergirding each "fact" on the line. The facts most easily conveyed on a time line tend to be
policy changes, such as when laws were passed or Supreme Court decisions handed
down. These indicators of change, however, tend to represent a view of history by the
dominant culture: State policy changes typically mark the dominant culture's accom-
modation to social, political, and economic pressures for change that have emerged
in struggles with oppressed groups over a long period of time. The indicators are
much less accurate as representations of the most significant markers in the history
of struggles by oppressed groups as seen from the groups' own vantage points.

The time line refers, for example, to passage of the Voting Rights Act of 1965—
an event that culminated a century of struggle by African Americans to secure

the right to vote unimpeded by the numerous legal and extralegal mechanisms designed to deny them that right (e.g., dual registration, poll taxes, literacy tests, and harassment at the polls). Few would deny that the Voting Rights Act of 1964 was one of the most significant events in group struggles for rights in this century. However, as Lani Guinier (1998a, 303) relates, it was not all:

> As one local sharecropper told SNCC (Student Non-Violent Coordinating Committee) organizer Bob Moses, the most important accomplishment of the civil rights movement, as far as blacks in Mississippi were concerned, was not the vote. It was the opportunity to meet. Coming together in small groups at citizenship schools or attending large mass meetings in black churches gave people a way to speak their stories and amplify their voices. Voting, which was a means of expressing that voice, could never substitute for the process of formulating, articulating, or pursuing a citizen-oriented, community-based agenda. The vote was crucial, but it wasn't all. In retrospect, maybe not even the most.

More recently, it is widely recognized that President Obama's election was in part the consequence of his community organizing strategic approach—supporting thousands of planning meetings in the homes of his supporters, many of whom were first connected via Internet and text messaging communications. It has yet to be seen whether these activist networks will be maintained after the election and deployed in the process of governing—a goal President Obama clearly seeks. Even though it is more difficult to convey the significance of thousands of group meetings in this time line, they are no less important in understanding and historically situating the meaning of race, class, gender, and sexuality systems. Furthermore, it is worthwhile to remember that changes in national laws often reflect changes that have already taken place in people's behavior and that are already law in some states. Seventeen states, for example, had already extended women the right to vote by the time the U.S. Constitution was amended in 1920.

Every transformation of the race, class, gender, and sexuality order—the ways that society is organized to reinforce the existing hierarchies—is socially created through a process of conflict and compromise that takes place over time between resistance movements and the dominant culture as embodied in the state. Gramsci (1971) and Omi and Winant (1994) categorized these processes as taking place in different ways depending on the place and power of the subordinate groups in the social hierarchy at any given time. They describe two general kinds of conflict: a "war of maneuvers" and a "war of position."

War of Maneuvers

A "war of maneuvers" takes place when subordinate groups lack democratic rights (e.g., the vote, representation in legislative and other government bodies), property, and any substantial basis on which to challenge the dominant social order. So challenges to dominant groups have to take place outside—in the margins of society. In a war of maneuvers, groups develop an alternative internal society as a counter to the repressive social system. Many racial ethnic communities before the racial liberation movements of the 1960s and 1970s, and many gays and lesbians before the Stonewall riot in 1969 and the early movement following it, resisted oppression in the margins of society by managing to survive despite severe repression and particularly by developing internal communities that countered that repression. When you look at the time line, you will notice that during a war of maneuvers, there are significantly fewer indicators of positive progress in dominant culture arenas—congressional representation, educational and occupational attainment, representation in the military.

War of Position

More recent history suggests that oppressed racial ethnic groups and sexuality groups are moving from the *war of maneuvers* to the *war of position*, in which subordinate groups have access to diverse institutional and cultural terrains on which to develop strategies to challenge oppression. In a war of position, subordinate group members, strengthened by the sense of community and political power developed in the war of maneuvers, are strategically positioned to challenge the state's race, class, gender, and/or sexuality hierarchies. This shift can be seen in the time line as the much more rapid pace of change evidenced in the past forty or fifty years. Even though the White working classes and White heterosexual women have had legitimized access to some forms of democratic participation much longer than people of color or gays, bisexuals, and lesbians, White women in particular have continued to improve their strategic position to resist oppression during the recent period of increased democratization and cultural change. Yet their progress is much more pronounced in some areas, such as in education, than in others, such as in income, in corporate leadership, or in the financial services industry.

Just as during wars of maneuvers, group process and progress are more obscured in the time line, other processes obscure the actual histories of oppressed groups—for example, the ways the state gathers and reports data on the population. Because government allocations of resources for schools, welfare, roads, and health care are dependent on accurate and up-to-date information about the size, composition, and distribution of groups, one of the struggles that oppressed groups face is simply the struggle to be counted. For the first time, for example, the 2000 U.S. Census collected data on same-sex couples by counting couples who were living together and identified as unmarried partners. Of the 5.5 million couples who identified as living in this kind of arrangement, 594,000 (1 in 9) were same-sex couples (U.S. Census Bureau 2003).

The struggle to be counted is one that racial ethnic groups, especially small groups and those with large, poor, transient, and rapidly growing populations, still face. Only since 1980, for example, has it been possible to more accurately identify Hispanics in government statistical reports of the population, and only since 2000 have Asian and Pacific Islanders and Native Americans been included in the annual statistical summaries of major indicators. Figure 2.1 shows the racial

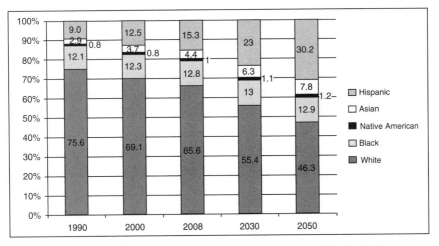

Figure 2.1 Percentage of the Population by Race, 1990 to 2008 and Projections

Sources: U.S. Bureau of the Census, 2002. Table 1: United States—Race and Hispanic Origin: 1790–1990. Available from http://www.census.gov/population/www/documentation/twps0056/tab01.xls, accessed October 12, 2008.

U.S. Bureau of the Census, 2001. *Overview of Race and Hispanic Origin: 2000.* Available from http://www.census.gov/prod/2001pubs/cenbr01-1.pdf, accessed October 12, 2008.

U.S. Bureau of the Census, 2008. Table 4: Percent of the Projected Population by Race and Hispanic Origin for the United States: 2008 to 2050. Available from http://www.census.gov/population/www/projections/tablesandcharts/table_4.xls, accessed October 12, 2008.

Figure created by: Christina E. Griffin

composition of the U.S. population since 1990 and the growing diversity of the population, which is projected until 2050, especially the rapid growth of Asians and Latino/as.

Still, racial groups have more accurate representation in government records than do gays, bisexuals, and lesbians, who have never been officially counted and who have been reluctant to self-identify in no small part because the government itself has a continuing history of oppression of gay people (Duberman, Vicinus, and Chauncey 1989). For example, in the first six years of the "Don't ask, don't tell, don't pursue," military policy purportedly designed to protect gays and lesbians in the military, expulsions of gays and lesbians increased by 73 percent, leading President Clinton to label his policy a failure (Burelli and Dale 2006). After 2001, however, expulsions of gays and lesbians from the military dropped as demand for American soldiers substantially increased in the Middle East. In 2001, 1,273 gay and lesbian soldiers were expelled from the U.S. military, whereas the yearly average of discharges between 2003 and 2006 was 702.

Another problem is that time lines are brief representations of broad sweeps of history and are necessarily selective. The data for this time line, for example, highlight the three domains of oppression and present separate time lines for significant markers in education (ideological), citizenship rights and representation in federal government and the military (political), and work and income (economic). Cross-cutting all three of these dimensions is the family, here marked by dates in the area of marriage and reproduction. Also, because the time line depicts events significant for a variety of groups, no single group is likely to see its historical line presented in a complete progression. Finally, the time line may be more useful as a set of markers or guides to changing patterns of relations that might point us in a direction to search for deeper understandings—to ask more questions.

HIGHLIGHTS OF THE TIME LINE

Despite its limitations, the time line reveals a number of significant processes and events in the history of race, class, gender, and sexuality struggles in the United States. Primarily, it shows that struggles of oppressed groups for full inclusion in a democratic society have been continuous. And often the gains secured by a single group broaden the inclusiveness of the society for everyone. The Civil Rights Acts of 1964, 1965, and 1968, for example, were won primarily through the efforts of African American citizens to expand representation in government and to secure fair treatment in education, in the workplace, and in housing. When written, the Civil Rights Acts outlawed discrimination on the basis of race (including all racial groups), sex, color, religion, and national origin. The protection against sex discrimination prohibits sexual harassment, and some gays and lesbian students harassed in school have successfully brought suits by charging that their civil rights to equal protection were violated (cf. Lambda Legal Education and Defense Fund 2000).

But even when political rights are secured legally, realizing and maintaining those rights often remain a struggle and are more difficult for oppressed groups because dominant groups use their power to find new ways to oppress. For example, after *Roe v. Wade* in 1972 guaranteed a woman the right to an abortion, actually securing an abortion has been made more difficult, particularly for poor women, by a series of political actions: the 1977 Hyde Amendment that eliminated federal funds for abortions, legislation placing restrictions on abortion such as parental approval and twenty-four-hour waiting periods, and harassment of doctors and clinics that provide abortions (Woliver 2002). Likewise, after the Fourteenth and Nineteenth Amendments to the Constitution extended the right to vote to all citizens, discriminatory practices, such as poll taxes, dual registration, and literacy tests, made it difficult to exercise that right for many years. Significant numbers of women and people of color were not elected to state or federal offices until the very recent past and still constitute only 29 percent of Congress (156 of 538 members) in 2009 (Congressional Research Service 2008).

The same processes of oppression are evident in education. Even after the *Brown v. Board of Education* decision of 1954 ruling that separate but equal educational facilities were unconstitutional, it was not until the pressures of the civil rights movement in the 1960s and even into the 1970s that governments began to intervene to eliminate the practice. Today, racially segregated and unequal schooling remains a problem for the poor, people of color, and inner-city and rural residents.

Finally, gays, bisexuals, and lesbians have faced numerous obstacles to obtaining full and equal rights, privileges, and treatment in U.S. society. Although they were never denied some citizenship rights, such as the vote, realizing full civil rights has still been extremely difficult because of pervasive hostility, repression, and discrimination.

HISTORICAL TIME LINES OF RACE, CLASS, GENDER, AND SEXUALITY CONTESTS IN THE UNITED STATES

(See the appendix to this volume for references)

Education

Education is a central site of contests over race, class, gender, and sexuality in the United States both because knowledge is key to resisting oppression and because educational credentials are essential to getting good jobs, salaries, benefits, and better quality of life. The time line suggests several critical trends in education contests.

First, because race, class, and gender segregation in schooling has been a primary mechanism for reinforcing hierarchies, school desegregation has been a key goal among oppressed groups. The time line reveals the intense resistance to school desegregation and how quickly the gains made during desegregation can recede when there is no longer intervention to ensure that desegregation continues. Significant changes in the racial order occurred with the passage of the Civil Rights Act of 1964, but more recently poorer school districts—typically those in rural and inner-city areas—have also begun to bring lawsuits to challenge the unequal resources that go to schools when school funding is based on property taxes (cf. Burkett 1998; Young 1999). In Illinois, for example, where high-poverty school districts annually receive $2,235 less per student than low-poverty districts (the second largest state funding gap in the country), charges of educational discrimination have led to protests and legal action (Arroyo 2008; Ihejirika 2008). And in the 1990s women successfully desegregated the remaining male-only bastions, the military academies, by charging that they denied women equal educational opportunity, prohibited under Title IX legislation for schools receiving federal funds.

Second, the time line also highlights the fact that the government can be a site both for protecting privilege and for redistributing power by steering funds to support education. For example, the 1944 G.I. Bill of Rights supported the education and training of thousands of mostly White working- and middle-class men who fought in World War II, but it now serves a much more diverse military. Likewise, funding for the disabled, for bilingual education, and for poor students helps to empower subordinate groups, although seemingly never enough to shift the balance of power significantly.

Finally, it is difficult to record much of the historical struggles of gays, bisexuals, and lesbians in education because many gay and lesbian schoolteachers still do not publicly identify themselves as homosexual for fear of losing their jobs. Homophobic fears that homosexuals thrive on molesting young children and recruiting them to a gay lifestyle, particularly promoted among conservative Christian groups, have led fundamentalists to oppose antidiscrimination measures that would protect homosexuals in schools and to exclude mention of homosexuals from the curriculum (Carlson 1997; Eisenmenger 2002; Kosciw, Diaz, and Greytak 2008).

1896 In *Plessy v. Ferguson*, the Supreme Court endorses the principle of "separate but equal." It upholds the segregation of public facilities but asserts that Whites and Blacks should be accommodated on "separate but equal" terms.

1944 The G.I. Bill of Rights, also known as the Serviceman's Readjustment Act, is passed, creating a massive socioeconomic shift upward for the American working class. The G.I. Bill establishes a system to reintegrate military personnel into the civilian economy and a system to compensate veterans of World War II for their service. The bill provides tuition, fees, books, and a monthly subsistence payment to the veterans while they are in school, as well as providing them the opportunity to set up their own businesses, to buy their own homes, and to receive financial aid.

1948 The Supreme Court rules in *McCollum v. Board of Education* that there may be no religious instruction or activity in public school facilities.

1954 In *Brown v. Board of Education* of Topeka, Kansas, the Supreme Court strikes down the "separate but equal" doctrine of *Plessy* and orders all public schools to be desegregated.

1955 The Supreme Court orders the implementation of *Brown*, stating that all public facilities and accommodations be desegregated "with all deliberate speed."

1964 Despite the Supreme Court's order, desegregation is not widely implemented until the Civil Rights Act of 1964.

1965 Congress passes the Elementary and Secondary Education Act. It is the first law to extend federal funding to elementary and secondary schools. It also provides grants for the purchase of library materials and textbooks.

Congress passes the Higher Education Act, providing federal scholarships and federally guaranteed student loans for poor students. The act also funds college libraries, graduate fellowships for prospective elementary and secondary school teachers, and a teacher corps, whose members will augment the faculties of schools in poverty-stricken areas.

1966 Congress extends the existing school milk and lunch programs for poor children to include breakfast.

1968 The Bilingual Education Act, an amendment to the Elementary and Secondary Schools Act, provides assistance to local educational agencies in establishing bilingual educational programs.

1969 The Navajo establish Navajo Community College, the first college operated by Native Americans.

1970 College students receive a total of $2 million in grants, loans, and interest subsidies for guaranteed loans, compared with $247,000 in 1964. The money reaches one in four students.

1971 The Supreme Court rules in *Swann v. Charlotte-Mecklenburg Board of Education* that busing to achieve racial balance is constitutional in cases in which segregation has received official sanctions and officials have offered no alternatives.

1972 Congress passes Title IX of the Education Amendments of 1972, prohibiting discrimination on the basis of sex in most federally assisted educational programs and related activities, including sports. Title IX opens the way for increased participation of women and girls in athletic programs and professional schools.

1973 The Vocational Rehabilitation Act mandates that "no handicapped individual shall be excluded from any program or activity receiving federal financial assistance."

1975 The Education for All Handicapped Children Act passes, guaranteeing all handicapped students ages three to twenty-one a right to free public education.

1978 For the first time, more women enter college than men.

In *Regents of the University of California v. Bakke*, the Supreme Court upholds the constitutionality of affirmative action but does not affirm racial quotas in admissions processes.

1979 The Supreme Court rules unanimously that federally funded colleges do not have to admit all handicapped applicants or make extensive modifications to accommodate them.

1983 In U.S. colleges and universities, women earn more than one-half of the undergraduate degrees, one-half the master's degrees, and one-third of the Ph.D.s. However, women make up only 27 percent of the full-time faculty and 11 percent of the full professors.

1988 In response to the Supreme Court's ruling in *Grove City College v. Bell*, Senate Bill 557 is passed, stating that Title IX of the Civil Rights Act applies to all higher education programs regardless of whether they draw federal funds.

1994 Congress adopts the Gender Equity in Education Act to train teachers, promote mathematics and science learning by girls, counsel pregnant teens, and prevent sexual harassment.

1996 California passes a law banning the use of race and sex in college admissions, contracting, and public employment.

In *Hopwood v. Texas*, a federal court invalidates the program of affirmative action in admissions at the University of Texas Law School.

The Supreme Court rules that Virginia Military Institute must admit women to its student body. The Citadel follows suit.

1997 University of California, Berkeley, reports a 57 percent drop in Black admissions and a 40 percent decline in Latino/a admissions. For the University of California, Los Angeles, the decline is 43 percent for Black students and 33 percent for Latino/as.

At the University of Texas Law School, five African American students are offered admission, down from sixty-five in 1996.

The Supreme Court expands the meaning of Title IX by ruling that to qualify for federal support, college athletic programs must actively involve fairly equal numbers of men and women.

In response to the Supreme Court's ruling in *Hopwood v. Texas*, Texas implements the "Texas 10 Percent Plan." Under this plan, the top 10 percent of graduating seniors from all high schools in Texas are offered admission to the University of Texas at Austin. Before this, 75 percent of UT's freshmen class had been drawn from only 10 percent of the state's high schools. The plan gains widespread support, in part because it offers a remedy to both the race- and class-based biases in college admissions. All public universities in Texas follow suit and begin to admit the top 10 percent of graduating seniors. California (1999) and Florida (2000) also adopt similar plans. States implementing these percentage plans will later face a backlash from middle-class families who claim that their children have been denied admission under the plan.

1999 Nancy Mace is the first woman to graduate from the Citadel.

U.S. District Court Judge Robert Potter rules that Charlotte, North Carolina, educators must dismantle their thirty-year-old policy of school integration mandated by *Swann v. Charlotte-Mecklenburg Board of Education* because they may no longer use race when deciding where to assign school children.

In *Weaver v. Nebo School District* (Utah), a federal judge rules that a school district cannot prevent a gay or lesbian teacher from being "out" in his or her life outside the classroom.

2001 The federal No Child Left Behind (NCLB) legislation is signed into law. NCLB funds basic public school programs and requires adequate yearly progress if schools are to maintain their federal funding.

2002 Charlotte-Mecklenburg school district implements its revised system for school choice. Under this new plan, school segregation increases. In 2001, there were forty-seven district schools in which the percentage of White or Black students was more than 15 percent different from their percentage among the school-age population. In 2002, under the new system, the number of these schools rises to eighty-one.

2003 The Supreme Court hears two affirmative action cases from postsecondary schools in Michigan. In *Grutter v. Bollinger*, the Supreme Court rules five to four to uphold the University of Michigan law school's narrowly tailored use of race in admissions. In *Gratz v. Bollinger*, however, the Supreme Court rules six to three that the University of Michigan undergraduate school's use of race is too mechanistic and therefore unconstitutional.

Thirty-one percent of the nation's schools do not meet the adequate yearly progress standards set by NCLB, including 78 percent of the Florida schools given an "A" rating by President George W. Bush's brother, Florida Governor Jeb Bush.

2005 At U.S. colleges and universities, women earn 57 percent of the bachelor's degrees, 59 percent of the master's degrees, and 49 percent of the PhDs. Women make up 41 percent of full-time instructional faculty and 36 percent of full-time tenured and tenure-track professors.

NCLB is shown not to have improved basic skills: Reading scores have not improved, and the rate of improvement of math scores has decreased under NCLB. Leaders in forty-seven states have called for changes in NCLB.

2006 Citadel President John Rosa initiates a survey among students about sexual harassment and assault. More than 68 percent of the women and 17 percent of the men surveyed reported that they had "experienced some form of sexual harassment since becoming a cadet."

2007 The Citadel has graduated 145 women since 1999. In the fall of 2007, the Citadel enrolls 53 women in an incoming class of 709, bringing total female enrollment to 130 of the 2,036 member corps of cadets (6.4 percent).

In *Parents Involved in Community Schools v. Seattle School District No. 1, et al.*, the Supreme Court considers for the first time "whether a desire to achieve a racially diverse student body is a constitutionally valid goal for public elementary and high school students." In a five to four decision, the Supreme Court rules that racial balancing is not constitutional.

2008 6.1 million students at American colleges and universities take out $85 billion in student loans, more than double the amount that 4.1 million students borrowed one decade earlier.

Some recent indicators of educational attainment for various groups can perhaps give another perspective on the ways that inequality is played out in the educational arena. Perhaps the single most important credential to qualify for most middle-class, professional, managerial, and administrative jobs is a college degree. Figures 2.2a and 2.2b display the percentage of men and women in the five major racial designations who are over twenty-five years old and who have completed college from 1970 to 2007. The data show several patterns:

- The college-educated population has increased dramatically in the thirty-eight-year period, either doubling or tripling for almost every group.
- Black and Hispanic women's educational attainment is higher than that of men in their group. In 2007, 19 percent of Black women and 18 percent of Black men had completed college; 13.7 percent of Hispanic women and 11.8 percent of Hispanic men had.
- In 2007, White women were 1.6 times as likely to complete college as Black women and 2.2 times as likely as Hispanic women. In 2007, Asian Americans, although less than 5 percent of the total U.S. population, had the largest college-educated population of all racial groups. They also experienced the greatest percentage point increase in college education from 1970 to 2007 (31.7 percent for men and 32 percent for women compared with a 15.5 percent and 19.9 percent increase for White men and women, respectively). This increase is in part the result of the Immigration and Naturalization Act of 1965, which allowed immigration among people who worked in targeted high-technology occupations, such as engineers and computer specialists, that required a college degree. Immigration produced a 75 percent increase in the Asian or Pacific Islander population between 1960 and 1970, a 127.5 percent increase between 1970 and 1980, and a 107.8 percent increase from 1980 to 1990 (Roberts 1995).

The Hispanic population increased 61 percent between 1970 and 1980 and 53 percent between 1980 and 1990 (Roberts 1995). By 2000, 40 percent of the Hispanic population and 69 percent of the Asian population were born in foreign countries.

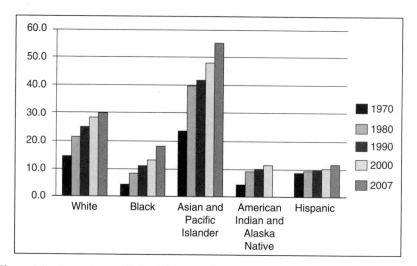

Figure 2.2a Percentage of Males 25 Years and Over Who Have Completed College, by Race, 1970 to 2007

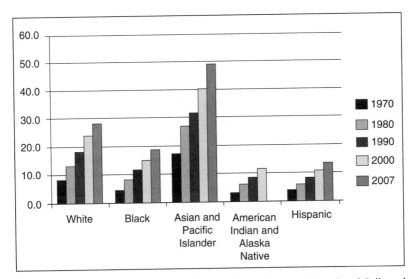

Figure 2.2b Percentage of Females 25 Years and Over Who Have Completed College, by Race, 1970 to 2007

Source: U.S. Census Bureau. 1998 Current Population Survey. *Educational Attainment in the United States,* 2007. Table A-2. Percent of People 25 Years and Over Who Have Completed High School or College, by Race, Hispanic Origin and Sex: Selected Years 1940 to 2007. Available from http://www.census.gov/population/www/socdemo/educ-attn.html, accessed October 12, 2008

U.S. Census Bureau. A Half-Century of Learning: Historical Statistics on Educational Attainment in the United States, 1940 to 2000. Table 4: Percent of the Population 25 Years and Over with a Bachelor's Degree or Higher by Sex, Race, and Hispanic Origin, for the United States: 1940 to 2000. Available from http://www.census.gov/population/www/socdemo/education/phct41.html, accessed October 12, 2008.

Tables created by: Christina E. Griffin

In contrast, only 3.6 percent of the White non-Hispanics and 6.3 percent of the Blacks were foreign born. In part because Latin Americans are recruited to low-wage jobs (e.g., farm labor), the percentage of the Latino/a population that has completed college remains low (11.8 percent for men and 13.7 percent for women in 2007), whereas the college-educated Asian population, recruited for high-tech and managerial jobs, remains high (U.S. Census Bureau 2001, 2004a, 2004b). This systemic difference is important to remember when Asian educational attainment is held as a standard to compare against that of other minorities. Many educated Asians were not educated in the United States, whereas African Americans, Native Americans, most Latinos, and native-born Asian Americans attend a race- and class-structured school system.

Polity

Several patterns stand out in the political time line. The pattern of patriarchal privilege that White, property-holding men had known in Europe was written onto the American landscape after the initial struggle for settlement was over. Whites took firm hold of the land and of the rights to make decisions about the lives of its occupants. Citizenship rights, including the right and the ability to vote and hold office, were first extended to property-owning White men and were denied to all women, to Native Americans, to African Americans—slave and free—and to White men who owned no property. These oppressed groups have worked for more than two hundred years to achieve in law and in practice what property-owning White men claimed at the founding of the nation.

One way to assess changes in the balance of power among groups is to track representation in government offices and in the military. The time line reveals a story of slow progress that nonetheless changes to a "war of position" after World War II, when the force of racial and gender liberation movements significantly changed the position of groups.

Gay and lesbian representation has been slower to come. Gays and lesbians have historically been the target of particularly oppressive government actions, such as being excluded from immigrating to the United States after the passage of the McCarran-Walter Act of 1952, identified as traitors during the 1950s, expelled from the military, and harassed by the police (Blasius and Phelan 1997; D'Emilio 1983; Duberman, Vicinus, and Chauncey 1989). During World War II the United States and its allies continued the imprisonment of homosexuals they found in Nazi concentration camps on the grounds that their incarceration was justifiable (Duberman, Vicinus, and Chauncey 1989).

Cities such as Tampa, Florida, and Boulder, Denver, and Aspen, Colorado, that passed antidiscrimination measures in the early 1990s witnessed extensive political mobilization to reverse the measures, including the passage of statewide legislation to nullify the antidiscrimination measures. Barney Frank was elected as a gay congressman in 1988, but only after he had been "outed" and had already served his Massachusetts district successfully for seven years. Today, twenty states and the District of Columbia prohibit employment discrimination on the basis of sexual orientation, and thirteen of those also include gender identity (Badgett, Ramos, and Sears 2008).

Citizenship

- **1778** The U.S. Constitution limits the right to vote to taxpayers or property owners, who make up a large proportion of the White male population. By the time Andrew Jackson is elected president (1829–1837), the right to vote is extended to include almost all White males.
- **1790** In a first effort to define American citizenship, Congress passes the Naturalization Law, which states that only free White immigrants are eligible for naturalized citizenship.
- **1830** The Indian Removal Act mandates the removal of Native Americans (including Seminoles, Choctaws, Creeks, Chickasaws, and Cherokees) from east of the Mississippi River to the newly established Indian Territory in present-day Oklahoma. In 1838, the Cherokee tribe is driven along the "Trail of Tears" after being forcibly removed from its land.

1848 The Treaty of Guadalupe-Hidalgo ends the Mexican-American War and incorporates half the land area of Mexico (i.e., the states of Texas, New Mexico, Arizona, and California and parts of Nevada, Utah, and Colorado) into the United States. Mexicans remaining in the new territory are granted full citizenship rights. Because language or cultural rights of the new citizens are not protected, over the next fifty years language laws inhibit Mexican American participation in voting, judicial processes, and education.

1857 The Supreme Court rules in *Dred Scott v. John F. A. Sanford* that a slave is not a citizen of the United States and has no right to sue in federal courts.

1866 The Fourteenth Amendment is ratified, guaranteeing newly freed slaves the right to vote but also limiting the vote to males.

1870 The Fifteenth Amendment is ratified, guaranteeing all citizens the right to vote regardless of race or color. Nevertheless, men of color continue to face obstacles to voting, such as literacy tests, dual registration, and poll taxes.

1874 In *Minor v. Happersett*, the Supreme Court rules that the clause guaranteeing equal protection under the laws of the Fourteenth Amendment does not include women. The Court concludes that although women are citizens, the right to vote is not a privilege of citizenship. Most states continue to disenfranchise women, although some, notably Western, states extend them the franchise.

1882 As a direct result of economic downturn and White workers' competition with Chinese men for jobs in agriculture, railroads, and the shoe, rope, and cigar industries, anti-Asian sentiment flares and leads to the passage of the Chinese Exclusion Act. The first legislation to restrict immigration for any group bans Chinese immigration and denies future citizenship to all Chinese already in the country. It is broadened by 1900 and renewed indefinitely in 1902.

1887 The Dawes Allotment Act grants the president the right to break up reservations and allot land to individual Native Americans. More than 80 million acres of land belonging to Native Americans is opened for settlement. Every Native American receives 160 acres of land, and any land left over is sold. The Act forces individuals to live on small farms, destroying the communal lifestyle of the Native American.

1902 The Reclamation Act in 1902 dispossesses many people of Mexican descent living in the Southwest from their lands.

1920 The Nineteenth Amendment is ratified, giving all citizens regardless of sex the right to vote. But when trying to vote, women and men of color still face property tax requirements, dual registration, literacy tests, and other obstacles.

1924 The National Origins Law, also know as the National Quota System, seeks to maintain Western European ethnic dominance in the United

States by imposing limits on the number of immigrants coming into the country. The limits are quite stringent for Eastern and Southern Europe but much broader for Western Europeans. To provide cheap labor in the Southwest, Latin American countries are exempt from this law. Asian immigration is banned.

Native Americans are granted citizenship in the United States, but some states continue to disenfranchise them.

1926 The American Eugenics Society is founded. American eugenicists believe that the wealth and social position of the upper classes is justified by a superior genetic endowment. They support restrictions on immigration from nations they consider inferior, such as Italy, Greece, and the countries of Eastern Europe. They argue for the sterilization of insane, retarded, and epileptic citizens in the United States. As a result of their efforts, sterilization laws are passed in twenty-seven states, and isolated instances of involuntary sterilization continue into the 1970s.

1934 Since 1887, 62 percent of the Native American land base has been transferred to Whites.

1942 The War Relocation Authority is established to administer the forced evacuation of all persons of Japanese ancestry living on the U.S. West Coast and their relocation to inland detention centers; more than 110,000 persons of Japanese ancestry are placed in ten war relocation centers, victims of mass hysteria following the Japanese attack on Pearl Harbor in 1941. These war relocation centers, in which military police are armed with machine guns, are like concentration camps.

The U.S. Army decides to enlarge Camp Gruber, a military installation with an extensive reservation not far from Muskogee, Oklahoma. To accomplish its plan, the government sees to it that eight tracts of restricted Cherokee property, including the homes of forty-five Cherokee families, are condemned. The government forcibly removes the Cherokee from the land and orders that the land be vacated within forty-five days.

1945 The war relocation centers that housed persons of Japanese ancestry during World War II are closed.

1948 For the first time, Native Americans in Arizona and New Mexico are allowed to vote in state and national elections.

1952 The Walter-McCarran Act allows the naturalization of non-White immigrants. Asian immigration is legalized but kept to low levels. England, Ireland, and Germany represent two-thirds of the quota for the entire world. The Western hemisphere, including Latin America, is exempt from limits except that applicants must clear a list of barriers designed to exclude homosexuals, Communists, and others.

1957 Utah allows Native Americans living on reservations to vote. It is the last state to do so.

1964 The Twenty-fourth Amendment to the U.S. Constitution prohibits poll taxes.

1965 The Immigration and Naturalization Act gives all nations equal opportunity to immigrate to the United States. An annual limit of twenty thousand immigrants is set for any given country, including countries in Latin America.

   The Voting Rights Act suspends racially discriminatory voting practices, chiefly intending to reverse the disenfranchisement of African Americans, but obstacles to voting continue to affect all people of color.

1971 The Twenty-sixth Amendment to the U.S. Constitution lowers the minimum voting age to eighteen.

1975 The Voting Rights Act Amendment requires bilingual ballots in certain areas.

1983 United States English is established, an organization seeking to secure the passage of the English Language Amendment that would declare English the official language in the United States. In 1995, this organization will have four hundred thousand members and an annual budget of $5 million.

1984 Wilma Mankiller becomes the first woman installed as principal chief of a major Native American tribe, the Cherokee in Oklahoma.

1988 The U.S. Government apologizes for the internment of Japanese Americans during World War II and passes legislation providing reparations of $20,000 to the approximately sixty thousand surviving Japanese Americans who had been interned.

1990 The Immigration Act continues to permit immigration of immediate relatives of U.S. citizens but puts a flexible cap of approximately seven hundred thousand for the fiscal years 1992–1994 on all immigrants. A preference system is based on family relationships, employment, and diversity. (See Figure 2.3 for a historical picture of the immigration patterns in the United States.)

   The Americans with Disabilities Act requires access to the polls and to the ballot.

1992 Congress passes the Voting Rights Language Assistance Act, which makes bilingual voting information readily available.

1993 The National Voter Registration Act, also known as the "Motor Voter" bill, makes voter registration more uniform and accessible by requiring states to allow mail-in voter registration and to let voters register at other state agencies, such as driver's license bureaus, welfare offices, and unemployment agencies.

2000 In October, a federal court rules that Puerto Ricans living in Puerto Rico cannot vote in the presidential election even though they are U.S. citizens. Neither can residents in the U.S. territories of Guam, American Samoa, and the U.S. Virgin Islands. Together with Puerto Rico, the population of these U.S. territories is nearly 4.1 million people. Residents of

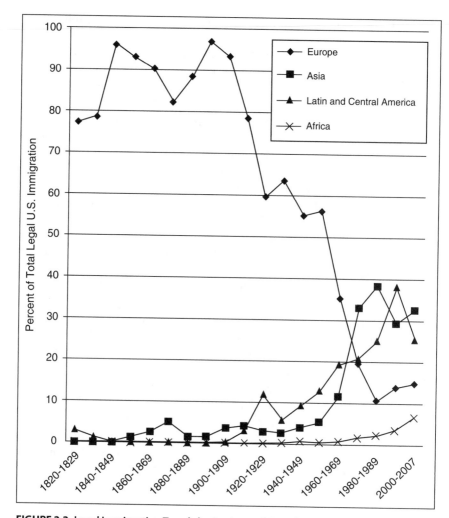

FIGURE 2.3 Legal Immigration Trends by Region and Decade, 1820–2007
Source: U.S. Department of Homeland Security. *Yearbook of Immigration Statistics:* 2007 Table 2: Persons Obtaining Legal Permanent Resident Status by Region and Selected Country of Last Residence: Fiscal Years 1820 to 2007. Available from http://www.dhs.gov/ximgtn/statistics/publications/LPR07.shtm, accessed October 12, 2008.

Figure created by: Christina E. Griffin

the U.S. territories also do not having voting representation in the U.S. Congress.

The presidential election is marred by accusations of voter fraud and suppression that delays the final outcome of the election by weeks: Thousands of eligible voters are not allowed to cast ballots; more than 1 million ballots go uncounted; almost 2 million ballots are disqualified because machines read multiple or no votes when counting them. The outcome of the presidential election is ultimately decided by the Supreme Court.

2001 The National Commission on Federal Election Reform recommends that all states grant voting rights to felons who have completed their criminal sentences. Nearly 4 million U.S. citizens cannot vote because of past felony convictions.

2002 The Help America Vote Act is passed to address the voting problems that emerged in the 2000 presidential election.

2008 Barack Obama (Democrat–Illinois) wins the presidential election with 53 percent of the popular vote to John McCain's (Republican–Arizona) 46 percent. Because of his decisive victory, the outcome of the presidential contest is known on election night. At the state level, however, the pattern of very close elections without a clear winner continues in senate races in Oregon, Alaska, Minnesota, and Georgia.

Government Offices

1822 Joseph Marion Hernandez (Whig–Florida), is the first Latino/a elected to Congress.

1870 During Reconstruction, the first African American men, Hiram R. Revel (Republican–Mississippi) and Joseph Hayne Rainey (Republican–South Carolina), are elected to Congress.

1892 Charles Curtis (Republican–Kansas) is the first Native American to serve as a representative in Congress (1893–1907) and as a senator (1907–1913). He will later serve as vice president during Herbert Hoover's presidency (1929–1933).

1917 Jeanette Rankin (Republican–Montana) is the first woman elected to Congress.

1958 The first Japanese American, Daniel Ken Inouye (Democrat–Hawaii), is elected to Congress.

1969 The first African American woman, Shirley Chisholm (Democrat–New York), is elected to Congress.

1970 The first Asian American woman, Patsy Mink (Democrat–Hawaii), is elected to Congress.

1974 The numbers of women in elective office begins to rise. Women hold 8 percent of the seats in state legislatures and 16 (3 percent) of the 535 seats in Congress.

1976 Daniel K. Akaka (Democrat–Hawaii) is the first Chinese American elected to Congress.

1981 The first woman Supreme Court justice, Sandra Day O'Connor, is seated.

1984 Geraldine Ferraro (Democrat–New York) is the first woman to run as a vice presidential candidate on a major party ticket.

1986 Women hold 14.8 percent of the seats in state legislatures and 24 (4.5 percent) of the 535 seats in Congress.

1988 After publicly disclosing his homosexuality in 1987, Barney Frank (Democrat–Massachusetts) becomes the first openly gay person to be elected to Congress. First elected in 1980, he is elected to his fifteenth term in 2008.

1989 Ileana Ros-Lehtinen (Republican–Florida) is the first of three Latinas and the first Cuban American to be elected to Congress.

1992 The first Korean American, Jay C. Kim (Democrat–California), is elected to Congress.

　　　Ben Nighthorse Campbell (Republican–Colorado) becomes the first Native American elected to the Senate in more than sixty years.

　　　Nydia Velazquez (Democrat–New York) is the first Puerto Rican woman to be elected to Congress. Lucille Roybal-Allard (Democrat–California) becomes the first Mexican American woman to be elected to Congress. Carole Moseley Braun (Democrat–Illinois) becomes the first African American woman to be elected to the Senate.

1997 Madeleine Albright's appointment as the first woman Secretary of State makes her the highest ranking woman in the history of the U.S. government.

1998 Tammy Baldwin (Democrat–Wisconsin) becomes the first "out" lesbian elected to Congress.

1999 Women hold 67 (12.4 percent) of the 539 seats in Congress. Twenty (3.7 percent) of the Congressional seats are held by women of color. Men of color hold 46 (8.5 percent) seats.

2000 1,669 (22.5 percent) of the 7,424 state legislators are women; 251 (3.4 percent) of all state legislators are women of color.

2007 Nancy Pelosi (Democrat–California) becomes the first woman Speaker of the U.S. House of Representatives, the highest-ranking woman in the history of U.S. government. She is second in the line of presidential succession after the vice president.

2008 Barack Obama (Democrat–Illinois) is the first African American to run on a major party ticket and to be elected president.

　　　1,749 (23.7percent) of the 7,382 state legislators are women. 355 (4.8 percent) of all state legislators are women of color. Since 1971, the number of women serving in state legislatures has more than quintupled.

　　　Eight women (five Democrat, three Republican) serve as governors. Governor Sarah Palin (Republican–Alaska) is selected as the first woman vice presidential candidate for the Republican Party.

2009 Women hold 92 (17 percent) of the 535 voting seats in the 111th U.S. Congress, 17 (17 percent) of the 100 seats in the Senate and 75 (17 percent) of the 435 seats in the House of Representatives. Twelve (13 percent) are women of color, all serving in the House of Representatives. No women of color serve in the U.S. Senate (Carol Moseley-Braun remains the only woman of color ever to have served in the U.S. Senate). Three additional women, two of whom are women of color, also serve as nonvoting delegates in the House of Representatives from Guam, the Virgin Islands, and Washington, D.C. Donna Christian-Christensen, the representative from the Virgin Islands, is the first female physician to serve in the U.S. Congress.

The U.S. Congress is the primary body establishing policy for the nation. Control of this body has a tremendous impact on the health and well-being, rights, and opportunities of all U.S. citizens. Congress has 539 members, whose composition in 2009 is displayed in Figure 2.4. Although White men constituted only 40 percent of the total U.S. population in 2009, they controlled 82 percent of the seats in the U.S. House of Representatives—more than doubling their power over their actual population representation. In the U.S. Senate, their control is even greater, constituting 83 percent of that body of one hundred. Only five men of color (three Hispanic and two Asian Americans) and seventeen White women were senators in 2009. Figure 2.4 shows the overrepresentation of White men in congress. There is one White male congressman for every 313,000 White men in the country, whereas White congresswomen each represent 1.7 million White women, Black congresswomen 1.45 million Black women, and Hispanic congressmen 980,000 Hispanic men.

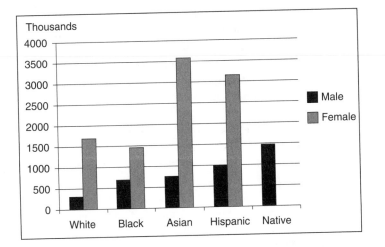

Figure 2.4 Number of Constituents Represented Per Congressperson of the Same Race and Gender, 2009
Note: Values in category "Native Hawaiian and Other Pacific Islander" were added to category "Asian" for data consistency. At the time of publication, there were 3 vacancies in congress: 2 in the HOR and one in the Senate.
Sources: U.S. Census Bureau. 2009. *Statistical Abstract of the United States 2009.* Table 6: Resident Population by Sex, Race, and Hispanic-Origin Status: 2000 to 2007. Available from http://www.census.gov/prod/2008pubs/09statab/pop.pdf, accessed January 7, 2009.
Congressional Research Service. 2008. *Membership of the 111th Congress: A Profile.* Available from http://assets.opencrs.com/rpts/R40086_20081231.pdf, accessed January 2, 2009.

Figure created by: Christina E. Griffin

Military

1792 Although more than five thousand African American men served during the Revolutionary War, the United States requires only that all White males between the ages of eighteen and forty-five take up arms and report for training. The states that previously admitted free African Americans into their militias interpret the law as a ban and expel them.

1812 Like the militias, the new National Army accepts no African Americans until the War of 1812 compels it to do so.

1917 The Selective Service Act is passed, authorizing conscription for the nation's armed services and requiring all males between the ages of twenty-one and thirty to register for the draft.

1948 President Truman issues Executive Order 9981, directing the armed forces to provide equal treatment and opportunity regardless of race.

The Women's Armed Forces Integration Act of 1948 incorporates the women's armed service nursing corps into the regular services, further opening military careers to American women.

1973 "Women-only" branches of the U.S. military are eliminated. But women are still barred from participating in combat.

1976 The first women are admitted to the U.S. military academies.

1980 The first women graduate from the service academies: Coast Guard, fourteen; U.S. Military Academy, sixty-one; Naval Academy, fifty-five; Air Force Academy, ninety-seven.

1991 More than forty thousand women serve in the Persian Gulf War; 7 percent of the active duty troops and 17 percent of the reserve forces and National Guard are women—the largest deployment of women in U.S. history.

1993 100 percent of the positions in the Coast Guard, 99.4 percent of the positions in the Air Force, 91.2 percent of the positions in the Navy, 67.2 percent of the positions in the Army, and 62 percent of the positions in the Marine Corps are open to women.

1994 The "Don't ask, don't tell, don't pursue" policy goes into effect, requiring that military personnel not inquire about a service member's sexual orientation. It also requires that gays and lesbians not identify themselves as homosexual.

By act of Congress, most Navy combatant ships are opened to women (excluding submarines and some smaller ships).

2001 More than fifteen thousand American women have served in the U.S. military peacekeeping mission in Bosnia, begun in 1996.

2002 100 percent of the positions in the Coast Guard, 99 percent in the Air Force, 91 percent in the Navy, 70 percent in the Army, and 62 percent in the Marines are open to women.

Race of Enlisted Women in the Active U.S. Military:

	WHITE	BLACK	HISPANIC
Army	37%	45%	11%
Navy	48%	31%	12%
Marine Corps	55%	22%	18%
Air Force	61%	27%	7%

2003 On March 23, combat operations in Iraq mark the beginning of the Iraq War. On May 1, President George W. Bush declares "mission accomplished" in Iraq and the end of major combat operations.

2006 11,704 service members have been discharged from the U.S. military under the "Don't ask, don't tell, don't pursue" policy since 1994. Of the service members discharged, 30 percent are women. Discharges have significantly declined during the War on Terror.

2007 More than 1.4 million active military and more than 410,000 National Guard and Reservists have served in Iraq or Afghanistan. More than 28 percent of these soldiers have been deployed more than once. The "stop loss" policy, which keeps soldiers from leaving even after reaching their enlistment end date, has been used on more than fifty thousand troops.

Women in the military (not including the Coast Guard) number 195,991—14.3 percent of the total active force, both officers and enlisted. 15.1 percent of all officers in the U.S. military are women; 14.2 percent of all enlisted soldiers are women. The Air Force has the highest percentage of women (19.6 percent) and the Marine Corps the lowest (6.3 percent).

2008 Between March 19, 2003, and August 2, 2008, 4,122 U.S. soldiers (4,023 men and 99 women) were killed in Iraq and 30,490 were wounded. 74.7 percent of soldiers who died were White, 10.69 percent Hispanic, 9.48 percent African American, and fewer than 2 percent each were Asian, Native Hawaiian or Pacific Islander, American Indian, Alaska Native, or "multiple races, pending, or unknown."

The total number of deaths of soldiers in the "Coalition of the Willing" (the U.S. and its allies) in Iraq is 4,469.

Estimates are that between January 2006 and September 2008, 42,263 Iraqi security forces and civilians have died during the war.

Approximately 97 percent of U.S. military casualties in Iraq have occurred since "mission accomplished" was declared.

Some estimate that the Iraq War will ultimately cost the United States $2.7 trillion. In testimony before the U.S. Congress, Senator Charles Schumer (Democrat– New York) stated that the war was costing U.S. taxpayers approximately $430 million a day.

Work/Economy

This section of the time line emphasizes legal changes that alter the status of various categories of workers. At first, laws and policies tended to focus on making work policies and practices uniform across the country (e.g., child labor laws, unemployment compensation, Aid to Families with Dependent Children [AFDC]). Later, the focus shifted to address concerns about inequities in the workplace (e.g., hiring practices, pay, and discrimination).

1848 A New York state law, the Married Women's Property Act, grants married women the right to own property in their own names, to sue and be sued, to run their own businesses, to work outside the home and claim the wages as their own, and to make a will disposing of their own property as freely as their husbands could. This law serves as a model for subsequent married women's property acts passed across the country between 1848 and 1895. Before this law, the property of a woman became her husband's to control on her marriage.

1904 The National Child Labor Committee forms in twenty-five branches in twenty-two states, demanding that child labor be outlawed.

1910 It is estimated that more than two million children are employed in industrial settings.

1933 Congress authorizes the Civil Works Administration to give work to the unemployed.

1935 Known as the cornerstone of the New Deal, the Social Security Act is passed, providing monthly payments for Americans age sixty-five and older. This Act and the others that follow ensure federal responsibility for public welfare.

Aid to Dependent Children (ADC), initially a minor provision of the Social Security Act, provides single mothers with a means to subsist. In the 1960s its name would be changed to AFDC (Aid to Families with Dependent Children) as part of President Johnson's "Great Society." AFDC is built on the existing tradition of state pensions for widows who were mothers of small children.

President Roosevelt establishes the Works Progress Administration (WPA). During its eight-year existence the WPA put some 8.5 million people to work (more than 11 million were unemployed in 1934) at a cost to the federal government of approximately $11 billion. The agency's construction projects produced more than 650,000 miles of roads; 125,000 public buildings; 75,000 bridges; 8,000 parks; and 800 airports. The Federal Arts Project, Federal Writers' Project, and Federal Theater Project—all under the aegis of the WPA—employed thousands of artists, writers, and actors in such programs as the creation of artwork for public buildings, the documentation of local life, and the organization of community theaters.

1938 Congress passes the Fair Labor Standards Act, limiting work to forty hours a week, after which workers must be paid overtime, and establishing a minimum wage of 25 cents an hour. This law affects 12.5 million workers. The establishment of the minimum wage significantly discourages the employment of minors.

1939 The Department of Agriculture introduces food stamps.

1941 In part as a response to a threatened march on Washington to demand jobs for Blacks, President Roosevelt issues Executive Order 8802, designed to end racial discrimination in government agencies, job training programs, and industries with defense contracts. It also establishes the Committee on Fair Employment Practices.

1947 Congress passes the Taft Hartley Act, written by the National Association of Manufacturers, to cripple unions that had gained strength during the labor shortages of World War II. The act outlaws closed shops (which required all employees in workplaces with unions to be union members), sympathy strikes, and secondary boycotts; requires union representation to be determined by a percentage of the workforce as a whole, not just of those voting; prevents foremen from joining unions; allows strikebreakers to vote in union elections and to vote to decertify a union; allows the President of the United States to halt strikes; makes union leaders subject to arrest for failing to break wildcat strikes; and requires union members to sign loyalty oaths stating that they are not communists.

1962 President Kennedy issues an Executive Order that requires federal employees to be hired and promoted without regard to sex. Before this order, federal managers could restrict consideration to either men or women.

1963 The Equal Pay Equity Act is the first federal law that prohibits sex discrimination and guarantees to men and women the same wages for the same work performed under the same conditions. It does not cover those employed in domestic or agricultural positions, executives, professionals, or administrators.

1964 Congress passes Title VII of the Civil Rights Act, prohibiting discrimination in employment because of sex, race, color, religion, and national origin. It does not include sexual orientation.

1968 The Fair Housing Act of 1968, also known as Title VIII of the Civil Rights Act, is passed, making it for the first time illegal to advertise any preference, limitation, or discrimination based on race, color, religion, or national origin. It will be amended in 1974 to prohibit sex discrimination in financing, selling, or renting housing or in the provision of brokerage services.

1969 Congress passes the first of three major Tax Reform Acts (others follow in 1976 and 1986) purportedly designed to reduce tax loopholes for the rich. It does not work. Between 1969 and 1989 the number of persons with incomes over $200,000 who paid no income taxes rose from 155 to 1,081.

1970 Women make up 38 percent of the civilian workforce, rising to 42.5 percent by 1980, 45.2 percent by 1990, and 46.2 percent by 1996.

1972 The Equal Pay Act of 1963 is amended to include executive, professional, and administrative positions.

East Lansing, Michigan, is the first community to protect its workers from discrimination on the basis of sexual orientation. As of January 2000, however, the State of Michigan still does not protect its workers from this discrimination.

1974 The Equal Credit Opportunity Act is passed, allowing married women for the first time to obtain credit cards in their own names.

1975 For every dollar earned by White men, Black men earn 74 cents; Hispanic men, 72 cents; White women, 56 cents; Black women, 55 cents; and Hispanic women, 49 cents.

1980 CEOs in the United States take home just over forty times the pay of average American workers.

1986 The Supreme Court declares sexual harassment to be a form of illegal employment discrimination.

1988 Employment and training, transitional health and day care benefits for persons leaving public assistance, and extension of public assistance to families with both parents present are only a few of the reforms that the Welfare Reform Act enacts. The law also provides for improved enforcement of child support orders.

The Fair Housing Act of 1968 is amended to prohibit discrimination against the elderly, mentally or physically handicapped people and families with children.

1994 One person in every two-parent family who receives payments under AFDC must participate in job searches.

1995 For every dollar earned by full-time year-round employed White men, Black men earn 76 cents; Hispanic men, 63 cents; White women, 71 cents; Black women, 64 cents; and Hispanic women, 53 cents.

1996 The Personal Responsibility and Work Opportunity Reconciliation Act replaces the previous welfare system with block grants to states through the Temporary Assistance to Needy Families (TANF) program. There is a lifetime limit of five years on receiving benefits. Welfare recipients are required to work after twenty-four months of benefits or they become ineligible for further assistance.

2000 The U.S. Equal Employment Opportunity Commission receives 15,836 charges of sexual harassment, 86.4 percent of which were filed by women.

2005 TANF is reauthorized under the Deficit Reduction Act of 2005.

2007 45.7 million Americans are without health insurance; 10.4 percent of Whites, 19.5 percent of African Americans, and 32.1 percent of Hispanics do not have health insurance.

CEOS in the United States take home 521 times the pay of average American workers. Between 2003 and 2007, the average annual increase in pay for CEOS was 9.7 percent, compared with 3.5 percent for average executives and 0.7 percent for average employees.

Indicators of Economic Inequality

To highlight current levels of economic inequality, a set of indicators follows.

National Income Inequality Key to the well-being of groups is control over material resources, particularly income and wealth, and freedom from poverty. A major distinguishing characteristic of the U.S. economy is the vast gap between the material resources of the rich and the poor.

The United States has the greatest income disparity of any nation-member of the Organization for Economic Co-Operation and Development (OECD)—thirty advanced industrialized nations—in part because the rich receive more here than elsewhere but mostly because the poor receive so much less (see Figure 2.5). In the United States, the poor earn 39 percent of the U.S. median income, whereas their counterparts in the other OECD nations earn between 44 and 57 percent of the median income in their countries (Mishel, Bernstein, and Allegretto 2007).[1]

Who Controls Material Resources? Race, class, gender, and sexuality hierarchies are maintained in part because dominant groups have greater control over the material resources of society. Therefore, women, people of color, and working-class people have higher poverty rates, lower incomes, less wealth, and fewer prestigious occupations, and they pay a greater portion of their earnings in taxes (Abramovitz and Morgen 2006; Mishel, Bernstein, and Allegretto 2007; Lovell, Hartman, and Williams 2008). Although the economic status of gays, bisexuals, and lesbians as a group is not reported in government documents, some clear material advantages are denied to homosexuals, among them the special economic privileges that accrue to married couples: spousal benefits on the job, survivor benefits in Social Security, and tax advantages. Furthermore, promotions and other forms of advancement in many work settings are still difficult to obtain for gay men and lesbians (Badgett, Ramos, and Sears 2008).

Who Are the Poor? Because 66 percent of the U.S. population in 2007 was White, there are of course more poor Whites than any other group. In fact, there are five times as many White as Black families and four times as many White as Hispanic families living below the poverty level. However, families of color, and especially single-parent women of color and their children, bear a much greater portion of the poverty burden than their share in the population would indicate. Families

---

[1]More information about OECD is available at http://www.oecd.org, and data on income disparity among OECD countries is available at http://www.stateofworkingamerica.org /tabfig/08/SWA06.

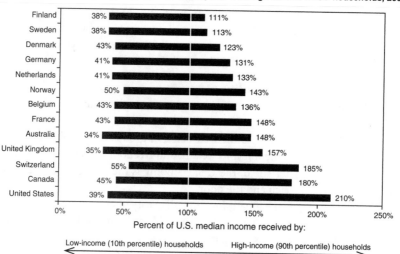

Share of U.S. median income received by low- and high-income OECD households, 2000*

Figure 2.5 Share of U.S. median income received by low- and high-income OECD households. 2000*

* These relative income measures compare the gap between the top 10% and the bottom 10% of household income in each country to the U.S. median income in purchasing-power-parity terms.
Source: Smeeding, Timothy, and Lee Rainwater. 2001. "Comparing living standards across nations: Real incomes at the top, the bottom, and the middle. "Luxembourg Income Study Working Draft Paper. Luxembourg: Luxembourg Income Study.
Smeeding, Timothy. 2006. "Poor people in rich nations: The United States in compative perspective." *Journal of Economic Perspective* 20(3):69–90.
From Mishel, Lawrence, Jared Bernstein, and Sylvia Al Ieqretto, *The State of Working America 2006/2007*. An Economic Policy Institute Book. Ithaca, N.Y.: ILR Press, an imprint of Cornell University Press, 2007.

of color have higher poverty rates than the White family rate of 6.0 percent in 2007: Asians, 8.11 percent, Hispanics, 20.6 percent, and Blacks, 23.8 percent (see Figure 2.6).

Single-parent mothers and their children have the highest poverty rates of any family group, but single-parent women of color and their children are most likely to be poor. Poverty rates for families headed by single mothers are: Whites, 21.4 percent; Asians, 14.8 percent, Hispanics, 39.6 percent, and Blacks, 39.7 percent.

Who Has the Wealth? Wealth is a much better indicator of total economic resources than income because it includes income and all other assets (e.g., stocks and bonds, checking and savings account balances, homes), as well as liabilities (e.g., mortgage debt, amount owed on credit cards). In other words, wealth represents the net worth of an individual or family. Wealth inequality is much more extreme than income inequality and has worsened over time. Over the past forty years, the wealthiest quintile (20 percent) of Americans has held over 80 percent

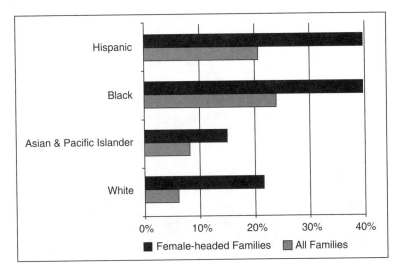

Figure 2.6. Poverty Rates by Race, 2007
Source: U.S. Census Bureau. 2007. *Income, Poverty and Health Insurance Coverage in the United States: 2007*. Table B-1: Poverty Status of People by Family Relationship, Race, and Hispanic Origin: 1959 to 2007. Available from http://www.census.gov/prod/2008pubs/p60-235.pdf, accessed October 12, 2008.

Figure created by: Christina E. Griffin

of the nation's wealth, with the top 1 percent controlling one-third of it. By 2004, the poorest quintile of households held only 15.3 percent of the wealth, down 3.4 percentage points since 1983 (see Figure 2.7).

It is a challenge for middle- and lower-income families to accumulate great wealth in part because so many have significant debt and are unlikely to inherit assets, as many upper-class people do (Beckert 2008). And yet a family's wealth can make all the difference when crises such as a serious health problem, loss of a partner or spouse, job loss, or natural disaster threatens their livelihood and stability. Wealth is also a much better indicator of the racial gap in economic vulnerability because racial wealth disparities are much greater than income disparities between Whites, African Americans, and Latinos. Whereas non-White income was 55.6 percent of white income in 2004, non-White net worth was just 27.3 percent of White net worth. In contrast, the net worth of the average African American household was equal to just 19 percent of the average White household. African American households also disproportionately faced zero or negative net worth: 29.4 percent of African American households had zero or negative net worth, compared with 13 percent of White households (Mishel, Berstein, and Allegretto 2007)

At the top of the wealth scale, the rapid globalization of capital markets in the past decade has created billionaires in other countries who now join elite White men in the United States as the richest people in the world. Still, the top twenty-five richest people in the world include only one woman, Liliane Bettencourt

Distribution of wealth by wealth class, 1983-2004

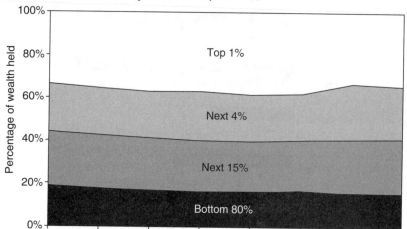

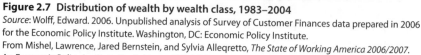

Figure 2.7 Distribution of wealth by wealth class, 1983–2004

Source: Wolff, Edward. 2006. Unpublished analysis of Survey of Customer Finances data prepared in 2006
for the Economic Policy Institute. Washington, DC: Economic Policy Institute.
From Mishel, Lawrence, Jared Bernstein, and Sylvia Alleqretto, *The State of Working America 2006/2007*.
An Economic Policy Institute Book. Ithaca, N.Y.: ILR Press, an imprint of Cornell University Press, 2007.

of France (Kroll 2008). And by 2008, only twenty-four women were CEOs on
Fortune magazine's list of the top one thousand companies in the United States
(Catalyst 2009).

Who Gets the Income? Most of the population, however, makes a living not
through corporate ownership but rather through the wages earned from working for an employer. The income distribution of the United States also reveals
the effects of race, class, and gender inequality. And as with other indicators,
income inequalities have deepened in recent years. For example, between 1979
and 2005 the after-tax income of the poorest quintile of income earners increased by 6 percent, whereas the middle quintile increased by 21 percent, and
the top .01 percent saw their incomes increase by 480 percent (Congressional
Budget Office 2007).

One major economic disadvantage to people of color and working-class people is that they have higher rates of unemployment, part-time work, and seasonal
work. Although they do not have higher unemployment rates, White women are
more likely to work part time and seasonally than White men. However, even
comparing only people working full time and year round, White men continue to
earn significantly more than White women or people of color.

Men earn significantly more than women in every racial group. Asian men
are the only group that surpasses White men, earning $1.04 for every $1.00 earned

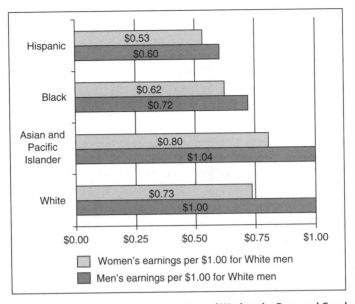

Figure 2.8. Median Income for Full-Time Year-Round Workers by Race and Gender, 2007
Source: U.S. Bureau of the Census, 2007. Table P-38. Full-Time, Year-Round All Workers
by Median Earnings and Sex: 1960 to 2007. Available from http://www.census.gov/hhes/www/income/
histinc/p38AR.html, accessed January 5, 2009.

Table created by: Christina E. Griffin

by White men. Every other group earns at least 25 percent less than White men. Hispanic women earn 53 percent, and Hispanic men and Black women earn about 60 percent the earnings of White men.

Figure 2.8 presents median income data in 2007 for all race and gender groups.

Marriage/Reproduction

Controlling marriage and reproduction and its attendant privileges has been a primary mechanism of race, class, gender, and sexuality oppression throughout the history of this country. The data in this section implicitly show the story of attempts to control women and some of the ways that those controls vary by race, class, and sexual orientation. For example, after *Roe v. Wade* legalized abortion, the Hyde Amendment effectively took away the right for many poor women, in practice more frequently women of color, by eliminating federal funding for abortions. The contests over sexuality have also been fought largely in this arena. For example, gays and lesbians still have not realized the legal right to marry and obtain related rights, including spousal health benefits, joint tax filing, and in almost all states, adoption. And many lives were lost because the government was slow to respond to HIV/AIDS, which was initially believed to be a disease affecting only homosexual men.

1873 Congress passes the Comstock Law, defining contraceptive information as "obscene material" and making it a crime to import or distribute any device, medicine, or information designed to prevent conception or induce abortion and even to mention in print the names of sexually transmitted diseases. Connecticut makes use of contraceptives illegal; twenty-four states decide to prohibit publication or advertising of abortion or birth control information; and fourteen other states also prohibit speech about birth control and abortion.

1921 Margaret Sanger organizes the American Birth Control League, which later becomes the Planned Parenthood Federation of America. She does this in an effort to assist the poor, because birth control is primarily available to the wealthy. Sanger arranges to get doctors for the poor and to educate them about birth control.

1922 The Cable Act passes, discouraging Chinese Americans from marrying immigrants who could gain exemption from naturalization laws and laws preventing them from owning land by marrying citizens. This act intimidates Chinese Americans and severely restricts their ability to build families in the United States.

1931 The Cable Act of 1922 is amended to allow American-born Asian women to regain their American citizenship on termination of their marriages to noncitizens.

1936 The Cable Act is repealed.

1965 In *Griswold v. Connecticut*, the Supreme Court upholds the right of married couples to use contraceptives.

1966 Seventeen states have laws against interracial marriage. All fifty states regulate marriage between Whites and other races.

1967 In *Loving v. Virginia*, the Supreme Court overturns all antimiscegenation laws (against marriage between different races), deeming them a violation of the Equal Protection Clause of the Fourteenth Amendment.

1972 In *Eisenstadt v. Baird*, the Supreme Court invalidates state laws restricting the access of single persons to contraceptives.

1973 The Supreme Court decides in *Roe v. Wade* that the decision to have an abortion must be left solely to a woman and her physician.

1977 The Hyde Amendment is passed, cutting off federally funded abortions for low-income women.

1978 The Pregnancy Discrimination Act of 1978 is passed as an amendment to Title VII of the Civil Rights Act, requiring all firms of fifteen or more employees to treat pregnancy the same as any other medical disability. As a result, discrimination against women because of pregnancy, childbirth, or related conditions is prohibited.

1981 The first cases (422 in the United States) of AIDS are identified in Los Angeles, California. Initially, most cases of AIDS in the United States are diagnosed in gay men and intravenous drug users.

1987 After a six-year silence, President Ronald Reagan uses the word "AIDS" in public for the first time. Of the 71,176 people diagnosed with AIDS in the country, 41,027 have died.

1988 The Reagan administration sends an eight-page booklet, "Understanding AIDS," to every household in America. According to the Centers for Disease Control (CDC), the epidemic will not spread widely in the heterosexual population.

1990 The 1990 Census shows that about 1.1 million interracial couples live in the United States, constituting approximately 2 percent of married couples.

In *Ohio v. Akron Center for Reproductive Health*, the Supreme Court upholds a state law requiring teenagers who seek abortions to notify one parent before doing so.

1992 The Supreme Court affirms in *Planned Parenthood v. Casey* that it is the right of states to restrict abortions if the restrictions do not pose an "undue burden." Specifically, the Court upholds twenty-four-hour waiting periods and mandatory antiabortion counseling for women seeking abortions.

1993 The Pregnancy Discrimination Act is superseded by the Family and Medical Leave Act, requiring employers with fifty or more employees to allow time off for pregnancy, a medical condition, or care of a sick family member.

All fifty states have revised their laws so that men can be prosecuted for sexually assaulting their wives, cohabitants, or dates.

1994 The Freedom of Access to Clinic Entrances Act, the first abortion rights legislation, is signed into law. It imposes severe fines and jail sentences and makes it a potential felony to block access to clinic entrances and to intimidate or harass clinic workers.

1996 Hawaii becomes the first state to recognize that gay and lesbian couples are entitled to the same privileges as heterosexual married couples.

The Defense of Marriage Act is passed, acknowledging that states will not be obligated to recognize gay and lesbian marriages performed in another state.

1998 Hawaii voters approve a constitutional amendment that expands the power of state lawmakers to restrict marriages to opposite-sex couples, thereby invalidating the 1996 Hawaiian court ruling.

1999 Since 1995, twenty-five states have enacted antimarriage laws targeting gay couples.

The Vermont Supreme Court grants gay and lesbian couples the right to enter into legal contracts that confer the same rights and protections as state-sanctioned marriage.

The U.S. Food and Drug Administration approves the prescription morning-after pill, commonly called "Plan B." The morning-after pill provides women the ability to prevent a pregnancy after unprotected sex.

Deaths worldwide from AIDS total 16.3 million. An estimated 33.6 million people worldwide are living with HIV/AIDS. The major mode of transmission of HIV is heterosexual intercourse, which accounts for 70 percent of all HIV infections. The overwhelming majority of people (95 percent of the world total) with HIV live in developing countries.

2000 The Vermont House of Representatives passes a bill to create "civil unions," giving gay and lesbian couples virtually all the benefits of marriage.

The U.S. Food and Drug Administration approves RU-486, a nonsurgical method of terminating a pregnancy.

2006 The U.S. Food and Drug Administration rules that women over age eighteen can purchase Plan B without a doctor's prescription.

2007 Globally, there are an estimated 33 million people living with HIV. Sixty-seven percent of all people currently living with HIV and 72 percent of people who have died from AIDS are from sub-Saharan Africa. New HIV infections decreased from an estimated 3.0 million in 2001 to an estimated 2.7 million in 2007.

Since 1995, states enacted 557 antichoice measures. In 2007, states considered 464 antichoice measures. The most common antichoice measures considered were: biased counseling and mandatory delays, mandatory ultrasounds, separate legal status for embryos and fetuses, abortion bans, and restriction on young women's access to abortion. Ultimately, nineteen states enacted forty-three antichoice measures this year.

2008 Thirty-two states and the District of Columbia fund abortions only in the cases of life endangerment, rape, and incest. Seventeen states use state funds to provide all or most medically necessary abortions. One state, South Dakota, funds abortion only in the case of life endangerment.

Two states have granted same-sex couples the right to marry: Massachusetts (2004) and Connecticut (2008). New York recognizes marriages between same-sex couples legally entered into in another jurisdiction (2008). Three states provide civil unions for gay and lesbian couples: Vermont (2000), New Jersey (2006), and New Hampshire (2008). Additionally, the District of Columbia, Oregon, and California provide state-level spousal rights to same-sex couples through domestic partnerships within the state. Hawaii, Maine, and Washington State provide some spousal rights within the state.

The Supreme Court of California rules in May that same-sex couples have the same right to marry as different-sex couples under the state constitution. Between June 17 and November 4, 2008, more than eighteen thousand same-sex couples marry in California. The right of gay and lesbian couples to marry in California and the status of the same-sex couples who married in 2008 is, however, under threat after voters passed Proposition 8, an antigay ballot measure in the November election.

Since the beginning of the epidemic, twenty-five million people have died from "HIV-related causes."

Eighty-seven percent of U.S. counties do not have an abortion provider.

SUMMARY

The historical record of oppressed groups in U.S. society reminds us that this nation was built by first extracting the land from Native Indians, by building the agricultural base through the forced labor of African slaves and the cheap labor of Mexican migrants, by expanding the land base through the conquest of Mexico and building the railroads with the cheap labor of Chinese workers, and by the factory, farm, and service work of the White working class. Women of each of these groups worked in these arenas while they cared for families and raised their children to participate in the society without themselves being fully accepted as equal participants. The historical time line gives us a sense of the persistence of both oppression and of the struggles of oppressed groups for full access to the rights, privileges, and opportunities of U.S. society.

Current social and economic indicators such as poverty, income, wealth, education, and congressional representation confirm that race, class, gender, and sexuality systems of oppression are persistent, pervasive, and severe. They persist through time, pervade every institution in society, and have severe consequences for oppressed groups. These historical markers and statistical indicators alert us that race, class, gender, and sexuality oppression exist. How these systems are created, maintained, challenged, and transformed is not apparent in these indicators. The remainder of this book seeks to describe how these systems operate in the United States today.

A Conceptual Framework—
Five Themes

CHAPTER 3

❧

The Story of Margaret Welch:
A Case Study

Everyone thinks that if you try hard enough, you can make it in America. I thought so, too, but when I found myself a widow at age thirty-three, with two children to support, and forced to go on public aid, I discovered how the welfare system works.

I have tried hard to make a better life for myself and my girls. I have studied hard to get an A average after being out of school for sixteen years, and it hurts to have to give up my dream, but the system won't let me out of the "welfare class." There are a great many of us who want out of the welfare class, but the system won't let us out.

—Margaret Welch[1]

Letters to the Editor, Chicago Tribune, March 26, 1987

Margaret Welch is a White woman who moved to Chicago from Tennessee in 1982 after the death of her first husband. When her second husband "walked out" five years later, leaving her with two girls, ages nine and five, she was forced to go on public aid. What follows is an excerpt from an interview conducted with Margaret Welch by Studs Terkel, a Chicago writer.

An Interview by Studs Terkel

The image people have of public aid is black women with a lot of kids. Before I went on public aid, I had that impression: the more babies you have, the more money you get. I realized that you get three dollars a day if you have another baby. That's not going to raise a

---

[1]Although this interview took place in the early 1990s, as the data in Chapter 2 suggest, the social and economic conditions affecting Margaret Welch and other women like her have not improved and by most indicators have worsened. Whites now constitute one-third of welfare recipients, but access to funding under the Temporary Assistance for Needy Families (TANF) program instituted in 1996 is more difficult because the primary purpose of that legislation was to move people out of welfare and into work. Although the welfare rolls were significantly reduced during the ensuing decade, research suggests that conditions of life for the poor, especially poor women, have worsened. Educational opportunities for welfare recipients are limited, and employment prospects are typically in low-wage jobs that offer no health benefits and cannot offset the increases in the cost of living engendered by working (e.g., day care and transportation) (Lein and Schexnayder 2007; Seccombe and Hoffman 2007).

kid. I thought they were freeloaders, who like to live off other people. But when I was forced on public aid, my opinion changed. I was on an even keel with them. We all sat there in the office and waited five or six hours at a time. They weren't getting special treatment. They were having hard times, too.

What gets me is this: I'm on public aid. I'm trying to stay in school and apply for all these scholarships. Blacks and Hispanics have hollered so much, they've got these scholarships. Even single white men can get scholarships if they have kids. But it's hard for a single white woman to get a scholarship, because you're not a minority. If you're a woman, you're supposed to take care of your kids if you're left alone with them. If men are left with kids, it's "Oh, that poor guy."...

I've just registered for my last year in nursing school. I won't be able to go back because the scholarship I got last year was just denied me. They said it was a Hispanic scholarship, and enough Hispanics applied, so I lost out.... I can't afford the tuition, so I don't know if I'm ever going back....

I went on public aid when my job at the hot-dog stand ended and my house burned down. I lost everything. On public aid, they gave me $711. That was supposed to get me an apartment, replace all my furniture and all the kids' clothes. The cheapest apartment called for a $600 deposit. It doesn't leave anything. I noticed a poster on the wall: public aid helps returning to school. I had a GED. I took the test and placed into the highest class. They were telling me about the scholarships and said I was a cinch. I got one last year and carried straight A's. But I found out last week I'm not a minority and out.

There goes...my dream of becoming a registered nurse....I got so close. "I'm sorry, but this time we have enough Hispanics."

This is the first time in my life I'm really mad this way....My boyfriend is Mexican and my best girlfriend is Puerto Rican and very Black. I've never been prejudiced, but why the hell are you doing this to me? I've been through enough. I was widowed at seventeen and

married again and my husband took off, leaving me with two kids. Just because I'm White, I don't get something?...

I feel like I've been robbed of a chance to finish school....I already had a job promised me in a hospital. I would be making $15 an hour for the first time in my life. I could feed my kids without begging, borrowing, or stealing. Selling food stamps is considered stealing. I get $308 a month to live on. My rent's $250. So that leaves me $58. You can't pay lights and gas and everything else. So you end up selling a few food stamps to buy laundry detergent.

For food, you buy a lot of rice and flour, make tortillas. That's all your kids have. They're the ones who are punished, whether you're white, black, or anything else. I was so sure that in a year, I'd have a job where I could feed my kids without feeling the way I do. I wouldn't have them laughed at in school because they get free meals. They wouldn't have to suffer that any more. Now....

My Puerto Rican black friend and I always applied for the same scholarships. We were always among the top in grades....We were promised jobs at the same hospital. We were in school together since the first day. This year, she got the scholarship, I didn't. She came to the house and said, "Don't be mad at me." I'm not. She's still my best friend. It's just—why?

We were sitting in my truck. I told her I got my letter. She ran out, checked her mail, and she's gotten hers. We didn't open them until we were together. She could tell by the look on my face. "What's the matter?" "I didn't get it. Did you?" She mumbled, "Yeah," and wouldn't let me see her letter. For a minute I was so mad at her. "I just want to kill you." [Laughs] We're still great friends. I'm glad she's making it, she deserves it.

I think blacks are going ahead. They speak out, they fight for their rights, and they're getting them. We're almost afraid of them and let them push us back.

If you see one black guy walking by, it's okay. But if you see three or four standing on a corner, you cross to the other side of the street. I was mugged about two years ago by a couple of Hispanic guys. Now if I see several Hispanics standing together, I cross the street.

Terkel: Suppose there were three or four tough-looking White guys?

I'd just walk through them….I've never been scared of a fight. I'm a big woman. I can handle myself.

Not far from my house is a motorcycle gang, Hell's Henchmen….When I was tending bar, I'd walk past them at two, three in the morning by myself and not think anything of it. But there's no way I'd walk by a black club.

I myself really don't feel hostility, but I feel that a lot of whites are becoming more and more afraid of blacks….

Somehow, people have to talk about this. You shouldn't feel "I'm too dumb to get up and say something"; talk in your words, say whatever. If enough people talk, good ideas may come out of it. Nobody wants to give up whatever power they got. To me, that's the whole thing, power….

You see the old slave-day movies. They were scared of their masters, their owners. They did what they were told. It seems like they've almost turned the tables. It's like we're scared to stand up against them….

Terkel: Would you prefer it the old way?

No-o-o-o! When I went to City-Wide College, my supervisor was a black lady. She just knew when there was something wrong. I'd sit at my desk half-crying. I'd gotten my second five-day notice that month to move out of my apartment. One of my classmates told her. When I came back from my break, there was a check on my desk to cover my rent. I tried to pay her back, but she said, "No, that's my gift to you." I would never have dreamed there was a black person like that when I was in Tennessee [where she grew up].

I don't believe Black people should be pushed back. But I don't feel because I'm white, I should be either. It goes both ways. I don't think the gap is that big on a street level, not in my neighborhood. But when you get into the bureaucracy, business, and school, it's those big people making the noise….

(Terkel 1992, 69–73)

INTERPRETING MARGARET'S STORY

Margaret Welch is angry. She is also hurt, discouraged, resentful, envious, confused, empathetic, proud, and self-confident. In short, she is a complex person trying to comprehend her life circumstances in light of the race, class, gender, and sexuality hierarchies in society, in the welfare system, in her college, in her neighborhood, and in her most intimate relationships with her boyfriend and her best girlfriend. She vents her anger at a social system that leaves her without the resources to finish her education and get off welfare. More intensely, she vents her anger at people of color—who have secured scholarship programs to which she is told she cannot apply, even as she struggles to control and understand that anger. In the same breath she says that she wants "to kill" her Puerto Rican best friend, that she is glad for her, and that her friend deserves the scholarship.

- Is Margaret racist?
- Is her lack of effort or talent the reason she is on welfare?
- Will cutting back her welfare payments or requiring that she work or go to school solve Margaret's dilemma and get her off welfare?
- If she were Black or Puerto Rican and had been turned down for a scholarship, where might she place her anger?
- Why did someone attribute the denial of Margaret's request for a scholarship to Latino/a students' funding?

- Is Margaret a criminal for selling food stamps?
- If Margaret were living in the 1950s or 1960s, how would her situation have been different? How would it have been different in 2009?
- Why is she afraid of anonymous Black men on the street but not of White Hell's Henchmen?
- If Margaret were lesbian, would her children be taken from her?
- What does it mean to be a White, heterosexual mother on welfare?

These are but a few of the many questions raised by Margaret's life that are centered in race, class, gender, and sexuality hierarchies. These questions have no simple answers. But they do illustrate the complexity of race, class, gender, and sexuality in our everyday lives and provide an avenue to explore the many ways that social location in these hierarchies shapes how we experience the world and how we view the experiences of others.

Race, class, gender, and sexuality are deeply embedded in society's basic political, economic, and ideological institutions: the state, the economy, the family, and the educational and religious systems. They are also fundamental elements of personal identity, how we define who we are. Yet every day, the meanings of these hierarchies are negotiated and renegotiated as individuals like Margaret encounter institutions such as the college or the welfare office and attempt to understand, to conform to, and to challenge the patterns of behavior and beliefs that are associated with race, class, gender, and sexuality.

As Margaret begins to react to her scholarship denial, she believes she is a victim of discrimination because she is a White woman. Yet, as the data in Chapter 2 show, the major institutions of society are primarily structured to support the advancement of White people, not of people of color. At the time, White women were 1.6 times as likely to graduate from college as Black women and 2.8 times as likely as Puerto Rican women (Ortiz 1994). Living in poverty are 39.7 percent of families headed by Black women, 39.6 percent of families headed by Hispanic women, and 21.4 percent of families headed by White women, like Margaret's family (see Figure 2.6). But because of scholarships targeted to increase enrollments of these groups, Margaret still feels discriminated against as a White woman.

Interestingly, Margaret does not overtly consider the role of class in shaping her situation. Instead, class appears more in the background of her life. She does not question the fact that higher education is not free and open to all, as elementary and secondary schools are. Like most Americans, she takes the costs of higher education for granted. Instead, she needs financial aid because college costs money and she is poor. Yet she seems to feel "put down" and blocked, not so much by these class realities as by Blacks and Latinos/as—other oppressed groups—who collectively and successfully have pushed for rights in the political arena and have won key struggles, including those for college financial aid.

Because Margaret was told that her scholarship was for Latinos/as, it is not surprising that Margaret would blame Black and Latino/a progress for her own ill fortune. But one of the things that an analysis of race, class, gender, and sexuality reveals is that in any social situation how we define the situation, what we take to be real, is shaped by our social location. Thus any particular situation can be described as having multiple "truths"—realities, understandings—representing the interpretations that different actors make based on the earlier experiences and perspectives they bring to the encounter.

[handwritten margin note: Social location]

Consider for a moment Margaret's interpretation, her "truth." Margaret said she was told that

- The scholarship she had received in the past was in fact a Latino/a scholarship
- "Enough" Latinos/as had applied this semester
- Because she was White and not Latina, she could not have a scholarship

A Latino/a student, on hearing of Margaret's plight, might see the situation from a different perspective, have a different "truth," and wonder

- Why Margaret was given a Latino/a scholarship in the first place
- Whether the money could have been held until enough eligible Latinos/as applied
- Why were there not enough applicants
- Whether Latinas on welfare knew the money was available
- What the welfare office was doing to encourage Latinos/as to attend college

A financial aid officer might wonder

- Why funds earmarked for Latino/a students would be given to an White student
- Whether restricted funds are being commingled (a violation of proper procedure and law in many cases)
- Whether Margaret had been told of the scholarship money that was available and open to *anyone* based on need and/or merit
- Why Margaret is being told that she was denied a scholarship because Latinos/as applied when she was never really eligible for that form of aid in the first place

Each of these actors takes different "truths"—understandings, interpretations—from this situation. We have seen Margaret's understanding of it: "All of a sudden, they're ['the minorities'] giving me the short end," and the questions she asks:

- Just because their skin's darker than mine, why should they get it and I don't?
- I've never been prejudiced, but why the hell are you doing this to me?
- Just because I'm White, I don't get something?

Margaret believes that White women don't have a chance. Even though her best girlfriend and her boyfriend are Latina and Latino, her neighborhood is racially mixed, and she has had many positive experiences across racial lines, Margaret appears to see her disadvantage as directly connected to a presumed advantage of people of color—and she is angry. Interracial hostility, even though it is very uncomfortable for her, is an understandable, if not desirable, outcome. Margaret also raises the issue of the "welfare system's" not wanting people to get off welfare. Here she implies, but does not directly state, that if welfare is designed to help people become self-sufficient, she, as a poor person, should be able to get the financial aid she needs to finish her education and to get a job as a nurse. Race is not her focus here. Poverty and the class structure of the educational system are. And this "truth," although it is a part of Margaret's worldview, is not the one that is reinforced in the way that her loss of the scholarship was explained to her. This truth lacks the power, therefore, of the racial-advantage "truth" and appears to recede in Margaret's understanding of the situation.

How we interpret our "truths"—our lives, the meanings we take from our experiences—is also revealed as much in our silences and the things we take for granted as in our spoken words. Those silences are most likely to occur in areas where we experience privilege. So one of the issues that Margaret does not consider is her heterosexuality: It poses no special problem for her. Because she is heterosexual and White, Margaret is presumed (by the welfare office and larger society) to have the capacity to be a good mother—if she can get a degree and a good job and thus provide for her children. If Margaret were lesbian, however, she would face the prospect of having her children taken away from her by child protective services, as many lesbian mothers have (Benkov 1994; Lapidus 2004; Mink 2001). If she were lesbian, fearing the possible loss of her children, she might be less likely to even go to the welfare office to seek aid, and she and her children would suffer even worse economic hardship as a result. But these problems do not emerge in Margaret's life. She takes for granted that her sexual orientation had nothing to do with the scholarship denial, that her children won't be taken away or harassed in school because of her sexual orientation. It is simply not an "issue" for her; it is a silence in her story, but it is a powerful "truth" in her life.

And what of Margaret's best girlfriend? What truths might she take from this situation? First, she obviously feared that her friendship would be damaged by the attribution of Hispanic responsibility for Margaret's being denied the scholarship. She implored, "Please don't be mad at me." When she begins to reflect on the situation, she might also feel justifiably angry that Hispanics are being blamed for the ineptitude and/or policies at the scholarship office. She might also feel angry that the limited funds earmarked for Hispanic students were used to support a White student.

- Facing Margaret's racial anger, will she become hurt and angry herself and begin to think of Margaret as racist, as the enemy?
- Will she blame the welfare office for its racially divisive practice or blame herself for taking a scholarship that Margaret might have deserved?

Partial Truths: Race, Class, Gender, and Sexuality as Separate Systems

Clearly, there are many ways of understanding Margaret's dilemma, many truths in her life. Dominant perspectives in modern social science, as well as in the media, tend to interpret complex lives in very isolated and limited ways by attending to only a single dimension. To illustrate the important—but partial—insights that might be gained by such perspectives, following are examples of issues that might be raised, questions that might be asked, and "truths" that might be unearthed when Margaret's complex life is examined through the lens of only a single social system.

Race: Race scholars would emphasize the ways that ideas about and structures of race influence Margaret's life. Her story, in fact, was originally printed in *Race: How Blacks and Whites Think and Feel About the American Obsession*, a book of interviews conducted by Studs Terkel (1992). By focusing on the racial dimension alone, we might explore:

- The racial animosity expressed by a White toward Blacks and Latinos/as. The power of racial "otherness" or racial stereotypes was clearly illustrated in Margaret's generalization of her denial of a scholarship intended for Latino/a students to hostility toward and fear of both Blacks and Latinos/as inside the academic setting, on the street in her neighborhood, and in the public political arena.
- The institutional practice that promotes racial animosity between White and other racial groups by pitting them against one another for scarce resources such as scholarships.
- The ramifications of the fact that Whites made up the majority of welfare recipients in the 1990s and still constitute one-third of them—despite the stereotypical association between welfare and people of color—even though Blacks and Latinos/as are much more likely to be poor, reflecting their racial disadvantage in the economy.
- Whether it is appropriate to label Margaret as racist. What is a racist? Can a person *be* racist? Do people incorporate racial beliefs into their personalities as permanent and unchangeable character traits? Or are configurations of racial beliefs, attitudes, and behaviors more malleable—subject to change in different situations, at different times?
- The seeming irony that a racially privileged group member would perceive herself as the victim of racial discrimination. How might that happen? What are the implications for how Whites come to see their race? How do their views of themselves affect their views of people of color? And how do the views and resistance of people of color shape how White people view their Whiteness?
- The significance of nursing as a predominantly White profession, with 88 percent of registered nurses having been White ten years ago (U.S. Census Bureau 1999: Table 645) and 77.4 percent being so now (U.S. Census Bureau 2008d: Table 598). When Margaret finally does receive her nursing degree, she is unlikely to face *racial* discrimination in the job market, whereas her Puerto Rican friend is much more likely to face it. Yet if Margaret has

difficulty finding a job, how will she understand that difficulty? Whom will she blame? What will she do about it?

- How White people maintain their position of power in the racial hierarchy by structurally excluding people of color from political and economic advancement and by promoting and maintaining stereotypes of racial ethnic peoples, including notions that they are inferior, less deserving, and to be feared.

Class: Class scholars would emphasize the way that ideas about and structures of economic class influence Margaret's life. What questions might these scholars raise and what class truths might they extract from Margaret's story?

- How are Margaret's difficulties in meeting the basic survival needs for her family a product of her class position and her poverty? Because she worked at a hot dog stand and then lost her job, she was forced onto public aid to survive. Could Margaret and others like her in the 1990s have found a way out of poverty in an economy in which the increase in job opportunities was largely for part-time work and in which even full-time workers in minimum wage jobs received wages that were lower than poverty level? And fifteen years later, the situation is unchanged (Mishel, Berstein, and Allegretto 2007).

- If education and training are to be seen as an answer to Margaret's and other workers' low wages, what social forces are inclined to further this cause when much of the economy is dependent on low-wage work?

- Although sympathy with the labor unions has remained high among the American public, union membership is at an all-time low, in part because of the global portability of large-scale capital and the immobility of labor here and across the globe (Panagopoulos and Francia 2008). What is the relationship between the plight of American workers such as Margaret and the weak position of labor today? What avenues do workers have for improving their collective position in the economy?

- What are the processes through which our class system is reproduced and challenged? How do the privileged classes, the middle and upper classes, restrict access to higher education, to particular positions in the labor market, and to inherited wealth? How are controlling images (stereotypes) of the poor and working classes—as exerting less effort, being less talented, and being less deserving than those in the privileged classes—maintained? How do the poor and working classes resist those images?

Gender: Gender scholars would emphasize the ways that ideas about and structures of gender influence Margaret's life. If we were solely to focus on gender, what are some of the questions we might ask and the truths we might reveal?

- White women earned 73 percent of the wages of White males in the labor market (see Figure 2.8). Margaret feels responsible, and the state (the whole political and governmental domain) sees her as responsible, for child rearing. As Margaret says, "If you're a woman, you're supposed to take care of your kids if you're left alone with them. If men are left with kids, it's 'Oh, that poor guy.'" But she is not provided with the financial wherewithal either from the state or in the job market to support her family. What does Margaret's poverty have to do with her being both widowed and divorced and a single mother?

• Margaret plans to enter nursing, still a female-dominated profession that pays much lower wages and takes fewer years of schooling than male-dominated health professions, such as medical doctor. Why? What are the social and psychological processes that produce sex-segregated labor markets?

• She fears for her personal safety in the streets of her neighborhood. What is the connection between violence against women and patriarchy, the system of male dominance?

• If Margaret and her friend were Mike and Juan, and if Mike were denied a scholarship to engineering school while his Puerto Rican friend Juan got one, would they have reacted as the women did? How might their reactions have been different?

• What are the processes through which men maintain their position of power in the gender hierarchy? How do men and gender systems structurally restrict women's advancement in the economy, threaten women with violence, and promote stereotypes of women as weak, as more suited to home and family than to market work, and as less competent than men?

Sexuality: In addition to race, class, and gender, ideas about and structures of sexuality also shape Margaret's life. In the hierarchy of sexuality—the system of heterosexual privilege—cross-sex relationships are defined as the norm, and same-sex relationships are defined as abnormal or deviant and are rigidly restricted. Strong sanctions against homosexuality, in fact, help to maintain rigid and extremely different versions of what is "masculine" and what is "feminine." People conform to rigid sex roles—expectations for acceptable behavior for women and men—in part out of homophobia, the fear that they will be associated with gays or lesbians and will be mistreated as a consequence. What questions can be raised and truths revealed about Margaret's life arising from her position in the sexual hierarchy as a heterosexual woman?

• How would her story be different if Margaret decided to live with another woman to make ends meet? Would she be suspected of being lesbian and be treated differently by her friends, the school, the welfare office, her children? What might happen if she were lesbian or bisexual?

• What are the processes through which heterosexuality is socially constructed and legally enforced as a prerequisite for being seen as a "good mother"? What are the implications of being a heterosexual, bisexual, or lesbian mother for such issues as adoption, child custody, welfare benefits, and employment?

- To what extent is Margaret's reproductive life controlled by the low benefits afforded her for each child under AFDC and welfare? How are social policies constructed to control the sexual behaviors of poor women?
- To what extent is the hyperaggressive behavior of Hell's Henchmen based on the need to claim masculine power by asserting forcefully that the members are not "feminine," not gay?

These are only a few of the questions raised and the insights or "truths" that can be gleaned from Margaret's life. Each of these questions may reveal a significant aspect of Margaret's life, but when juxtaposed with the total complexities of Margaret's life and with each other, they seem at best to be very partial truths, for each ignores the other. And Margaret's own attempt to make sense of her situation reveals clearly that when she thinks of her situation, she does not—and cannot—separate her race from her class from her gender from her sexuality.

Margaret is like each of us in that her race, class, gender, and sexuality are all fundamental sources of her identity. Margaret is a woman. She is also White, poor, and heterosexual. All of these factors shape how she views herself and her situation, how others view her, and how the policies and practices of social institutions affect her. We can ignore some aspects of our social location at any time, but because they are fundamental elements of society's organization, we cannot render them inactive or unimportant.

FIVE THEMES: AN OVERVIEW
OF THE CONCEPTUAL FRAMEWORK

Rather than analyze Margaret's or any other life or group experience through a single lens alone, a much richer analysis is achieved through the analysis of race, class, gender, and sexuality as interrelated systems of oppression. Five common themes characterize these interrelated systems and can be used as a framework for analysis. The systems are (1) historically and geographically contextual (2) socially constructed (3) power relationships that operate at (4) macro social-structural and micro social-psychological levels and are (5) simultaneously expressed. They are described in detail in the chapters that follow but are briefly summarized here.

1. *Historically and Geographically Contextual*: Race, class, gender, and sexuality can be understood only in their *historical and geographic contexts*. So analyses focus on specific times and places and avoid the search for common meanings of race, class, gender, and sexuality that would apply in all times and places.

    Remember Margaret's life. Her dilemmas would have been very different in the 1950s, when the welfare system was almost solely serving White women. She would not have been told that she lost a scholarship to a Latina, but would education scholarships have been available for women at all?

2. *Socially Constructed*: Race, class, gender, and sexuality are *social constructs* whose meaning develops out of group struggles over socially valued resources. Although they may have biological or material referents, race, class, gender, and sexuality are not fixed properties of individuals nor of materially defined groups. Their meaning can and does change over time and in different social contexts.

Think again of Margaret. Part of her lament is that it doesn't *mean* the same thing to be White that it once did, and the change raises key questions for her. She asks: "Just because I'm White, I don't get something?" One could almost finish her thought, "Then what does it mean to be White anymore?"

3. *Power Relationships*: Race, class, gender, and sexuality are *power relationships of dominance and subordination*, not merely gradations along a scale of resources—who has more than whom—or differences in cultural preferences or gender roles. They are based in relationships of exploitation of subordinate groups by dominant groups for a greater share of society's valued resources. They change because oppressed groups struggle to gain rights, opportunities, and resources—to gain greater control over their lives—against dominant groups who seek to maintain their position of control over the political, ideological, and economic social domains—over their own lives, as well as over others' lives.

Margaret's story is certainly a story of power relationships—structural, external powers that shape her life because of her gender, sexuality, race, and class:

- The power she had to provide for her children while married
- The power she lacked to do the same when widowed and divorced
- The power she lacked to command a decent wage in the economy
- The power she had to keep her children while on public aid, when women of color and lesbian mothers might have lost theirs

And there are her internal, psychological senses of power: her sense of powerlessness to overcome the obstacles to completing her degree, her fear of and sense of powerlessness relative to Black and Latino men, and yet the power she feels to walk without fear through a group of Hell's Henchmen.

4. *Macro Social-Structural and Micro Social-Psychological Levels*: These power relationships between dominant and subordinate groups are embedded in society's *macro* social institutions and in the *micro* face-to-face interactions that constitute the everyday lives of individuals. Specifying the linkages between these two levels is a key component of a race, class, gender, and sexuality analysis.

Margaret's plight can be understood by looking at the opportunities and restrictions, the options and limits, that social systems of class, race, gender, and sexuality place on her—from occupational restrictions to low wages to legal and social expectations for poor, White, heterosexual mothers. And these macro systemic patterns are played out in her everyday interactions with her boyfriend, her best girlfriend, her children, the school, and the welfare office.

5. *Simultaneously Expressed*: Race, class, gender, and sexuality *operate simultaneously* in every social situation. At the societal level, these systems of social hierarchies are connected to each other and are embedded in all social institutions. At the individual level, we each experience our lives based on our location along *all* dimensions, and so we may occupy positions of dominance and subordination at the same time.

Many of the ways that macro systems of class and gender shape Margaret's life are relatively apparent. But race and sexuality systems—systems in which she occupies a privileged location—also shape her life in critical ways, even though they are somewhat more obscured. Her racial privilege is masked by a dominant ideology that blames racially oppressed groups for White people's class disadvantages. So Margaret is told, and she accepts, that the reason for her inability to pay for college is that scholarships are available for racially oppressed groups. Further, because Margaret is heterosexual and has not violated sexual norms, the system of heterosexual privilege is somewhat hidden in her story, but it nonetheless supports her in a way that she doesn't see, as is typically the case with privilege.

SUMMARY

Margaret Welch's story illustrates the importance of social location in shaping what we come to see as real, in shaping our understandings of the world. And because our social locations represent our positions in all the social hierarchies—including race, class, gender, and sexuality—within which we live our lives, analyses that focus on only a single dimension, although useful for some purposes, are ultimately partial. To develop understandings that are more useful in the pursuit of social justice, we need complex analyses that attend to the multiple social hierarchies as they intersect with one another, both in individual lives such as Margaret's and in the society as a whole.

To analyze race, class, gender, and sexuality as intersecting systems of oppression, this book puts forth a conceptual framework. The framework represents these systems as socially constructed, historically and geographically specific power relations that simultaneously operate at the macro social-structural and micro social-psychological levels.

CHAPTER 4

Themes: Historically and Geographically Contextual, Socially Constructed Power Relations

In this chapter I examine the first three themes in the analysis of race, class, gender, and sexuality: They are (1) historically and geographically contextual, (2) socially constructed (3) power relations. I begin by reviewing some of the historically and geographically varying meanings of each of these systems. That the meanings of these systems vary over time and place demonstrates that they are socially constructed. Next, I explore in more detail what is meant by social construction. Finally, I address how conceiving of these dimensions as power relations pushes us to see them as relational and thus to examine both privilege and oppression.

Race, class, gender, and sexuality are interdependent, socially constructed power relations. Their meanings develop and change in group struggles that are firmly rooted in particular geographic locales and in particular historic time periods. From these group contests, new racial categories, new social classes, new gender constructions, and new sexual communities arise, transform, and dissolve. Through similar processes of biologizing, dichotomizing, and ranking, race, gender, and sexuality systems of power and privilege are created and, through the resistance they engender, they are transformed. The social class system produces a similar dynamic of oppression through a slightly different process of construction—not biological determinism but an extreme notion of individual determinism that uses concepts of ability and effort to justify the dominant group's position of power.

HISTORICALLY AND GEOGRAPHICALLY CONTEXTUAL

Although they persist throughout history, race, class, gender, and sexuality hierarchies are never static and fixed but are constantly changing as part of new economic, political, and ideological processes, trends, and events. Their meaning varies not only across historical time periods but also across nations and regions within nations during the same period. Because these systems must always be understood within a specific historical and geographical context, race, class, gender, and sexuality analyses tend to avoid the search for common meanings of the systems that would apply in all times and places.

Race

Consider for a moment the major shifts in the dominant conception of race that have taken place in the United States in the past century. The concept of race—the grouping of people with certain ancestry and biological traits into categories or groups for differential treatment—emerged initially in the United States as a justification of slavery (Fields 1990; Omi and Winant 1994; Winant 2000). People of many different African nations and tribes were defined as all one group, and that group was associated with evil, sin, laziness, bestiality, sexuality, and irresponsibility. This new racial conception of Africans rationalized the exploitation of their labor in slavery and justified holding humans in bondage, whipping them, selling them, separating them from their families, and working them to death (Spickard 1992, 19). In "The Illogic of American Racial Categories," Paul Spickard (1992, 18) illustrates the historical and geographical ways that races are defined and redefined by the state from 1870 through 1980. The U.S. Bureau of the Census used the following racial classifications:

1870   White, Colored (Blacks), Colored (Mulattoes), Chinese, and Indian
1950   White, Black, and Other
1980   White, Black, Hispanic, Japanese, Chinese, Filipino, Korean, Vietnamese, American Indian, Asian Indian, Hawaiian, Guamanian, Samoan, Eskimo, Aleut and Other(Spickard 1992)

More recent shifts include:

1990   *5 races*: White, Black (or African American), Asian or Pacific Islander, American Indian, Eskimo, Aleut
            2 ethnicities: Hispanic, non-Hispanic (O'Hare 1992)
2000   *15 races*: White; Black, African American, or Negro; American Indian or Alaska Native; Asian Indian; Japanese; Native Hawaiian; Chinese, Korean; Guamanian or Chamorro; Filipino; Vietnamese; Samoan; Other Asian; Other Pacific Islander; Some Other Race
            5 ethnicities: Mexican, Mexican American, Chicano; Puerto Rican; Cuban; Other Spanish/Hispanic/Latino; Not Spanish/Hispanic/Latino (U.S. Bureau of the Census 1998b)
2010   In the past few years, the Census Bureau has been testing options for changing the U.S. racial and ethnic classifications once again, this time by eliminating the "Some Other Race" category—the third largest racial group in the 2000 census, 97 percent of whom were Hispanic (Lewis 2006).

As late as the 1980s, racial groups were differently defined in different countries:

England	White, West Indian, African, Arab, Turkish, Chinese, Indian, Pakistani, Bangladeshi, Sri Lankan, and Other
South Africa	White, African, Coloured, and Asian
Brazil	The many gradations of *White* and *Black* were: *preto* (black), *cabra* (slightly less black), *escuro* (dark, lighter than *preto),* *mulato escuro* (dark mulatto), *mulato claro* (light mulatto), *pardo* (light mulatto), *sarara* (light skin, kinky hair), *Moreno* (light skin, straight hair), and *branco de terra* (some Black heritage, seen as White) (Degler 1971; Nobles 2000).

Although some of these U.S. and British categories are also nationality labels, many people in the United States and Great Britain treat them as domestic racial units (Spickard 1992). And census classifications directly affect access to housing and employment, social program design, the organization of elections, and the disbursement of local, state, and federal funds (Omi and Winant 1994; Nobles 2000). Each of these national systems of racial classification, in fact, reflects a different social, economic, and political reality. When these social conditions change, so do racial categories. Before the 9/11 attacks, the U.S. Census included in its definition of "White" those people having origins in "the Middle East and North Africa." Shortly thereafter, this group went from being classified as White to the category "Other," a fact that Charles Gallagher (2007) cites as an example of how "Whiteness" and the privileges associated with it can be revoked.

Brazil has a history of extensive miscegenation and for years was touted as a "racial democracy," free of the racism so widespread and intense in the United States (Degler 1971; Kivisto 2007). However, in recent years many scholars have challenged this view of Brazil as less racist because, despite structural changes in the economy, peoples of African descent in Brazil remain on the bottom of the economic hierarchy and face discrimination and subtle forms of racism routinely in everyday life (Bailey 2004; Twine 1998; Winant 2001). Further, Twine (1998) and Winant (2001) suggest that the myth of a racial democracy in Brazil effectively stymied antiracist struggles through ideologically masking difference and inequality.

In the post-civil rights era in the United States, the racial signifiers *Latino/ Latina, Asian American, people of color,* and *Native American* developed when people from different cultures, tribes, and national origins were treated as a single racial group by a dominant culture that failed to recognize differences among "racial" ethnic groups. Many members of these groups subsequently organized politically to resist their joint oppressions, and out of those political movements new racial identities were forged. These labels did not exist before the 1960s, and even today some people identify with them and others do not, signifying the fluid, political, historically specific, and social meaning of race.

Also, following the 1967 repeal of the last laws against miscegenation (race mixing), a "biracial baby boom" began to be recorded in the United States (Root

1992). Even though interracial and intergroup marriages totaled about one million, or 4 percent, of all marriages in 1990, this figure is more than triple the 321,000 in 1970 (Harrison and Bennett 1995). Today 13 percent of all marriages are interracial, a figure that could rise to 21 to 25 percent by 2050. As a consequence, one in forty persons now identifies as multiracial, and youths under eighteen are twice as likely as older groups to do so (Lee and Bean 2004). The growth of this racially mixed population is literally transforming the face of the United States and is directly challenging the foundation of a social order predicated on the notion of biologically distinct and fixed races:

> The increasing presence of multiracial people necessitates that we as a nation ask ourselves questions about our identity: Who are we? How do we see ourselves? Who are we in relation to one another?... Such questions of race and identity can only precipitate a full-scale "identity crisis" that this country is ill equipped to resolve. Resolving the identity crisis may force us to reexamine our construction of race and the hierarchical social order it supports. (Root 1992, 3)

This identity crisis can be seen in the refusal of many mixed-race people to identify themselves on such things as job applications and school records as Black, White, Hispanic, Native American, or Asian. Many multiracial people argue that because they are more than any one of these, having to choose one of these designations negates their identity—and they are insisting on a new designation: mixed-race or multiracial. Their impact is being felt: The 2000 census allowed citizens to check off as many racial designations as they desired, and the number of multiracial identifiers dramatically increased (Lee and Bean 2004). In the past twenty years, more high-profile Americans have claimed their mixed-race heritage, most notably President Barack Obama, but also Tiger Woods, Nicole Richie, Alicia Keyes, and Derek Jeter.

Class

The social class system is also historically specific. Today, for example, many scholars—even those studying class from a Marxist perspective—no longer contend, as Marx originally did, that the proletariat (workers) and the bourgeoisie (capitalists/owners) are the only two major classes in modern capitalist societies. And although they disagree about the exact composition of the new class, almost all modern class theorists agree that today's capitalist class system contains a third major actor, the "new middle class" that exists between labor (workers) and capital (owners) (cf., Vanneman and Weber Cannon 1987; Van den Berg 1993; Wright 1997).

The middle class controls workers both directly and indirectly. Managers and supervisors exert direct control; mental laborers (e.g., lawyers, teachers, social workers) exert indirect control. The middle class sells its labor to the capitalist/owning class (sometimes defined as the upper class) and exerts control over the workers below it. For controlling workers and increasing production and profits and for promoting the ideas that justify the current class system, the middle class is rewarded with higher wages, job security and benefits, prestige, and respect.

As evidence of their location as a class "in the middle" and not as the most powerful economic class, the middle class since the 1970s has been challenged and transformed by changes in the economy that have shifted greater power and resources to the owning (upper) class:

- Increasing technological control (and a decreasing need for supervisory control) over the workforce
- Corporate downsizing
- Shifting of the tax burden away from corporations and the wealthy to individuals in the middle, working, and lower classes
- Stagnating or declining wages
- Globalization of markets and the workforce
- Increasing costs of housing, health care, and higher education

The negative economic effects of these shifts have been mitigated somewhat in two-parent, heterosexual, middle-class families by the increased participation of women in the workforce and by the declining number of children in families. But the standard of living among single mothers and among the poor—particularly among people of color—and their children declined significantly during the period (Brobeck and Montalto 2008; Farley 1996; Mishel et al. 2007).

Just as the power of the middle class relative to the owning or upper class has declined in recent history, so too has the power and standard of living of the working class and the lower class, or poor. In addition to being affected by many of the same processes as the middle class, working-class and poor people were affected by the increase in part-time employment, the loss of high-paying blue-collar jobs, the decline of unions, and reductions in government programs, such as welfare benefits and college grants and scholarships. As a result of these changes and as more resources are concentrated at the top of the class system, each of these classes has become less able to resist further changes that benefit the wealthy. Thus, for example, the ability of workers to demand and obtain higher wages, better working conditions, better benefits is less in most industries today than it was thirty years ago (cf. Bravo 2007; Farley 1996; Freeman 1994; Mishel, Berstein, and Allegretto 2007).

In short, the social class structure changes over time as new classes are created and existing classes gain or lose power in their struggles with other classes for resources. Further, the class system is structured by race, gender, and sexuality as women and men, people of color and Whites, heterosexuals and gays, lesbians, bisexuals, and transgender people have different opportunities to attain higher class positions, to reap the full benefits of those positions, to stay in those positions, and to pass the advantages accruing to those positions on to their children (cf., Badgett et al. 2008; Lareau and Conley 2008; Oliver and Shapiro 1995; Wright 1997, 2008).

Gender

Although gender—the socially structured relationships between women and men—is constructed, like race, with reference to biological categories (male and female), its meaning too has drastically changed throughout different historical eras. Not until the Industrial Revolution in the nineteenth century did the workplace become increasingly separated from the home and today's dominant conceptions of masculinity and femininity begin to take shape. During this time, dominant culture (White, heterosexual, middle- and upper-class) conceptions of femininity became associated with the warm, personal, "private" sphere of home, and masculinity became associated with the cold, "public" sphere of the labor market. The daily lives of women and men began to diverge as dominant-culture men were increasingly pulled away from the home to work in factories and were extended the "family wage," a wage large enough to support their entire families. Dominant-culture women were expected to remain out of the paid labor force and to tend to the home (Coontz 1992).

Carol Tavris (1992, 265) describes these newly emerging heterosexual conceptions of masculine and feminine:

> People began to attribute to inherent male and female characteristics what were actually requirements of their increasingly separate domains. Thus, women were expected to provide warmth, nurturance, and care, and forgo achievement; men were expected to provide money and success, and forgo close attachments. The masculine ideal, tailored to fit the emerging economy, was to be an independent, self-made, financially successful man. Masculinity now required self-control: no gaudy displays of emotion; no weakness; no excessive self indulgence in feelings. Femininity required, and soon came to embody, the opposite.

Despite the pervasiveness of the images, intersectionality scholars have noted that not *all* women and men were included in these ideals of masculinity and femininity. Men of color were not extended a family wage, and women of color were already in the paid labor market, doing domestic work, other low-wage service work, or agricultural work (Amott and Matthaei 1996). The ideal traits held up for men and women of color contrasted sharply with those for White women and men. After Reconstruction, for example, the ideal dominant culture image of the "good" African American man was the Sambo image: a happy-go-lucky, silly, stupid darky who was often afraid of the dark (Goings 1994). The image provided a justification for slavery and at the same time reduced the perceived physical and sexual threat posed by real African American men. The Mammy image was the female parallel to Sambo: a happy, asexual servant who so loved the master's family—and slavery itself—that she would willingly give over her life to the care and nurturance of White families (Collins 2000; Goings 1994). As the ideal White man was strong, independent, and emotionless, Sambo—like White women—was weak, dependent, and full of emotion. White women were to nurture their families, whereas emotionally strong Mammies could have no families of their own, just as they could have no sexuality.

In sum, gendered social relationships between women and men are differently constructed throughout history, in different social groups, and in different locations through social processes that consistently produce and maintain a patriarchy—a system of male dominance—that is racialized, class-bound, and heterosexist.

Sexuality

For as long as recorded history, people have engaged in heterosexual and homosexual sexual relations. Only recently, however, has sexuality come to be constructed as a fundamental element of social structure, as a source of community, and as a source of personal identity. Just as late-nineteenth-century shifts in the economy brought changes in gender meanings, they also brought about the conditions that made possible for the first time the development of a homosexual community and identity.

John D'Emilio (1993, 2006) argues that as wage labor spread, work became dissociated from family and the household. And families and heterosexual expression came to be a means of establishing intimacy, promoting happiness, and experiencing pleasure—not a means of surviving. The free-labor system thus released sexuality from the "imperative" to procreate (to produce more workers for the family) and made it possible for men and women to survive outside of the household economy. These changes in the relationship between the economy and family structures made possible the appearance of many of today's non-normative family forms: single parents, families without children, gay and lesbian families, and cohabiting heterosexual families. They also established the conditions for a collective gay life:

> By the end of the [nineteenth] century, a class of men and women existed who recognized their erotic interest in their own sex, saw it as a trait that set them apart from the majority, and sought others like themselves....In this period, gay men and lesbians began to invent ways of meeting each other and sustaining a group life. Already, in the early twentieth century, large cities contained male homosexual bars....In St. Louis and the nation's capital, annual drag balls brought together large numbers of Black gay men. Public bathhouses and YMCAs became gathering spots for male homosexuals. Lesbians formed literary societies and private social clubs. Some working-class women "passed" as men to obtain better paying jobs and lived with other women—lesbian couples who appeared to the world as husband and wife. (D'Emilio 1993, 470)

Yet the communities that developed in the early twentieth century remained rudimentary and difficult to find until World War II severely disrupted traditional patterns of gender relations and sexuality and temporarily created new situations conducive to homosexual expression: in sex-segregated settings as GIs or as WACs (Women's Army Corps) and WAVES (Women Accepted for Volunteer Emergency Service) and in same-sex rooming houses for relocated workers. Through the 1950s and 1960s, the communities grew, particularly in urban subcultures, and became easier to find as newspapers, magazines, and novels published stories about gay life and as bars and other gathering sites increased.

The modern gay rights movement was ignited by the Stonewall Riot in New York City in 1969, when a group of gay men in the Stonewall Inn fought back when police raided the bar to harass and arrest them. The movement was generated in part because a gay community already existed and as a response to the severe oppression and scapegoating of gays during the cold war era of the 1950s and 1960s:

- President Eisenhower imposed a total ban on employment of gay men and lesbians by the federal government.
- The FBI instituted widespread surveillance of gay organizations.
- Purges of gays from the military had risen sharply (D'Emilio 1993)

In sum, the nature of the system of heterosexual privilege and the experience of homosexuality has varied extensively from its early expressions in the nineteenth century to the much more open and stable communities of the post-Stonewall era. Race, class, and gender, as well as geographic location (especially rural-urban and coastal-interior differences), also critically shape the nature of communities and the life experiences of gay people. For example, Mama Rene, a Filipino gay man arrested at Stonewall, was interviewed twenty-five years later, along with other Filipino gay men, for a study of gay transnational politics by Martin Manalansan IV. When asked how he felt about that historic event, Mama Rene said:

> They say it was a historic event. I just thought it was funny. Do I feel like I made history? People always ask me that. I say no. I am a quiet man, just like how my mom raised me in the Philippines. With dignity. (Manalansan 1995, 433)

Manalansan found that Mama Rene's belief that "coming out," or the public avowal of identity, is not necessary for self-fashioning was common among Filipino gay men:

> They see "coming out" as the primary preoccupation of gay men from other ethnic and racial groups. In fact, visibility can be dangerous for gay Filipinos. Until the late 1980s, U.S. immigration laws both criminalized homosexuality and categorized it with Communist Party membership. And not all gay venues are open to these immigrants.... Some tell of being "hounded" out of predominantly white or black gay bars. (Manalansan 1995, 434)

More important, Manalansan argues, the "closet" and the coming-out process are not culturally constituted in the same way:

> Filipino gay men argue that identities are not just proclaimed verbally, but are "felt" (*pakiramdaman*) or intuited as well. The swardspeak expression *ladlad ng kapa*, which literally means unfurling the cape and has been translated as "coming out," reveals gay identity to be something "worn" and not necessarily "declared." And it is this act of "wearing" identity that makes other public modes of gay identity articulation superfluous for many of my informants. (Manalansan 1995, 434)

Bayard Rustin, an out gay man, was the major African American civil rights leader who organized the 1963 March on Washington at which Martin Luther King, Jr., gave his "I Have a Dream" speech. Yet fears that homophobia and charges of sexual impropriety would harm the cause led Rustin to stay in the background and allowed King to become the spokesperson and figurehead for the march and the movement (D'Emilio 2003).

Thus even the political and personal nature of "coming out," which has been a cornerstone of the political and personal liberation strategies of U.S. White gays and lesbians, has very different, and even contradictory, implications for Filipino gay men, African American men, and other men and women of color. What liberates Whites may actually lead to the repression of men and women of color (cf. Almaguer 1993; Collins 2004; D'Emilio 2003). No single strategy for fighting oppression is "right"; no single strategy alone can work.

Likewise, because lesbians also face gender oppression, their experience of sexual oppression is different in many ways. For example, because women face discrimination in the labor market—earning less, having fewer options for high-wage employment, and higher poverty rates—the loss of jobs because of sexual discrimination can potentially have a greater impact on lesbians than on gay men, making them more likely to face poverty as a result. The lesson to be learned is that race, class, gender, and sexuality as interrelated systems of oppression are created and maintained in specific historical and geographic contexts and within specific groups. They cannot be fully understood or applied as abstract constructs independent of specific times and places.

SOCIALLY CONSTRUCTED

These brief examples of the historical and geographical specificity of race, class, gender, and sexuality systems of oppression foreshadow the second major theme in the scholarship on these dimensions: that they are *socially constructed*. Race, class, gender, and sexuality are historically and geographically specific because they are social constructs whose meaning develops out of group struggles over socially valued resources. These struggles vary over time and in different places as the ability of dominant groups to maintain their position changes as a result of numerous forces, most notably of the effectiveness and strength of subordinate groups' resistance to oppression but also of the dominant group's strength at any given time, which is affected by such factors as global competition and internal group cohesiveness.

I discuss race, gender, and sexuality first because there are some shared elements—biological determinism and dichotomizing—in the ways that race, gender, and sexuality systems are socially constructed. Social class is socially constructed on slightly different building blocks—a ladder, not dichotomous categories, and individual choice, not biological determinism—and yet the result is a similar system of oppression. The case of social class makes it clear that systems of oppression can be constructed on somewhat different grounds and still achieve similar ends.

The dominant culture defines the categories within race, gender, and sexuality as polar opposites—White and Black (or non-White), men and women, heterosexual and homosexual—to create social rankings: good and bad, worthy and unworthy, right and wrong (Fausto-Sterling 2000; Lorber 1994). It also links these concepts to biology (most clearly with race and gender, less consistently with sexuality) to imply that the rankings are fixed, permanent, and embedded in nature. That is, dominant groups define race, gender, and sexuality as ranked dichotomies in which Whites, men, and heterosexuals are deemed superior. Dominant groups typically justify these hierarchies by claiming that the rankings are a part of the design of nature, not the design of those in power. Subordinate groups resist the binary categories, the rankings associated with them, and the biological rationales used to justify them. Critical examination of either process—polarizing or biologizing—reveals that race, gender, and sexuality are not based in polar opposites nor in biology but rather are social constructs (American Sociological Association 2003; Gamson and Moon 2004; King 1981; Lorber 1994; Weber and Fore 2007).

When we say that the meanings of race, class, gender, and sexuality are not fixed biological traits, we also mean that we cannot *fully* capture their meaning in everyday life in the way that social scientists often attempt to do by employing them as variables in traditional quantitative research. When race, gender, and sexuality are treated as discrete variables, individuals are typically assigned a single location along each dimension, which is defined by a set of presumably mutually exclusive and exhaustive categories. This practice reinforces the view of race, gender, and sexuality as permanent characteristics of individuals, as unchangeable, and as polarities—the view that people can belong to one and only one category. So race, gender, and sexuality are not treated as social constructions whose existence and meaning depend on social relations among groups opposing one another for societal resources but rather as fixed and permanent characteristics of individuals—more like eye color than group membership (Hancock 2007; McCall 2005).

This practice also fails to grasp the historical specificity and the conflicting meanings of race, class, gender, and sexuality that arise in everyday life. "Mixed race" people, for example, often have no place in the schema provided. And what of the people who are bisexual or heterosexual at one time of life and gay or lesbian at another? Neither do people who identify as transgender—living parts or all of their lives in a gender expression different from their sex—have a place in these schemas.

Race

Biologists and physical anthropologists recognize that all humans have an essential commonality, that there have never been any pure races. What we call races are geographic and biologically diverging populations that in particular locales are distinguished by statistically significant frequencies of various genetic or physical types—from blood types to sickle cell anemia. Yet the variations within these divergent populations are greater by far than the variations among them (American Sociological Association 2003; Weber and Fore 2007; Zuberi 2001). As geneticist James King (1981) states:

> Whether two individuals regard themselves as of the same or of different races depends not on the degree of similarity of their genetic material but on whether history, tradition, and personal training and experiences have brought them to regard themselves as belonging to the same group or to different groups.... There are no objective boundaries to set off one subspecies from another. (cited in Spickard 1992, 16)

More important, the presence of similarities or differences in physical makeup is significant only when social meaning becomes attached to those differences and when society's valued resources are allocated on the basis of them (Spickard 1992, 15).

As Michael Omi and Howard Winant (1994, 96) suggest, race is a social phenomenon that "suffuses each individual identity, each family and community, yet also suffuses state institutions and market relations." Struggles over the meaning of race are fought in the political, economic, and ideological arenas as subordinate racial groups press for full incorporation in all aspects of society. In the modern era, the 1960s witnessed the success of social movements that were racially based and inspired and that transformed the meaning of race. Racial equality had to be acknowledged as a desirable goal, but its meaning and the proper means to achieve that equality were open for debate.

In the economically troubled periods since the 1960s, the dominant culture has reacted to the gains of the 1960s by claiming to favor equality and a "color-blind society" (Bonilla-Silva 2003; Winant 2000). But many of the rights won in the 1960s have been opposed at the level of implementation, just as affirmative action has come under vehement attack. Today, the rise in Native American, Asian, and Latino/a populations is again changing the nature and meaning of race, as these groups become large enough to press demands and as Whites seek to maintain control by implementing repressive policies aimed at limiting their power.

Gender

Even though gender is socially defined by referring to biological differences related to reproduction, as new work on intersex suggests, there is significant biological and anatomical variation in what bodies are socially defined as male and female (Preves 2009). Further, the biological and physical similarities between women and men far outweigh the differences. Gender, too, is socially constructed in the struggles between groups over society's scarce resources (Fausto-Sterling 2000).

Even in the area of reproduction and mothering, the biological relationships of women to children are socially constructed and given meaning in race, class, gender, and sexuality hierarchies. For over a century, social expectations of women's work and family roles, for example, have been rationalized by the biological fact that women can bear children. Middle-class women who stay at home to care for their children are often viewed by the dominant culture as "good mothers," yet poor women who do the same are viewed as lazy or "welfare queens." How can women's biological reproductive capacities prescribe their roles as mothers when we have different expectations for mothers of different classes, races, and sexual orientations?

Furthermore, the biological connection of women to their children is far more complex than ever before and is now being challenged—particularly by White, middle-class, heterosexual women and by some lesbians and gay men who seek to adopt children—as a basis for legal rights to motherhood (Solinger 1998; Woliver 2002). Today, when women and men have so many different biological and social relationships to their children, the courts are increasingly asked to mediate questions of who should rear children— of who can *be* mothers. Consider the following "mothers":

- *Traditional mothers,* who have a genetic, gestational, and legally sanctioned social relationship to the child
- *Lesbian mothers,* whose biological relationship may or may not be the same as that of traditional mothers and yet whose legal status as mothers is subject to challenge and denial because of their sexual orientation
- *Surrogate mothers*: *genetic and gestational mothers* who provide an egg and bear the child but do not raise the child, and *gestational mothers* who have no genetic relationship to it but bear the child for another couple
- *Social mothers:* *foster mothers,* whom the state assigns as temporary mothers but who have no genetic or gestational relationship to the child; *adoptive mothers,* who are legally recognized mothers but who have no genetic or gestational relationship to the child; *"other" mothers,* who have no legal, genetic, or gestational relationship to the child but who play a significant role in raising the child (cf. Collins 2000; Mezey 2008; Millbank 2008).

Each of these ways of mothering is constructed in race, class, gender, and sexuality hierarchies that shape the meanings attached to them and the legally prescribed rights of these mothers to rear children. The rights of some women to be mothers depends, in fact, on the lack of rights among other women to retain their status as mothers. In the era of "choice," following the *Roe v. Wade* Supreme Court decision in 1971, for example, large numbers of White, unmarried girls in the United States began to choose either abortion or to keep their babies. These choices reduced the pool of adoptable White babies, producing both an increase in the market value of available White babies (and increased "trading" in the underground sale of those babies) and a boom in foreign adoptions. As Solinger (1998, 390–391) states:

> Probably most Americans did not realize how profoundly the motherhood "choices" of (White) middle-class women—to get abortions, or to become single mothers (both of which choices diminished the pool of babies who might have been available to others), or to become adoptive mothers—indirectly created or directly depended on the definition of other woman as having weak, or coercively transferable, motherhood rights. Nor was it always clear how much motherhood "choices" had to do with money, for both the women who had it and the women who did not.

Annette Appell's (1998) research focuses on one of those groups with weak and transferable motherhood rights: the mothers of the roughly one-half million children in foster care in the United States, mothers whose children were removed because they failed to meet a government agency's standard of proper mothering. They are disproportionately poor and women of color. Appell notes that only a small minority of these women have physically harmed or abandoned their children. The rest lose their children because they use illegal drugs, consume too much alcohol, are abused by husbands or boyfriends, or leave their children with family or friends without making a "proper" care plan. Yet these women have their children taken away in part because their poverty means that their lives intersect with official entities and bureaucracies on a number of levels: the government pays their medical bills; public hospitals, clinics and emergency rooms provide their health care; public building inspectors and police enter their homes. Middle-class mothers have private health care, privacy in their homes, and are more likely to use alcohol and prescribed antidepressants than crack cocaine. In short, poor mothers with problems come into contact with the legal system and face losing their children; middle-class mothers seldom do.

Chesler (1986, 280) also highlights the impact of race, class, gender, and sexuality on motherhood in discussing why we have the phenomenon of surrogate mothers:

> Racism is the issue, and why thousands of babies are "unsuitable" (for adoption). Ownership is the issue, and the conceit of patriarchal genetics. "Barren women" are the issue, and why some women must come to feel an excruciating sense of failure because they cannot bear a child.... And guilt and money, and how women can earn both, are the issues that need honest attention.

In sum, although our biological relationship to children can be fairly easily determined (even when one party denies the connection) with DNA testing, it tells us very little about the way that relationship shapes our lives. The meaning of our biological relationship to children is socially constructed in race, class, gender, and sexuality hierarchies and cannot be understood independent of these systems.

Sexuality
Despite evidence to the contrary, dominant culture perspectives on race and gender contend that they are biologically distinct categories and that their biological base does—and should—affect the social position of people in different race and gender groups. Dominant culture perspectives on sexuality are more contested in the political and ideological arenas, yet, much like gender, sexual orientation is conceived of as binary opposites—gay or straight. From this perspective the presumed "cause" of sexual orientation is equally polarized as either genetically determined or as a personal lifestyle choice.

Much like the issue of "choice" in pregnant women's decisions to abort or to bear a child, when the notion of choice enters any debate in the U.S. context, it is assumed to be a free choice made by various individuals having the same basic options, opportunities, and resources at their disposal. But this notion pays scant attention to the social structural constraints—powerfully shaped by race, class, gender, and sexual systems of oppression—within which these choices are made (Mezey 2008; Solinger 1998; Woliver 2002). "Choice" in the dominant culture context implies individual responsibility. If the choices individuals make are not the choices that dominant groups approve, then individual responsibility implies blame, and blame sets the stage for unequal treatment.

Thus whether homosexuality and, of course, heterosexuality are viewed as genetically determined or as lifestyle choices to a large extent shapes how homosexuals and heterosexuals will be treated in the social order. Despite extensive biological and genetic research, there is, in fact, no strong evidence that gay, lesbian, bisexual, or heterosexual orientations are genetically determined (Fausto-Sterling 2000). In no way could the people who identify themselves as and who are seen by others as gay, bisexual, or lesbian be classified on the basis of physical traits, just as heterosexuals cannot be so identified. Yet many groups (some religious groups, for example, that view homosexuality as morally wrong) have based policies of tolerance for gays and lesbians on the belief that sexual orientation is genetically determined and is not a matter of choice and thus of responsibility. The *Catechism of the Catholic Church*, for example, states that homosexuality is serious sin and "gravely hinders them [homosexuals] from relating correctly to men and women."[1] In September of 1997, the National Conference of Catholic Bishops affirmed that homosexual sex is wrong, and yet it urged parents of gay children to demonstrate love for their sons and daughters and to recognize that "generally, homosexual orientation is experienced as a given, not as something freely chosen" (Cloud 1997). Many gays and lesbians have also promoted this idea in the hopes of finding greater acceptance in society at large.

Yet, as John D'Emilio (1993) points out, this strategy is ultimately self-defeating because it does not attack the underlying belief that homosexual relations are bad, a poor second choice. The gay, lesbian, bisexual, and transgender political movements of recent times have in fact made it easier for people to make the choice. As a consequence, there are more self-identified homosexual people and better developed and more visible communities now than ever in history.

Out of the struggle to define sexuality, the images, rights, and treatment of gays, bisexuals, and lesbians emerge. And race, class, and gender significantly shape the experiences and perspectives that homosexual groups bring to the conflict (Anzaldua 1987a, 1987b; Collins 2004; Duberman et al. 1989; Lorde 1995). The largest and politically most visible group, for example, is White, middle-class, gay men. They have the economic self-sufficiency to survive outside of heterosexual marriage, and they have the gender and racial advantages that enable

---

[1]Congregation for Catholic Education. 2009. "Instruction concerning the criteria for the discernment of vocations with regard to persons with homosexual tendencies in view of their admission to the seminary and to Holy Orders." Available online at http://www.vatican.va/roman_curia/congregations/ccatheduc/documents/rc_con_ccatheduc_doc_20051104_istruzione_en.html#_ftn8. For complete catechism see http://www.vatican.va/archive/ccc/index.htm Accessed January 17, 2008.

them to combat and overcome many of the restrictions imposed on their lives by homophobic social policies and practices (D'Emilio 1993; 2002).

Other groups, such as lesbians of color, may have less institutionally supported economic or political power—for example, to press for biological or choice ideologies of sexuality. But because their status as women of color makes clear that biologically based ideologies can be equally constraining, they may also be less likely to push for a genetic explanation as a way to greater social acceptance.

Social Class

Social class provides an instructive contrast to race, gender, and sexuality ideologies. The dominant ideology of social class is that it is not binary, polarized, or biological. Instead, the United States is represented as having an open economic system in which talent and hard work, not inherited physical traits, are the primary determinants of one's economic location (Beckert 2008; McNamee and Miller 2004). Our system is not depicted as polarized between rich and poor, capitalists and workers, or middle and working classes. Rather, it is portrayed as a continuous ladder of income and resources that people can slide up and down based on their own efforts and abilities, not on their biology (Vanneman and Weber Cannon 1987; Wright 2008). Because anyone is presumed to be potentially able to "make it," people can be held personally responsible for where they land in the class system. This ideology is labeled the *American Dream* to contrast with the economic ideologies in other industrial nations, particularly in European nations, where the aristocracy and the presumably more rigid class systems are deemed to be more closely tied to biology and inheritance.

The belief that biology and inheritance *do not* and *should not* determine class is deeply ingrained in American dominant culture ideology. Although this belief in the American Dream was far more prevalent when the economy was expanding during the 1950s and 1960s, some social scientists even today assert that the American economic system is so open that classes do not exist (Clark and Lipset 1991; Kingston 2001). Research on the relative ease with which individuals can move up the class hierarchy suggests, however, that the American class system is not uniquely open (Goldthorpe and Jackson 2008; McNamee and Miller 2004). Comparing the United States with Canada, a capitalist economy, and with Sweden and Norway, more social democratic and less purely capitalist economies, Mark Western and Eric Olin Wright (1994) found that the United States exhibits similar patterns of openness to class mobility. They also found that in the United States and Canada, friendships and intermarriage across class lines are no more prevalent than in Sweden and Norway. In short, class transmission has as much to do with inheritance in the supposedly more open United States system as it does elsewhere.

If class location is largely inherited, is class biological? A long-standing tradition in the United States does link poverty to genetically inherited traits, beginning with the social Darwinism of the late nineteenth and early twentieth centuries and continuing to the present in works such as Richard Herrnstein and Charles

Murray's *The Bell Curve* (1994). In that widely read book, the authors argue that genetic differences explain the fact that poor people have consistently low IQ scores, that IQ measures intelligence, and that low IQ explains poor people's lack of achievement and poverty. However, Murray and Herrnstein, as well as others who have made similar claims, provide no direct evidence of the connection between genetics and IQ because they do not study genetics at all and ignore evidence of cultural, class, race, and gender bias in the IQ test. But even this biological class argument runs counter to the dominant ideology of class as substantially an "earned or achieved," not a biologically determined, position. The upper classes presumably "earn" their position because of their superior traits (values, intelligence, skills, effort), and the lower classes "earn" their inferior location.

Neither of these two extreme positions—that class is either genetically determined or purely a function of individual talent and effort—captures the more complex reality of social class. Like race, gender, and sexuality, social class is a pattern of hierarchical social relationships that is deeply ingrained in the social order and that shapes the lives, options, and opportunities of individuals from birth. It is also deeply intertwined with other dimensions of inequality.

Consider, for example, the ways in which social class influences and is maintained in college and law school admissions, along with gender and race. As Lani Guinier and Gerald Torres (2002) conclude about affirmative action in college and law school admissions, procedures that are not targeted to Whites, men, and the affluent and that admit people of color and women but that have more universally applicable standards (such as admitting any applicants who finished in the top 10 percent of their class regardless of the schools they attended) increase the racial and gender diversity in admissions more than most affirmative action policies employed to date. Standard admissions procedures that are based in large part on cultural knowledge (estimated through tests with known race, class, and gender biases), on attendance at private elite schools, and on social connections (e.g., special consideration given to the children of law school graduates) are strongly biased in favor of White men from affluent backgrounds (Karabel 2005; Sturm and Guinier 1996).

If we actually changed the standards to base them more on experience (e.g., grades) and not on prediction through tests, people from less culturally and socioeconomically advantaged backgrounds would be admitted in much greater numbers than any affirmative action adjustments could achieve. And evidence from schools such as City College in New York that have had open admissions programs suggests that these students will succeed at similar if not higher rates than other students admitted in traditional ways (Guinier and Torres 2002; Sturm and Guinier 1996). This is not to say that progress toward greater inclusion for oppressed groups lies in the elimination of affirmative action but, rather, that it lies in social change of a more fundamental sort: addressing the interactions of these dimensions—change that has also been more powerfully resisted (cf. Gutfeld 2002).

Although American social class ideology disavows biology and categorical binaries, it justifies hierarchy and dominance nonetheless. The case of social class makes very clear that ideologies are created to justify hierarchies and need not be constructed as binaries or as biological, nor need they be internally consistent or logical. To justify the power and control of the dominant group, ideologies of dominance develop in different ways over time and in different social contexts and can rest on fundamentally very different, even seemingly contradictory, beliefs.

In sum, race, class, gender, and sexuality are social constructions that are constantly undergoing change at both the level of social institutions and the level of personal identity. They are not fixed, static traits of individuals, as is implied when they are treated both as biological facts and as categorically fixed variables in a research model. They are, however, deeply embedded in the practices and beliefs that make up our major social institutions. The permanence and pervasiveness they exhibit illustrate their significance as major organizing principles of society and of personal identity.

POWER RELATIONSHIPS

Race, class, gender, and sexuality are historically specific, socially constructed *systems of oppression;* they are *power relationships.* Race, class, gender, and sexuality do not merely represent different lifestyle preferences or cultural beliefs, values, or practices. They are power hierarchies in which one group exerts control over another, securing its position of dominance in the system, and in which substantial material resources—such as wealth, income, or access to health care and to education—are at stake (Baca Zinn and Dill 1996; Connell 1987, 1995; Glenn 1992; Stewart and McDermott 2004; Vanneman and Weber Cannon 1987; Weber 2007; Wright 2008; Wyche and Graves 1992). Race, class, gender, and sexuality are thus fundamental sources of social conflict between groups.

The centerpiece of these systems is the exploitation of one group by another for a greater share of society's valued resources. That they are based in *social relationships between dominant and subordinate groups* is key to understanding these systems. There can be no controlling males without women whose options are restricted, there can be no valued race without races that are defined as "other," there can be no owners or managers without workers who produce and deliver the goods and services that the owners own and the managers control, and there can be no heterosexual privilege without gays and lesbians identified as "abnormal," as "other."

Race, class, gender, and sexuality are not just rankings of socially valued resources—who has *more* education, income, or prestige. They are power relationships: who exerts power and control over whom; how the privilege of some results from the exploitation of others (Goldthorpe and Jackson 2008; Vanneman and Weber Cannon 1987; Wright 2008). The groups that have power in a social system influence the allocation of many types of resources. In one sense, then, the procurement of socially valued resources can be seen as the end product of struggles for power: the spoils to the victors. To maintain and extend their power and control in society, dominant groups can and do use the resources that they command. So socially valued resources such as money and prestige both accrue to those in power and, once procured, serve as tools for maintaining and extending that power into future social relations.

Heterosexism, like racism, classism, and sexism, is, for example, a system of power relations in which, to justify the privileges of heterosexuality, heterosexuals gain and maintain control over gays, lesbians, bisexuals, and transgender people by defining them as "other," as less than fully human, as "deviant." Heterosexual marriage is established as the standard against which all other ways of conducting adult intimate life are measured. People who depart from this script are commonly seen as deviant and (except in rare cases) are denied the legal privileges afforded heterosexuals, including the right to marry, to adopt children, to receive survivor benefits from Social Security, to file taxes as married, to receive health insurance from a spouse's employer, to inherit from one's partner, to claim a legal family connection in medical emergencies (Egan and Sherill 2005; *Harvard Law Review* 1990).

Scholars studying race, class, gender, and sexuality tend to see these systems as power relations, but this perspective is not universally accepted. The ethnicity approaches to race (reviewed in Omi and Winant 1994), gradational perspectives on class (reviewed in Vanneman and Weber Cannon 1987; Wright 2008), sex-differences and sex-roles approaches (reviewed in West and Fenstermaker 1995; Stewart and McDermott 2004), and moral or biological perspectives on sexuality (reviewed in D'Emilio and Freedman 1988) conceive of these dimensions as differences that are not ultimately power based. In these alternative approaches, differences between women and men, between gays and straights, and among racial and ethnic groups are taken as primarily centered in women's and men's social roles and in cultural variations in traditions such as food, clothing, rituals, speech patterns, leisure activities, child-rearing practices, and sexual practices.

These perspectives, however, often downplay or ignore the very real struggles over scarce resources that accompany location in these different groups and systems of oppression. The "gradational" approach, for example, sees class inequality as represented by relative rankings along a scale of prestige or income (a ladder image), not by the struggle between opposing groups for scarce resources (for reviews, see Lucal 1994; Vanneman and Weber Cannon 1987; Wright 2008). No oppositional relationships exist between positions on a scale; some people simply have more than others. And these approaches see race as a group of ethnicities, different cultural practices, and preferences that have roughly equal value. White is treated more as an absence; *race* is a term used to refer to people of color, a process that hides the privileged status of Whites and their relationship of dominance with other races (Gallagher 2007; McDermott and Samson 2005). In a similar process, heterosexuality is also viewed as an absence, whereas gays, lesbians, bisexuals represent the "presence" of sexuality (Herek 1987; Lucal 1994).

Perhaps because intersectional studies primarily emerged from the experiences and analyses of groups who face multiple dimensions of oppression and perhaps because power relationships are simply much more apparent when more than one dimension of inequality is addressed, "cultural difference," "gradational," or "ranking" perspectives are almost nonexistent in intersectional studies. The view that power relations are central is almost universal.

Looking at the *relational* nature of these systems of inequality, not simply at the differences in rankings of resources that accompany these systems, forces us to focus on *privilege*, as well as on oppression. Because the one cannot exist without the other, any analysis of race, class, gender, and sexuality must incorporate an understanding of the ways that the privilege of dominant groups is tied to the oppression of subordinate groups. The scholarship in this field explores the social construction of Whiteness (cf. Ferber 1998; Gallagher 2007; McIntosh 1998), of masculinity (cf. Brod and Kaufman 1994; Connell 1995; Kimmel 2009) and of heterosexual privilege (Gamson and Moon 2004; Jackson 2005; Rich 1993). One common theme is that the experience of privilege is associated with a failure to understand the connection between privilege and oppression but that the experience of exploitation gives a unique angle of vision on the nature of oppression (Collins 2000). As Albert Hourani, an Arab philosopher, described it:

> To be in someone else's power…induces doubts about the ordering of the universe, while those who have power can assume it is part of the natural order of things and invent or adopt ideas which justify their possession of it. (quoted in Terkel 1992)

To understand these relationships of privilege and oppression, we must ask who gains and who pays in the events and processes we observe. How are the economic, political, and ideological resources and control of privileged groups produced by the low wages, labor, political disenfranchisement, and controlling images and devaluation of others? By focusing on power relations among groups, we move away from dominant culture conceptions of race as about people of color, of gender as about women, of class as about the working classes and the poor, and of sexuality as about gays, lesbians, bisexuals, and transgendered people. Instead, we make visible the invisible norms, the dominant groups, the standards against which others are judged to be inferior: Whites, middle and upper classes, men, heterosexuals.

To understand power dynamics, it is revealing to look closely at social critiques and social policies that fail to take these power relationships into account. Many political analysts, for example, consider the most significant legacy of many 1990s politicians—from President Clinton to Mayor Rudolph Giuliani of New York—to have been spearheading welfare reform and removing as many as one million welfare recipients from government support during the decade of the 1990s—four hundred thousand in New York alone (DeParle 1998). And they consider welfare reform an unprecedented success. As Giuliani stated, "This is by far the best thing we're doing for the city. It is much more significant than the reduction in crime"(DeParle 1998, 53).

But if we look beyond the declarations of the politicians who embrace the policies and look through the lens of race, class, gender, and sexuality, we ask about power relationships, and we ask, "Success for whom?" Is the policy a success for the (mostly) women whose lives have been changed by it? Have they benefited? Most are working minimum wage for many of the service industries that exploded in the 1980s and 1990s and that rely on a cheap and unskilled labor force—fast food restaurants, retail sales, domestic work. A growing number of reports contend that women receiving welfare much prefer to work, yet they cannot live independently on the wages they make in minimum-wage jobs (Lein and Schexnayder 2007; Seccombe and Hoffman 2007).

Barbara Ehrenreich (1999), a journalist, tried for a month to live and work in Florida to find out if it is "really possible to make a living on the kinds of jobs currently available to unskilled people?" She found out—it is not. She began by cleaning hotel rooms, and before the month was up, she had taken a second job, was essentially working all of her waking hours, and could not afford to get sick. She had become so tired and run down that she finally "broke" and just walked out on her restaurant job when, after a particularly grueling day, a customer entered the kitchen to complain about the slow service. She left feeling a failure and concluded:

> How former welfare recipients and single mothers will (and do) survive in the low-wage workforce, I cannot imagine. Maybe they will figure out how to condense their lives—including child-raising, laundry, romance, and meals—into the couple of hours between full-time jobs. Maybe they will take up residence in their vehicles, if they have one. All I know is that I couldn't hold two jobs and I couldn't make enough money to live on with one. And I had advantages unthinkable to many of the long-term poor—health, stamina, a working car, and no children to care for and support. (1999, 50)

In a broader study undertaken to understand whether poor women could really live on the wages they would make without welfare payments, economists and sociologists at the Center for Research on Women in Memphis, Tennessee, studied what it took to earn a "living wage" in Memphis in 2002 (Ciscel 2002). They defined a living wage as the level of income it takes for women to live independently of government subsidies, private charity, and other assistance. Even assuming a bare-bones budget—one that allowed for no extras, such as eating out in a restaurant, going on a vacation, buying a new car, or saving for children's college, a single parent with one child working full time would need to earn $31,284, or $15.64 an hour—triple the minimum wage. In fact, the living wage was more than double the official federal poverty thresholds for 2002, meaning that the government does not even define a family as in poverty, and therefore eligible for assistance, unless it makes less than one-half of a living wage.

When we think about the race, class, gender, and sexuality power dynamics at work in this story, it is difficult to see the welfare recipients—one-third White women but disproportionately women of color—as benefiting from the "success" of welfare reform. When the policies were instituted, few welfare recipients were consulted (Hancock 2004). They lacked power, a voice. Barbara Ehrenreich's individual attempt to live on the minimum wage and research on the living wage in Memphis lead us to question the benefits for the women themselves. Furthermore, studies of the impact of welfare reform on single mothers indicate that for a variety of reasons women on welfare faced less hardship than women who left welfare rolls for low-wage work, particularly because work brought new expenses that their low wages could not offset, such as child care and transportation (Edin and Lein 1997; Lein and Schexnayder 2007). They also lost income and incurred higher expenses because other government supports—Medicaid, housing subsidies, and food stamps—were reduced as their incomes increased when they took jobs.

If the poor women did not benefit, who did?

- The owners of businesses who employ workers at low wages
- The politicians who claimed credit for a "social engineering" victory
- The groups whose taxes are lowered as welfare benefits are eliminated from the federal budget
- The agencies and programs that receive funding that might otherwise have gone to welfare benefits—hospitals, schools, highways, businesses, the military

And yet how is this process debated and discussed in the public arena? Women who receive welfare are racialized—pictured as women of color (even though a third are White women, as Margaret Welch came to understand) and dehumanized, for we are asked to believe that their poverty is centered in their lack of skills, motivations, and values, not in the choices that the powerful make (Hancock 2004). When we are asked to see the poverty of women and children in this way, "requiring them to work," as the policy now does, seems to be a viable solution to rid the country not just of welfare recipients but of poverty itself. The policy and public discourse around it deny, however, the real work, energy, and creativity that it takes to survive in poverty, whether on welfare or in low-wage employment, as well as the benefits that accrue to the powerful when a large sector of the nation is either unemployed or employed in low-wage work (Lein and Schexnayder 2007).

A race, class, gender, and sexuality analysis pushes us to confront the power relationships at the core of these systems of inequality. These systems are sometimes described as interlocking dimensions in a matrix of domination in which race, class, gender, and sexuality represent axes. Individuals and groups can be identified by their locations in a position of dominance (power) or subordination (lacking power) along each dimension (cf. Collins 2000; Baca Zinn and Dill 1994). However they are pictured, thinking of these systems as relational encourages us to consider the nature of their relationship to each other. They are not completely independent but, rather, are interdependent, mutually reinforcing systems. One of the ways that sexuality, gender, and race privilege and power are maintained by White male heterosexuals, for example, is by maintaining power in the social class system and by restricting access to valued economic resources (e.g., wealth, jobs) by other sexuality, gender, and racial groups, as the case of women and welfare so aptly suggests.[2]

SUMMARY

Race, class, gender, and sexuality are historically and geographically specific, socially constructed power relations of dominance and subordination among social groups competing for society's scarce valued resources in the economic, ideological, and political domains. The structures of oppression and groups' differences within systems vary over time and in different social locations. Because race, class, gender, and sexuality are social constructions, their nature and meaning is generated in significant patterns of human social interactions—not predetermined by biology, not fixed at birth, but still persistent and pervasive. Race, class, gender, and sexuality are also significant because they represent power relations of dominance and subordination, not simply cultural preferences, gradations on a scale of prestige or money, gender role expectations, or moral or biological sexual differences. Dominant groups have access to greater economic, political, and ideological resources and employ these resources to control subordinate groups and to maintain their power. At the same time, subordinate groups resist economic, political, and ideological oppression. It is in this struggle between dominant and subordinate groups that the meaning of race, class, gender, and sexuality is transformed in different places and at different times.

---

[2]For descriptions of this process in graduate and professional schools, see Guinier, Fine, and Balin 1997 and Granfield and Koenig 1992 for law; Margolis and Romero 1998 for sociology.

CHAPTER 5

✦◯

Themes: Macro and Micro Levels, Simultaneous Expression

In this chapter I discuss the final two themes of the framework. Race, class, gender, and sexuality systems operate at both the (4) macro structural (institutional) and micro social-psychological (individual) levels and are (5) simultaneously expressed, intersecting systems. These themes remind us that these inequalities are embedded simultaneously in both societal structures and our personal identities. So analyses should look for the connections and intersections of race, class, gender, and sexual inequalities at the macro and micro levels of the social order.

Race, class, gender, and sexuality relations are simultaneously embedded and have meaning in the macro level of community and social institutions, as well as in the micro level of individual's everyday lives. As Table 1.1 in Chapter 1 summarized, we can think of society as organized into three major domains, each supported by major social institutions:

- *Ideological*   education, media, religion
- *Political*   the state, law
- *Economic*   industry, work

Institutions in each of these domains represent social arrangements and practices that are relatively stable and pervasive and that persist over time. The primary ways in which education, government, and work are conducted in U.S. society are relatively stable. For example:

- Education is required in most states through age sixteen.
- College is not required.
- The main model for teaching is a teacher with a class (ideal size fifteen to twenty).
- Common tests are used to measure performance.

Embedded in the arrangement and practices of each institution, race, class, gender, and sexuality systems are created, maintained, and transformed as dominant and subordinate groups struggle for self-definition, self-valuation, empowerment, full participation in political processes and outcomes, and a fair share of society's valued economic resources.

The practices and arrangements exist at both the macro social-structural level of institutions—broad societal and community-level patterns—and also at the micro social-psychological levels of families and individuals, small groups, and personal identity. A key aspect of an intersectional analysis, in fact, involves explicating the linkages between broad societal-level structures, trends, and events and the ways in which people in different social locations experience and interpret the structures and make meaning of their lives.

Macro social-structural trends often are represented analytically as a set of lifeless statistics about different populations. When we look at statistics summarizing national trends in economic or political indicators, such as those presented in Chapter 2, for example, it is difficult to know exactly what they mean for the way that people actually live their lives—their micro realities. This understanding is especially difficult when the people whose lives we study occupy different social locations from our own in the race, class, gender, and sexuality hierarchies. On the other hand, when we closely follow the micro trends in everyday life for a group of people, we may see how they live with financial constraints: how they feed their families, how they deal with life's stresses, how they manage work and family life, how they stay healthy.

But when we focus in detail on the lives of a small group of people, we have difficulty knowing how representative or pervasive the patterns that we observe may be. Thus we must examine both macro societal processes and the everyday lives of people in different social locations in race, class, gender, and sexuality systems. And we must explore connections between both levels—how people's everyday lives reinforce or challenge the macro systems and how the macro systems influence people's individual lives.

We can pursue this understanding by

- Identifying trends in the major social institutions and the race, class, gender, and sexuality relations in them
- Looking for patterns and themes in the ways that individuals and groups in similar and different social locations confront the options, opportunities, and strictures posed by their locations in these race, class, gender, and sexuality systems within major institutions
- Recognizing that individuals may respond differently to similar circumstances—even individuals in the same social locations
- Sharing in an ongoing dialogue the patterns and themes that we observe with the individuals and groups whose lives we seek to understand. This dialogue enables us to evaluate the validity of our understandings and to support the self-definition, self-actualization, and empowerment of the people we study, as well as of ourselves.
- Reflecting on the macro social-structural and micro social-psychological influences in our own lives

MACRO-MICRO PROCESSES IN THE IDEOLOGICAL DOMAIN

Macro

Ideologies represent sets of beliefs that help us to make sense of the contradictions in our social world. Leith Mullings describes ideologies:

> How ideologies—used here in the sense of production of meanings—are generated, maintained and deployed is intimately related to the distribution of power. Dominant ideologies often justify, support and rationalize the interests of those in power: they tell a story about why things are the way they are, setting out a framework by which hierarchy is explained and mediating contradictions among classes, between beliefs and experiences. (1994, 266)

If few people believe them, ideologies serve no purpose and cannot exist. Social systems built on inequality thus rely heavily on ideologies disseminated in institutions such as education and the media to provide the explanation for inequality that will justify the status quo and will thus discourage people from challenging the inequality. The American Dream is one such ideology—it explains all forms of inequality by suggesting that the privileged are more talented and work harder and, by implication, that those who are in subordinate positions work less hard, have less talent, and deserve less.

Dominant ideologies (also referred to as hegemonic ideologies) are pervasive societal beliefs that reflect the dominant culture's vision about what is right and proper. Controlling images (stereotypes) are dominant-culture ideologies about subordinate groups that serve to restrict their options, to constrain them. Although society has many conceptions of working women, for example, only one is dominant, hegemonic, taking precedence over other conceptions and serving as the standard against which the value or worth of "other" conceptions of working women is measured.

When you hear the phrase "today's working woman" mentioned in the media or in a popular magazine, what kind of woman comes to mind? In all likelihood, no matter what your race, class, gender, or sexual orientation, you thought of a White, heterosexual, professional woman working hard in a position of some power in the labor force. She is most likely married, but if she is single, she is certainly young. This image of today's working woman is not only atypical but also antithetical to the reality of work for most women today. Only 40.1 percent of working women are in professional, managerial, and related positions, and many of those hold little real power in the workplace. Furthermore, 17 percent of those women are not White, some are more than fifty years old, and many (although we cannot know exactly how many) are lesbian or bisexual (U.S. Bureau of Labor Statistics 2008a).

Why would such an atypical image come to mind? Because this image is the dominant, hegemonic conception of working women. It represents the image of the most powerful group of women. It is grossly overrepresented in the media because it is set up as the model, the ideal, against which other working women are to be judged. By its repeated presentation in the media (e.g., most women seen on television are White, middle-class, professional women), the image distorts the public perception, leaving the impression that the attainment of positions of power among women is far more possible than is actually the case. By masking the true nature of race, class, gender, and sexuality oppression, the image helps to preserve the status quo.

Ideologies such as this that pervade the macro structures of society affect how people come to view themselves and others—the micro level. This hegemonic controlling image of working women further sets up a standard for judgment that most women cannot possibly attain. So the experience of most women does not match the prevailing ideas about who working women are. Ideologies, then, are meant to explain the contradictions: Talent and hard work place some women above the rest. If most women come to believe that their failure to measure up is a product of their personal limitations—lack of talent, desire, effort—they internalize the oppression. They may experience a loss of self-esteem and a lower sense of self-worth and, because they feel less worthy, they may accept the obstacles they face in trying to improve their positions in the labor market.

Because of the distorted images of subordinate groups that pervade education and the media, members of these groups are often viewed as weak human beings who passively accept and even deserve less of society's socially valued resources. To comprehend the human agency, resilience, creativity, and strength of oppressed group members, however, one must view the actions and motivations of oppressed group members through their own lenses, not through the lenses of dominant culture controlling images. For example, Leith Mullings, Alaka Wali (2001) and their research team conducted a multiyear ethnographic study into the reasons for the high infant mortality rates in largely African American central Harlem. They spent years observing in the community, talking to people, attending meetings, and working with a community oversight board to make sure their work was accurately tapping into the community's life.

When the researchers began to prepare their findings for presentations to the community and to the key policy leaders whose decisions affected the community, they did what most researchers do and prepared a report with PowerPoint slides. Those slides included fairly standard descriptors used when describing minority and low-income communities—levels of unemployment, poverty, number of residents on public assistance, number without high school degrees, and so forth. What the community members showed Mullings's team, however, was that this method painted an inaccurate and potentially damaging image of the community because it reinforced stereotypes and failed to see the strengths in the community. So they changed the presentation to include the flip side of these, as well as their traditional, indicators: the 71 percent who were not on public assistance, the 41 percent of adults over age sixteen who were fully employed, the 20 percent of employed adults in executive/managerial or professional jobs. In this way, the researchers presented a more holistic representation of the weaknesses, as well as the strengths, of the community and avoided inadvertently reinforcing images of the community as undeserving and lacking in resources and assets (Mullings and Wali 2001).

When we look through the lenses of oppressed groups, it is clear that they actively resist oppression and devaluation in numerous ways every day. Not all women, for example, come to view themselves as less worthy as workers if they do not attain the hegemonic ideal. And not all central Harlem residents see their community as lacking in resources and assets. Daily acts of resistance range from an individual's rejecting negative images and replacing them with positive ones (e.g., a domestic worker's taking great pride in her work) to mass social protests. Acts of resistance also range from passive forms, such as work slowdowns or excessive and carefully planned use of sick leave (to ensure maximum disruption of the workplace), to active measures such as public protests, marches on Washington, strikes, or violence (Bookman and Morgen 1988; Naples 1998).

Recognition of the history of oppressed-group resistance helps to counter myths and beliefs in the dominant culture that oppression is a "natural" aspect of social life. Through public protest and the persistent demand for civil rights laws that made racial discrimination in education, housing, employment, and other areas of social life illegal, for example, African Americans were able to shift greater educational and economic opportunity and earning power in their own direction and in the direction of other oppressed groups (e.g., other people of color, White women, religious groups). Social movements such as the civil rights movement; racial and ethnic pride; gay, lesbian, bisexual, and transgender pride; the labor movement; and women's movements are collective manifestations of resistance to negative and controlling images of and structures constricting oppressed groups. In part through these movements, individuals become aware of the ideological nature of and the structural barriers to attaining the "ideal." They resist internalizing the oppression and have the potential for self-definition and self-valuation, a process critical to the survival of oppressed groups. The mass movement that elected Barack Obama and supported him in the early months of his presidency emerged largely from the efforts of previously disenfranchised peoples in the United States—people of color, women, gays, lesbians, bisexuals, and transgender, working-class, young, and poor people. They came to see his success and the part they played in it as a strong valuation of themselves and others like them. Positive self-valuation both moved people to action and grew as a consequence of their actions.

Micro Processes

Identity At the individual level, race, class, gender, and sexuality are fundamental sources of identity formation for all of us: how we see ourselves, who we think we are. They are, in fact, so fundamental that to be without them would be like being without an identity at all.

Racial group membership, for example, not only shapes how we see ourselves but how others see us. People of color are often viewed in limiting ways based on controlling images—stereotypes of who they are and how they ought to act. When White people say to a Native American, "You don't seem Indian to me" or "I don't think of you as Indian," they are acknowledging that the Native American is acting out of line with their stereotypic images of Native Americans. They also imply that although contradictory evidence may make them willing to change their views of a single person ("you're not like them"), it does not challenge their stereotypes and in fact reinforces the power of these controlling images ("they can't possibly be like you").

Members of oppressed racial groups may also seek to control the behavior of group members by holding them accountable to *oppositional* expectations for group loyalty and resistance to oppression—by insisting that they *not* act like the dominant White group. Most racial groups, for example, have developed derogatory terms to refer to members of their own group who may deny or devalue their racial identity. *Oreo, coconut, apple,* and *banana* are terms for African Americans, Latinos/as, Native Americans, and Asian Americans who "act White," who appear to devalue their heritage by denying or ignoring it. In short, both dominant and subordinate groups hold expectations for the way racial group members should be. And even though these expectations often differ across class, gender, and sexuality systems, they are powerful structures in our lives.

Psychosocial Resources The barriers of oppression are both material and ideological; the resources associated with one's social location in the matrix of dominance and subordination are both material and psychological (Collins 2000; Weber, Hancock, and Higginbotham 1997). Nonmaterial psychosocial resources have important consequences for social and psychological well-being that in turn affect one's ability to secure material resources. Psychosocial resources associated with one's social location include positive feelings of well-being and self-respect that result from a strong connection to and identity with a group of people who share a common history and life experiences (Comas-Dias and Greene 1994; Sellers et al. 1998).

Developing positive identity and feelings of self-respect is made easier for dominant groups whose own experiences serve as the public model for how all people should live their lives. Because social institutions such as schools are structured to support the White middle class, for example, White, middle-class children are usually raised with successful role models and in families with greater access to the resources that will help the children succeed in school. They enter school with greater expectations for success; teachers expect their success and give them more attention. Teachers' positive orientations enhance the children's sense of self-worth, thus improving their performance and their chances for school success (Sacks 2007; Saenz et al. 2007; Schultz 2008).

Occupying a subordinate location in the race, class, gender, and sexuality systems does not, however, necessarily equate with a lack of psychosocial resources. Some research has consistently demonstrated that African American adolescent girls, for example, have higher overall self-esteem and a stronger sense of self than do White adolescent girls (American Association of University Women 1991, 1994, 1999). Working-class Latino/a children growing up in the barrio may develop a strong sense of self-worth if they are surrounded by loving family members and neighbors who convey a sense of each child's special worth as an individual and as a Latino/a. And this psychosocial resource can serve as the foundation for a healthy defense against negative or rejecting messages from the dominant society. Resistance to pressures of structured inequality within subordinate group communities can, in fact, be a psychosocial resource that can be used in a collective struggle against oppression and in a personal journey toward self-appreciation and good mental health.

MACRO-MICRO PROCESSES IN THE POLITICAL DOMAIN

Macro Processes

As the historical time line in Chapter 2 suggests, the struggle for full citizenship rights, for inclusion in the political process, and thus for an equal voice in public policies—from defining racial groups to taxation to family, welfare, immigration, school, and international policies—has been long and difficult. Participation in the political institutions of society defines groups' relationships to the policy enforcement institutions—law, criminal justice, the police, and the military. Control over the political domain also increases control in the ideological and economic domains by increasing power over the production of controlling ideologies about subordinate groups and by increasing access to greater economic resources. The prevalence of upper-class, White, heterosexual men in the U.S. Congress, for example, enables them to pass tax legislation, business legislation, and other policies that support the continued dominance of this group in the economy.

But macro political processes also affect other domains that seem less obvious, such as a group's physical health. Thomas LaVeist (1992) demonstrated that the political empowerment of communities of color is an important determinant of their health. In communities with more people of color on the city council, health indicators (e.g., life expectancy, disease rates) were better than for communities with few people of color on the councils. When people of color are elected to city councils, their presence affects the community's health in at least two ways:

- Council members can direct resources that improve health to communities of color (e.g., health clinics).
- Council members can divert projects that might threaten community health (e.g., toxic waste dumps).

Subordinate-group resistance through political action can affect and has affected the well-being of oppressed communities. But for these macro community-level changes to take place, individuals must also feel empowered and involved enough to participate in the process—running for office, lobbying, protesting, voting, working for candidates, talking to others in the community about the issues and candidates, writing letters (see also Basu and Dutta 2008; Moore, Townsend, and Oldroyd 2006).

Micro Processes

When people in oppressed groups internalize the negative views and limits on their lives in the political realm, they may feel unable to effect change in their environments and be unlikely to act in ways that would change their own or the group's status. They lack a sense of control over their environment and a sense of efficacy—the belief that what you do can make a difference. So, for example, they are unlikely to participate in the political process. When large numbers of people in a community do not participate in the political process, political change that favors their community is unlikely to take place. During the past fifty years, for example, voting participation in federal elections declined precipitously from 1960, when 62.8 percent of the voting age population participated, until 1996, when 49 percent did so. And although a final accounting is yet unavailable for the 2008 election, some estimates suggest a return to near 1960 levels (Nonprofitvote. org; U.S. Census Bureau 2009, Table 402). Congressional, off-year elections are always characterized by lower voter participation than presidential years, and voting in those elections has also declined from 58.5 percent of the voting age population in 1960 to 33.1 percent in 1998, followed by a modest increase to 35.8 percent in 2006 (U.S. Census Bureau 2009: Table 402.

This decline in popular voting coincides with the period of a great shift of wealth and power away from segments of middle-class, working-class, and poor populations. Still, White, middle-class, educated middle-aged voters remain the most likely to turn out, in part because dominant group status provides people with access to resources and options that enable them to influence the political process and thus increases their sense of personal control and efficacy. To achieve the same end—a sense of personal control, efficacy, empowerment—members of oppressed groups must reject negative images, self-blame, and limitations. President Barack Obama's message of "Change We Can Believe In" for the 2008 election, punctuated by the chant "Yes We Can!" were messages intended to confront directly the belief so prevalent over recent history that voting—especially by the traditionally disenfranchised—could not lead to change, could not make a difference. And Obama encouraged the sense of personal control by employing strategies to engage people—especially the young, gays and lesbians, the working and middle classes, and people of color—in working for the campaign with their friends, families, and neighbors, in participating in the process, not simply in voting.

Patricia Collins discusses the ways in which Black women's empowerment involves rejecting the dominant view of reality, including the pervasive cultural stereotypes of Black women as subjugated and devalued people in American society. Collins describes the creation of a separate reality for Black women as they confront and dismantle controlling negative images of themselves as matriarchs, mammies, welfare mothers, physically unattractive women:

When Black women define ourselves, we clearly reject the assumptions that those in positions granting them the authority to interpret our reality are entitled to do so. Regardless of the actual content of Black women's self-definitions, the act of insisting on Black females' self-definition validates Black women's power as human subjects. (Collins 2000, 114)

When Black women and other oppressed groups feel validated as human beings, they will be empowered in many ways to further their own lives, as well as those of others.

MACRO AND MICRO PROCESSES IN THE ECONOMIC DOMAIN

Control over economic resources (e.g., wealth, income) enables dominant groups to control other critical social resources: housing, education, transportation, health care, and jobs, the primary means by which most adults obtain their financial resources and by which many define their sense of self-worth. So a critical intersectional analysis must examine economic resources (wealth and income) and jobs, both how they are distributed across different groups and how the distributions have changed in the recent past. Recent changes indicate a shifting balance of power across different race, class, gender, and sexuality groups and thus foretell different everyday struggles for people in different locations in these systems.

Macro Processes

Since the 1970s, economists, sociologists, and even politicians agree that changes in the U.S. economy have seriously reduced the standard of living for most Americans. These changes include:

- The decline of manufacturing and the increase in the service sector that brought permanent layoffs, the loss of higher paid blue-collar jobs, and the creation of lower wage white-collar jobs
- The rapid technological advances, especially the applications of the computer chip, that led the push to a service economy
- The increased global competition from foreign companies that have cheaper labor costs
- The flight of U.S. businesses to locations abroad to find cheap labor and to reduce their U.S. taxes
- The loss of union strength—private-sector unionization dropped from 40 percent of the labor force in the 1950s to 12 percent in 2006
- The outsourcing of government functions to private contractors whose wages and benefits do not typically match government employment
- The increased corporate debt and risky investment practices contributing to the failure of major corporations, particularly in the financial services, housing, and auto industries. The failures were met by unprecedented

government "bailouts" in 2008–2009 because these companies were deemed to be "too big to be allowed to fail."

• The shift in the tax burden from corporations to individuals and from the wealthy to the middle class, working class, and poor. By 2007 individuals contributed 50.8 percent of the country's total tax revenues, slightly more than in 1960, whereas corporations contributed only 14.7 percent, down from 24 percent in 1960 (Freeman 1994; Internal Revenue Service 2008, Table 6; Klein 2007; Mishel, Berstein, and Allegretto 2007; Timmer, Eitzen and Talley 1994; U.S. Bureau of Labor Statistics 2008a; 2008b).

Income and Jobs The power structures of race, class, gender, and sexuality put groups in different positions both to shape these processes and to structure their relationships to them—producing advantage for some and disadvantage for others. From the 1980s to the present, both wealth and income inequality increased, and the middle class declined for the first time since the 1920s and the Great Depression of the 1930s:

• The very rich got richer.
• Middle-income groups lost numbers, wealth, and income.
• The ranks of the poor grew, and the people in them got poorer (Hacker 1997; Institute for Women's Policy Research 2008; Mishel, Berstein, and Allegretto 2007).

These shifts in the class structure are also differentially distributed across race, class, gender, and sexuality systems: The ranks of the poor are increasingly composed of women (particularly women of color) and children. Growing poverty and a shrinking middle class are produced primarily by job loss, by lower wages in the new jobs created in the 1980s (more women's than men's jobs), by reduced wages in the remaining jobs, and by the increased costs of health care.

Recovery after the recession of 2001was a "jobless" recovery—productivity (gross domestic product) increased, but the economy lost jobs for two years and added them in very small numbers until the recession began in 2007, when job losses and involuntary part-time employment began a rapid increase. At the beginning of 2009, the nation was experiencing record job losses, with an unemployment rate of 7.2 percent, or 11.1 million people. Unemployment hit African Americans and Latinos much harder than Whites: The White rate was 6.6 percent, Black 11.9 percent, and Latinos 9.2 percent. Although manufacturing continued to suffer the worst declines, technology, retail and wholesale sales, and construction also saw losses. Health care was one of the only areas in which job growth occurred (U.S. Bureau of Labor Statistics 2008c).

Since the 1980s U.S. workers have also seen long-term deterioration in job quality:

• The ability of the U.S. economy to generate "good jobs"—those paying $16 an hour, $32,000 a year, with employer-provided health insurance and pension—declined 25 to 30 percent over the past twenty-five years.

- Twenty-five percent of the workforce earned poverty-level wages before the recession of 2007.
- The young and less educated have experienced the greatest decline in good jobs, but higher education provides less protection against unemployment than it used to.
- Since 1995, 30 percent of the work force has been employed in nonstandard work—not regular full-time work—including part-time, temporary, day, or contingent labor. The trend in this work is to more permanent nonstandard work, or "perma-temping." Women are more represented in this kind of work, and it is 3.5 times less likely to provide health insurance.
- The increased involvement of women in the labor force since the 1960s led to more two-earner families, even in the middle class. Middle-income families consisting of married couples with children now work 30 percent more hours a week than they did in 1975, amounting to twenty-two weeks, or more than five months, of full-time work a year.
- Older workers are staying in the labor force longer to keep health insurance and to offset the losses they suffered in their pensions from the stock market crash beginning in 2008 (Mishel, Berstein, and Allegretto 2007).

Women and Work Women's labor force participation rates have dramatically increased since the 1970s. In 2007, 46.4 percent of the workforce were women (U.S. Department of Labor 2007). Historically, the number of Black women employed outside the home has been high because they worked to offset their husbands' low pay, which resulted from discrimination in hiring and in wage structures (Ortiz 1994). The number of White women employed outside the home, however, has increased until their rates (59 percent) almost equal those of Black women (61.1 percent) (U.S. Census Bureau 2008c). This increase has been especially dramatic among women with children. In 1960 only 27.6 percent of married women with children were employed, but by 2008 66.4 percent were employed. Most families now include two income earners, and between 1996 and 2006 the number of dual-income families increased by 31 percent, from 25.5 to 33.4 million families (U.S. Department of Labor 2007).

Wealth Wealth is in many ways a better indicator of economic well-being because it is the total, at a given moment, of a person's accumulated assets (e.g., ownership of stocks, money in the bank, real estate, business ownership) less the debt held at one time. Income is less inclusive and refers only to the flow of dollars (salaries, wages, and payments from an occupation, investment, government transfer) over a set period, typically a year. The richest people accumulate very little of their wealth through work for wages. Wealth is thus a good indicator of the relative economic power of race, class, gender, and sexual groups:

- Although people of color average 55.6 percent of White incomes, they own only 27.3 percent of Whites' net worth.

- The inequality of wealth (representing total financial assets) between White people and people of color—the racial wealth gap—has remained very high during this period. In 1983 the median wealth for Blacks was 7 percent that of Whites; by 2004 it was only 10 percent.
- The only major wage gap to *decline* since the 1980s was the gender gap in wages. But progress in closing the gender earnings gap slowed considerably since 1990: Women increased their annual earnings relative to men's by 11.4 percentage points from 1980 to 1990 but by only 6.2 percentage points over the next seventeen years to 77.8 percent of men's earnings. Most of the change was the result of a decline in men's wages, not an increase in women's wages (Institute for Women's Policy Research 2008; Mishel, Berstein, and Allegretto 2007, 162–3).

The racial wealth gap also varies by gender and family status. In 1989 the average wealth among people of color who were

- married was 35 percent that of Whites who were married
- single male heads of households was 62 percent of White single male heads of households
- single female heads of households was 20 percent of White single female heads of households

These gaps are different from income differences between the races, but they present a more accurate picture of the total financial resources available to families. In this picture, single women of color who are heads of households are by far the most disadvantaged group financially relative to White women and men, to men of color, and to married women of color (Mishel and Bernstein 1994, 252; for recent data on gender but not race see Brobeck and Montalto 2008).

Micro Processes

These changes in the macro structure of the economy have clearly affected everyday life in the United States for everyone. Occupying a privileged location in the economic class system facilitates one's life in many ways. As a consequence of the macroeconomic shifts in the past thirty years, for example, many poor and working-class people have lost their jobs, work multiple part-time jobs, can no longer afford education, have transportation problems getting to work, cannot afford quality child care, may lack health care coverage or have minimal coverage, cannot afford to own their own homes, need multiple incomes in a family to meet basic needs.

For many middle- and upper-class people, none of these needs is likely to be a cause for concern; their economic resources either render them nonexistent (difficulty getting to work) or easily remedied (finding child care or paying for college). Consequently, people in the dominant group often fail to grasp the realities of life for those living on the economic margins. They also can feel validated by a dominant system that in many ways equates money with success and success with worth. In contrast, people in subordinate groups must, as Patricia Collins (1998) points out, resist the negative association in our society between lack of material/economic resources and lack of worth as human beings.

Communities often resist this dominant culture association between wealth and worth by putting forth alternative systems of valuation, such as valuing loyalty, honesty, hard work, respect for elders, and nurturing others. People who show these valued traits can receive community validation and develop a positive sense of self-worth, even in the face of a dominant society that actively devalues them.

SIMULTANEOUS EXPRESSION

Race, class, gender, and sexuality are interrelated systems at the macro institutional level. Because they are created, maintained, and transformed simultaneously and in relationship to one another, they cannot be understood independently of one another. At the micro level of the individual, these systems are experienced in our lives simultaneously. Each contributes to our identities, our views of the world. In a very real sense they cannot be separated.

This feature has been highlighted by women of color involved in feminist movements who are often asked to place their gender before their race in deciding where they will work for social justice and the kinds of positions they should take on social issues. In a similar vein, the Black Power movement of the 1960s was undermined and lost women's participation in part because of its patriarchal insistence that racism, not sexism, was the primary oppressor and that Black women should play traditional women's roles in the organization. As former Black Panther Elaine Brown said, the party was "a very misogynistic organization" (Jackson 1998, 45). The pressure to separate oneself into different (and competing) parts was eloquently resisted in the often quoted title of one of the first anthologies about Black women's studies: *All the Women Were White, All the Blacks Were Men, But Some of Us Are Brave: Black Women's Studies* (Hull, Scott and Smith 1982).

Although one system may appear prominent in a particular historical moment or social situation or in an individual's identity, close examination will always reveal the relevance of the other dimensions. Race, class, gender, and sexuality systems of oppression often reinforce one another, but they are also unique systems of dominance with unique histories and current manifestations. What is unique about an intersectional analysis and what differentiates it from analyses of a single dimension of inequality is that it

- Simultaneously examines all four dimensions and may also incorporate other related dimensions, such as ethnicity, nationality, disability, or age. In this way, the analysis is much more complex than one that isolates a single dimension for examination.
- Focuses attention on the unique expressions of social reality that exist at the points of connection, the intersections of the four dimensions. Thus the

lives of groups such as women of color are not excluded from but become the central focus of much research.

One's social location in the intersecting systems of race, class, gender, and sexuality produces varying social experiences:

- One can be privileged in all social systems—a White, heterosexual, middle-class, professional male.
- One can be privileged in some social systems yet disadvantaged in others—middle-class people with a subordinate racial ethnic position, working-class men, and middle-class White women. Gay, middle-class, White men, for example, have the advantage of gender, class, and racial privilege, yet this advantage cannot protect them from negative social sanctions aimed at controlling their sexual orientation.
- One can be disadvantaged in all the social systems—lesbian women of color who have few job skills and little formal education.

That we almost all occupy both dominant and subordinate positions and experience advantage and disadvantage in race, class, gender, and sexuality systems means that there are no pure oppressors or oppressed in our society. Race, class, gender, and sexuality are not reducible to immutable personality traits or seemingly permanent characteristics. They are social constructions that often give us power and options in some arenas while restricting our power and options in others.

We cannot argue from this principle, however, that "we are all oppressed" so that our oppressions can simply be added up and ranked to identify the most oppressed group or the greatest victims. We cannot say that disadvantage on any two dimensions is the same as on any other two. No simple mathematical relationship can capture the complexity of the interrelationships of these systems (Hancock 2007). And yet recognizing that we each simultaneously experience all of these dimensions can help us to see the often obscured ways in which we benefit from existing race, class, gender, and sexuality social arrangements, as well as the ways in which we are disadvantaged. Such an awareness can be key in working together across different groups to achieve a more equitable distribution of society's valued resources.

SUMMARY

Race, class, gender, and sexuality systems are generated, extended, and challenged in the ideological, political, and economic societal domains. At the micro level, the everyday actions of individuals as they live their lives in unequal social relations both generate those systems and challenge them. At the macro level, structures of oppression provide a powerful framework, a hierarchy that persists through time and across places and that has serious consequences for social life. Understanding the ways that our individual lives are shaped by larger social forces is a key process in coming to understand race, class, gender, and sexuality as systems of oppression that shape all of our lives, all of the time. Further, these systems are interrelated and so are our identities and places within them. Because we simultaneously experience our location along all dimensions, they must all be taken into account in every analysis of social life.

Questions to Ask When Analyzing Race, Class, Gender, and Sexuality

As you read the rest of the book, I hope that you develop and strengthen your ability to analyze the interconnected systems of race, class, gender, and sexuality and to see how to use your analyses to further your personal development and for social betterment. When you analyze situations and events, remember that the tools that you bring to the analysis are the questions you ask and the knowledge you have of the dynamic character of race, class, gender, and sexuality oppression: that these systems are *historically and geographically contextual*, *socially constructed power relations*, *simultaneously expressed* at both the *macro level* of social institutions and the *micro level* of individual life and personal identity. When we think of race, class, gender, and sexuality systems in this way, a more complete and more complex understanding of social life provides us with a firmer foundation on which to develop effective strategies for promoting social equity and a more humane social order.

When you conduct your analyses, recall the five basic themes in a race, class, gender, and sexuality analysis. Each theme can be associated with some general questions you might want to consider. The questions posed here are not meant to be comprehensive—you will surely think of others—but to be general guides, a starting place. I will also revisit the case of Margaret Welch by raising a few questions that highlight the simultaneous and interrelated dynamics of race, class, gender, and sexuality in her life.

Historically and Geographically Contextual

First, race, class, gender, and sexuality are *contextually rooted in history and geography*. When we examine situations, it is important to know the histories and global contexts of particular groups so that we can come to understand their current situations and their interpretations of events. Taking a broad historical and global view also enables us to see the tremendous changes that have taken place in each of these systems over time and the diversity across social geography and to recognize the potential for change in situations we face every day. Ask yourself:

- How have the relevant ideologies, controlling images, developed over time? In this location?
- What political processes have shaped this situation over time? In this location?
- What historical economic conditions have affected the situation? Regional economic conditions?

- How would this situation be understood at a different historical time? In different regional and geographic locations?

About Margaret Welch, we might ask: How have controlling images of poor women, welfare recipients, developed over time in the United States? How are they different for White women and women of color and for heterosexual, bisexual, and lesbian women? How have the political forces that shape today's welfare policies (e.g., prescribed schooling and work for benefits) developed over time? Margaret lives in Chicago—do rural poor women face different obstacles? How have the economic shifts of the past thirty years in the United States affected poor women's lives? If Margaret were lesbian, would she have better protections against discrimination in New York or San Francisco than in Chicago, Des Moines, or the rural South?

Socially Constructed

Second, race, class, gender, and sexuality are *socially constructed,* not biologically determined. Their meaning develops out of group struggles over socially valued resources. Ask yourself:

- Are race, class, gender, and sexuality taken to determine how people should be out of some notion of biological imperative or of inherent inferiority?
- Are race, class, gender, and sexuality seen as immutable "facts" of people's lives or of social situations?
- Are people's economic resources, power, prestige, education, health—their total status—seen as something they earned through individual effort?
- How might you view the situation differently if people of different race, class, gender, and sexuality locations were in it?

In Margaret's life, we might ask: Does the welfare system operate under the assumption that women like Margaret can actually improve their life conditions? Does Margaret blame herself for her current plight? Are there any people apparent in her life who believe in her ability to escape from poverty permanently? Imagine that Margaret were Chinese American and gay. How would her story change?

Power Relationships

Third, race, class, gender, and sexuality are *power relationships* of dominance and subordination in which dominant groups exploit the labor and lives of oppressed groups for a greater share of society's valued resources. Try not to confuse personal power with social power. Individuals can be powerful by virtue of their insight, knowledge, personalities, and other traits. They can persuade others to act in ways they want. But this personal power can be achieved in spite of a lack of socially institutionalized power. It is the power that accrues from occupying a position of dominance in the race, class, gender, and sexuality systems that we seek to understand here. Ask yourself:

- What are the institutional arrangements that benefit the powerful and cost others in this situation?
- Which group or groups gain and which group or groups lose in the institutional arrangements we observe?
- Have the participants come to believe (internalized) that they lack or have power in the situation? How have their beliefs affected their actions?

In Margaret's case, we might ask: Who are the groups that gain because Margaret and others like her (White, heterosexual, women) are poor? Who benefits from poverty? Does Margaret internalize her lack of power? If so, how does this internalization affect her actions? If Margaret became involved in the welfare rights movement (cf. Abramovitz 1996; Hancock 2004), would her view of herself and of the causes of her poverty change? How?

Macro and Micro Levels

Fourth, race, class, gender, and sexuality systems operate at both the *macro level of social institutions* and the *micro level of individual life*. When you analyze a particular social event, seeing the interpersonal and psychological manifestations of oppression is often easy. Because the broad macro level forces that shape events are more remote and abstract, they are more difficult to see.

Which group or groups gain and which group or groups lose in the institutional arrangements we observe? When many people of color and White women look at White male backlash against affirmative action, for example, they can easily see angry White men out to push back gains made by people of color and women and to maintain their position of power and control. They can dismiss White men as "oppressors" or bad people. But when we ask about the broader race, class, gender, and sexuality forces that shape this relationship, we also see that the recent decline in our economy has rendered many White men vulnerable to loss of jobs, income, and health. White men's anger in part comes out of their different expectations—out of their sense of privilege (cf. Newman 1993; Ferber 1998). If we are to collaborate to achieve economic change that benefits most people, we must recognize the real ways in which many White men, as well as many other people, are vulnerable in the present economy. Ask yourself:

- What are the ideological, political, and economic institutional arrangements and practices that are shaping each actor's actions and views in the situation?
- Imagine changes in key macro institutional conditions, such as the onset of an economic recession. How would this change alter the situation?
- How does each actor view the situation? Is that view different for people in different race, class, gender, and sexuality locations?
- Are oppressed group members aware of the race, class, gender, and sexuality power structures in the situation? Is there evidence that they resist controlling images in their views and their actions? Is there evidence that they have accepted the controlling images, the limits on their lives? Why?
- Are dominant group members aware of their privilege in the situation? What does it mean to them? What views do they hold of oppressed groups? If they do not refer to oppressed groups, why not?

And thinking of Margaret, we might ask: What are the macro economic conditions that render Margaret poor? The political conditions? The ideological, controlling images? How is Margaret's view of the institutions (welfare, education) she faces limited by her social location? How might a wealthy White woman view Margaret's situation? Has Margaret internalized the social limits on her life, resisted them, or both?

Simultaneous Expression

Fifth, these systems are *simultaneously experienced*. All operate to shape everyone's lives at all times. Ask yourself about all of the systems in every situation you examine. Although one may appear to be in the foreground, go behind the obvious and ask about the less visible dimensions. Ask yourself:

- If we take account of only a single dimension of oppression (e.g., gender) and ignore the others, how might we interpret the situation differently?
- What are the dimensions that are foregrounded, that are fairly obvious, in this situation?
- What dimensions are not so apparent? Why?
- How does the power of the individuals involved shape our perspective on what dimensions are important?

And for Margaret, we might ask: Even though race, class, and gender are in the forefront of her story, how does sexuality also shape her life? If Margaret were lesbian, how might her story be different? If Margaret were not White, how might her story be different? If we looked only at her gender, how might we miss key elements in understanding her situation?

Implications for Social Action and Social Justice

Finally, when you conduct analyses, make the connection between *activism for social justice* and the analyses you conduct. Ask yourself about the implications for social justice of the perspective you have, the questions you ask, and the answers you obtain.

- Do your analyses provide insights that in a political context would likely serve to reinforce existing power relations?
- Do your analyses illuminate processes of resistance or avenues for self-definition or self-valuation that could transform the race, class, gender, and sexuality hierarchies?
- How might people in different social locations react to and employ your analyses? To what ends?

When you take race, class, gender, and sexuality into account in every situation, you arrive at a richer, more complete, more complex, and more useful understanding of society.

✦⊃

A Race, Class, Gender, and Sexuality Analysis of Education

When exploring how the intersecting systems of race, class, gender and sexuality are generated, maintained, challenged, and transformed, I seek an analysis that is complex, that does not rank oppressions, that addresses their intersecting nature, and that moves us toward social justice. The conceptual framework presented here suggests that the analysis should be historically grounded and should address the simultaneous expressions of socially constructed power relationships at both the individual (micro) and societal (macro) levels.

In this section, I attempt to further explicate the framework by applying it to a specific case, the American system of education. Rather than analyze a particular group's experience in the educational system at a specific historical moment, I seek to illustrate the framework and to guide future work by raising questions and identifying some of the kinds of issues and social relationships that must be addressed in a comprehensive analysis of the reproduction of race, class, gender, and sexuality systems in education in the United States today.

In Chapter 6, I open the discussion with two brief educational biographies. Theo Wilson is a teenage African American male whom I met and observed in the late 1990s when he was participating in an after-school program in a Northeastern city. Lynn Johnson is an African American baby boomer who was interviewed in the late 1980s for a research project on Black and White professional-managerial women, which I conducted in Memphis, Tennessee. In this segment of her interview, Lynn reflects on her educational experiences in the 1960s and 1970s. Taken together, these two cases reveal many of the complexities of race, class, gender, and sexuality as they are played out between women and men of the same racial group in different places and times.

Education is an institution whose primary identity is in the domain of ideology: It is focused on the production and transmission of ideas that prepare people to work in and to contribute to the smooth functioning of society. Consequently, any discussion of the social processes endemic in the institution of education must first address the cornerstone ideology on which it rests: the American Dream ideology. Chapter 7 presents and critiques the basic premises and paradoxes of the American Dream, particularly as they lay a foundation for the race, class, gender, and sexuality conflicts in and about the U.S. system of education.

Chapters 8 and 9 explore the production of race, class, gender, and sexuality in education within the rubric of each of the themes in the framework. I chose not to limit my analysis to a single group, such as Chinese American women, or to a single social process, such as the resegregation of public schools, a focus that would enable more depth of analysis but would limit the opportunity to raise a variety of issues and questions for further consideration—a purpose of this book. Nor is there space to provide a comprehensive race, class, gender, and sexuality analysis of the U.S. education system. Instead, these chapters illustrate the framework by highlighting some of the ways that addressing these themes complicates, illuminates, and renders our analyses more useful in the pursuit of social justice. I chose breadth over depth, using a variety of group experiences to suggest avenues to pursue in more comprehensive analyses.

One of the fundamental social processes through which race, class, gender, and sexuality hierarchies are produced and sustained, particularly in education, is segregating and isolating groups for differential treatment. Understanding segregation processes in education—into different schools, different tracks in schools, different areas of study, different curricula—is key to unraveling the dynamics of race, class, gender, and sexuality. I examine segregation processes in the historical roots of the modern school system, as well as in current macro institutional and micro individual processes. Macro institutional power relations in the economic, political, and ideological domains are illustrated as they play out in education (e.g., in politicization of educational issues, in the curriculum, in labor market outcomes). Micro individual power relations are examined in classroom dynamics of race, class, gender, and sexuality in kindergarten through twelfth grade, and the simultaneity of race, class, gender, and sexuality systems is examined through a review of cases presented in this section.

Chapter 10 concludes the section with a discussion of how our analyses of race, class, gender, and sexuality systems can lead us to act for social justice. In deepening our understanding of how power relationships are created and sustained and resisted, we gain new perspectives on social institutions, learn to ask new questions, and begin to see new paths to social equality.

✦◯

CHAPTER 6

A Case Study: Theo Wilson and Lynn Johnson

Dream Variations
Langston Hughes

To fling my arms wide
In some place of the sun,
To whirl and to dance
Till the white day is done.
Then rest at cool evening
Beneath a tall tree
While night comes on gently,
    Dark like me—
That is my dream!

To fling my arms wide
In the face of the sun,
Dance! Whirl! Whirl!
Till the quick day is done.
Rest at pale evening...
A tall, slim tree...
Night coming tenderly
    Black like me.

The Case of Theo Wilson[1]

I observed the following exchange between Theo Wilson and Marie Carucci during a writing tutoring session in an after-school program in 1996.

---

[1]"Theo Wilson" is a pseudonym, as are all other names in the story. These names and some details of the story have been changed to protect the identities of those involved.

"Write a poem about a dream you have," Marie Carucci said to Theo Wilson, after they read and talked about "Dream Variations."

Puzzled, Theo asked, "What do you mean? Do you mean the things that happen when you're asleep?"

Marie replied, "Well, yes, dreams do happen when you're asleep, but I mean the kind you have when you're awake—perhaps something you might like to do, if you could do anything you wanted."

"I don't know," said Theo and his leg began to jitter.

"Just something you really want to do, anything—dance in the sun like Hughes, something serious, something silly." And they talked some more about Hughes's poem.

Finally, Theo said, "Well, I can't do anything I want. Everything takes good math skills, and I'm not good at math."

"Well, just pretend you can."

Dreams
Theo Wilson

I would like to be a Secret Service agent,
    Protecting important people,
    Saving lives,
And getting no acknowledgment—
Just knowing that my job and
people
    Depend on me.

When Theo got to this point, he quit and shoved the paper at Marie, his leg jittering furiously. Marie asked him why he dreamed this, and he continued:

Why?
To slow down crime or
Make criminals fear me.
To hear thanks or
A smile.

I would love to do this.
But I doubt it would happen.
Bad luck seems to
Follow me.
Whenever I get good at something,
Something or someone messes it up.

Theo stopped, shaking his head and muttering that he just didn't know why "this stuff" happened to him all the time. Marie probed, "What stuff? Give an example."

Take last year in October—
I had the best week of practice all year.
Even the Varsity guys were noticing me.

> Coaches tried me out for new things in practice.
> But in the JV game versus [Our Town],
> I dropped a touchdown pass—
> In the end zone.

Theo quit again, hanging his head and trying to laugh off his remembered humiliation. They talked for a while about bad luck and good luck and choices, and Marie said, "How could you change things?"

> How could I change things?
> Have a magical surgery
> To take my hands off me and
> Put Jerry Rice's hands on me.

Theo Wilson and Marie Carucci met when she and another faculty member, Bill Nichols, from a local urban university campus began to tutor youths in writing and math after school at the community center a few blocks from their campus. They are working against the limits of race, class, gender, and sexuality hierarchies to envision and facilitate a future for Theo that is not a dead end—one that allows dreams.

Theo Wilson is a fifteen-year-old, African American male who lives in the urban Northeast. Like many young teens, he is of average height, lanky, and a bit awkward and shy. His major interest is sports, especially football. He lifts weights fanatically, hoping to make the varsity team someday. And now he has decided to play lacrosse. Although he was completing his freshman year, his academic performance in high school was already very poor, especially in math. And he was in a technical English class rather than in a college prep one, even a "slow" section.

Like many poor, urban youths, Theo "lives" in a variety of places—sometimes with his father (before he died), sometimes with his paternal grandparents, but mostly with his maternal grandmother. His mother, a drug addict who is in and out of rehab, appears sporadically in his life. Taking advantage of the G.I. Bill, his father went to college and for a while held a low-wage administrative job. But when Theo was about ten years old, his father was diagnosed with a rare degenerative disease and spent much of his energy fighting to stay alive. He died less than six months after Theo wrote "Dreams." Before he died, however, Theo's father tried to stay involved in Theo's education. In the spring of 1996, when he learned of the free tutoring sessions, he enrolled Theo.

After his father died, Theo was left even more adrift than before. Since then Theo has turned more and more to Marie and Bill for parenting and nurturing, but Marie is moving out of town and Bill is working hard at his own family and career. Only a few months after his father died, Theo called Marie late one Sunday evening, telling her he had to talk to her "right away." After much stumbling and embarrassed laughing, he blurted out that while everyone was out of the house, he liked to dress up in "different kinds of clothes. Know what I mean?" So in addition to grappling with everything else, Theo—the football player, weight lifter, and now lacrosse player—is struggling with his preference for this "inappropriate" gender expression and what, if anything, it might mean for his sexual identity, which is also developing. When Marie asked him whether his teachers had ever discussed cross-dressing, transgender issues, or homosexuality in class, he burst out laughing, "They couldn't talk about *that* stuff!"

Marie began helping Theo identify sources of information and support. They found a number of sources that offered support for gay, lesbian, and bisexual youths, but none for young cross-dressers. For a while, Theo spent much of his free time searching for answers, primarily on the Web but also by calling support and hotline numbers. His search for answers ended, at least for a while, when he called a number he found in his high school newspaper. It promised help for young people with problems. When Theo explained his "problem," the voice at the other end of the phone first denounced him as a sinner and then began reading Bible verses to him. Theo turned his attention and energy to finding a date for the prom and became focused on girls and having a girlfriend. But his "thing," as he calls it, continues to cause him pain and anxiety.

As part of teaching Theo writing, Marie talked to him about Standard English. When Marie teaches Standard English to working-class students, immigrants, students of color—to anyone other than White middle- and upper-class students—she teaches it as a second language.

Working with Theo on a grammar assignment, identifying transitive and intransitive verbs, Marie asked an increasingly distracted and frustrated Theo why he thought he had to do this work. She also talked to him about levels of language, about how arbitrary the "rules" are, and about why even though you may say, "I ain't got no money," it's a good idea to know the standard way of saying the same thing. During the conversation, Theo talked a great deal about how useless this stuff is and how boring and how teachers make you do the same stuff year after year.

> MARIE: But why do they make you do it? Why do I think you should know Standard English?
> THEO: *I don't know. 'Cause you're a English teacher, too?*
> And they both laughed.
> MARIE: Well, here's one good reason why: Unless you're going to be a rock star or a professional athlete or a famous artist—if you're going to be a regular person who goes to work every day—you make more money if you can speak and write Standard English. And if we just work at all of this and you learn it this year, you won't have to bother learning it over and over again—just get it over with.
> THEO: *Why ain't nobody ever told me that before?*
> He set to work with a little more focus and determination.

Unlike the other youths in the program, Theo from the beginning launched himself into the work, never missing a single session and often coming to Bill's office for extra math sessions. And although Marie and Bill gave their work and home phone numbers to all the youths, Theo was the only one to use them, to go after help actively. He even came to math tutoring sessions during the summer.

After a semester of active tutoring and mentoring by Marie and Bill, Theo began to think differently about his options and future prospects: He began to dream. Theo Wilson now says he wants to go to college. And one thing he learned was that his technical English course and basic math are not college preparatory classes. In these classes, he would not learn what he needs to know to score well on the SATs or ACTs or to keep up in college. So in his sophomore year, he enrolled in college prep courses, continuing to work with Marie and Bill. Bill is even mentoring Theo through the SATs. Now that he's in the tutoring program, Theo may get a chance to go to college. But he still faces tremendous obstacles.

The Case of Lynn Johnson[2]

Lynn Johnson is a successful forty-five-year-old African American hospital administrator who attended elementary and high school in the 1950s and 1960s in Memphis, Tennessee. She grew up living in public housing projects with her mother, who was on welfare (AFDC), and her six siblings. When she was sixteen, Lynn had a baby but continued school and graduated with her class from her inner-city, all-Black high school. Lynn was among the first African American students to attend a local, private liberal arts college in Memphis. When she was interviewed in 1987 for a research project I conducted with Elizabeth Higginbotham, she was asked the following questions:

> INTERVIEWER: Is there anything about your early childhood and schooling which you think has influenced your career plans?
>
> LYNN: *Yeah, the teachers. Elementary school was one of the most outstanding experiences for me. Being a poor kid and going into that environment, you think that the rich people—or the great people of the world—are teachers. They're the ones with the pretty clothes and the big cars and the big money and all that kind of thing. I had in my environment some teachers who really knew you. Who knew about you, took time to find out about you, cared about you, pushed you, who beat your tail if you didn't do it the way that you were supposed to be doing it, who told you what you could do in life. And they always told you that you could do EVERYTHING. Who didn't put limitations on you and who made you excel. I think if a kid does not have that, especially when they grow up in the kind of environment I grew up in, if they don't have that, they'll lose their motivation real quick. The teachers wouldn't allow me to lose it.*
>
> INTERVIEWER: Is there anything particular in your high school experience which stands out as important to you?

---

[2]"Lynn Johnson" is a pseudonym. Her name and some other details in the story have been changed to protect her identity.

LYNN: *The support that system gave me. I got pregnant when I was sixteen years old, and I was supposed to have been kicked out of school.*

When I found out I was pregnant, I said, "Oh, my god!" You know, just the embarrassment of it all. And so I was going to stay at home.

My principal came to my house and he said, "What are you doing here? You've been out of school a week. What are you doing at home?"

And I said, "Mr. Springer,"—first I tried to be on my high horse—"I'm not [says her maiden name]."

He said, "Yeah, I heard you got married."

And I said, "Yeah, I did."

And he said, "But I also hear that you're pregnant."

And I said, "Yeah, I am."

And he said, "Well what are you doing here?"

And I said, "I can't come back to school."

He said, "Who said so?"

I said, "Well that's the rule, and I know it's the rule, and I wasn't going to come in there for you to put me out."

He said, "I wasn't planning on putting you out. Get your butt back over here."

I talk about it like it was my experience [pregnancy]—but it happened to a lot of girls—I mean, those who weren't going to go anywhere. Teachers in that day and time defined what they had—what kind of young people they were working with. Those that they knew didn't care one way or another, they said, "Get out of here, you done had the baby, you're on your way to having two babies, get out of here." Those who had the potential, who could go somewhere, who made an error or whatever, they worked with them. They worked with them. They said, "All right, you did your dirt. Let us dust you off and you come on back in here and let us see if we can't move you forward." And they did.

...Oh, honey, from the tenth grade on you had to take the ACT. They would write the checks themselves cause they'd know we didn't have the money. They had the best people caring about those kids. Not anymore....

Lynn is now very active at work and through her church, both individually and in programs to provide working-class African American youths with options, skills, and the motivation to succeed. Lynn mentors Black workers at the hospital, sharing knowledge and information and advising them, in hopes of facilitating their mobility in the workplace. She feels a strong commitment to give back to her community. She was taught that her achievement was not accomplished alone and that it carries with it a responsibility to the community that helped her.

PARTIAL TRUTHS: RACE, CLASS, GENDER, AND SEXUALITY AS SEPARATE SYSTEMS

The stories of Theo Wilson and Lynn Johnson each reveal some of the ways that the social relations of race, class, gender, and sexuality are produced, challenged, and transformed every day in the context of education. They simultaneously highlight both the powerful social forces that guide, steer, and push individuals into particular life paths based on their social location in race, class, gender, and sexuality hierarchies and the powerful personal and group forces that resist, reject, redefine, and overcome structural and psychological limits. We cannot fully understand these forces by isolating them one from another nor by treating only one as primary.

Race

Even though Theo and Lynn are of the same race, they have very different senses of themselves. Lynn is optimistic, working to give back to her community and believing that what she does can make a difference. Thirty years later in the North, Theo, at least at first, believed that no matter what he did he could not even dream about a better life, much less envision attaining one. The irony of the Southern racially segregated schools that Lynn attended is that they were grossly underfunded and deemed inferior in many ways. But because they were controlled by local African American communities, they served as sites of resistance, as training grounds for future leaders of that community (cf. Gilkes 1994). In Lynn's story there is a clear sense of community commitment to her success, a commitment missing in the story of Theo and often missing in the stories of White working-class women (Weber and Higginbotham 1992).

Class

Even though Theo and Lynn come from working-class families, they appear to be headed for different class outcomes. Lynn, bright and talented, was selected by school officials and tracked for college. She ultimately had relatively easy access to college admission, despite having gotten pregnant at sixteen. But because Lynn Johnson was a working-class African American, marriage as an avenue of mobility into the middle class was less available than it would have been for White working-class women, both because there are fewer Black middle-class than White middle-class men and because of the still relatively low rates of intermarriage between Blacks and Whites (Lee and Bean 2004). Instead, she was socialized to rely on her own academic and professional success.

Theo may make it to college, but the obstacles he faces to completing a degree, especially the weakness of his educational preparation and the high cost of education in the 1990s, are enormous. Making it into the middle class without a college degree is difficult.

Gender

Although Theo is male, male privilege is revealed to have a very class and race specific meaning in these stories. It was Lynn, not Theo, who was encouraged in academics and selected by teachers, family, and community for mobility. Despite his lanky body build, Theo, like many young African American boys, was encouraged in sports—though professional sports are a remote possibility for most excellent male athletes and even more remote for females.But he was tracked for a vocational education in preparation for minimum-wage work (Messner 2002, 2007).

Lynn's story also reveals the constraints imposed by gender. In Lynn's generation, it was common for teenage girls who became pregnant to be either required or pressured to drop out of school and often to give their babies up for adoption (Solinger 1992). Lynn benefited, however, from her African American community's greater tolerance of pregnant girls, particularly those who were seen as having the potential for mobility.

Sexuality

Although Lynn is heterosexual and Theo is still forming his own sexual identity, they both developed their sexual identities in raced, classed, and gendered ways. Her young marriage ended in divorce, and Lynn is now a single, professional, African American mother. She has a particular orientation toward men, marriage, and motherhood that is shaped by her social location, which differs from the orientations of many upwardly mobile White professional women (Weber and Higginbotham 1992).

If he comes to identify as a cross-dresser and/or as gay, Theo may have an even more difficult time finding positive models, accurate information, and validation for his sexual practices and identity than if he were White and middle or upper class (D'Emilio 1993, 2002, 2003; Sears 1992). And to claim masculine privilege, Theo may be even more inclined to pursue contact sports such as football, despite his lanky build, because they represent accepted arenas for achieving masculinity among Black working-class men (Messner 2002, 2007).

RACE, CLASS, GENDER, AND SEXUALITY AS INTERRELATED SYSTEMS: QUESTIONS TO ASK

As these examinations reveal, attempting to look at these two lives solely from the perspective of a single dimension obscures the complex intersections of race, class, gender, and sexuality. To capture the richness and intricacy of Lynn's and Theo's lives, we need to look at them from multiple dimensions and consider the meanings of those dimensions. If we look at their lives from the perspective of the themes of a race, class, gender, and sexuality framework, we might ask the following questions.

Historically and Geographically Contextual

If Theo, like Lynn, had been growing up in the 1950s or 1960s, how might his situation have been different? Would he have the community support that Lynn got to overcome obstacles to his mobility? How might his sexuality issues have been received? Would he have even spoken of his cross-dressing at all? And what would he face today?

If Lynn were growing up now, how might her story be different? What was/is the cost of a college education? What forms of aid were/are available? How have changes in the Black community changed the influences on young people (e.g., Lynn is now middle class and does not live near poor African Americans)?

In the 1950s and 1960s, how did Southern segregated urban communities differ from Northern ones, and how do they differ today?

Socially Constructed

What are the social forces in Theo's and in Lynn's lives that operate to support their personal development? Their social mobility?

How did the schools operate to restrict or support their sexual development? Class mobility? Gender identities?

How might the school and the community respond if Theo were Asian American? If Lynn were?

Power Relations

How is vocational tracking for Theo and other working-class African American males related to the success of dominant-culture, White middle-class heterosexual men?

In what ways does Lynn's success challenge a power structure of race, class, gender, and sexuality? Does it also reinforce dominant power relations? How?

How does Lynn's teen pregnancy and Theo's developing gender expression and sexual identity put them at risk in a patriarchal heterosexual society?

Macro Social Structural

In what ways did the schools help to create different futures for Theo and Lynn? How did the practice of school tracking—sorting students into different classes (e.g., college prep, basic, technical) in preparation for different futures—affect each of them?

Think of the prevailing stereotypes of young, poor, urban African American males. How do they restrict options for young men like Theo?

At the hospital, Lynn now has few women and people of color in the ranks above her. How might controlling images of Black middle-class women affect her chances for further mobility?

Micro Social Psychological

In what ways does Theo resist oppression? What are the implications for Theo of his methods of resistance? In what ways did Lynn resist oppression? What individuals and groups in their environments supported resistance? What are the broader social ramifications of each of their methods of resistance?

What is the evidence that Theo internalized race, class, gender, and sexuality oppression? Is there any evidence that Lynn has? What are possible personal ramifications of accepting restrictive views of their potential? What are the ramifications for society's race, class, gender, and sexuality hierarchies when individuals come to accept society's negative views of their group?

What people and processes support Theo's sexual identity development?

Simultaneously Expressed

Where do dreams come from? Why does Theo Wilson have so much trouble understanding the concept of a dream? How is the dream Theo describes a reflection of his social location as a poor, African American male who is as a teenager coming to terms with his sexuality? What is lost when we ignore any aspect of his reality?

How are dreams reflected in the story of Lynn Johnson? In what ways are they consistent with what you might expect, based on her social location? In what ways do they challenge your expectations?

Implications for Social Activism and Social Change

How have social movements (e.g., civil rights, gay, lesbian, and bisexual, women's, labor) shaped Lynn's and Theo's experiences of race, class, gender, and sexuality? Lynn Johnson was active in civil rights activities while she was in college. Thus far, Theo shows little interest in political activities. How might their different relationships to social movements affect their life chances and worldviews?

SUMMARY

The stories of Lynn Johnson and Theo Wilson—and the questions raised by them—highlight a variety of ways that race, class, gender, and sexuality shape and are shaped by people's educational experiences–from school tracking and college attendance to segregated housing and community support for mobility, from the condition of the economy and the cost of higher education to the availability of financial aid and scholarships, from teen pregnancy to sexual identity. Race, class, gender, and sexuality systems are produced and reinforced in the domain of education every day.

꜒◯

Education and the American Dream

The institution of education supports both the political and economic structures of society, but at its core it is an ideological institution, intended to create and transmit the ideas on which the society is organized and which will support its continuation. The American Dream ideology—that those who are talented and work hard can get ahead—is dependent on a system of education to provide opportunities and to explain its failures. In this way, the American Dream ideology, a fundamental belief system rationalizing the current social hierarchies, is intricately intertwined with education. This chapter examines the American Dream ideology and its connection with the system of education to lay the ideological foundation for using the themes of the conceptual framework to explore the ways that race, class, gender, and sexuality hierarchies are produced and challenged in education.

DREAMS AND OPPRESSION

What's in a dream? *What do dreams have to do with oppression?* A great deal. Dreams contain what we know, what we want, what we think we can and cannot have, what we can imagine is possible. They tell us a great deal about people's lives. They tell us when people are free in their minds, as Lynn Johnson was when she thought she could be anything she wanted to be. They also tell us when people are controlled, contained, or trapped in their minds, as Theo Wilson was when he could not dream because "Everything takes good math skills, and I'm not good at math." And

> Bad luck seems to
> Follow me.
> Whenever I get good at something
> Something or someone messes it up.

Writers attempting to convey a central truth about oppression have often relied on dream metaphors. Lillian Smith, a White Southern woman who fought for civil rights, entitled her biography *Killers of the Dream* (1949). Langston Hughes, a gay African American poet, ponders what happens when dreams are shattered by racism:

Harlem (A Dream Deferred)
Langston Hughes

What happens to a dream deferred?

Does it dry up
like a raisin in the sun?
Or fester like a sore—
And then run?
Does it stink like rotten meat?
Or crust and sugar over—
like a syrupy sweet?
Maybe it just sags
like a heavy load.

Or does it explode?

The connection of dreams and oppression is especially relevant in the American context. The American Dream is a uniquely American ideology: the basic belief that hard work and ability will pay off with personal success. In a major address on education, presidential candidate Barack Obama recalled Thomas Jefferson's declaration that "talent and virtue, needed in a free society, should be educated regardless of wealth or birth." And he reaffirmed the American Dream in his own words: "no matter what we look like or where we came from or who our parents are, each of us should have the opportunity to fulfill our God-given potential" (Denverpost.com 2008; Obama 2008).

And the educational system, more than any other social institution, is supposed to be the place of opportunity for all, the institution that makes the American Dream possible.

PREMISES OF THE AMERICAN DREAM

The American Dream ideology gives citizens a basis for continuing to believe that American society provides equality and the promise of financial success to all its citizens, even when people's experiences in no way reflect that belief: Most people are not financially successful, and only a few people accumulate enormous wealth. As Jennifer Hochschild (1995) notes, this ideology has four components:

1. *Equality of Opportunity*: The concept of equality means equality of opportunity; our society purports to provide equal opportunity for everyone to pursue money, property, and other desirable social resources. As President

Obama said, we should be given *the opportunity* to fulfill our God-given potential."

2. *Reasonable Anticipation of Success*: Because, according to the Dream, all Americans have equal opportunity to pursue success, they may reasonably anticipate success—however they define it. As long as resources and opportunities seem to be available to all, people may continue to believe that success is possible for them in the future, even though they may not feel successful now.

3. *Individual Responsibility for Success*: Because, according to the Dream, all Americans have equal opportunity, people who succeed are seen as responsible for their success, and those who fail are held to blame for their failure. This belief—that because everyone has an equal opportunity to succeed, failures are the fault of the people who fail—is compelling because all people want to believe that they can succeed.

4. *Success as Virtue, Failure as Sin*: Because people who succeed are seen as solely responsible for their success, success implies virtue, and, by extension, failure implies sin. And the presumption of virtue is more readily awarded to and less easily removed from the successful who occupy dominant social locations—Whites, men, and heterosexuals. The very public downfall of many politicians in the recent past illustrates this belief. Because their sometimes long-term success in politics and their wealth implied virtue in their private lives, many Americans were shocked at the revelations of sexual indiscretions among powerful politicians: affairs (former senator and presidential candidate John Edwards, D-NC), involvement with high-priced call girls (New York Governor Eliot Spitzer, D), sexual harassment of male congressional pages (Congressman Mark Foley, R-FL), and solicitation of sex in a public restroom (Senator Larry Craig, R-NE).

And "rehabilitation" of one's image is much easier for the successful. John McCain, 2008 Republican nominee for president, for example, had an affair with and later married his current wife, Cindy, while his then wife was recuperating from an auto accident. But throughout the 2008 campaign, he was touted as a "true American hero" for surviving prisoner-of-war status in Vietnam years before the affair and many years before the 2008 election. His affair was not just dismissed but "forgotten."

In contrast, many Americans find the welfare reforms of 1996 and 2002 acceptable, even desirable—even though they punish primarily poor women by eliminating their financial assistance—because poverty is presumed to be a result of their own failure, their sinfulness, their laziness. Punishment thus becomes a way of properly addressing the problem.

In her examination of the "welfare queen" controlling image, Ange-Marie Hancock (2004, 56) calls on Wahneema Lubiano, a former welfare recipient who is now a university professor, to characterize the term:

welfare queen is a phrase that describes economic dependency—the lack of a job and/or income (which equals degeneracy in the United States); the presence of a child or children with no father and/or no husband (moral deviance); and finally, a charge on the collective U.S. Treasury—a human debit. (Lubiano 1992, 337–338)

Today, in the words of many conservative talk show hosts, you can hear the racialized and gendered demonization and disgust expressed about the poor and those who receive public assistance. Bill Cunningham, for example, is a Cincinnati-based nationally syndicated talk show host who received the National Association of Broadcasters Award for large-market "Personality of the Year." Here is what he has to say about the poor (Media Matters for America 2009):

> People are poor in America…not because they lack money but because they lack values, morals, and ethics….Unlike many countries in the world…we have fat poor people. We don't have skinny poor people. Ours are fat and flatulent. (Media Matters for America October 28, 2008)
>
> The reason people are poor in America is not because they lack money, it's because poor people in America lack values, character, and the ability to work hard. (Media Matters for America October 23, 2008)
>
> Among the so-called noble poor in America…birth control is not used so illegitimate children can be brought into the world, so the mom can get more checks in the mail from the government. (Media Matters for America October 27, 2008)

PARADOXES OF THE AMERICAN DREAM

Democratic capitalism—the belief in political democracy but not in economic democracy—is based on a paradox:

- Democracy is a political system in which supreme power is vested in the citizens—government *by* the people—and is justified by the principle of social *equality*.
- Capitalism is an economic system based on the pursuit of profit and private ownership, resulting in pervasive economic *inequality*. Capitalism is organized on social class relations of dominance and subordination—with the upper and middle classes reaping greater economic rewards because they own the workplace and design, supervise, and control the labor of the working and lower classes.

Resolving this basic paradox of democratic capitalism—the belief in social and political *equality* amidst severe economic *inequality* —necessitates reconceptualizing the notion of equality to mean equality of opportunity, not of outcome. The idea of equality of opportunity lends itself to a social system based on "meritocracy" or the "belief that because the race for social rewards is fair, those who reach the finish line must be faster and thus more meritorious runners than those who came in last" (Oakes et al. 1997; see also McNamee and Miller 2004). This view creates the commonsense notion about difference that people become wealthy and powerful through a "natural" sorting process that is fair and that separates the best from the rest. It also promotes the related notion that those who are not powerful will never acquire power because they lack the ability and that we therefore live in the best of all possible worlds. In short, the American Dream ideology provides a powerful explanation for the fundamental contradiction of democratic capitalism. But consider what happens when we look more closely at the premises of this ideology:

1. *Equality of Opportunity*: In his speech, Barack Obama did not say—nor does the Dream imply—that financial success or even a minimal standard of living should be *guaranteed* to everyone. He says only that people should be given "the opportunity to fulfill our God-given potential."

   Does U.S. society give everyone a chance? Does everyone start on a level playing field? Are the rules the same for everyone? Does a student going to school in the South Bronx have the same chance as a student in Beverly Hills? Does Theo have the same chance as an upper-class White girl in his same city?

2. *Reasonable Anticipation of Success*: In the past thirty years, the declining standard of living among the poor and the working and middle classes and the redistribution of wealth to the very rich have made this premise increasingly difficult to sustain, particularly for people of color. Many signs of despair in the population—one outcome of the breakdown of the Dream—have risen dramatically, particularly among youths: violent crime rates, school dropout rates, drug abuse, teenage pregnancy. And some argue that the anger of White men and the push to institute repressive social measures, such as anti-immigrant and punitive welfare reforms, are the results of declining opportunities for working- and middle-class White men in the economy (Ferber 1998; Newman 1993; Powell et al. 2006).

   Can everyone reasonably anticipate success? Could Theo Wilson have reasonably anticipated success before he reached out to Marie and Bill? Could he now? Could youths today, as many have in the past, reasonably anticipate that they will be more successful than their parents—that they will be better educated, have better jobs, make more money?

3. *Individual Responsibility for Success*: Assigning responsibility for their place in life to individuals rather than to unjust social systems maintains the dominant group's power and position. When people truly believe in the American Dream, understanding that capitalism is an economic system based on the exploitation of the labor of most people for the benefit of the few is difficult to achieve. Directing attention to individuals rather than to the system obscures the absolute impossibility that *all* talented and hard-working people will become financially successful in capitalist societies (McNamee and Miller 2004).

   When you believe in the American Dream, the fact that some individuals get ahead serves to reinforce the belief that success is possible for all and that the unsuccessful must, therefore, be untalented and lazy at best, morally corrupt at worst. Success stories such as that of Lynn Johnson are often construed to be the result of the talent and hard work of the individual. Although Lynn Johnson is in fact talented and hardworking, other systemic factors contributed to her success:

- The support of the school principal and teachers
- Her placement in a college preparatory track
- The involvement of the community in her mobility
- The ready availability of college scholarships and loans
- The lower cost of higher education in the 1960s

When Lynn's efforts are seen as the only forces responsible for her success, the urge is strong to blame Theo and other poor and working-class youths if they fail to succeed.

Theo, too, is talented and hardworking, but many systemic factors work toward his failure:

- School tracking, which ensures that students like Theo will be placed in vocational or general tracks
- His mother's drug problems, his father's death
- Lack of positive role models, both in his community and in his school
- The rising cost of a college education and the difficulty of moving into the middle class without one
- Lack of sex education and support for dealing with his developing sexual identity and gender expression
- Controlling images of young, inner-city, working-class Black men as dangerous and unruly

Those like Theo, who do everything they can but still fail may come to see that effort and talent are not necessarily the keys to success, but they have trouble convincing others—because, after all, why should we listen to losers? As Hochschild (1995, 29) notes:

> Because success is so central to Americans' self image, and because they expect as well as hope to achieve, Americans are not gracious about failure. Others' failure reminds them that the dream may be just that—a dream, to be distinguished from waking reality. Their own failure confirms that fear. As Zora Neale Hurston puts it, "There is something about poverty that smells like death."

Why in our society does poverty "smell like death"? Why do we equate success with money, failure with poverty? What other measures of success do we have? How seriously do we take them? Do you know people who go to high-paying jobs every day even though they hate the jobs and what the jobs are doing to their lives? Why don't they leave these jobs and take ones that are more satisfying? And finally: Was Theo solely responsible for his failure in school? Was Lynn solely responsible for her success?

4. *Success As Virtue, Failure As Sin*. This equation ignores the structures of society that support the success of some and the failure of others. It ignores the fact that in our society many of the major wealth holders inherited their wealth (Beckert 2008; McNamee and Miller 2004). It ignores the fact that wealth is achieved for a relative few at the expense of the many—that the nine-figure salaries of top CEOs depend on their ability to increase their companies' earnings and that the increase is frequently the result of "outsourcing" (i.e., moving production to countries with cheaper labor) and "downsizing," i.e., putting people out of work.

Most Americans would find humorous the following description by nineteenth-century reformers:

[Prostitutes are]...daughters of the ignorant, depraved, and vicious part of our population, trained up without culture of any kind, amidst the contagion of evil example...[they] enter upon a life of prostitution for the ratification of their unbridled passions, and become harlots altogether by choice. (cited in Hochschild, 1995, 30–31)

We certainly would recognize today that unbridled passion—amidst the contagions of evil—is not the prime reason for prostitution. Economic hardship; sexual and physical abuse by parents, spouses, and partners; and the limited employment options for poor women are the prime reasons. But if we were to substitute "welfare recipient" for "prostitute" and "welfare queen" for "harlot," the quotation would sound quite familiar today.

Humorist Fran Liebowitz describes the paradox of this premise succinctly:

The misfortune of the fortunate, it seems, always appears as an act of God. In other words, "no fault of their own." The misfortune of the unfortunate is, on the other hand, perceived to be a direct result of the slothful, irresponsible, ill-intended, but not unanticipated bad choice of the embryo that insists upon taking up residence in the body of a 14-year-old crack addict—not, apparently, an act of God. (1997, 220)

Is the child of a fourteen-year-old crack addict a sinner? Is the fourteen-year-old crack addict a sinner? Thinking back to Margaret Welch, is she a sinner? Are Bill Gates, the Mellons, the Waltons, the Rockefellers, the duPonts more virtuous than the rest of the population? Are highly paid CEOs always virtuous people? Are the people who lose their jobs through "downsizing" sinners? Is Lynn Johnson more virtuous than Theo Wilson?

Given all of the evidence that the American Dream is just that—a dream— why do most Americans continue to believe so strongly in it? Why, instead of attacking unjust systems of power, do they attack each other? Blaming "losers" is critical to preserving the current system. It is the flip side of rewarding the winners, and it encourages everyone, including those near the back of the pack, to distance themselves from "losers" instead of joining with them in challenging an unfair system.

EDUCATION: THE CORNERSTONE
OF THE AMERICAN DREAM

Through its central role in reproducing race, class, gender, and sexuality hierarchies and in justifying those hierarchies, the institution of education is a cornerstone on which the ideology of the American Dream rests. To have an equal opportunity to pursue success, particularly financial success, citizens need equal access to the skills necessary to that pursuit, and schools are charged with providing everyone with these basic skills. Schools are also charged with identifying the talented and hardworking and providing them with the extra knowledge, skills, and certification to "reach the top," to become successful. Given its critical role in reproducing the American Dream ideology, the educational system must be seen as free of bias—not as racist, classist, sexist, or heterosexist. Otherwise, the premise of equal opportunity cannot stand. All people must be seen as having a chance to succeed, or we cannot blame them if they do not.

How is the ideology of the American Dream reproduced and reinforced in the educational system? Ideologies are believable only if they emerge when ordinary people act out the stories daily. And every day, as people act out the social relations of race, class, gender, and sexuality hierarchies within schools, some do "make it." Lynn Johnson's story, an excellent example of someone's living the American Dream, reinforces the Dream. If Theo is successful, the Dream will be reinforced. But individual success stories obscure the "failures" of the vast majority. These exceptions, which prove the possibility of success, justify our sealing the coffin of restricted life chances on most people while opening the door of almost unlimited choice for a few.

Individuals, Education, and the Dream

Every day children drop out of school, are suspended, are tracked into lower classes, and are retained in grade for reasons of discipline, poor standardized test performance, and teacher bias (Anyon 1997; Brantlinger 1993; Entwisle, Alexander, and Olson)1997; Kozol 2005; Sacks 2007). The education of thousands of poor and working-class students, students of color, and immigrant students is much like that of Theo Wilson, who until his sophomore year was in classes that were not preparing him for college, whose education was preparing him only for menial jobs.

As these children go through their day—some, in separate and inferior schools whose entire curricula are less challenging (cf. Spade et al. 1997; Kozol 2005); others, sometimes in the same school with upper-track children and middle-class, often White teachers—they may come to recognize, as Theo Wilson did, that they are being tracked for a particular place in the world. They may come to see that their education has cut them off from many desirable options in life. The education that Theo was receiving was inferior by most criteria: He was learning less, and what he did learn would have been less useful for securing decent employment if he graduated. Whatever employment options students in poor and working-class schools and lower-track students in all schools have after graduation are severely restricted by the failure of their education to prepare them for college.

As students in tracks similar to Theo's end up unemployed or working in the menial-labor jobs they were tracked for, people in positions of greater power (children in higher tracks, middle-class teachers, and employers) will find it easy, logical, and even "natural" to assume that these students lack ability, talent, desire, effort, or all of these. In this way, the American Dream is reinforced in conjunction with race, class, gender, and sexuality hierarchies.

And as a result of the American Dream ideology, Theo Wilson and others are encouraged to believe that they are inferior, and they find trying to resist internalizing their oppression more and more difficult. They increasingly lose motivation: It is difficult to stay motivated when schoolwork is trivial and menial. They lack skills: An inferior education leaves them less able to compete in the marketplace. Before he began taking charge of his own education, Theo had already internalized limits and the belief in his own inferiority. He said he couldn't dream because "Everything takes good math skills, and I'm not good at math."

Groups, Education, and the Dream

Although the consequences are felt by individual students, the process of reproducing race, class, gender, and sexuality hierarchies by sorting people for different treatment and then of justifying the unequal outcomes of this sorting process by promoting beliefs about group inferiority is fundamentally a group process. These group processes are less apparent than the processes that shape our individual lives, but we are led to consider them by group indicators such as national racial differences in educational outcomes. Race and gender data indicate, for example, that in 2006, 18.1 percent of Hispanic girls and 27.5 percent of Hispanic boys ages sixteen through twenty-four were high school dropouts. These rates were roughly double the percentage of high school dropouts among African American girls (11.7%) and boys (9.7%) and four times the percentages for White girls (5.3%) and boys (6.4%) (National Center for Education Statistics 2007, Table 105).

Think about these statistics for a moment. Were you surprised to see how high the rates were for Hispanics? How about for girls? Did you realize that girls drop out of school at rates so similar to boys? If you were not aware of these facts, you are not alone. Perhaps the people most discussed in the media as high risk for dropping out are urban, African American males and, secondarily, Latinos. But the dropout rate of Latinas is double the rate of African American males and similar to that of Latinos. And female high school dropouts earn only 63 percent of what male dropouts earn (National Women's Law Center 2007, 8–9).

If the public is uneducated about *who* is dropping out, we tend to be even less knowledgeable about *why* these youths drop out. What comes first to your mind if you try to explain the high Latino/a rates? How would you explain these patterns? If you first thought about negative traits that you have come to associate with Hispanic culture—devaluing education, valuing family over work, or lacking the work ethic—your explanation rests on the notion that the beliefs and values of the group members are to blame, a critical tenet of the American Dream ideology. But if you think of macro system factors, you might consider:

- The problems of learning in English-only schools when English is your second language
- The inferior quality of education in most bilingual classrooms (cf. Valdes 1996; Ortiz 1988)
- The significantly lower per-pupil expenditures in districts with high concentrations of English-language learners (Arroyo 2008)
- The impact of family dislocation on the children of recent immigrants and farm workers
- The lack of community links between educational institutions and families
- The failure of schools to educate youths about sexuality and pregnancy and to provide support for continuing school after childbirth
- The inferior quality of education for the urban and rural poor (Kozol 2005)

Because these kinds of explanations challenge rather than reinforce the American Dream tenet that everyone is given an equal opportunity to succeed, they are not promoted or encouraged. People offering these kinds of explanations are, in fact, often disparaged. For example, in 1999 the newly installed Democratic governor of South Carolina, Jim Hodges, put forth a plan to the legislature to improve public schools in the state. School improvement—particularly early childhood education and school readiness—had been the major focus of his election campaign, because South Carolina schools consistently rate among the bottom two or three states on almost every standard indicator of educational performance, from ACT and SAT scores to achievement tests to dropout rates. Some estimates are that as many as 60 percent of ninth graders in the state do not complete high school (EPE Research Center 2008). The rates of poverty among the largely rural, African American population are among the nation's highest, whereas indicators of children's health, such as infant mortality and low-birth-weight babies, are among the poorest (Stroud 1999a).

With strong backing from the business community, Hodges proposed legislation entitled First Steps, modeled after Smart Steps, a similar program in North Carolina targeted to improve the health and educational performance of the state's children. First Steps included provisions for school construction, class size reduction, and other changes within schools, as well as state government grants to underwrite grassroots efforts to provide day care, immunization and other health services, parenting classes, and transportation—resources needed to address related problems associated with poverty that also impede children in school (Robinson 1999; Stroud 1999b).

Despite its eventual adoption and widespread support in the state, when his proposal first reached the legislature, it faced stiff opposition. House Majority Leader Bobby Harrell, R-Charleston, said committee members balked at funding First Steps because it "looks more like a social program than an education proposal." He and others later called the proposal "a disguised attempt to expand the welfare state" (Stroud 1999a). And Representative Dan Tripp, R-Greenville, repeatedly called it "creeping socialism" (Robinson 1999), insinuating that addressing sources and consequences of inequality outside the individual efforts and abilities of the oppressed is somehow anticapitalist and thus anti-American.

This process of denying structural sources of oppression—and thus denying structural change as a solution—is reinforced not only by promoting images of inferiority of some groups but also by promoting equally damaging constructions that others are superior. Just as Lynn Johnson may be cited as proof that success is possible for all Americans if they work hard enough, entire groups are identified as "model minorities." The educational attainment levels of these groups, especially of Asian Americans, who have levels higher than those of other racial groups, including Whites, are cited as proof that the educational system is not racially biased. (See Figures 2.2a and 2.2b.) And, as a result, the dominant ideology—that the lower educational attainment and higher poverty rates of African Americans, Native Americans, and Latinos/as are evidence of these groups' lack of motivation, of ability, or of both, not evidence of racial bias—is reinforced.

This argument obscures not only racial bias in the schools but also

- The discrimination that Asian Americans have faced in U.S. higher education, including quotas limiting their numbers, and in everyday life (Chou and Feagin 2008; Karabel 2005; Takagi 1993).
- The fact that many Asian people with high educational attainment were not educated in the United States and were allowed to immigrate only *because* of their professional status and high education. The 1990 Immigration Act's employment preferences, for example, included "outstanding professors," "researchers," "multinational executives," "professionals with advanced degrees," and those able to invest $500,000 in certain businesses. These migrants tend to come from particular countries (China, Taiwan, Korea), whereas others of lower socioeconomic status are more likely to have come as refugees (Laotians, Cambodians, Vietnamese) (CARE 2008).
- The wide variation in socioeconomic status and educational attainment across Asian ethnic groups and the extreme diversity in the category itself. In the 2000 census, forty-eight different ethnic groups were included under the broad umbrella of "Asian American and Pacific Islander" (CARE 2008).
- The fact that when people believe the dream is attainable, as immigrants are more inclined to do, they work harder to achieve and are willing to tolerate less humane treatment because they see it as finite: They believe it will end

And as long as we focus on these "model minorities," we can ignore the daily reality of students like Theo Wilson. These students, for whom the schools predict failure and who see generations of dropouts in their neighborhoods, are less able to hold out hope for their own success and thus are less able to sustain the same work ethic as that of students who see success as possible.

SUMMARY

The American Dream ideology is used to justify the extensive social inequality in U.S. society. And it does so by promoting four basic tenets:

- Equality of opportunity
- A reasonable chance of success
- Individual responsibility for success
- Success as virtue, failure as sin

In the end, belief in the American Dream supports the current race, class, gender, and sexuality hierarchy. And because it is the cornerstone on which the belief that all citizens have an equal chance of success is built, education is central to promoting the ideology. Thus the promise of education in America is that it will be the great equalizer. That it produces race, class, gender, and sexuality oppression is a contradiction that demands explanation.

CHAPTER 8

✦⌾

Themes: Historically and Geographically Contextual, Socially Constructed

This chapter focuses on the first two themes of the framework: the historical and geographically contextual and socially constructed nature of race, class, gender, and sexuality hierarchies. Race, class, gender, and sexuality intersections must be understood in their historical context, in specific places, with careful attention to how these patterns of relationships are socially constructed—generated, preserved, challenged, and transformed through social contests. Understanding the ways that these hierarchies are socially constructed in education must begin with an examination of the historical roots of the U.S. education system, how the modern patterns of these hierarchies were established, and how they have changed as a result of resistance by subordinate groups. How did the ideology of the American Dream shape and how was it reinforced by the social organization of education in the twentieth and twenty-first centuries in the United States?

Rather than trying to explicate the entire history of a single group or of all race, class, gender, and sexuality struggles in the United States, this chapter illustrates the ways that hierarchies are socially constructed in time and place by focusing the discussion around a particular theme—segregation—that weaves its way through the history of and contemporary struggles between those who control the institution of education and those who have sought unfettered access to knowledge despite their lack of control over it.

The term *segregation* is most often associated with racial residential segregation, and its deleterious effects on poor communities of color have been well documented. For many years, scholars have noted how segregation isolates communities and sets up the conditions of control over the poor by concentrating poverty and setting in motion mutually reinforcing and self-feeding processes of decline (Massey and Denton 1993; Patillo 2008; Powell et al. 2006). When communities are poor and people lack work, skills, education, and other resources, businesses leave and are less inclined to locate there, schools lack a tax base and have fewer resources, and many good teachers choose not to teach there. So residential segregation is a structural process that produces and increases inequality. As Massey and Denton state in their study of Black residential segregation:

> The effect of segregation on black well being is structural, not individual. Residential segregation lies beyond the ability of any individual to change: it constrains black life chances irrespective of personal traits, individual motivations, or private achievements. (1993, 2–3)

Because schools are differentiated by class and neighborhood, understanding segregation processes is critical to understanding race, class, gender, and sexuality inequalities produced in and by schooling.

When groups have different educational experiences, a host of other aspects of life are affected: income, occupation, employment status, job security, health status, life expectancy, and life satisfaction. And when entire groups have lower incomes, lower status occupations, poorer health, and higher mortality, the American Dream ideology, along with other dominant-culture influences, encourages people to explain and to understand these facts by referring to notions of group inferiority—not to system-wide practices that segregate and exclude, discriminate against, and harm less powerful race, class, gender, and sexuality groups.

Once groups are segregated and educated differently, ideologies of group inferiority are rather easily generated and maintained. The historian Barbara Fields (1990), for example, pointed out in her study of slavery and racial ideology that African people were enslaved in America *before* the notion of racial inferiority was developed by slave owners to "explain" the inhumane treatment of their slaves. And underfunded systems such as the reservation schools for Native Americans, the segregated schools for African Americans that prevailed until the 1960s, and the resegregated urban schools of the 1990s and 2000s also isolated these groups, enhancing the dominant ideology of racial inferiority and facilitating differential treatment in other realms, such as the labor market.

The "war of maneuvers," the processes of resistance that take place when a group lacks full citizenship, economic resources, and other bases of power, took place in the racially homogeneous communities created by the pervasive residential segregation before the 1960s—in Black communities of the urban North and the South, on reservations, and in barrios and Chinatowns (Omi and Winant 1994). And although not residentially segregated, for most of the nineteenth and early twentieth centuries, women's education, particularly in higher education, typically took place in separate schools. When groups are physically segregated and isolated from one another, the type of control described earlier is possible, but so are the close conditions among the oppressed that foster group identity, awareness of the oppression and of the common plight of others, and collective action for survival.

There are also other forms of segregation when dominant and subordinate groups occupy the same physical space. One example is school ability group tracking, which dominated American education into the 1990s, a process highly organized by race, class, and gender. In a formal system of de jure (by law) tracking, students in the same school are sorted into groups who attend different classes, use different texts, study different curricula, and spend their days largely with their group or track. And although formal systems of tracking have fallen out of favor and "choice" of courses and curricula have become the norm, recent research suggests that students remain equally segregated into different educational careers that continue to prepare students in these more informal de facto tracks for the same unequal outcomes (Heck, Price and Thomas 2004; Yonezawa, Wells and Serna 2002).

Even in situations in which dominant and subordinate groups sit next to each other in the same class, there is a kind of segregation of ideas into different intellectual spaces. Women, people of color, gays, and lesbians are often either excluded from classroom texts or segregated into certain parts of a text in which they are presented in stereotyped ways that serve to reinforce the dominant ideologies: women in family roles, not as workers; internationals as immigrants, not as families; men of color in sports or as criminals, not as leaders in business or industry (American Association of University Women 1999; Feree and Hall 1990; Peterson 2008).

Dominant groups also employ new mechanisms of social control, such as "surveillance," in the race- and class-desegregated spaces more common today (e.g., residential, workplace), in which select members of subordinate groups have attained access to centers of power not open before. Surveillance represents a politics of control—in plain view—reminiscent of the mechanisms of racial control in the South during slavery and over domestic workers even until today (Collins 1998). In this situation, subordinate group members are present in the same space—they are seen and watched, are even on display—but they lack the institutional power to change the race, class, gender, or sexuality balance of power. Surveillance methods of control have perhaps always been the prevalent method in the control of women, who have not been segregated as a group into different communities.

Surveillance control methods range from violence, such as the violence women experience in households and in public spaces, to fairly elaborate social interaction rules. The South, for example, takes pride in being a place that is polite, hospitable, genteel. In large part this self-definition derives from the rules of social interaction that accompanied the close living and working conditions of slaves and masters in a plantation economy. These rules included, for example, prescriptions that people be addressed by title as a way of acknowledging different statuses and signaling the kind of treatment that people should receive. Even today, these rules have a different significance than in other parts of the country. In the past twenty years, legislators across the country considered many varieties of reforms to address the problems of poor-performing schools particularly in poor, rural, inner-city, and minority school districts. But it was conservative Southern states—Louisiana, Alabama, South Carolina—that led the way in passing "character education" legislation requiring, among other things, schoolchildren to address their teachers as "Sir" or "Ma'am." Character education has since broadened its definition and has become an integral part of former President George W. Bush's signature education reform of 2001, the No Child Left Behind Act (NCLB). Part of the appeal of character education, especially for conservative politicians who controlled many state legislatures, Congress, and the White House for much of the recent past, is surely a desire to institute more subtle mechanisms of control in the face of dominant culture fears about people of color, immigrants, and the poor as unruly, lawless, and dangerous.

Given the centrality of the segregation process in developing and challenging race, class, gender, and sexuality hierarchies, it is not surprising that a fundamental struggle of some groups for equality has centered on eliminating segregation in schools. If we think of the process of segregation as broader than its typical referent—to racially segregated schools, especially in the South before the civil rights movement, we can use the concept to identify critical social processes that generate and maintain race, class, gender, and sexuality hierarchies in society, not just see these processes as conflicts between poor Whites and African Americans in the South. These processes of segregation and surveillance, isolation, exclusion, and control resonate throughout the following overview of the historical and contemporary social constructions of race, class, gender, and sexuality in education.

HISTORICAL CONSTRUCTION OF RACE, CLASS, GENDER AND SEXUALITY IN EDUCATION

The foundation for the current political, economic, and ideological domains of oppression within our education system was laid during the rapid industrialization of the late nineteenth and early twentieth centuries. At that time, particularly in urban centers, an unprecedented population explosion occurred, primarily of poor, uneducated, unskilled immigrants from Eastern Europe, as well as of rural migrants from the United States, who sought the promise of a better life through industrial labor. From 1880 to 1918, student enrollment across the nation increased from 200,000 to 1.5 million, and by 1909, 58 percent of students in thirty-seven of the largest U.S. cities were foreign born (Oakes 1985, 19–20). As a result of these changes, secondary schools came under increasing pressure to do more to meet the many conflicting social needs:

> Colleges and universities wanted a more standardized pre-collegiate education. Many of the middle class called for free public education available to all youth. Poor and immigrant families were eager for the economic benefits they believed schooling would provide their children. Businessmen were interested in acquiring a more productive and literate work force. Organized labor was concerned about who should control the training of workers. Progressive reformers sought humane solutions to the immense social problems confronting the burgeoning population of poor and immigrant youth. But most of the population increasingly feared the potential dangers that could result from what was seen as unrestrained hordes of urban immigrants, and a perception of a need for the exercise of greater social control was widespread. (Oakes 1985, 20)

The Educational Model

The public comprehensive high school was envisioned as the answer to these demands. And its particular form was shaped largely by three dominant themes:

- *Social Darwinism:* The application of Charles Darwin's theories of evolution to human social life, suggesting that those holding power in the competitive social world survived because of their superior moral and biological fitness. This theory provided scientific justification for the social dominance of Anglo-Saxon White men and the inferior makeup (lower evolutionary stage) and subordinate status of others—immigrants, the poor, people of color, and women. At the same time, its proponents argued that human intervention could exert some positive influence on the evolutionary process, thus justifying the education of "others."
- *Americanization Movement:* The movement to preserve the dominance of White Anglo-Saxon Protestant (WASP) culture in the face of mass immigration by eliminating immigrants' "depraved life styles" and making cities safe by teaching immigrants the "American values of hard work, frugality, modesty, cleanliness, truthfulness, and purity of thought and deed."
- *Belief in the Unlimited Potential of Science and Industry:* The factory model of industrial efficiency, based on the division of labor and principles of scientific management. It was hailed as the solution to all problems of human organization. In popular constructions, schools were seen as factories, turning the raw material of children into a finished product: educated, productive, Americanized adults (Oakes 1985, 20–25; see also Nicholson 2003; Schneider and Keesler 2007).

From these principles, the modern, comprehensive public high school was forged:

- Students were grouped according to ability. Theories of human evolution, which postulated superior and inferior groups, justified separation of the curriculum into vocational education and academic education.
- Anglo-Saxon culture was valued and promoted as superior to all others. To develop common American ideals and modes of thought, school curricula unabashedly promoted Anglo-Saxon culture and excluded other cultures, values, and histories.
- Schools were organized on the scientific management principles of the factory. Schools were structured on the industrial model of bureaucratic organization, with authority and central decision making at the top, specialization, division of labor, established rules and regulations, and an impersonal attitude toward the individual (Anyon 1997; Katznelson and Weir 1985; Oakes 1985; Schneider and Keesler 2007).

This stratified model of public education was justified by referring to democratic ideals and to the American Dream ideology. In 1908, the superintendent of the Boston public schools espoused this "new view" of equal opportunity, taking individual needs, interests, and abilities into account:

> Until very recently (the schools) have offered equal opportunity for all to receive *one kind* of education, but what will make them democratic is to provide opportunity for all to receive education as will fit them *equally well* for their particular life work. (Cited in Oakes 1985, 34)

Writing in *Scientific Monthly* in 1921, another educator stated:

> We can picture the educational system as having a very important function as a selecting agency, a means of selecting the men of best intelligence from the deficient and mediocre. All are poured into the system at the bottom; the incapable are soon rejected or drop out after repeating various grades and pass into the ranks of unskilled labor.... The more intelligent who are to be clerical workers pass into the high school; the most intelligent enter the universities whence they are selected for the professions. (Cited in Oakes 1985, 35)[1]

By 1918 the National Education Association recommended that the following nonacademic vocational programs begin in junior high school: agriculture, clerical, industrial, fine arts, and household arts. And students were openly classified by race, ethnicity, economic backgrounds, and gender into different programs.

Testing

Also at this time, the burgeoning field of psychology and testing entered the political educational arena when a group intelligence test, the IQ test, became the "scientific" means to separate the rich from the poor within a common school. Initially developed by a group of psychologists that included Alfred Binet, H. H. Goddard, Lewis Terman, Robert Yerkes, and Edward Thorndike, the tests reflected their belief that intelligence was a single, general attribute that was innate, stable, and inherited (Oakes et al. 1997). The IQ test was first administered on a mass scale during World War I to army recruits and to immigrants entering Ellis Island as a mechanism for ranking and sorting individuals in terms of their perceived mental abilities. The fact that according to the test 80 percent of immigrants were determined to be "feeble-minded" merely reinforced the prevailing theories of social evolution and raised no concerns of test bias, in part because the use of scientific and sophisticated statistical techniques lent an air of objectivity to the tests.

What Thorndike and other test developers actually accomplished was a self-fulfilling prophecy:

- They based intelligence tests on knowledge common to Anglo-Saxon, middle-class culture, deemed the superior culture.
- Because prediction of future school success was based on test performance, test results were used to sort students into different tracks—academic or vocational—to train students for future work roles.

---

[1]At the time, clerical workers were mostly male and represented the lowest level of the white collar/managerial track. Clerical jobs were not the female-dominated, highly technical, and low-authority jobs they have come to be today.

- Students ended up in occupations and earning incomes commensurate with their IQ and the educations they received: Anglo-Saxon, middle-class men in the top professions and immigrants and the poor in the trades and on the bottom.
- These educational "results," which had been predicted from the test scores, thus reinforced belief in the "scientific merit" of the test.

Still, the commitment to testing as a mechanism for sorting in the educational system and in public life persisted throughout the twentieth century, despite periods of progressive reform (1920s–1930s, 1960s–1970s) that emphasized different educational goals beyond intellectual skill building and traditional courses (Schneider and Keesler 2007). The SAT developed at midcentury as an outgrowth of IQ testing to promote a "new meritocratic order," although the persistence of race and class inequalities in test scores belies the claims of objectivity (Lemann 1999, cited in Klein 2005).

The NCLB is the latest and most comprehensive attempt to organize American education around standards, testing, and accountability. NCLB mandates that every student in every state be tested every year "to provide more feedback to administrators, teachers, students, and their parents so that instruction can be focused on where it is most needed" (Schneider and Keesler 2007, 206). And the testing has consequences for the schools, as well as the students. If their students fail to make "adequate yearly progress" toward the goal of 100 percent proficiency by 2014, as measured by performance on each state's math and reading tests, the failing schools and school districts face severe sanctions, including reductions in funding and even closing.

Even though a bipartisan coalition in Congress passed both the initial legislation and the reauthorization in 2002, the critics of NCLB have grown from every possible corner of American life. Most notably, Michael Petrilli, the former Assistant Deputy Secretary in the Office of Innovation and Improvement in the Bush Department of Education who described himself as a "true believer" in NCLB and who worked diligently to implement it has now concluded that NCLB failed, that it is "fundamentally flawed and probably beyond repair" (Petrilli 2007). The research has also mounted on NCLB's string of failures at enormous costs in time, money, and morale to schools, students, and teachers, especially in the poorest and least advantaged schools and school districts:

- *Failure to Fully Fund the Program.* The federal government has never fully funded the program, leaving states to spend large amounts on testing and reporting when almost all states ran deficits resulting from declining tax revenues because of the recessions at the beginning of the decade and the extreme fiscal crisis at its end. Meanwhile, costs to the states for everything from health care, education, and prisons to highway maintenance have increased.
- *Failure to Allocate Funds Equitably.* Failing schools are the least equipped to succeed. NCLB resources are not allocated on the basis of need, and yet

schools in high-poverty districts, more likely to have minority populations, have greater resource needs. When they fail to live up to standards, funding is withheld, encouraging a spiral of decline.

• *Focus on High-Stakes Tests and Subsequent Narrowing of the Curriculum.* Because the consequences are so serious, especially for disadvantaged schools, many schools opt to focus the curriculum around test taking, math, and reading. Subjects not on the test get short shrift or are eliminated altogether. Some schools have eliminated recess and physical education, even as we have an epidemic of childhood obesity, and have also eliminated or severely curtailed arts, music, career-related training, and extracurricular activities.

• *Lack of Improvement on Overall Performance, Race and Socioeconomic Gaps.* Perhaps most significantly, the primary aims of NCLB—to improve overall student achievement and to close the gaps between racial minority and poor students and their more privileged counterparts—has not happened. Instead, the evidence indicates that the basic trends in achievement gains are almost exactly what they were before the act became law: modest gains in math and no gains in reading. If the current trends persist by 2014, there will be only 24–34 percent proficiency in reading and 29–63 percent in math, well below the 100 percent mandated under the law (FairTest 2007; Lee 2006; Meier and Wood 2004; Nicholson 2003; Schneider and Keesler 2007).

Educating "Others"

While the White working class and poor and Eastern European immigrants were being tracked for different educations and different places in the social order, "other groups" (e.g., people of color, women, and gays and lesbians) faced multiple forms of discrimination in the educational system. Although I cannot review all of those histories here, following are some select highlights to illustrate the kinds of treatment different subordinate groups have historically faced in the United States.

African Americans In the early nineteenth century, African Americans were prohibited from attaining an education. Not until the Reconstruction period, 1865–1877, did private missionary groups and the War Department's Freedmen's Bureau establish separate private and public schools for African Americans. By 1900, one-third of African American children five to nineteen years old were enrolled in school—a dramatic increase from 10 percent in 1870 (Meier, Stewart and England 1989, 41). Yet the distribution of government resources to African American and White schools was grossly unequal. Legal challenges to the constitutionality of this inequality culminated in the Supreme Court ruling in the case of *Plessy v. Ferguson* (1896) that affirmed the "separate but equal" doctrine and legally slammed the door shut on any hope for equal opportunity for nearly sixty years.

Schools remained separate and unequal until the decision was overturned by the Supreme Court's *Brown v. Board of Education* (1954) decision that concluded that over a half-century of evidence proved that separate facilities were inherently unequal in education. Widespread implementation of *Brown*, which called for desegregation of schools with "all deliberate speed," did not take place until after the Civil Rights Act of 1964, when, under pressure from the civil rights movement, the federal government began to withhold funds and to bring lawsuits against recalcitrant school districts. By the 1970–1971 school year, 79 percent of Black students in the South were attending school with Whites, and enforcement efforts began to focus on the urban centers of the North (Meier et al. 1989, 48).

Meier and colleagues (1989) called the exclusion of African Americans from education and education in separate and grossly unequal schools that occurred before the *Brown* decision "first-generation discrimination." Although segregation in unequal schools still exists, what they call "second-generation discrimination" also occurs now within desegregated schools to deny equal educational opportunity to African Americans. This type of segregation represents a consistent pattern of action that actually increased after 1954, including discrimination in ability group tracking and use of discipline to track and to encourage dropouts, with resulting differentials in educational outcomes (Meier et al. 1989). Second-generation discrimination was possible in part because African Americans entered into a system already well organized and functioning to sort the powerful from the undesirables—a system originally designed to discriminate against White immigrant, poor, and working-class men at the beginning of the nineteenth century.

May 17, 2004, marked the fiftieth anniversary of *Brown*, but scholarly reexaminations of the state of African American education have been critical of the shift in educational policy from desegregation to strategies of providing some poor districts with "adequate" funding while maintaining a high degree of racial and socioeconomic segregation. Though more funding for poor schools is an admirable aim, Orfield and Lee (2007) note that if things remain the same—rich and poor students in different rich and poor communities—there is no reason to believe that funding alone will create equal educational opportunities (see also Gantz 2004).

Native Americans Also in the late nineteenth and early twentieth centuries, many Native American children were removed from reservations and sent to a system of boarding schools, day schools, or schools in converted Army posts for as many as ten years. These schools were developed by missionaries to "save" Indians who were facing extermination by settlers, prospectors, and the U.S. Army. The missionaries proposed to educate Indians to work as farmhands, laborers, and chambermaids. In the midst of the Americanization movement, obliterating Indian culture and replacing it with European culture was deemed both economically productive and humane. Mary Crow Dog, for example, attended the same mission school in the 1960s that her grandfather had attended earlier in the century. This poster had been given to her grandfather by missionaries to post in his room:

1. Let Jesus save you.
2. Come out of your blanket, cut your hair, and dress like a white man.
3. Have a Christian family with one wife for life only.
4. Live in a house like your white brother. Work hard and wash often.
5. Learn the value of a hard-earned dollar. Do not waste your money on giveaways. Be punctual.
6. Believe that property and wealth are signs of divine approval.
7. Keep away from saloons and strong spirits.
8. Speak the language of your white brother. Send your children to school to do likewise.
9. Go to church often and regularly.
10. Do not go to Indian dances or to the medicine men (Crow Dog and Erdoes 1996, 511).

The educational goal of "Americanizing" Indians and preparing them for menial labor (e.g., be punctual, work hard, wash often) and promoting the American Dream ideology (e.g., property and wealth are signs of divine approval) could not be more clearly stated.

Women From the inception of vocational education, working-class White girls were tracked for home economics and garment work, and Black, Native American, and Chicana girls were trained to be servants, laundry workers, and farm laborers (Amott and Matthaei 1996; Wrigley 1992). Although middle-class Anglo-Saxon women were not denigrated using the same biological referents as those for people of color, most White immigrants, and the poor, women were deemed to be biologically suited for different social locations than men: for the private sphere of the home and for occupational roles that became associated with that sphere. Some middle- and upper-class White women were supported in pursuing higher education, yet college curricula for these women were designed to prepare women for

- Sex-segregated occupational roles (e.g., teacher, nurse, librarian)
- The social roles of homemaking, marriage, and motherhood and to impart cultural capital—key for status maintenance (Ostrander 1984; Streitmatter 1999)

In more recent times, women's colleges have continued their popularity with a substantial group of women. Even so, excepting some elite schools with large endowments (e.g., Wellesley), most of these largely tuition-based, private women's colleges have struggled to stay open, and many have gone coeducational because of the rising costs of higher education (Schemo 2006b).

Gays, Lesbians, Bisexuals, and Transgender Youths (GLBT) Although gay, lesbian, bisexual, and transgendered youths were not segregated into different schools, since its beginnings U. S. culture has sanctioned only heterosexual sex within marriage and has relegated other sexual practices, even heterosexual ones, and gender expressions to the darkness of the closet. And the people who engage in anything other than heterosexual sex within marriage are defined as sinful, sick, and morally depraved. Silence, judgment, and punishment have thus been the primary modes of addressing homosexuality. Throughout this century, homosexuals have been marginalized in education by

- Exclusion from the curriculum
- The closeting and witch hunting of gay and lesbian teachers
- Verbal and physical assaults (Carlson 1997)

Early in the twentieth century, Freudian psychoanalytic theory validated heterosexual development as healthy and homosexuality as immature and psychologically unhealthy, thus scientifically justifying and legitimizing the prevailing moral and religiously based discriminatory treatment. Throughout the first half of the twentieth century, dismissing gay and lesbian teachers was justified on the grounds that it kept young people from exposure to improper role models, lechery, and child molestation. In pervasive disease metaphor, homosexuality was viewed as contagious, and homosexuals were presumed to be lecherous and immature and to desire sexual relations with their young students (Carlson 1997).

Although witch hunts no longer prevail, the "contagion theory" is still prevalent, and the "don't ask, don't tell" policy of many school districts effectively silences gay and lesbian teachers and students, leaving them alone in their "otherness." Further, as Pascoe (2007) notes, today's schools reaffirm normative sexual and gender identities through school rituals, pedagogical practices, and disciplinary procedures that include school dress codes emphasizing gender differences, school policies that encourage abstinence and discourage homosexuality, curricula drawing on conceptions of heterosexual pairing and marriage, and the naturalization of heterosexuality through such events as school dances and proms.

Higher Education and Credentials

At the same time that the modern comprehensive high school forged its place in the social order, U.S. higher education established its relationship to these high schools and to the new economic order as the credentialing institutions for the new middle class of professionals, managers, and administrators. From the early twentieth century, certain occupations (e.g., medical doctor, lawyer, and teacher) became accessible only to people with college degrees.

Interestingly, the social learning necessary to perform these middle-class occupations is obtained incidental to the pursuit of a college degree. It is not the focus of the curriculum. Not surprisingly, from early in the century, athletics and sororities and fraternities were incorporated into higher education as places where social-class capital was explicitly developed in highly gendered and racialized ways ("Black Colleges with White Golfers," 2000–01; Brown 1995; Messner 2007). As Larabee (1995) notes, it is this corporate structure of student life—not the curricular content—that most prepares students for middle-class occupations. The process of getting admitted to college and completing a college education gives students an enhanced sense of social superiority and qualification for leadership.

In sum, since the late nineteenth century, the American system of education has served a key role in creating, reinforcing, and justifying race, class, gender, and sexuality hierarchies and in creating and reinforcing the American Dream ideology. A system of mass public education was structured to support the mobility and social dominance of middle- and upper-class heterosexual Anglo Saxon males. The system segregated and excluded people of color and ranked and educated differently—often within the same schools—Eastern European immigrants, the working class and the poor, and middle-class Anglo-Saxon women. Both formal and informal tracking of students for different educations and different places in the social order remains a primary source of social inequality today (Anyon 1997; Entwisle, Alexander, and Olson 1997; Hallinan 1995; Heck, Price, and Thomas 2004; Lucas and Berends 2002; Yonezawa, Wells, and Serna 2002).

CONTEMPORARY SOCIAL CONSTRUCTIONS OF RACE, CLASS, GENDER, AND SEXUALITY IN EDUCATION

Segregation and isolation processes take place both at the macro level in different schools and different academic tracks and at the micro level in different classroom experiences. Segregation of women and men; of heterosexuals and homosexuals; of poor, working, middle, and upper classes; and of Whites and people of color into different roles both at work and in the home is a societal process that enables differential distribution of valued societal resources such as income, health care, and housing. This societal segregation both reinforces and is reinforced by educational segregation processes that begin very early. To understand why the labor market is so segregated, for example, we must understand how early education begins by segregating people along the lines of race, class, gender, and sexuality. In these processes of segregation, students meet different people, learn different things, and develop different hopes, dreams, and expectations for their futures.

Entire race, class, and gender groups are segregated and educated differently in several macro social processes when they

- Follow a curriculum that excludes or includes their experiences and backgrounds
- Attend different schools
- Attend the same schools in different formal and informal academic tracks
- Drop out of school at different rates

School Segregation

Although segregation into different schools is much less central to gender hierarchies and plays little to no part in maintaining sexuality hierarchies, it is a central process supporting class and race hierarchies. From kindergarten through postgraduate education, most poor and working-class students and people of color attend different schools from those of middle- and upper-class students. And our educational system is made up of many different types of schools.

- *Kindergarten-twelfth grade:* Racially homogeneous schools (including reservation, barrio, and ghetto schools); class homogeneous schools (including many racially homogeneous schools, as well as desegregated schools); same-gender schools; rural, urban, and suburban schools; public and private schools; college preparatory and vocational schools
- *Post-high school:* Community colleges, technical schools, four-year colleges, universities; elite private schools, religious schools, state public schools; women's colleges; traditionally Black colleges and universities; and military colleges

Many processes support this segregation:

- The legacy of a history of de jure (by law) racial school segregation that lasted effectively until the 1960s
- Extensive class and racial residential segregation since the 1960s, including the shift of the White middle-class population and businesses from urban to suburban spaces and increased class stratification as deindustrialization and the rise of the service economy have prompted the bifurcation of the labor force into highly paid professionals and low-wage service workers
- The financial requirements of private school education.
- The knowledge and political clout of White middle-class parents who pressure local school boards to provide their children special schools such as magnet or charter schools within the public school system (Frankenberg and Siegel-Hawley 2008; Meier, Stewart, and England 1989)
- School voucher plans (Kohn 2004; Schemo 2006a)

Class Segregation

From preschool programs through twelfth grade, public education is fundamentally organized around neighborhoods, reflecting the class and socioeconomic segregation of U.S. housing, and private education is restricted to those who can afford it (cf. Kozol 2005; Frankenberg, Lee, and Orfield 2003; Patillo 2008). Valerie Polakow describes the class segregation of children that begins as early as preschool:

> In contemporary practice a two-tiered system means that poor children go to Head Start and other at-risk public preschools (if they gain access), and middle- and upper-income children attend fee-based child care centers where parents choose the kind and quality of program they wish their children to enroll in. Not only does this two-tiered system create economic and racial segregation, but it also ensures that children, in their earliest developing years, are placed in stratified educational landscapes. Cost-benefit accountability for poor children's early education is demanded, whereas fee-based centers do not

have to prove their right to provide a place for children to play and to learn. In the absence of a national child care system, public education becomes a gift bestowed by the haves upon the have-nots. It is not surprising that the two-tiered system is fostering a separate and unequal education—a pedagogy for the poor. (1993,128–29)

Kindergarten through high school education is also class stratified. Jean Anyon (1980) studied fifth-grade classrooms in five working-class, middle-class, afflu-ent, and elite elementary schools, documenting the varied kinds of elementary education that students receive to prepare them for different places in the class system. She called the process a "hidden curriculum" because the differences she observed occurred even though the fifth grades were similar in many respects: All the schools, for example, used the same math textbook, and all language arts classes included aspects of grammar, punctuation, and capitalization. Similar pro-cesses have been observed by other scholars (Brantlinger 1993; Page 1991; Spade et al. 1997; Thorne 1993).

Working-Class Schools The children of manual laborers and clerical workers were taught to follow orders and to perform routine tasks and mechanical work in the service of others—not to think for themselves, to plan ahead, or to be creative. Teacher priorities included disciplining and controlling the class. Language arts focused on the mechanics of punctuation, capitalization, and the four kinds of sentences. Math focused on rote learning:

> The teacher in one school gave a 4 minute lecture on what the terms are called (i.e., which number is the divisor, dividend, quotient, and remainder). The chil-dren were told to copy these names in their notebooks. Then the teacher told them the steps to follow to do the problems, saying, "This is how you do them." The teacher listed the steps on the board, and they appeared several days later as a chart hung in the middle of the front wall: "Divide; Multiply; Subtract; Bring Down."(Anyon 1980, 73–4)

This learning approach was retained by teachers even when students were having difficulty understanding. One teacher said:

> "You're confusing yourselves. You're tensing up. Remember, when you do this, it's the same steps over and over again—and that's the way division always is." When some students still had problems several weeks later, she said they "needed more practice." (Anyon 1980, 74)

Middle-Class Schools Students whose parents were low-level bureaucrats (e.g., so-cial service workers or business managers) were prepared for bureaucratic roles in which self-expression is denied. In these schools, students were rewarded for knowing the answers *and* for how to find them, but not for creativity.

The primary goal in this middle-class school was to "get the right answer." As in working-class schools, students had to follow directions to get the right answer, but the directions usually called for some choice and decision making.

The children were often asked to figure out themselves what the directions asked them to do to find the answer.

Language arts consisted of simple grammar but also involved writing in forms they would need to know, such as business letters and thank-you letters. Math involved some choice: Two-digit division was taught in two ways—the long and the short way. Providing both ways of dividing, the teacher said, "I want to make sure you understand what you're doing—so you get it right." She also asked students to tell how they solved the problem and what answer they got (Anyon 1980, 77).

Elite or Affluent Professional Schools The children of the producers of culture—artists, intellectuals, legal, scientific, and technical experts, and other professionals—are prepared in school for creative roles in society. In these schools, creativity and working independently had priority over maintaining discipline or control, rote task performance, or getting the right answer. Work was evaluated for its interpretation of reality, for the quality of its expression, and for the appropriateness of its conception to the task at hand.

Language arts emphasized individual thought and expressiveness, and students produced written stories, essays, and editorials, as well as murals, graphs, and crafts. A typical math problem asked students to take home a sheet of paper and to have their parents fill in the number of cars, television sets, refrigerators, games, or rooms in the house. Each child then compiled the data from all the students and used the calculators provided in the classroom to compute the class average for each item.

Executive Elite Schools The children of top executives and owners are prepared to develop their analytical intellectual powers. These students were continually asked to reason through a problem and to conceptualize the rules that governed a system. This ability to analyze and to plan systems prepares elite students to own and control businesses. Language arts were seen as a complex system to be mastered, and grammar was emphasized in written and oral work for other classes. The math teacher taught area and perimeter by having the children derive the formulae for each:

> First, she helps them through discussion at the board, to arrive at $A = W \times L$ as a formula (not *the* formula) for area. After discussing several, she says, "Can anyone make up a formula for perimeter? Can you figure that out yourselves?" (Anyon 1980, 83)

The teacher discusses two-digit division as a decision-making process. She asks:

> "What's the first kind of decision you'd make if presented with this kind of example? What is the first thing you'd think? Craig?" Craig says, "To find my first partial quotient." She responds, "Yes, that would be your first decision. How would you do that?" Craig explains and then the teacher says, "OK, we'll see how that works for you." The class tries his way. Subsequently, she comments on the merits and shortcomings of several other children's decisions. (Anyon, 1980, 83)

The teacher made little effort to control students' movements about the class, and in stark contrast to the working-class students, her students never had to wait in lines to go anywhere—to the cafeteria, to the playground, to the bathroom.

Anyon's research documents critical social class differences in how and what—despite many surface similarities—students are taught in different schools. Differences in school resources were also pronounced between two school districts, one with the working-class and middle-class schools and the other with the affluent middle-class and executive elite schools. What Anyon found in her study has been reinforced with extensive research since. The affluent and elite schools had

- More variety and abundance of teaching materials
- Increased preparation time by teachers
- Teachers from higher social class backgrounds and more prestigious schools
- More stringent board of education teaching methods requirements
- More frequent and demanding evaluations of teachers
- More teacher support services
- Higher expectations for student ability and demands for student achievement
- More positive attitudes by teachers about students' future occupations
- Better student acceptance of classroom assignments (Anyon 1980, 87; see also Anyon 1997; Arroyo 2008; Condron and Roscigno 2003; Entwisle, Alexander, and Olson 1997; Kozol 2005; Mayer 2001; Sacks 2007)

Race Segregation

Although it has less effect on gender or sexuality hierarchies, the segregation of different social classes into different schools is greatly implicated in the educational outcomes of racially oppressed groups. Despite a history of school busing and court-ordered desegregation, most students still attend schools that remain largely segregated. In 2005–06 the average African American student attended a school that was more than 70 percent non-White; the average Hispanic, a school that was 73 percent minority. White students, however, were the most segregated group, with the average White student attending a school that was 77 percent White. In urban schools of the Northeast, where racial segregation is the greatest in the country, White, Black, and Hispanic students experienced extreme degrees of racial isolation. Fifty-one percent of African American students and 45 percent of Hispanic students attended schools whose student populations were between 90 and 100 percent non-White. Asian students are the most integrated group, attending schools, on average, with 48 percent White students, even though these schools tend to have higher concentrations of Asians than are in the population at large (Orfield and Lee 2007).

Public school teachers are similarly segregated by race. The overwhelming majority of teachers are White, and the average White teacher currently teaches in a school in which almost 90 percent of their faculty colleagues are White and over 70 percent of their students are White. Moreover, White teachers typically teach in schools with fewer poor and English-language-learning (ELL) students than the typical minority teacher (Frankenberg 2006).

From 1968 to 1972, segregation rates dropped precipitously nationwide, remained roughly constant over the 1970s, and increased slightly in the 1980s. In 1968, for example, 77.8 percent of all Black students in the South attended schools whose student bodies were at least 90 percent people of color, but by 1972 only 24.7 percent of Black students did so (Boozer, Krueger and Wolkon 1992). But more recent research documents the resegregation of public schools, a shift that began to take place between 1988 and 1991 and has continued ever since. For example, the percentage of White students in schools attended by most Black students is lower now—30 percent—than it was before the busing decisions of the early 1970s. The South and the border states (the six states bordering the Confederacy, from Oklahoma to Delaware) are now resegregating faster than other regions of the country, in spite of their being the least segregated regions (Orfield and Lee 2007).

In the first ruling on school desegregation in twelve years, the U.S. Supreme Court decided two significant cases in June 2007: *Parents Involved in Community Schools v. Seattle School District No. 1 et al.* and *Meredith v. Jefferson County Board of Education.* A closely divided court ultimately struck down the constitutionality of two school integration programs—both of which set goals for equitable representation of White and minority students. In a direct appeal to a "color-blind" ideology, the conservative Chief Justice John G. Roberts, Jr., author of the plurality opinion, portrayed the race-conscious programs as betrayals of the landmark *Brown v. Board of Education* decision. Justice Stephen G. Breyer, who delivered the dissenting opinion, wrote that "to invalidate the plans under review is to threaten the promise of *Brown.* The plurality's position, I fear, would break that promise" (Barnes 2007).

These patterns of segregation and resegregation of schools provide the context for the construction of White privilege through the mechanisms of segregation, exclusion, and surveillance.

Gender Segregation

Although the United States has a long history of all-women's and all-men's schools, they have for the most part been private schools and colleges. By the 1960s, several forces combined to bring about the beginning of a precipitous decline in enrollments and school closings at all-women's secondary and higher education institutions. First, higher education experienced its greatest-ever expansion, fueled by economic growth and the societal need to keep the baby-boom population out of the labor force. For the first time, large numbers of working-class women and men could afford to attend college. Furthermore, as a consequence of Title IX in 1972, which prohibited discrimination on the basis of sex in most federally assisted educational programs, and the Civil Rights Act of 1964, women increasingly gained access to all types of colleges and universities, as well as the promise of equal treatment once they entered coeducational institutions. Finally, even before Title IX, all-women's schools had already begun to decline because they were too expensive for most people and because the spirit of racial integration following the civil rights movement led most to believe that "separate could never really be equal" (Streitmatter 1999).

By the 1990s, however, enrollments at all-womencolleges began to increase as it became clear that Title IX and civil rights legislation had failed to eliminate gender inequities in a variety of areas: enrollments in science, technology, engineering, and math (STEM) programs; operating dollars for women's athletics; and sex segregation of women into training programs for low-wage jobs (American Association of University Women [AAUW] 2007; DeWelde, Laursen, and Thiry 2007; Women's Sports Foundation 2008). Schools began to argue convincingly that all-women environments are generally more supportive for women and that their students have higher self-esteem and self-control, more positive attitudes about the changing roles of women, more willingness to take risks, more confidence in science and math, and greater rates of attaining Ph.D. and M.D. degrees (Baker and Velez 1996; Streitmatter 1999). But the gains were short-lived as the rising costs of higher education, stagnant family incomes, and the recessions beginning in 2001 and 2007 have rendered it an extremely difficult time to keep any small colleges alive. The number of women's colleges has dwindled from about three hundred in the 1960s to fewer than sixty today, and only 3.4 percent of female high school graduates who took the SAT in 2006 reported that they would apply to a women's college (Schemo 2006b).

Ironically, just as many women's colleges have gone coeducational or closed, there is a rapidly growing movement toward single-sex K-12 education—segregation into both different schools and different curricula or tracks in the same school. The movement was fueled in part by the notion promoted in conservative political circles that boys are being surpassed by girls, are shortchanged in education, and need special attention (Corbett, Hill and St. Rose 2008). Gender segregation's dramatic growth since 2000 is largely attributable to the funds provided and the rule changes initiated through the NCLB Act and the Bush administration's department of education (McNeil 2008; Weil 2008).

The significance and impact of gender-segregated schools must be examined in light of the historical social relations of power and oppression among groups. Girls' schools and Black community calls for segregated education for Black males, for example, arise as a response to the negative effects of segregation among oppressed groups—lack of ideological, political, and economic resources and limited access to power. Recent support from powerful groups for single-sex education especially focused on the plight of males can be seen as an attempt to reassert male privilege in the face of gains by women in the educational arena over the previous thirty years (AAUW 2008). And as Pascoe (2007) asserts, schools normalize dichotomized and highly sexualized gender differences, leaving transgender students with few options to enact a different gender expression. As argued by the Gay-Straight Alliance Network:

Sex segregation can be especially difficult for transgender students who do not identify as either male or female. If such a student is only presented with the choice of a male or female restroom, the student is forced to make a choice that does not match their gender identity. And often times such a "choice" is meaningless because the student is harassed by other students regardless of whether the student opts to use the male or the female restroom. (2004, 2)

Sexuality Segregation

Although gay and lesbian students have not been historically segregated into different schools, same-sex schools such as men's and women's colleges have provided environments in which White middle- and upper-class gay and lesbian communities have developed and thrived. Gay and lesbian communities were more likely to develop in these class-restricted settings primarily because White middle- and upper-class people were better able to sustain their social class and identity in modern capitalism (D'Emilio 1993, 2002). In the 1990s, gay and lesbian youths began to organize student groups in high schools for many of the same reasons that race- and gender-segregated programs have developed—to serve as sites for self-determination, valuation, and resistance to oppression. According to the Gay, Lesbian, Straight Education Network (GLSEN; 2008), most of the groups are gay-straight alliances and are organized to support gay students and to oppose discrimination and harassment in schools. They have increased from two in 1991 to more than four thousand in 2008.

Harassment and discrimination are routinely encountered by GLBT students today. In a 2007 National School Climate Survey of GLBT students, one in five reported physical assaults, 86 percent verbal harassment, and 60 percent feeling unsafe in school. One-third reported missing class at least once a month because, as a result of their sexual orientation, they felt uncomfortable or unsafe. And GLBT students were more than twice as likely as the general student population to report that they were not planning to pursue postsecondary education (Kosciw, Diaz and Greytak, 2008). As a consequence, since the first school for gay students, the Harvey Milk School in San Francisco, opened in 1985, several gay schools and gay-friendly schools have opened in recent years—in Milwaukee, Los Angeles, San Francisco, and New York (Bethard 2004; Calefati 2008; GLSEN 2008). They have received both support and resistance: In 2008, for example, a proposal for a highly publicized Chicago Social Justice High School was withdrawn after religious community leaders and the mayor expressed reservations about the segregation of gay students (Bethard 2004; Calefati 2008).

Segregation Within Schools—Tracking

In addition to segregating students into different schools, segregating them into different academic tracks in the same schools to teach them differently is another critical process in the production of social hierarchies. In tracking, students are separated into different classes or into different groups within the same class to teach them at different speeds and at different levels of difficulty. Some form of tracking is practiced in nearly every public school in America today and begins as early as kindergarten (Entwisle, Alexander and Olson 1997; Heck, Price, and Thomas 2004; Sacks 2007). Peter Sacks summarized the American context of tracking well:

> Ability tracking in American schools begins as early as kindergarten, with the imposition of school "readiness tests," and continues through the elementary years with pullout programs, gifted and talented classes, and remedial classes for "slow" learners. By middle school and high school, tracking becomes integral to the American education system's structure and function. (2007:105)

Most educators justify tracking by arguing that differentiating students by "ability group" makes teaching easier and raises student achievement by allowing curricula and instruction to be tailored to students' abilities and interests. But research on the effects of school tracking in K-12 education reveals a much more complex reality. The few studies comparing homogeneous and heterogeneous groups suggest that tracking and ability grouping do not seem to raise the average achievement of students any higher than heterogeneous instruction does: The top group does better, the bottom group does much worse, and the middle group remains the same (Dougherty 1996; Entwisle, Alexander, and Olson1997; Kerckhoff 1995; Sacks 2007). Academic-track students later score better on math and verbal tests, have higher educational aspirations, and get more education than lower-track or vocational-track students. But there are so few heterogeneous groups to study that we cannot generalize confidently from these results. These studies also overlook the fact that students

- who are advantaged to begin with make up most of the top group
- are educated differently in different tracks, increasing the gap between advantaged and disadvantaged children
- live up to the expectations of their teachers, whether positive or negative.

We do know, however, that at the macro group level, tracking

- widens inequalities in academic achievement
- hinders the mixing of students of different social classes and races.

And at the micro level of students' individual lives, tracking

- undercuts the self-esteem and academic self-concept of lower-track students
- lowers educational aspirations of lower-track students
- increases the likelihood of delinquency and dropout rates among lower-track students (Anyon 1997; Dougherty 1996; Entwisle, Alexander, and Olson 1997; Heck, Price, and Thomas 2004; Kerckhoff 1995; Lucas and Berends 2002; Sacks 2007).

Two things are particularly distressing about these negative effects of tracking:

1. Students are supposedly tracked into different groups and provided with different educations because they have different academic abilities to begin with. Yet academic aptitude is only one of the factors that actually influence

how students are tracked—social class and race also affect placement both directly and indirectly (e.g., teachers' subjective assessments and parent preferences are also typically a part of the assignment process).

2. Academic aptitude is typically assessed by scores on tests that measure only one type of intelligence and that are race- and class-biased.

Studies attempting to predict how students are tracked based solely on their test scores accurately predict no more than 50 percent of student placements (Dougherty 1996). Race and class background of the students affects both teachers' perceptions of students' abilities and parents' influence on the placement process for their children—two factors that also affect track placement.

By the late twentieth and into the twenty-first century, tracking in American schools had become more concealed than in previous decades, often obscured by a more egalitarian-sounding rhetoric of "curricular choice" among educators. Consequently, scholars have observed a distinction between the formal tracking and classification schemes in times past and the more subtle forms of tracking relying on students' choices of their courses. These mechanisms have nevertheless continued to sort children harshly by class and race (Heck, Price, and Thomas 2004; Lucas and Berends 2002; Sacks 2007). As Lucas and Berends (2002) conclude, "The differentiated curriculum is still the dominant form of pedagogical organization in secondary schools in the United States."

Race, Class, Gender, Sexuality, and Tracking

Race, class, and gender affect track placement both directly and indirectly. White, middle-class students and/or girls are more likely to be placed in higher tracks, particularly in elementary school, than are poor and working-class students, students of color, and/or boys regardless of test scores. Poor and working-class students of color are more likely to be placed in vocational and lower tracks. But most of the difference in the track placement of Whites and people of color, which is considerable and apparent in almost any school setting, is a function both of the lower-class position of students of color, of teachers' perceptions of their potential, and of parents' involvement and of class and racial bias in the aptitude tests (Brantlinger 1993; Entwisle, Alexander, and Olson 1997; Kerckhoff 1995; Persell 1977; Sacks 2007).

Class In one study, high socioeconomic status students were found to be 46 percent more likely than low socioeconomic status students *with the same test scores* to end up in the academic rather than in the general track (Jones, Vanfossen, and Ensminger 1995). And in a study of high achieving (on nationally normed standardized tests) lower-income students, Wyner, Bridgeland, and Diiullio (2007) found that these students mirror the race, ethnic, and geographic distribution of America when they enter school. By the end of the first grade, however, only 28 percent of these high-achieving low-income students are performing in the top academic quartile, while 72 percent from high-income families are doing so.

Further, in elementary and high school, low-income students neither maintain their status as high achievers nor rise to high-achieving status as frequently as higher-income students. And although these low-income students perform over-all better than their underachieving counterparts, they never perform as well as their high-income counterparts. As a result, low-income students have lower rates of college graduation, of attending selective colleges, and of obtaining graduate degrees.

Gender Girls seem to have a slight advantage in access to the higher track in elementary school, but the advantage is gone by junior high school, when career tracking and gender socialization for different future lives is much more significant and overt. Girls are, for example, more likely than boys to be tapped for the gifted and talented programs in elementary school but are not retained in these programs to the same extent as boys once they reach middle school. And even though girls have increased their presence in science and math (but not computer science) courses and make higher grades throughout their school years, they still perform lower on high stakes standardized tests: ACT, SAT, and advanced placement (AP). They are also less likely to take advanced-placement tests in math, science, and computer science (AAUW 1994, 1999, 2004; DeWelde et al. 2007). And ultimately, women are still concentrated in certain disciplines, and most professions are still sex segregated (Commission on Professionals in Science and Technology [CPST] 2004).

Sexuality Gay, bisexual, lesbian, and transgender students are not systematically tracked into different classes, because sexual identity and expression does not become more developed until adolescence. And most GLBT students remain invisible in schools—much as Theo's sexual identity development and expression remained hidden from authorities at school. GLBT youths do, however, experience isolation and silencing in the curriculum and social life of schools, the negative effects of which inhibit their personal development and school progress. Increasingly they have organized to combat discrimination in schools. The Gay, Lesbian, and Straight Education Network, for example, has forty full-time staff members, a twenty-member governing board, and two advisory committees at the national level, as well as local chapters across the nation whose volunteers educate school officials about the need to pass nondiscrimination policies in schools, to train teachers to prevent antigay name calling, and to serve as community resources for teachers, parents, and students grappling with gay, lesbian, bisexual, and transgender issues. In addition, their Student Pride Project provides resources and technical support to more than four thousand school-based gay-straight alliances (GLSEN 2009).

Ethnicity Bilingual education has been championed as a mechanism for preserving culture among America's non-English-speaking minorities, primarily Latinas/os. But in a study of bilingual classrooms, Ortiz (1988) found that Hispanic children receive a lower quality of education than their White counterparts, whether that education was provided in separate schools or in separate classrooms in the same schools. The bilingual classes segregated Hispanic children from their class-mates, were crowded, and were often taught by teacher's aides. In addition, because teachers assumed that the students were less capable of learning, the instruction was remedial. The schools were often in poor districts and received few resources. And even when Hispanic children were in the same classrooms with Anglos, they were often ignored by teachers, spoken to in different tones, and given different (nonverbal) activities to perform (see also Callahan 2005; Crosnoe 2005; Padilla and Gonzalez 2001).

Race To illustrate the intimate connection between race, class, gender, and track-ing, a story from Reba Page's (1991) study of tracking in two predominantly White (less than 12 percent students of color), middle-class high schools is instructive. She discovered that the entire tracking system in the school had been established as an administrator's way of dealing with the race, class, and gender dynamics in the school. The administrator described it thus:

> Well, anyway…, there were three incidents in one day, and there had been a series of days with single incidents for over a week. It was a black-white thing. We had these girls who were coming to school, not going to class. Oh, they'd get their free lunch, but no attendance in classes. And, of course, they were bored. So they started fights: girl-girl fights with whites. They'd go around to classrooms, knock on the door, and ask for a kid, the kid would come to the door, and there'd be pushing and shoving. So I gathered them all up in the Commons and said, "Look, you're not getting any credits for all this time you've been putting in here at Southmoor. If you could have a class, what would it have to be like to make you attend?" (Page 1991, 116)

Note that the administrator identified the Black "free-lunch" girls as the prob-lem, "rounded them up," and proposed a resolution to their boredom that in no way required the school that created the alienating environment for those girls to change what it did for White middle-class girls and boys. The subordinate groups were defined as the problem, isolated, and tracked for a different education.

In an ethnographic study, Julie Bettie (2003) documented the ways that race, ethnicity, and class together shaped the identities, the social networks, the cultures, and the educational experiences and outcomes of Mexican American and White girls in a California comprehensive high school. Her close observation revealed how poor and working-class students, both White and Mexican American, were tracked into the vocational curriculum, effectively shutting down their future educational options:

> Some girls felt tracked into a vocational curriculum. When I asked Yolanda about tracking…she said:
> Oh, yeah, that happened to me. This counselor told me to take all the non-required classes. Now I'm way behind in English and math, so that is why

I can't go to a state school. The counselor said I wasn't ready. I heard she got fired for that.

When I asked Lorena how she decided which courses to take, she explained:

Well, the counselor suggests something or sometimes a teacher suggests what you are ready for.

When I pushed for why she had not been encouraged or did not choose (college) prep courses, she explained:

Well, college-prep classes are harder, and you have to write a letter to get in or something. If the counselor sees you are not smart, then they help you find the right classes. She'll try to find a way for you to get classes and meet requirements to graduate without taking the hard ones. (2003, 77)

And many students were also mindful of the financial constraints on their futures, opting for vocational or business curricula under the assumption that they would not be able to afford a four-year college.

Different School Continuation and Dropout Rates

As the high school dropout rates presented at the beginning of this chapter reveal, race and gender affect the rates at which groups continue in the educational system. Because continuing one's education beyond high school in different types of institutions significantly affects earnings and occupation, the transition to college is a critical juncture in the system of race, class, gender, and sexuality hierarchies. Social class is a key determinant of the likelihood that students will continue on. After high school, also, different educational options (community colleges, technical schools, colleges, universities, graduate schools) provide different experiences and prepare students for very different life chances.

Colleges are critical institutions in the reproduction of social class and related racial advantage, yet they hide that function under a thin veneer of merit. Even though *tests* and *performance* are foregrounded in higher education, students from middle- and upper-class families have a distinct advantage in admission to and completion of college, as well as in securing the best middle-class employment with their degrees in an overcredentialed market (Brown 1995; Karabel 2005; McNamee and Miller 2004).

Research on college access suggests that:

- By age twenty-four, 75 percent of students from high-income families have earned at least a bachelor's degree, whereas fewer than 9 percent of students from low-income families have done so.
- Low-achieving students from high-income families attend college at about the same rate (77 percent) as high-achieving students from low-income families (78 percent).
- In 2006, 81 percent of high-income students entered college directly from high school, 61 percent of middle-income students did so, but only 51

TABLE 8.1 SAT Scores and 1 Year Change by Race and Ethnicity, 2008

Group	Critical Reading	1-Year change, Reading	Math	1-Year change, Math	Writing	1-Year change, Writing	Total 1-Year Change
American Indian	485	⬇ −2	491	⬇ −3	470	⬇ −3	⬇ −8
Black	430	⬇ −3	426	⬇ −3	424	⬇ −1	⬇ −7
Mexican American	454	⬇ −1	463	⬇ −3	447	⬇ −3	⬇ −7
Puerto Rican	456	⬇ −3	453	⬇ −1	445	⬇ −2	⬇ −6
Other Hispanic	455	⬇ −4	461	⬇ −2	448	⬇ −2	⬇ −8
Asian American	513	⬇ −1	581	⬆ 3	516	⬆ −3	⬆ 5
White	528	⬆ 1	537	⬆ 3	518	no change	⬆ 4

SOURCE: Jaschik, Scott. 2008. "The SAT's Growing Gaps" *Inside Higher Ed* August 27. Available from http://www. insidehighered.com/news/2008/08/27/sat, accessed October 12.

Table created by: Christina E. Griffin

percent of low-income students continued—two-thirds the rate of their higher-class counterparts (Planty et al. 2008).

The data in Table 8.1 show 2007–2008 race and ethnic differences in SAT scores, the tests used by most colleges to determine admittance. Average incomes for these groups fall in roughly the same rank order as the test scores, reinforcing the association between class advantage and college admission. The changes from 2007 to 2008 also suggest that White and Asian students' advantage in standardized tests were increasing relative to Black, Hispanic, and American Indian students.

In 2004, 41.7 percent of White high school graduates ages eighteen through twenty-four were enrolled in college, whereas only 31.8 percent of Blacks and 24.7 percent of Hispanics were. In 2005, 30.5 percent of Whites, 49.2 percent of Asians, 14.5 percent of American Indians, 17.7 percent of Blacks and 12.0 percent of Hispanics ages twenty-five and older held bachelor's, graduate, or professional degrees (KewalRamani et al. 2007, 122).

SUMMARY

In spite of the ideology of equal opportunity, the gross differences in the kinds of schooling people receive based on their race, class, gender, and sexuality persist throughout American history. These differences happen in part because the American Dream ideology, in offering individual explanations for different school and group outcomes, diverts attention from systemic processes—segregation by school and within schools—that educate race, class, and gender groups in unequal ways. Those who are disadvantaged in the educational system—poor and working-class students, students of color, girls, and GLBT students—have the fewest economic resources (money), political resources (influence, control over school boards), and ideological resources (expertise, knowledge of the system, control of media) to bring about change. Changing systems that clearly advantage some and disadvantage others takes a shift in the ideological, political, and economic power arrangements of society.

＞

CHAPTER 9

Macro and Micro Level Power Relationships, Simultaneously Expressed

This chapter focuses on the last three themes of the framework: that race, class, gender, and sexuality are power relations simultaneously expressed at both macro institutional and micro individual levels. To explore these power relations, I look first at some of the macro institutional arrangements in political, economic, and ideological realms that structure educational inequality today. I then explore micro processes by looking at the various ways that race, class, gender, and sexuality relations are produced and challenged in the face-to-face encounters between teachers and students in the classroom every day. To give a sense of the way that students actually experience these classroom dynamics, I discuss them in the order that students pass through school: preschool and kindergarten, first to third grades, fourth to sixth grades, junior high and high school.

I briefly highlight the final theme of the framework by returning to the cases of Theo and Lynn to remind us of the simultaneous operation and interlocking nature of these systems, a fact that cannot be ignored when we look at how multiple social locations play out in an individual life. Finally, to assess the significance of the intersectional framework for promoting social justice, I review some of its implications for social justice in education.

MACRO SOCIAL-STRUCTURAL POWER RELATIONS

As the stories of Theo Wilson and Lynn Johnson suggest, schools are not passive mirrors of race, class, gender, and sexuality hierarchies in society today. Schools actively help to form those hierarchies in the political, economic, and ideological domains. Education is central to producing ideologies that undergird race, class, gender, and sexuality relations of oppression and resistance. It is also central to establishing and reinforcing political and economic power relations of race, class, gender, and sexuality.

Political Power and Education

Educational policy is a political arena where race, class, gender, and sexuality struggles are fought and relations shaped. Schools act as sites of oppression by assessing where people belong in the larger economy, preparing them for their place in it, and promoting ideologies that justify the very race, class, gender, and sexuality hierarchies they helped to create. As Pitirim Sorokin put it in 1927:

> The school, even the most democratic school, open to everybody, if it performs its task properly, is the machinery of the "aristocratization" and stratification of society, not of "leveling" and "democratization." (Sorokin 1927, 190)

Many, especially in the civil rights community, contend that the educational policy arena is the single most important site of political struggle against racial discrimination in the United States. People of color have long emphasized that resistance to oppression must take place in the educational arena, and many major conflicts of the twentieth and twenty-first centuries have been over educational issues:

- School funding
- School desegregation and busing
- Affirmative action in higher education admissions, minority scholarships, and faculty hiring
- The content of curricula (from sex education to multiculturalism)

Race, Class, Gender, and Sexuality Contests

How race, class, and gender inequalities are to be considered in college hiring and admissions policies has been the focus of some of the hottest political contests over the past thirty years. Ever since President John F. Kennedy introduced *affirmative action* into the national dialogue in 1961, when he directed government contractors to "take affirmative action to ensure that all applicants are employed... without regard to their race, creed, color, or national origin," higher education and government have been embroiled in conflict over how to achieve justice for all in the context of our democratic capitalist system (Levine 2007). How do institutions provide *individuals* with equal rights in education today when the legacy of systematic discrimination against subordinate *groups* has for centuries deprived some people of the opportunity to compete on an equal playing field? Ignoring the past does not make it go away and, in fact, tends to support policies that replicate the hierarchy of the past. But some mechanisms for redressing past *group* inequities, "for leveling the playing field," can themselves appear to create new injustices for *individuals* in the present.

In 1978 *Bakke vs. University of California*, Davis brought the language of "reverse discrimination" into public dialogue when John Bakke, a White medical school applicant, was denied admission while minority and disadvantaged applicants were considered separately in the admissions process. In a split decision, the United States Supreme Court ruled that the use of race in admissions policies was acceptable, but not the use of "quotas," which was the label given to the separate minority admissions process. Conservative activists took up the antiquota language and have used it as a rallying cry against affirmative action programs ever since.

Affirmative action policies were dealt an even stronger blow in 1996, again in California, when Proposition 209 outlawed "discriminating against" or granting so-called preferential treatment to "any individual or group" in California on the basis of race (Hunt 2008). The consequences were immediate and drastic. The following year, for example, African American enrollments at the University of California, Los Angeles, dropped dramatically and have never fully recovered, going from 6.5 percent of the student body in 1995 to 2 percent in 2006. After instituting a "holistic admissions" approach in 2006—including evaluating students' academic records (grade point averages and test scores), along with personal data (written statements, family circumstances, student activities, etc.), extensive recruiting, and fundraising for scholarships—admissions increased but still have not reached the level of 1995 (Hunt 2008; Levine 2007).

After race-sensitive admissions were eliminated in Texas in *Hopwood v. Texas*, the flagship schools of University of Texas at Austin and Texas A & M faced a problem similar to that in California and pursued a different solution. In 1997, led largely by rural and racial minority legislators of color, the Texas legislature passed a *10 percent plan*, requiring that the top 10 percent of seniors in Texas public high schools be admitted to any state public university of their choice. This policy obviously created a path for top students from African American and Latino schools, as well as for students from rural districts, to make it into the state's best colleges. Under the plan, minority enrollments increased at the flagship schools, but still not to previous levels (Guinier and Torres 2002; Tienda and Niu 2004).

Later, some parents of children in the dozen or so highly competitive public "feeder schools" of the more than one thousand public high schools in the state mounted resistance to the 10-percent plan. They argued that their children were being unfairly "squeezed out" of top schools by less qualified top-10-percent students and that the policy was causing a "brain drain" from the state. Extensive research on the preferences, choices, admissions, and attendance of 13,803 high school seniors across the state, however, did not support these arguments. Students who left the state for their education were planning to do so anyway, and almost everyone who chose to stay in the state—from feeder schools and the top 10 percent—was admitted to one of their top two choices of schools, the overwhelming majority to their top choice (Gutfeld 2002; Tienda and Niu 2004). And the top-10-percenters performed as well as or better than peers entering UT Austin with SAT scores hundreds of points higher, raising even more questions about the purpose and function of high-stakes tests (Sacks 2007).

A more recent salvo in the fight to end affirmative action came again in California in 2003. As in the case of the California Proposition 209 and a similar Michigan referendum, the attack was led by conservative activist Ward Connerly and the American Civil Rights Institute, which he founded and headed. In 2003, the group put forth Proposition 54, designed to eliminate all racial data gathering—in public education, public contracting, or public employment—in the state of California (Pollack 2004). The measure was vehemently opposed by many groups who feared that the proposition would make tracking discrimination in housing, education, or other arenas impossible. The American Sociological Association (2003), for example, along with other professional associations, issued a statement on the continued need for collecting data and doing social scientific research on race. Even though Proposition 54 did not pass in California, the goal to eliminate affirmative action through lawsuits, ballot initiatives, and highly polarized political rhetoric continued to move from California and Texas to other states. Florida, Washington, and Michigan passed versions of Proposition 209, and in 2008, the measure was pushed in five more states. Three did not make it to the ballot, Colorado narrowly defeated the measure, and Nebraska passed it (Levine 2007).

These "color-blind" approaches to public policy represent aggressive attempts to eliminate recognition of groups and thereby our ability to track group injustices and to redress those injustices through public policy. These arguments can have popular appeal because advocates couch them neatly in the language of individual rights and equal treatment under the law. But the plaintiffs in the suits and the beneficiaries of the "color-blind" policies belie the appeals to justice because they have uniformly been privileged Whites, as the higher education cases demonstrate (Gutfeld 2002; Pollack 2004; Reskin 1998; Tienda and Niu 2004).

In recent years, class and economic inequality have also been the basis for political clashes over K-12 educational policy. Since the 1990s, for example, mostly rural, poor school districts have brought suit against their states to challenge school funding formulas that allocate resources to schools based on the property taxes raised in the school district. Such formulas benefit already rich school districts, particularly well-to-do suburban schools, and disadvantage poor rural and inner-city school districts with higher concentrations of racial minority students (Anyon 1997; Burkett 1998; Kozol 2005). And NCLB has created perhaps the greatest political conflict in recent times on many fronts: funding of the program and of poor schools, emphasis on high-stakes tests, requiring poor schools to compete to achieve accountability goals without the resources to do so, censuring schools that fail with threats of closing, and a voucher system that encourages students to leave poor-performing schools but does nothing to improve them (Meier and Wood 2004; Nicholson 2003; Schneider and Keesler 2007).

Massive disasters such as war or major hurricanes like Katrina provide a unique context, a blank slate if you will, to literally remake education from the ground up, and this context becomes fertile ground for public contests over *how* to remake schools (Klein 2007). After Hurricane Katrina, the City of New Orleans fired all of its public school teachers, reopened only a fraction of the former schools, and created most of them as charter schools—a move advocated by conservative leaders that supported their aims of privatizing public education. Ken Saltman summarizes the effort:

> A number of privatization schemes are being initiated through a process involving the dismantling of public schools followed by the opening of for-profit,

charter, and deregulated public schools. These enterprises typically despise teachers unions, are hostile to local democratic governance and oversight, and have an unquenchable thirst for "experiments," especially with the private sector. These initiatives are informed by right wing think tanks and business organizations. Four examples that typify back door privatization are: No Child Left Behind, Chicago's Renaissance 2010 project, educational rebuilding in Iraq, and educational rebuilding in New Orleans. (Saltman 2007, 3).

Significant opposition has characterized each of these examples, a fact that led teacher organizations nationwide to support President Obama and Democrats in the 2008 election.

Political conflicts have also arisen over state support for all-male military academies; male admissions to all-female colleges such as Mississippi University for Women, Texas Women's University, and Mills College; gender bias in the curriculum; and unequal allocation of resources to women and men in higher education, centered in Title IX gender equity legislation of 1972.

Education is also a critical arena for contests over the institution of compulsory heterosexuality—the political pervasiveness and dominance of heterosexual norms throughout all areas of the culture (see Rich 1993). Elected and appointed school board members around the country exert political power when deciding how family life and sexuality will be treated in the schools. These decisions are hotly contested, particularly as they relate to who can teach in the schools and what the curriculum will contain about sexuality—both heterosexuality and homosexuality—and the family. Are female-headed families to be treated as real families? What of gay and lesbian marriages, parents, families? Openly gay men and lesbians, particularly those who teach in elementary school, have also faced harassment and have lost their jobs (Carlson 1997; Eisenmenger 2002). Lynn Phillips and Michelle Fine report that many public school teachers are inhibited from critically discussing issues of sexuality:

> They are evaluated on the basis of "value-free" discourse that privileges and "naturalizes" chastity, marriage, and heterosexuality; that denigrates teen motherhood; and that hesitates to discuss abortion lest they be "leading" the young woman (as if *not mentioning* is not "leading"). (1992, 243)

As C. J. Pascoe argues, advocates of abstinence-only sex education programs rely on "the twin assumptions that American teens are too innocent to know about sexuality and too sexual to be trusted with information" (2007).

Perhaps nowhere is the attack on gays and lesbians and its connection with attacks on other oppressed groups more clearly laid out than in the political agendas of right-wing groups such as Phyllis Schlafly's Eagle Forum and Beverly LaHaye's Concerned Women of America (CWA). These groups oppose

- Sex education in schools
- Female access to all-male educational institutions
- National standards
- The "extremist" National Education Association

- Bilingual education
- Antidrug programs
- Multicultural curricula
- Gays and lesbians in the classroom

In her study of women's activism on the political right, Susan Marshall (1998) reports that the Eagle Forum told its members that sex education teaches children how to engage in sex and with what devices and that CWA advised its members that these programs "countenance pedophilia, tell innocent children to indulge in promiscuity, and show eight-year-olds how to use a condom."

Marshall summarizes the positions of these movements as follows:

> Homosexuality is the most heinous moral result of the sexual revolution, and the gay movement is perceived as a conspiracy—"a nationwide assault on the Body of Christ and the traditional family"—that is pushing to "take over our culture, step-by-step," infiltrating business, the media, the schools, and even churches. Borrowing an imagery from science fiction, one CWA "expert" advises that gays have devised a plan to breed a counterculture by marrying and having children, and homosexuals who do not participate in this eugenics experiment get revenge by recruiting children inside the schools. Needless to say, these organizations support state antigay constitutional amendments and proposed legislation to bar gay teachers from the classroom as well as the federal Defense of Marriage Act [which bars states from recognizing gay marriages] ; Marshall 1998, 169–170).[1]

In sum, power relations of dominance and subordination in education are exerted and contested in the political arena. Struggles are waged over access to education, the content of curricula, and the treatment of groups in school. The interrelated nature of race, class, gender, and sexuality systems is especially evident as groups seek through political processes to shape education and control dominant ideologies about every aspect of society, from family to sexuality, from religion to business.

Although schools are sites of oppression, they are also key sites of resistance to oppression. The relative isolation of poor and segregated schools often makes them powerful sites for developing a collective oppositional consciousness for protest movements. Many student leaders and participants in civil rights activism during the 1950s, 1960s, and 1970s were located in traditionally Black colleges, just as many activists in the American Indian movement developed a consciousness and resistance strategies from the segregated space of the reservation (Carlson 1997; Reyhner and Eder 2004; Robnett 1997).

Many groups have fought against oppression in schools:

---

[1]Although the positions represented in Marshall's work reflect those expressed by these groups in the 1990s, they still represent the groups' positions (see Concerned Women for America, available online from http://www.cwfa.org/cfi, accessed April 4, 2009; Eagle Forum, available online at http://www.eagleforum.org, accessed April 4, 2009).

- Native Americans against culturally biased and inferior education in reservation schools and state-sponsored boarding schools (Carlson 1997; Reyhner and Eder 2004)
- Asian Americans and Jews against quotas in higher education (Karabel 2005)
- Latinos for bilingual education and against inferior education in bilingual classes (Callahan 2005; Crosnoe 2005; Gitlin et al. 2003)
- Women and people of color against exclusion from math and science tracks (Corbett et al. 2008; DeWelde et al. 2007; AAUW 2004)
- Gays and lesbians against the silencing of homosexuality in curricula and the oppression of gay teachers and students (Carlson 1997; Cho et al. 2004; Eisenmenger 2002; GLSEN 2008)

Both European immigrants and African Americans have emphasized education as a primary mechanism for uplifting their ethnic or racial groups. Lynn Johnson, for example, was clearly selected for mobility by her community and supported in whatever way necessary to see that she succeeded—from demanding that she attend school while pregnant to paying for her SAT tests. Lynn was chosen by her teachers and other community leaders to represent the African American community in Memphis as one of the first group to attend a local all-White, private liberal arts college. Her good performance was seen as a way of contradicting negative stereotypes about Black ability, as well as of producing a professional who would be expected to give something back to the Black community later. Lynn did become a successful professional with a strong sense of commitment to the African American community and to supporting others in their quest for fair treatment and upward mobility.

Economic Power and Education

The political struggle over educational policy is so intense in part because education is the primary determinant of income, providing access to good jobs, and is the key to upward mobility, to passing on middle-class standing, and to allowing intergenerational escapes from poverty (McNamee and Miller 2004). At the same time, however, because graduates are dependent on available jobs for employment, increasing the educational attainment levels of the population has not eliminated poverty. In the past thirty years, as middle-class employment opportunities have declined, employers have responded by raising the educational requirements for the same jobs. Jobs that once required a bachelor's degree, such as public school teacher, increasingly require some graduate work, if not a master's degree. And jobs that once required a high school diploma, such as sales representative, now often require a college degree (Bills 2003; Brown 1995, 2001; Van de Werfhorst and Andersen 2005).

Racial segregation of schools, consistently very high for Blacks and Hispanics, has a direct economic impact on wages and jobs. Black and Hispanics who attend racially isolated schools tend to obtain lower-paying jobs than Whites, and those jobs tend to be in racially isolated sectors of the labor force (Boozer, Krueger, and Wolkon1992; Eaton 2001; Wells et al. 2004). Desegregated schooling reduces racial differences in educational and occupational attainment and promotes interracial contact. African Americans who attend integrated elementary and high schools are more likely to

- Attend and persist in integrated colleges
- Enter scientific and business occupations
- Work in integrated organizations
- Work and socialize with White people
- Live in integrated neighborhoods (Dawkins and Braddock 1994; Eaton 2001; Wells et al. 2004)

But some African American students also note the downsides of schooling in desegregated environments outside their own communities: racial discrimination, assumptions made by Whites about their families and backgrounds, and a sense of disconnection from their own communities (Eaton 2001).

If anything is clear, it is that social class shapes both students' place in the educational system and their opportunities for employment. Working-class and poor students, educated differently and lacking the economic and social resources of their middle-class counterparts, fare less well in the labor market. Gender and racial discrimination have some of their greatest impacts on women and racial ethnic people by blocking their entry into the middle classes and thus relegating them in greater proportions than White men to the working classes, where they will be educated differently and prepared for working-class occupations.

The labor market is even more segregated along gender than along race and class lines, and occupational segregation (i.e., of women into low-paying, female-dominated occupations) is the primary explanation for the persistent gap in the earnings of women and men (McGuire and Reskin 1993, Reskin 1998). One process implicated in the sex segregation of the labor force is the differing preparation for the workforce that boys and girls and women and men receive in their education. Feminist scholars and national science organizations such as the National Academy of Sciences and the National Science Foundation have, for example, established initiatives to understand and to reverse the gross underrepresentation of women, especially women of color, in careers in science, mathematics, and engineering. The gender gap in these fields contributes not only to a wage gap but also to intellectual bias in the fields (AAUW 2004, 2007; Corbett, Hill, and St. Rose 2008; De Welde, Laursen, and Thiry 2007; National Research Council 1993, 1996; National Science Foundation 2007, 2009).

In the early 1990s, the American Association of University Women commissioned a review of more than one thousand articles and studies on girls and K-12 education. Published in 1992, *How Schools Shortchange Girls* brought national attention to its extensive findings, including that the limited participation of women in careers in science, mathematics, and engineering is linked to processes that take hold by junior high school, when girls become discouraged in the pursuit of these subjects, come to see themselves as inadequate, and are steered toward female-dominated occupations. In contrast, both girls and boys who like math and science have higher self-esteem, are more confident about their appearance, worry less about others liking them, aspire to professions, and hold on more strongly to their career goals. Discouraging girls and steering them away from these pursuits have psychological, as well as career, impacts. The AAUW recommended that girls must be educated and encouraged to understand that mathematics and science are important and relevant to their lives and must be supported in pursuing education and employment in these areas (AAUW 1992).

Follow-up studies—*Gender Gaps: Where Our Schools Still Fail Our Children* (AAUW 1999) and *Under the Microscope: A Decade of Gender Equity Projects in the Sciences* (AAUW 2004)—assessed programs and needs at the beginning of the twenty-first century. They found that great progress had been made: Innumerable programs debunked myths and stereotypes about the involvement of girls in math and science, and course enrollments and performance were now even. Computer science remained the exception: Early gender inequities in computer interest, use, and skills remained, and the proportion of girls pursuing degrees in computer science has actually declined since the mid-1980s (AAUW 1999, 2004; DeWelde, Laursen, and Thiry 2007; National Science Foundation 2007). If this gap persists, it could become enormously significant in promoting economic gender, race, and class gaps, because computer technology is one of the most rapidly spreading educational tools and sources of employment, including eight of the top ten fastest growing occupations today (Hecker 2001). Perhaps more significantly, the work of computer scientists in structuring the Internet is reshaping the way that learning is taking place in and out of schools and the way that the majority of people in the United States conduct their work every day. Having women, people of color, the poor and working classes left behind in this technological revolution could have a widespread and long-lasting impact in reinforcing and solidifying race, class, and gender systems of inequality.

As in other realms, the effect of sexuality on jobs is more difficult to assess, in part because so many gays, lesbians, bisexuals, and transgender people hide their sexuality. They fear discrimination, including the loss of jobs, if their sexual orientation becomes known. This fear is especially true for people who deal with young children, such as schoolteachers and child care workers (Button, Rienzo and Wald 1997; Carlson 1997). Still, some research documents the negative effects on wages of sexual orientation discrimination (Badgett 1995; Badgett, Ramos, and Sears 2008).

Ideological Power and Education

The realm of ideas is perhaps most central to the struggle for power in education. As an institution organized to create and promote the ideas that rationalize, justify, and explain the workings of the dominant social order and to prepare people to function within it, education is a critical locus in the struggle of groups to define themselves and to assert their value and worth. Within schools, these struggles are often critically fought over the content of the curriculum.

The Curriculum Some of the most bitter struggles have been and continue to be over the content of education—what we teach people, particularly what we teach about race, class, gender, and sexuality. Debates over multicultural and feminist content in curricula have been heated ever since the 1960s, when the civil rights, women's rights, and gay rights movements began to push for the revision of basic texts to include the histories and experiences of people of color, women, and gays and lesbians (see, for example, Lerner 1976; Minnich, O'Barr, and Rosenfeld 1988; Schuster and Van Dyne 1984). In the 1980s and 1990s, neoconservative politicians and intellectuals such as William Bennett, Allan Bloom (1988), Dinesh D'Souza (1991), and others began to develop an intellectual justification for maintaining the traditional curriculum and for rejecting the new histories and texts as divisive and threatening to the fundamental values of democratic capitalism. They defend the Western philosophical and literary tradition as superior and "universal in scope" and test scores as the "common index for all who seek to improve themselves, regardless of race, sex, or background" (D'Souza 1991, 255). Equating test scores with achievement and ignoring the dominant culture biases in standardized tests, D'Souza writes:

> High standards do not discriminate against anyone except those who fail to meet them. Such discrimination is entirely just and ought not to be blamed for our individual differences. (1991, 250)

Similarly, in advocating for his NCLB legislation, President Bush repeatedly argued that his program was intended to eliminate "the soft bigotry of low expectations," which presumably characterized those who advocated reforms not solely or primarily based in raising scores on standardized tests (Kozol 2005). Williamson M. Evers, for example, a member of President Bush's committee to oversee federal education research, stated that a list of high-flying schools—schools with significant numbers of minority and low-income children who tested high on standardized exams—"had proved that it was 'racist nonsense' to deny that accountability alone could generate equal outcomes for poor and middle-class students" (quoted in Rothstein 2002).

In this view of education

- Test scores are equated with achievement
- Abstract and arbitrary achievement standards are seen as a legitimate basis of discrimination in democratic capitalism
- Failure is the fault of the individual who does not achieve
- Redressing systemic biases that produce group "failures" (e.g., lower test scores of subordinate racial and economic groups) violates the tenets of democratic capitalism

These arguments, often put forth to end affirmative action, recall the Americanization movement of the early twentieth century, which proposed a curriculum that would create a unified America out of a diverse immigrant population by teaching immigrants the superior values, interests, and beliefs of middle-class,

Anglo-Saxon, patriarchal, heterosexual culture and that justified this curriculum in part with the newly created IQ test.

At stake in these debates is, among other things, what schools teach and students learn about

- Both dominant and subordinate groups in society
- The American Dream—why some groups get ahead while others lag behind in key societal resources
- Their individual abilities and the abilities of others like them in the race, class, gender, and sexual hierarchies

The prevalence of these attacks on multicultural, gay-positive, feminist curricula indicates that these curricula pose real challenges to dominant ideologies about who should be included at the center of our curricula and what should be taught about them. The new perspectives have been attacked because they have, in fact, taken hold and are reshaping what students expect and what large segments of the population want in education today. As our population becomes increasingly diverse, we must become increasingly aware of both the extent of diversity and the necessity for citizens to understand diversity and to be able to work with people who have different backgrounds, worldviews, lifestyles, values, and goals. In an increasingly global economy, major businesses and corporations need workers who can communicate and work with people from very different cultural backgrounds. The race, class, gender, and sexuality segregation of schools mitigates against this understanding, but critical gay, multicultural, and feminist curricula facilitate it.

In sum, macro institutional power relations of oppression and resistance in the political, economic, and ideological domains generate, challenge, and transform race, class, gender, and sexual inequality. As an ideological institution charged with equipping people with the knowledge, skills, and orientation to function as citizens, education becomes a key site of political and economic contests over access to quality schooling, the content of the curricula, and the treatment that youths of different race, class, gender, and sexuality groups receive in schools.

MICRO SOCIAL-PSYCHOLOGICAL POWER RELATIONS

Political, economic, and ideological domains of oppression are reproduced and transformed when individuals act out and resist race, class, gender, and sexuality hierarchies as they go about their lives every day, everywhere. In schools, these everyday experiences of domination, oppression, and resistance shape the way that students and teachers interact with and what they expect from one another.

What happens in classrooms? How do young people and their teachers interact every day? How do young people's experiences in school influence their self-esteem, their aspirations and dreams, their self-confidence, their identity, their views of and relationships to others?

When we focus on macro systemic processes, such as tracking and school segregation, that structure different life experiences, it is difficult to imagine that anyone could overcome or challenge such powerful structural forces. Yet these systems, although pervasive, are neither exact nor totally determining: They are social constructions. And individuals face these structures in many different ways, with different personal and social resources. Not all children who are poor, working class, children of color, girls, or gay, lesbian, bisexual, or transgender (GLBT) fail, drop out of school, get tracked in lower tracks, get pregnant, become drug addicts, or are destined to work in low-paying jobs.

Lynn Johnson grew up in public housing projects with six brothers and sisters and was a teenage mother whose own mother was on welfare. Yet her life was full of love, appreciation, and support both in her family and in her segregated public high school. She also received the academic training and encouragement she needed to succeed in college. Unlike Lynn, Theo Wilson was in a low track of his desegregated high school, his mother is a drug addict, his father had recently died, and he's now struggling with his sexuality and gender expression. Theo certainly faces obstacles to developing a positive academic and sexual identity that Lynn did not face. But, like Lynn, he is seeking out support where he can find it and is developing strong ties with Marie and Bill, who each support his healthy development.

How do we experience race, class, gender, and sexuality hierarchies in our everyday lives? Just as there are observable macro systems and trends, there are observable micro patterns of interaction—ways of dealing, expectations, behaviors—that are shaped by race, class, gender, and sexuality and that help to reproduce and/or challenge those hierarchies. In the educational realm these patterns of interaction begin as early as preschool and continue throughout all educational levels.

Preschool

Valerie Polakow (1993) documents gross inequities in the way that the poor children of single mothers are treated in public preschool programs. Classrooms can be a place of promise or of condemnation, and the children of poor women are often condemned, labeled "at risk," and subjected to exclusion, humiliation, and neglect. Poor children, especially children of color, are more often assigned one of a growing list of "at-risk" labels: language impaired (often used for children speaking nonstandard English), immature, Special Ed, ADD (attention-deficit disorder), ADHD (attention-deficit hyperactivity disorder), undisciplined, free lunchers, trailer-park kids, low skilled, LD (learning disabled), and socially maladjusted. Teachers often assign these labels based on their perceptions of the children's parents, act differently toward the children because of the label, and signal to the other children the "otherness" of the selected child (see also Diamond, Randolph, and Spillane 2004; Kozol 2005).

Like the work of Maccoby (1988, 2000), who demonstrated children's complex understandings of gender at very early ages, research by Debra Van Ausdale and Joe Feagin (1996) demonstrates that children as young as three years old use racial ethnic concepts to exclude others, to include others and teach them about racial ethnic identities, to define themselves and others, and to control others.

Conducting observations in preschool and day care programs, they recount the following illustrations of the use of racial ethnic concepts to exclude. In one encounter, Elizabeth, a three-and-a-half-year-old Chinese American girl, asked if she could play with Rita (3½, White/Latina) and Sarah (4, White), who were pretending to bake muffins and had all the tins:

> Rita shakes her head vigorously, saying: "No, only people who can speak Spanish can come in."
> Elizabeth frowns and says: "I can come in."
> Rita counters: "Can you speak Spanish?"
> Elizabeth shakes her head no and Rita reports: "Well, then you aren't allowed in."
> (Van Ausdale and Feagin 1996, 781)

In other encounters Van Ausdale and Feagin observed a White girl (four years old) tell a Chinese American girl (three years old) that she could not pull a wagon because "Only *White Americans* can pull this wagon." And in a third interaction, a four-year-old White girl tells a four-year-old Black boy that he could not possibly own a White bunny rabbit because "Blacks can't have Whites" (1996, 787).

In sum, teachers, parents, and even preschool peers hold different expectations for children and treat them differently depending on their own and their parents' locations in race, class, gender, and sexuality hierarchies. As early as preschool, children have learned that these are labels used to include and exclude, to define themselves, and to control others.

First, Second, and Third Grades

Although social scientists have paid much less attention to the race, class, gender, and sexuality sorting and ranking processes in preschool and the early grades than they have to middle and high school, Entwisle and colleagues (1997) review research demonstrating that race, class, and gender power relations are well established in the first grade. When children enter the first grade, parents and teachers tend to see children more in the context of their families' social location and less in terms of their potential. When parents are unemployed, for example, teachers hold lower expectations for their children, value the children's education less, and begin to view the children as having low ability. Positive ratings by teachers of how students "fit in" based on assessments of their classroom behavior in the first grade leads children to do well in the first year.

These first-grade ratings also affect the gains students make in the fourth grade more than the ratings of the fourth-grade teacher do, because the cumulative nature of the curriculum makes it hard for a child to achieve at a high level in the fourth grade without having achieved at a high level in earlier grades. This cumulative decline occurs even for students entering the first grade as high achievers on standardized tests (Wyner, Bridgeland, and Diiulio 2007). Males, students of color, and low-socioeconomic-status students more often fail or are entered into special education in elementary school, and these same children are later more likely to drop out of high school (Children's Defense Fund 2005; Entwisle, Alexander, and Olson 1997; KewalRamani et al. 2007; Laird et al. 2007). Thus the first grade is critical for setting the stage for later school performance, for academic self-concept, and for self-esteem. When children enter first grade, they continue to learn about and to act on their understandings of the social placement of children of various race, class, and gender groups.

Polakow (1993), for example, cites the cases of Tim, a nine-year-old White boy from a homeless family, and Heather, a seven-year-old White "trailer park kid." During the school year, Tim lived with his mother and sister in, variously, a truck, a shelter, a trailer, and a welfare motel. Children teased him because of his worn and unkempt clothes, and they picked up on the negative attitude of the teacher. Tim described how he felt:

> They think 'cos I haven't got no home that I haven't got nothing inside of me—they won't play with me—they won't be a buddy when we go on trips either and no kids will be my friends.... Also they all think I'm so dumb and I hate this school, and Mrs. Devon keeps saying she got no time when I ask her things. (Polakow 1993, 145)

Heather was defined by the teacher as a "problem" second grader. When Polakow visited, Heather's desk was in the hallway, and other children were not allowed to talk to her nor she to them. When asked what Heather had done, the teacher, Mrs. Mack, replied:

> The child just does not know the difference between right and wrong—she absolutely does not belong in a *normal* classroom with *normal* children.... I've given up on this child—she's socially dysfunctional—three times now we've caught her stealing free lunch and storing it in her desk to take home. (Polakow1993, 138)

Polakow learned that Heather had been taking lunches home on Fridays to have something to eat over the weekend. Mrs. Mack tried repeatedly to get Heather removed from her classroom, claiming Heather is learning disabled and emotionally impaired. Heather was eventually assigned to special education, which removed her from the classroom several times a day for remedial activities and made it impossible for her to finish her regular classroom assignments. As a result, she was said to have "poor work habits."

The overall orientation of teachers of poor children in these classrooms was toward containment and regulation: drilling children to produce the correct responses, regulating their imaginations, presenting them with tasks to complete rather than with opportunities to learn. Classrooms were rigidly segregated by ability and gender, with "out of order" children, often young Black boys from poor families, becoming classroom "deviants" subjected to disciplinary measures and exclusion and given limited views of their potential (see also Kozol 2005).

In an observational study of first and second graders in working-class, desegregated classrooms (30 to 90 percent Black), Linda Grant (1994) documented patterns of race and gender interaction. Focusing on the special roles played by Black girls in desegregated classrooms, Grant reports that teachers encouraged and assessed Black girls most positively in social rather than in academic roles. Perceived as intellectually average—equal to White boys, below White girls, and above Black boys—most were tracked in the middle or lower tracks. Even though rated equal to White boys, Black girls were seen by teachers as having less promise because White boys were defined as immature whereas Black girls were regarded as already mature socially and thus not as likely to improve academically.

Grant (1994) identified two social roles, the "helper" and the "enforcer," that were prevalent among Black girls. One social role, the "go-between," was occupied solely by Black girls. Although teachers sometimes punished them for assuming these roles, the teachers ultimately reinforced the behavior of these students because they helped to maintain order, peace, and social integration in the classrooms.

Helpers Black girls sought teacher attention and student respect by acting as helpers (e.g., locating lost materials, comforting emotionally distressed children, and keeping things tidy) One teacher even referred to a helper as "our little housekeeper." As Joyce Ladner (1972) notes, Black girls are often given adult responsibilities in the home and carry these over into the school where they are reinforced, even though the girls are occasionally reprimanded by teachers.

Enforcers Some Black girls urged peers to follow school rules in the teacher's absence. Grant (1994, 47) describes one such situation when the teacher left the room after asking the students to stay seated and be quiet:

> [S]everal students left their seats. When Gerald (White) walked past Pamela (Black), Pamela rose, placed her hands on his shoulders, gently kicked the back of his legs, told him to "move it," and pushed him several feet back to his desk. She then pointed a finger at Steven (Black) and threatened: "You're next." Steven quickly took his seat. She then shook her head sternly at Renee (White), who had started to rise but sat down in response to Pamela's action. (1994, 47)

The effectiveness of Black girls in this role shows that they have substantial influence with diverse peer groups.

Go-Between The most complex role, assumed only by Black girls, was as negotiator of deals and relationships between students and teachers and between other students. Consider the following interaction in which a go-between

- Identified one student as missing a shoelace, then asked a second student for an extra but came up empty
- Asked the teacher to send yet a third student (already on her way out) to another teacher's classroom to ask for a shoelace
- Thanked the student when she returned with the shoelace, because the teacher did not
- Asked a fourth student to pick up his coat from the floor
- Helped a fifth student with a reading word

- Got jelly beans from a sixth student and shared them with a seventh student

In all, this child interacted with the teacher and one-third of the class in one 10-minute period, with almost all of the interactions outside the teacher's awareness.

These roles, which require an understanding of the norms in different groups and a willingness to take personal risks for social harmony, begin to prepare Black girls for adult roles in service to others (e.g., as nurse's aides or teacher's aides, jobs in which Black women are overrepresented). Even though Black girls had the most diverse and extensive peer ties of any group, teachers responded by encouraging these social skills among the Black girls but simultaneously failed to encourage their academic interests and pursuits to the same degree that they did with White girls and even with boys. In contrast, Grant notes that Black girls in all-Black schools tend to be academic leaders and to be encouraged in academic pursuits.

As Grant (1994) and Polakow (1993) document, teachers' expectations for students are shaped by the race and gender of the students and powerfully influence students' behavior. Interestingly, the patterns of race-gender interaction (e.g., Black girls as go betweens) and teacher expectations (Black girls for social, not academic, achievement) occurred in the classrooms of both Black and White teachers.

Karl Alexander, Doris Entwisle, and Maxine Thompson (1987) explored the impact of teachers' backgrounds on their expectations and examined achievement among first graders. During this critical period of transition to school, teachers have a tremendous impact—both on how students will adjust and on how they will perform. Teachers' impressions of students' academic potential at this crucial entry point are often based on superficial and inappropriate cues, such as dress, style, language, and deportment. Sorting students into ability groups begins, and chronic underachievement starts early. And once started, it is difficult to reverse.

The researchers hypothesized that teachers from low socioeconomic backgrounds would be less likely to read cues such as "different" style of dress and language usage as fundamental failings because these cues would be familiar. They found indeed that teachers from high socioeconomic status backgrounds, both Black and White

- Perceived African American and low-status youngsters as relatively lacking in the qualities of personal maturity that make for a good student
- Held lower performance expectations for them
- Evaluated the school climate less positively (i.e., less pleasant and rewarding, more tense and frustrating) when working primarily with low-status students

One result is that Black and lower-status students who entered first grade with the same test scores as their White and high-status classmates had fallen well behind by year's end. The researchers also found that boys received worse conduct grades but that their academic grades were no worse. Later in the education process, racial ethnic youths, especially boys, are more often placed in lower tracks for nonacademic reasons of discipline.

Fourth, Fifth, and Sixth Grades

Many of the patterns of interaction begun in the early years are reinforced and elaborated as children grow older, and other issues, such as sexuality, develop and begin to shape race, class, gender, and sexuality dynamics. Barrie Thorne (1993) studied gender interactions in fourth, fifth, and sixth grades in a public working-class school and also found that race and class were related to student placement in ability groupings and that students were segregated by gender for many activities (e.g., seating arrangements, lines, lunch tables, and playgrounds).

Power differences were exhibited, especially in these segregated settings, for example, when boys had ten times more space on the playground and were more likely to interrupt girls' activities and space and to treat the space as "contaminating." But Thorne also points out that these relationships were fluid: They varied by location and activity, and some students crossed the gender borders. Interactions in schools were more segregated than in neighborhoods and more segregated on the school playground than in the classrooms: That is, schools are important sites for the reproduction of gender inequality.

Thorne's work is important because she points out that the "different cultures" research[2] exaggerates the differences and thus reinforces the hegemonic view of gender as oppositional dualisms attached to individuals—the belief that boys' groups are large, public, hierarchical, and competitive, whereas girls' groups are small, private, cooperative, and focused on relationships and intimacy. Instead, Thorne contends that gender dynamics are much more fluid than these oppositional images that come from research on White middle-class girls suggest. Thorne observed frequent "borderwork" activities—girls playing with boys, being competitive, and using insults and threats. She also noted that Black girls were marginalized more often than other groups and played the border-crossing role more often.

Jessie, for example, was the only African American in her class and was the most active and adept student at moving between boy and girl groups, even on the playground, where segregation was greatest. Her teacher once observed, "Jessie wants action with both groups," and occasionally someone would remark that the class has a "girls' side" and a "boys' side," "except for Jessie." Of Jessie, Thorne observes:

---

[2]See Carol Gilligan, Nona Lyons, and Trudy Hanmer, eds., *Making Connections: The Relational Worlds of Adolescent Girls at Emma Willard School* (Cambridge: Harvard University Press, 1990); and Mary Pipher, *Reviving Ophelia: Saving the Selves of Adolescent Girls* (New York: Putnam, 1994). Recent variations on these arguments have been made largely as rationales for single-sex schooling, particularly of boys (cf. Corbett, Hill, and St. Rose 2008; Weil 2008).

> During the part of the year when she had a desk with the girls, Jessie often went to the boys' side of the room to join an informal cluster or to find a spelling partner. Only one other girl, Tracy, ever practiced spelling with a boy. Jessie kept a continual eye on happenings in both sides of the room. One day when Miss Bailey was moving from student to student, checking a spelling test, Jessie, who was then sitting with the girls, whispered loudly, "Kevin got his all right; me and him got one hundred." Making eye contact with John from across the room, she added, "I was watching you make mistakes." (Thorne 1993, 128)

Jessie's behavior looks very much like the go-between identified by Grant and fore-shadows the "outsider within" status identified by Patricia Hill Collins (2000) as the unique social position occupied by adult Black women. A "peculiar marginality," this role provides Black women with a distinct view of the contradictions between the dominant group's actions and ideologies and a unique standpoint on self and society. This peculiar marginality is created not only in adult work roles such as domestic worker but also in the social roles that Black girls play in early school settings.

As children grow older, Thorne notes that boys receive greater sanctions for crossing boundaries than do girls, who have much more latitude to play multiple roles before adolescence. As children approach adolescence, however, the forceful intrusion of the system of compulsory heterosexuality begins to take precedence in gender interactions. The segregation of boys and girls increases, and by the fifth grade terms such as "sissy," "fag," and "faggot" are serious insults used to enforce heterosexual norms. Focusing on girls' bodies and changes, sex education defines girls in terms of sexuality.

Junior High School and High School

As girls enter adolescence (twelve to fourteen years old), they have already begun to develop

- Higher rates of depression
- Lower self-esteem
- More negative images of their own bodies
- Declining academic performance in science and math
- A social position that is increasingly derived from their relationships to boys

The "decline" happens for all girls but more so for White and Hispanic girls than for African American girls, whose overall, although not academic, self-esteem is higher than that of Whites to begin with (AAUW 1991, 1994, 1999).

Research in the 1990s focused extensively on the differential treatment of boys and girls in classrooms. Initially reported by the AAUW in *How Schools Short-change Girls* (1992) and reiterated in follow-up studies *Gender Gaps* (1999) and *Where the Girls Are: The Facts About Gender Equity in Education* (Corbett, Hill, and St. Rose 2008), girls, relative to boys, received

- Less teacher attention
- Less complex, challenging interaction with their teachers
- Less constructive feedback from teachers
- Less wait time on their responses (time to respond once called on)

In addition, gender bias in teacher-student interaction was greater in science and math than in other subject areas (AAUW 1992, 1999; Corbett, Hill, and St. Rose 2008).

Young people struggling to understand and come to terms with their sexuality, particularly young people who are gay, lesbian, bisexual, or transgendered, have few affirming markers about what they feel and think and are disciplined into dress and manners considered gender appropriate (Morris 2005; Pascoe 2007). Official school policies across the country on homosexuality are much like the military's "don't ask, don't tell"—official silence about the subject and about the sexual orientations of teachers and students. So even gay teachers often studiously avoid discussing homosexuality when it comes up in class, leaving gay youths feeling isolated and devalued. It is estimated that GLBT youths are more than twice as likely to attempt suicide and are more likely to suffer from depression, to abuse drugs, to drop out of school, and to become homeless (Poirer et al. 2008). Because the most visible gay people in society—as portrayed in the media and in the public political arena—are White, middle-class men, adolescence is especially hard for gay working-class and racial ethnic youths and for young lesbians. Some conservative forces in minority communities have even used this visibility to portray homosexuality as a White issue (Collins 2004).

In junior high school and high school, ability group tracking is pervasive and is highly correlated with race and class. And although it is possible to change tracks, as many students do, racial ethnic and low socioeconomic status students are most likely to drop to lower tracks, not to jump to higher tracks (Hallinan 1995; Heck, Price, and Thomas 2004). Think of Theo and Lynn, tracked differently. Theo has tremendous obstacles to overcome even to make it to college: lack of academic credits, lack of readiness for the SATs, and his own sense of having few options. His situation is a stark contrast to Lynn's: Tracked for mobility and encouraged by teachers, she feels she can do most anything she wants in life.

Comments from high school students in Jeannie Oakes's (1985) study reveal these different attitudes and knowledge bases in tracks. Here, we can begin to see the longer range effects of the processes described among much younger children. When asked about the most important thing they have learned or done so far in class, these students replied:

- I want to be a lawyer and debate has taught me to dig for answers and get involved. I can express myself. (high-track English)
- How to present myself orally and how to listen and to think quick. (high-track English)
- To understand concepts and ideas and experiment with them. Also to work independently. (high-track science).

- To behave in class. (low-track English)
- I learned about being quiet when the teacher is talking. (low-track social studies)
- I have learned that I should do my questions for the book when he asks me to. (low-track science)(Oakes, 1985, 86–9)

In sum, classrooms are powerful settings where teacher expectations, specific curricula, and students' interactions with one another create and reinforce race, class, gender, and sexuality hierarchies every day. In subtle and not so subtle ways, young people are treated differently across race, class, gender, and sexuality and are taught to think about and to treat each other unequally as well.

SIMULTANEOUSLY EXPRESSED

Macro systems of race, class, gender, and sexuality operate simultaneously, and individuals experience them in their own lives all at once. Theo Wilson is African American, male, and working class and is unsure about his sexual identity. Lynn Johnson is African American, female, middle class but raised in the working class, and heterosexual. All of these dimensions form critical aspects of their lives and identities.

Marie and Bill have been tutoring Theo to help him to develop skills, to get a better education, to have more life options. Marie saw herself as teaching writing to a Black working-class teenage boy who was struggling in school in a low track. She never expected the phone call she got from Theo to discuss his gender expression and his sexuality. Yet Theo's worldview, the issues he confronts and the sense he develops of himself, are shaped all at once by the many realities of his life that include his sexual orientation and gender expression, as well as his race, class, age, and urban home.

Lynn Johnson is older than Theo, and some things are clear to her: She did succeed in the education system and in the working world. She has a strongly positive sense of herself that was shaped in her development as a working-class African American girl in a segregated community in the 1960s and 1970s. She was pregnant at age sixteen, and had she been White or Latina, the community response to her pregnancy might have been different. But because Lynn's gendered heterosexual experience of pregnancy took place in a racial context in which the African American community was focused on racial uplift through education, Lynn was encouraged and supported in continuing in school.

As we look at these lives, it is clear that the intersections of race, class, gender, and sexuality are at play all the time. Yet most of the research and writing about these dimensions addresses only one, or sometimes two, of them but rarely more than two at once. So we must bring our understanding of the complexities of race, class, gender, and sexuality to our reading of others' research and to our own analyses of social life. In any analysis we should ask the following:

- What was left out?
- What difference does the omission make?
- What would change if it were included?

Think back to the observation made about Elizabeth, the Chinese American girl who was excluded from baking with her schoolmates because she could not speak Spanish. Van Ausdale and Feagin's analysis (1996) focused on race. But we can ask: What is the significance of the fact that the racial exclusion took place in a gendered activity? The girls were pretending to bake. This dimension was not considered in the study, but these girls were practicing racial exclusion and developing gender identities simultaneously.

Attending to these simultaneous dynamics enables us to address different issues. A common contention in political analyses, for example, is that women, oppressed by gender, are or should be more empathetic to others and more socially active in redressing other oppressions, such as racism, classism, or homophobia. But attending to gender in Van Ausdale and Feagin's racial analysis would not lead to that conclusion. Quite the contrary, these young girls are learning racial exclusion while they are learning to play traditional female roles. This coexistence is further borne out by Kathleen Blee's research on women in Ku Klux Klan (1991) and on modern right-wing movements (1998).

We might also ask:

- What of social class? Would upper-class girls have been pretending to bake?
- What if a White, non-Spanish-speaking boy and not Elizabeth had been the one to ask to enter the game. Would he have been excluded? Called a sissy?

As we hypothesize answers to these questions, we can see that all of the dimensions, some foregrounded and some backgrounded, operate in every situation.

IMPLICATIONS FOR ACTIVISM AND SOCIAL JUSTICE

What will it take to seriously challenge the system of education as a primary site for the reproduction of race, class, gender, and sexuality hierarchies? Thinking first of the micro realities of the lives of Lynn Johnson and Theo Wilson, some of the implications for social activism become clear. Both Theo and Lynn came of age in segregated African American communities, Theo in the Northeast in the late twentieth and early twenty-first centuries, Lynn in the South in the 1960s and 1970s. Poor African American girls have always needed strong supports to attain an education in a society organized to deny their worth, intelligence, and access to knowledge. Over the past century, African American civil society resisted this oppression in many ways, perhaps most significantly by emphasizing education as a means of racial uplift and as a form of resistance to oppression and by organizing and functioning in ways to make education happen not only for Black but also for all oppressed peoples. When Lynn Johnson was growing up, she had access to the full benefit of that African American tradition; she was valued for her intelligence, not just allowed but encouraged to remain in school after she became pregnant, funded to take the ACT, and guided in the curriculum and grooming she needed to be prepared to become one of the people who desegregated higher education institutions across the country in the 1960s.

By the 1990s, when Theo and other poor African American youths across the country entered high school, the Black civil society that supported Lynn had undergone dramatic changes. Shifts in the global economy, the denial of the deeply entrenched racial practices in the United States, and the ubiquity of the color-blind ideology have fostered major changes (Bonilla-Silva 2003; Winant 2000, 2001). Although the Black middle class has increased dramatically, poor African Americans are increasingly concentrated in racially segregated inner-city neighborhoods, a shift that fostered the breakup of community organization, crumbling family structures, unemployment, gangs, drugs, and other social problems (Kozol 2005; Patillo 2008; Thompson-Miller and Feagin 2007). Consequently, Collins (1998, 31) argues, "the structures and experience of Black poverty have radically changed." What this change meant for Theo was that the resources available to Lynn—the stable families around her own, community members able to foster her mobility financially and intellectually, were not there for Theo. Theo and his father continued to look for supports for Theo, but they could not find them in the traditional places. Instead, they found them in an outreach program run by White professors from an urban branch campus.

These stories, taken in combination, point to the kinds of support that poor women and men of color need to succeed, and they caution us that these needs cannot be met in the same ways today that they were thirty years ago. If the family and community network cannot provide what youths need to succeed, we need programs in place that can.

Scholars whose work is discussed in this chapter look closely at the harsh truths of life structured by the inequalities of race, class, gender, and sexuality—not at the dream but at the reality. Yet they undertake their research out of a desire for social change, to find ways to make a more humane and egalitarian social order. In the process of looking closely at and precisely describing the ways that inequality operates, they develop specific ideas about ways to promote inclusive and egalitarian social ideals and specific ideas for educational reform.

These researchers also develop hope, a hope that arises out of the concrete struggles currently being waged by dispossessed groups for freedom, equity, and social justice in U.S. education. As long as the state remains so heavily influenced by economic elites who benefit from social inequalities, the hope for serious reform must come from these social movements of the dispossessed. Most of these authors draw some conclusions about the current condition of education in the United States and recommend educational reforms that their research suggests would reduce inequalities and promote a more inclusive educational system and society. They also look to social movements as a necessary pressure to having the reforms implemented (Anyon 1997; Carlson 1997; Neill 2004 Sacks 2007).

Many Americans, for example, clearly believed that President Obama's 2008 election would bring significant reforms, and they organized and worked to make it happen. Fundamentally altering the unequal distribution of our society's resources both inside and outside of government is an enormous challenge, and time will tell whether the mobilization for change in 2008 persists. Much activity has surrounded the President's first major legislative proposal—his $800 billion economic recovery package, the largest in the history of the United States, aimed at beginning to bring the country out of its deep recession and what for many was already a depression. Within that bill, President Obama and the newly empowered Democrats in the House (no Republican voted for the bill) included significant new funding for education and infrastructure development. The inclusion of funds for education, along with those for other social programs (health care, unemployment benefits, etc.) provided some of the rationale for Republican opposition to the bill—on the assumption that social programs do not provide the best way "to get the economy moving again."

Yet the recognition of a history of deeply entrenched inequalities and their devastating impact on education was never clearer than in a clause inserted into the 647-page recovery bill by Representative James Clyburn of South Carolina, the powerful house Democratic whip. Clyburn crafted a clause requiring that "at least 10 percent of all rural-development funds go to the poorest counties—those in which one-fifth or more of the residents have lived at or below the federal poverty level *for at least 30 years* [emphasis added]" (Rosen 2009). Twelve counties in South Carolina, all along the Interstate 95 corridor, meet that standard. In fact, a statewide coalition of citizens' groups has been active for several years in attempting to raise consciousness about the abysmal state of schools in rural South Carolina, especially along the corridor, and to require the state to adequately fund those schools. At present, the state's constitution requires that its youth be provided only a "minimally adequate" education, and the group is seeking a constitutional amendment to change that requirement to "a high quality education allowing each student to reach his highest potential." In 2005, the group also produced an award-winning documentary entitled *Corridor of Shame: The Neglect of South Carolina's Rural Schools* as a part of their effort (Goodbyeminimallyadequate.com 2009).

When all other social institutions are structured unequally, we cannot hope to achieve equality in the educational system. Even though Americans believe, for example, in an educational system that gives everyone a fair chance, they want their own children to succeed in the competition for economic and social advantage and thus seek an unequal education to help in that process (Sacks 2007; Tyack and Cuban 1995). Reformers who moved for "detracking" in schools learned firsthand just how powerful the forces promoting inequality can be. Jeannie Oakes and her collaborators (Oakes et al. 1997; Oakes and Wells 1998) conducted a study of ten racially and socioeconomically mixed secondary schools across the country that are participating in detracking reform. Attempting to provide access to high standards for all students, the schools implemented reforms based on the latest scholarship that reflects the multidimensional, developmental, and culturally varied nature of intelligence, as well as people's unlimited potential for learning. They eliminated the lower track, developed common curricula, put all students on a college preparatory track for some subjects, designed a customized school calendar and after-school programs for students having difficulty, adopted classroom strategies that allowed students to demonstrate knowledge in new ways, developed multicultural curricula, and created a wide range of innovative learning projects to challenge each student.

Yet these projects ran into enormous opposition from teachers and administrators within the schools who continue to believe conventional, normative conceptions that intelligence is

- Essentially unchangeable–either for biological or cultural reasons or both
- Unidimensional—reflected in the speed of getting right answers on standardized tests;
- "normally" distributed across a bell curve
- Readily apparent—associated with the way that students comport themselves, an assessment that overlaps with race, class, and gender as reflected in such statements as the following:

Smart students…look like they're paying attention, turn in their homework, help classmates who don't understand something, and are good leaders.

We're getting fewer honors kids, and that's just demographics. (Oakes et al. 1997, 490)

In the final analysis, these educators believe that tracking students is the most effective way to educate a student population that is "naturally, innately" already ranked by intelligence.

The more significant resistance, however, has come from affluent White parents of high-track students who benefited from the unidimensional view of intelligence and the tracking system that is built on those views. These parents, often working in conjunction with resistant teachers in the schools, employed several strategies to stop the practice: threatening to leave the school, co-opting educational elites who see their roles as serving the elites of the community, buy-ins of not quite elite parents who accept the "commonsense" dominant ideology, and demanding preferential treatment for their children—smaller classes, the best teachers, the latest technology. What the reformers learned was that, while they had focused on the technical aspects of knowledge acquisition and learning, powerful social forces were invested in the role of the school to sort, rank, and reinforce the hierarchy of power that existed outside the school.

The efforts of these detracking advocates and others like them eventually made their mark across the nation and resulted in the end of formal de jure tracking in many schools. However as recent research shows, formal *de jure* tracking has been replaced by informal *de facto* tracking. The parents of the privileged know about academic college prep courses and, with the help of teachers who expect more from students of privilege, steer their children to them. As Bettie (2003) illustrates, poor and working class Latino/a and White youths are typically uninformed about the consequences of their curricular choices and face numerous barriers to opting for the academic track even when they do. As Carlson (1997, 57) states:

It is naive to believe that public schools can be detracked outside of a broad-based movement for democratic renewal in the culture, including a movement toward a more equitable economy and an improvement in the quality of people's working lives.

And addressing the inequities across schools, as well as within them, Jean Anyon similarly concludes:

> Attempting to fix inner-city schools without fixing the city in which they are embedded is like trying to clean the air on one side of a screen door. (1997, 168)

We cannot expect schools to be structured around principles of equity as long as they are implicated in preparing students for such unequal futures. Attaining educational equality will thus require improvements in the quality and pay of jobs and macroeconomic policies to counter the two-tiered economy that has developed over the past forty years. We cannot expect educational equality alone to reduce larger economic and occupational inequalities because, as we have seen, increasing the educational levels of the population when good jobs are not available merely leads to credential inflation (Bills 2003; Brown 1995; McNamee and Miller 2004).

Recommendations for Educational Reform

Most scholars who recommend educational reform to redress inequities emphasize several key bases for true reform.

Movements for Social Equity Reform must be accompanied by and tied to movements for social equity and social justice in society at large. If *all* children are to be educated, society must guarantee that basic human needs can be met. In addition to decent jobs and living wages, all citizens need health care, affordable housing, a child allowance, and a national child care system (including provision of full services for families in need), a national public early childhood education system, and reduced funding and resource disparities across schools (Arnold and Doctoroff 2003; Children's Defense Fund 2003 Polakow 1993).

Access for All to Programs That Work Effective reform must include access for all students to programs and opportunities with proven success in improving the learning of oppressed groups, such as preschool and full-day kindergarten, reduced class size (in the context of improved pedagogy and teachers' skilled in giving individualized attention), bilingual and English-as-a-second-language instruction, intensive curricular intervention programs, safe-schools programs, school-to-work and school-to-college transition activities, full-service schools (e.g., including health care, GED classes, job training), support for mainstreamed students and their teachers, and authentic accountability (Anyon 1997, 179; Neill 2004).

One such effort currently under way is the Harlem Children's Zone, "a holistic system of education, social-service and community-building programs aimed at helping the children and families in a ninety-seven-block area of Central Harlem (Harlem Children's Zone 2009)." The project began in 1997, when Geoffery Canada, the current president and CEO, drew a circle around a twenty-four-block area in central Harlem and initiated a network of social, health, and educational programs for the area's residents. In 2007, the project grew to encompass close to one hundred city blocks and to serve more than 7,400 children and 4,100 adults (Harlem Children's Zone 2009). This holistic approach to community uplift begins with a "baby college" for new parents and culminates with students' graduation from the Promise Academy (Severson 2005). Canada's approach has also drawn the attention of President Barack Obama, who announced during his campaign a plan to create "promise neighborhoods" (modeled after the Children's Zone) in twenty U. S. cities and included them in his first economic recovery bill. However, the U.S. economic crisis has threatened the viability of nonprofit programs such as the Harlem Children's Zone, which rely heavily on charitable contributions (Spector 2009).

Desegregation and Detracking Heterogeneous classroom experiences across race, class, gender, and sexuality are preferable to segregation and school tracking (Carlson 1997; Oakes et al. 1997; Orfield and Lee 2007; Sacks 2007). The unequal allocation of resources to schools—both human resources, such as well-trained teachers, and material resources, such as physical facilities, curriculum materials, and computers—based on race and class differences in the communities surrounding the schools is a continuing threat to equity in education and in society. Recent trends in the resegregation of schools are exacerbating that threat (Orfield and Lee 2007; Saenz et al. 2007). Likewise, recent economic trends have affected school tracking within schools. Primarily because of shifts from a manufacturing to a service economy, vocational education declined dramatically in the 1990s (50 percent in the past ten years), and the general education track has expanded to accommodate students who might have been in the vocational track, producing some "detracking"(Carlson 1997).

With the development of magnet schools,[3] however, these trends have served to increase—not to decrease—the inequality in the schools, as general track education receives even lower expenditures and lower expectations among teachers and as magnet schools and voucher systems further separate college-track students from the rest of the student population.

We need social policy that eliminates such unequal practices as funding schools through property taxes and "ability group" tracking within schools and that guides us in a systematic way to both housing and school integration. Instituting such a policy will require a major shift in the current political trends that focus on dismantling the desegregation plans of the 1970s but do not include

---

[3]The U.S. Department of Education established four criteria to define a magnet school: (1) a distinctive school curriculum based on a special theme or method of instruction, (2) a unique district role and purpose for voluntary desegregation, (3) voluntary choice of the school by students and parents, (4) open access to school enrollment beyond a regular attendance zone (Blank et al. 1983, 2). Magnet schools were founded primarily to solve the pressing political problem of preventing active, dramatic, and possibly violent resistance by some Whites to the creation of the desegregated schools required by the courts (Metz 1986, 15).

- Full discussion of how the new plans for school system structures will not deepen inequality
- Research to develop new strategies and to evaluate them
- Funding to implement strategies
- Oversight to monitor progress toward equity

Pedagogy of Equity A new pedagogy of equity is called for. Intersectional scholars offer significant promise for what a pedagogy of equity would address. The reforms that Carlson (1997), for example, demands as a necessary part of a democratic multicultural curriculum and pedagogy reflect the basic themes of race, class, gender, and sexuality scholarship:

Contextual, socially constructed: Challenge "essentialist" worldviews that take categories such as race, class, gender, and sexuality as "natural categories having a fixed meaning" in all times and places.

Power relations: Discuss race, class, gender, and sexuality as power relations antithetical to democratic "virtues," including protecting minority rights and individual freedoms, respecting difference, creating equity, and developing interlocking webs of caring and supportive relations among individuals. Within the context of human rights in a democratic community, teachers can, for example, involve young people in a discussion of gay identity.

Macro and micro levels: Discuss these issues at the structural level, as well as at the level of personal identity. Emphasize the connections between macro structures and personal experience, always looking for evidence of each in every discussion. Help students see that the success of a few people does not necessarily prove that the American Dream is a reality.

Simultaneously expressed: Seek to cross or rupture the borders that classify individuals into neat categories or camps. One way to rupture these borders is to emphasize the multiple subject positions we all occupy (i.e., race, class, gender, sexuality). A corollary is that because all truths are partial, classroom discussions should seek to clarify agreements and disagreements, not to identify a single truth.

Implications for social activism: Help students see the connection between knowledge about race, class, gender, and sexuality and social movements for equity.

The educational system holds promise as a potential site for increasing race, class, gender, and sexuality equity. It will require, however, a major transformation of the system at both the macro and micro levels. That transformation will depend on the success of social movements in providing the impetus for equity, as well as on the establishment of policies that are more likely to produce equity, including redistribution of fiscal resources, changes in organizational structures, a pedagogy that emphasizes promoting understanding and collaborating across diversity, and involvement of activists, community people, parents, and teachers in the process of designing reform.

SUMMARY

This section illustrates the conceptual framework by applying it in a comprehensive analysis of a major social institution, education. Education was selected for many reasons, but particularly because it is the first institution with which most people have extensive contact outside of their immediate families. This analysis, however, could have been conducted on any social institution—work and economy, religion, family, government/polity—or even applied to the circumstances of an individual life. Furthermore, as the analysis of education should have made apparent, none of these institutions operate in isolation from others. The race, class, gender, and sexuality processes that are generated and reinforced in one institution also affect the others.

CHAPTER 10

✦◯

Envisioning Social Justice

In 1955, one year after *Brown v. Board of Education of Topeka* removed the legal foundation of segregation, Mamie Mobley sent her fourteen-year-old son, Emmett Till, to Mississippi to visit his cousins. A few weeks later, her only child returned to Chicago—in a body bag. He had been beaten and shot, a gin-mill fan had been wired to his neck, and he was tossed into the Tallahatchie River. He was unrecognizable, identifiable only by the ring on his finger. Emmett Till was mutilated for allegedly whistling at a White woman in a country store. The two White men who killed him were quickly acquitted by an all-White male jury. Mamie Mobley was grief stricken: "Death at that time would have been welcome" (Terkel, 1992, 22).

Newspapers spread pictures of Emmett's corpse across the country. The sight of Emmett Till's body and the enormity of the injustice mobilized many people to action in the cause of civil rights. In 1985, Toni Morrison wrote *Dreaming Emmett*, a play commissioned by the New York State Writers Institute to commemorate the first national observance of Martin Luther King, Jr.'s birthday.

Nearly forty years later, Studs Terkel interviewed Mamie Mobley about those events and her life since Emmett's murder:

TERKEL: Don't you harbor any bitterness toward the two men—toward whites, for that matter? It would be unnatural not to—

MOBLEY: It certainly would be unnatural not to, yet I'd have to say I'm unnatural. From the very beginning that's the question that has always been raised: "What would you do to Milam and Bryant if you had the opportunity?" I came to the realization that I would do nothing. What they had done was not for me to punish and it was not for me to go around hugging hate to myself, because hate would destroy me. It wouldn't hurt them....

The Lord gave me a shield....If I had to, I could take their four little children—they each had two—and I could raise those children as if they were my own and I could have loved them. Now that's a strange thing to say, but I haven't spent one night hating those people. I have not looked at a white person and seen an enemy. I look at people and I see people. (Terkel 1992, 21)

After Emmett's death, Mamie Mobley went back to school, became a teacher, and taught for twenty-four years in the Chicago public schools. She also traveled across the country lecturing for the National Association for the Advancement of Colored People (NAACP) to inspire and to mobilize others to work for social justice.

> MOBLEY: My burning—the thing that has come out of Emmett's death is to push education to the limit: you must learn all you can. Learn until your head swells. This is what I was able to energize my children with, the desire for learning.
>
> There has been progress without a doubt. We cannot deny that. I see progress within myself and progress for those who will dare reach for it. Sometimes those steps are steep, they're not easy to climb, but as Langston Hughes said, "You have to keep on climbing" (Terkel 1992, 22)

Mamie Mobley framed her life in the pursuit of social justice. At her death in 2003, the Reverend Jesse Jackson, quoted in her *New York Times* obituary, described Mobley's impact on the civil rights movement:

> "What must be put into perspective is that we often say the modern Civil Rights movement began with Rosa Parks in Montgomery. That's really not accurate," Mr. Jackson said. He said Emmett's murder "broke the emotional chains of Jim Crow....Mrs. Mobley did a profound strategic thing....With his body water-soaked and defaced, most people would have kept the casket covered. She let the body be exposed. More than 100,000 people saw his body lying in that casket here in Chicago. That must have been at that time the largest single civil rights demonstration in American history." (Fountain 2003).

Mobley's story reveals the factors that can contribute to effective action for social justice. First, Mamie Mobley had a vision of justice that emerged from self-valuation, not internalized oppression—"not hugging hate to myself." It was a vision resting on caring, respect, and love for others and was fed by spirituality. It was a vision of justice as a collective enterprise of which she was a part, not as a personality characteristic that was hers alone. Second, her vision was based in a deep understanding of the structures of oppression that shaped her life, as well as that of others. And, finally, her vision of justice and deep understanding of oppression formed the foundation that motivated and sustained her in social action—to doggedly pursue knowledge and to teach children to do the same—an activist path in which she was joined by many African American women of her generation (cf. Gilkes 1994).

Over the past twenty-five years, I have looked to the lives of people like Mamie Mobley to guide my search for effective ways to promote social justice. From 1982, when Bonnie Thornton Dill, Elizabeth Higginbotham, and I began our work at the Center for Research on Women at the University of Memphis and into the mid-1990s, we wanted to make a difference in the way that women of color and that systems of race, class, and gender[1] were conceptualized, produced, and reinforced in higher education. To develop our understanding of race, class, and gender for our research and for our teaching, we began almost immediately to host national workshops for faculty in all areas of higher education so that we could develop a national community of change agents within our institutions to promote social justice. Over those years, we worked with large numbers of dedicated people in all kinds of institutions—from community colleges to private liberal arts colleges to research universities — to understand how to make an educational experience that promotes social justice. In that dialogue and in the dialogue with our students and our institutions, we learned much about working for justice, including incorporating sexuality into our analyses.

We tried to design the process, structure, and curriculum of our workshops to facilitate people's work for progressive social change. The design that we employed suggests what it takes to make change for social justice, and that design is reiterated in Mamie Mobley's story:

- A *vision*, a dream of a just society—one based in an ethic of caring, respect for others, and love that rings true and powerful enough to move and to motivate not only individuals but also communities of people to affirm their self-worth in the face of pervasive devaluation and to choose to struggle together for social change.
- A *deep understanding* of oppression contextually grounded in time and place, an understanding of the intersections of race, class, gender, and sexuality as socially constructed relationships of power that operate at both the societal and individual levels.
- Strategic *action:* action that is motivated by a vision of justice and grounded in a deep understanding of oppression and that is taken in principled group coalitions that understand and respect differences while pursuing common goals.

VISION

What is perhaps clearest in Mamie Mobley's story is that she had a vision of justice, one that sustained her, gave her hope, and motivated her to social action even in the face of pain. What is the vision of social justice that we can glean from activists such as Mobley who have struggled against injustice for their entire lives?

---

[1]In the early years of our work at the center, we did not incorporate sexuality into our analysis or workshops. Over time, the scholarship and political work of gays, lesbians, bisexuals, and transgender people increased our awareness of the significance of sexuality in shaping the other dimensions and as a primary system of oppression in American life.

Visions of social justice focus as much on the process of struggle for freedom from oppression as on what some ideal world would look like, in which honor, equity, and fairness prevail. Justice is more about the way we choose to live our lives every day than it is about what we will get if we work hard. This emphasis distinguishes it from dominant culture visions such as the American Dream that motivate people to act to achieve economic success and, in their more ruthless versions, valorize economic success whatever the means used to achieve it. So, for example, some people respect poor people who make lots of money by becoming drug dealers because they have achieved economic success against the odds. Or a man like Ross Perot, largely because he has billions of dollars, is held in enough esteem that in 1992 he was able to start a third political party and to wage a viable candidacy for president. The fact that in many years he paid no taxes and publicly denounces the work of the federal government—even though his own wealth was made by selling computer software developed by government researchers—does not tarnish his image because it is the achievement of wealth itself, not how he got it, that is honored in this model.

Many people admired the mortgage brokers, financiers, hedge fund managers, and investment bankers who accumulated billions of dollars in the past ten years for their success—even as the gap between their wealth and that of the rest of the nation had grown to unprecedented proportions. In fact, even as their firms and banks began to fail, the government's first actions were to "bail them out" because they were deemed to be too big, too important to be allowed to fail. Even after they had been paid over $300 billion in government money through the Emergency Economic Stabilization Act of 2008, the crisis did not end for many reasons: among them that the problems were already much deeper than many realized and, more important, that the government placed no meaningful stipulations on the expenditure of the bailout funds. So the firms opted to hold on to the money or to buy other banks, not to reinvest it in the economy. After receiving the bailout money, many of these firms continued to pay out bonuses in the millions to their CEOs and top managers, arguing that the bonuses were reasonable and fair (Collins 2008; CNN. com 2009; McIntire 2009). The wealth itself had signaled virtue not only in how CEOs and top managers saw themselves but also in how government lawmakers had come to see them. The assumption of good will and virtue inhibited both putting in place regulations that might have mitigated the disaster and later shaping the bailout so that expenditures would be overseen and managed.

We are much more apt to wonder why Mamie Mobley continues in her struggle than we are to ask why people continue to pursue economic success. Yet in America, the reality is that although many people pursue vast economic success, most never achieve it. And the pressures in our society to equate money and self-worth also help to reinforce the existing hierarchies of power by devaluing and even demonizing those who do not achieve economic success (e.g., "welfare queens") and valorizing those who do (e.g., we do not speak of "corporate welfare queens").

But that vision of economic success is clearly not the vision of Mamie Mobley or others seeking social justice. When we seek freedom and self-determination instead of economic success, the means involve caring, respect centered in a deep understanding of differences, and love. Moral authority accrues to the person whose own child is lynched and yet could "raise those children [of her son's murderers] as if they were my own and I could have loved them." That kind of moral authority empowers oppressed groups in the struggle for freedom.

The vision is also collective: It has life in the context of communities working together for change. When thinking about the ways in which policy changes in the 1980s made life more difficult for poor people, Mamie Mobley said:

> We can see what's happened to the income tax, the health insurance, and a whole lot of other things. You wonder how these things were allowed to come about. Then you think of dollars and cents, you can see that this is what it's all about: not the love of humanity, but the love of the dollar. *It's just another river we're going to cross.* (Terkel 1992, 25)

She speaks in the plural: "We can see." She is obviously a part of a community that sees policy changes in the same way. But it is also a community that is acting together for change, and her emphasis is on the process of getting there: She focuses on crossing the river, not on what it looks like on the other side. Perhaps most important for oppressed groups in the struggle for freedom is that the vision contain some hope for positive change. In this, Mamie Mobley's vision is perhaps at its most powerful. Despite the intense difficulty of making change when political, ideological, and economic power rests in others' hands, she doesn't equivocate: "It's just another river *we're going to cross.*"

UNDERSTANDING/KNOWLEDGE

The real promise of the intersectional analysis presented here is that it can deepen our understanding of oppression by opening up new ways of looking at social institutions, raising new questions, and suggesting more effective ways of addressing seemingly intractable systems of social inequality. And just as visions of social justice focus on the path to freedom, what we learn about race, class, gender, and sexuality is determined in large measure by the atmosphere, the context, the environment, and the process through which we learn. In the late 1980s, for example, I taught a night class on race, class, and gender to a group of students at the University of Memphis (then Memphis State University). The composition of the class was typical of the many classes I taught there—about fifteen working-class, first-generation college students, two-thirds women, about one-third African American, one or two international students, and the rest White men and women, almost all in their twenties and thirties and working full-time jobs during the day.

About halfway through the semester, after the students had gotten to know each other pretty well, Jim,[2] a White male student about twenty-five years old, said, "A White man doesn't have a chance anymore. The Blacks and women are getting all the jobs."

---

[2]"Jim" and "Anton" are pseudonyms.

In a matter of seconds the atmosphere in the room went from warm to boiling hot. Several of the students raised up, put their hands on the table. I knew I had to do something fast. I don't know where it came from, but I said to Jim, "Why do you feel that way?" The other students in the room sat back, and Jim looked at me as if I were crazy, as if the answer should have been obvious. He was speechless. So I tried another tack: "What makes you think that is true? Where did you get your information?"

Jim then told his story. He said he knew this was true because he worked at Memphis Light, Gas, and Water Division (MLGW), the public utility, and one of the largest employers in the city. He had been working there for five years as a meter reader, and he was due to get a promotion to supervisor because "that's the way it usually goes." Then he said, "And they went and hired a Black woman off the street and made her my supervisor." I asked Jim why he thought they had done that. He really didn't know. Instead, he relied on the reverse discrimination arguments so prevalent in public discourse.

But I knew. MLGW was under a court order to hire women and African American men because it had been successfully sued for discrimination. The settlement required hiring some supervisors and upper-level managers, as well as increasing the hiring of women and African Americans at the entry level, because the workforce was so out of line with the local labor market that simply changing the hiring practices at entry level could not hope to produce a balanced workforce in the foreseeable future.

I asked Jim, "How did it make you feel to lose out on your promotion?" He described in detail how upset he had been, how he had worked hard, how the money was going to contribute to his education. Students in the class were quite sympathetic with his plight, because they too were working hard to make ends meet while pursuing an education.

We then went back to the question that had started us off: "Are Blacks and women getting all the jobs, so White men don't have a chance?" We decided to focus attention on the labor market in Memphis and to get more systematic data. I asked Jim and several other students to gather information about the macro structures of the labor market—where women, African Americans, men, Whites, and other groups were actually employed in Memphis and at MLGW. The data they gathered and our discussions made eminently clear that Jim's impression was not true of the city and certainly not of the place he worked. In fact, quite the reverse was true.

During that class, Jim, the other students, and I developed a deeper understanding of the dynamics of race, class, gender, and sexuality. The understanding we developed was grounded in time and place—not in some abstract category of "the Blacks and women" but in the labor force in Memphis and at MLGW in the late 1980s. We analyzed the power dynamics involved: the power of a group of middle-class, White men to maintain control for years over a public utility paying among the highest wages in the city, in the midst of a city whose adults were over 50 percent Black and over 50 percent women. We examined the ideological power of dominant groups to promote the idea that reverse discrimination was a prevalent reality in the presence of a highly race-, class-, and gender-segregated labor market. And we self-consciously reflected on the power that the students—working-class, multiracial men and women—collectively took when they investigated the macro systems of inequality in Memphis and grappled with their effects in their individual lives.

My students were able to take power in part because the class had also developed an atmosphere of respect and trust, a foundation on which to challenge these tough issues. Because oppression has shaped all of our lives, often in harmful ways, and because many forces obscure these systems, seriously interrogating the meaning of race, class, gender, and sexuality—as my class did and as this text asks us to do—may be emotionally upsetting. Facing the ways in which our lives and those of others have been made easier by our privilege or have been harmed by oppression may be personally difficult. And yet, because our own experiences largely shape what we know and believe about race, class, gender, and sexuality, expanding our knowledge requires that we become clearer about our own social location in these systems and that we remain open to hearing about others' experiences, particularly about experiences that are different from our own.

It is especially important when examining our taken-for-granted everyday practices and beliefs connected with these systemic inequalities that we separate our emotional and intellectual reactions to a person's ideas—which can be quite negative—from our assessment of the person's value or worth as a human being. We can critically assess and vehemently disagree with others' ideas, beliefs, and even values without denigrating the people who hold them. Oppressed groups are routinely portrayed in society as different, as less worthy, and as responsible for their devalued status and for their lack of resources and options. In contrast, dominant groups are taken as the invisible norm, the standard, against which we are all asked to judge ourselves.

As Jim and the other students in the class struggled to understand labor inequality in Memphis, in their own and in each others' lives, they developed a growing respect for one another. Anton, a nineteen-year-old African American raised in a large and very close-knit family in rural Mississippi, was also working his way through college and showed great empathy for Jim. Over the course of the semester, they became good friends. One year after the class had ended, Anton stopped by my office with a huge grin on his face and said with great pride, "Guess what? Jim got his promotion."

Anton kept in touch with me off and on for the next twenty years. We talked as he faced terrible hardship in his young life. At nineteen he became a father, and although his baby's mother kept the child, she did not want to marry. He struggled to stay involved with his daughter, whom he loved deeply, while working and staying in college. Anton was also the oldest of his siblings and felt a great deal of responsibility to care for them and to be a good role model for them and for the other children in his small town. At twenty-four, he had a massive heart attack and underwent quadruple bypass surgery. His recovery was slow, but the heart attack and its aftermath gave him a wakeup call: He needed to learn to manage the stress in his life, including the stress from the intense pressure he felt to get his education and to do good in the world.

One of the stressors he came to face was his own homosexuality. Openly acknowledging that he was gay was extremely difficult, because Anton was both socially and spiritually deeply connected to the Black church in which he was raised and which roundly denounced homosexuality. Over the years he faced even more intense obstacles, developing HIV/AIDS. In each step of his journey, Anton talked about how his vision and understanding had propelled him to act for social justice. He worked in AIDS organizations, even organizing a choir of gay men of color with AIDS. The choir performed across the South, raising awareness and funds to fight AIDS in the Black community, including the Black church. He remained involved in the church and found Black ministers and churches that embraced him. He began to write essays, poems, and songs to share his struggle, his insight, and his vision of a just world. In 2003, Anton died of AIDS at the age of forty.

Michele Berger (2004) recently documented how sixteen HIV-positive African American women and Latinas who were multiply stigmatized by race, class, gender, and sexuality but also by past histories of drug use, sex work, and conflicts with the law came to political awareness in a community context and began to work as activists, advocates, and helpers. Not passive victims in any way, within that community context these women were able to reconstruct their lives and become effective political advocates for themselves and others through substance abuse treatment, recognition of gender as salient in their lives, and deploying non-traditional political resources.

Anton, Mamie Mobley, and the women in Berger's study faced unimaginable personal tragedy as a consequence of the deep inequalities in our society. And they employed the experience of tragedy to deepen their own understanding and vision, to share it with others, and to put it to action. It was neither the disease nor any of the other tragedies that Anton and these women faced that caused their activism, for there are many ways of confronting tragedy and deadly disease that do not involve activism for social justice. Instead, in community with others, they developed great understanding, expanded their vision, and acted, and in so doing they showed us how to engage in activism for social justice.

If we are to understand race, class, gender, and sexuality systems, we must be willing to have our stereotypes of subordinate groups challenged and to make the social privilege of dominant groups visible. To do so, we must be open to learning information and ways of thinking that may not have been included or validated in our education. We must also be aware that everyone holds stereotypes—that we may even have them about our own groups—and that we can challenge and change them. And because all of these systems operate in our lives at all times, recognizing the complexity in our own multiple statuses helps us to consider the complexity in the lived experiences of others.

In my teaching, I try to promote a classroom environment that encourages understanding and respect across difference. Jim, other students, and I developed a set of guidelines for classroom discussion that asks us to work to understand what oppression means in people's lives (for a discussion, see Weber 1990, 2005). The guidelines ask us to consider that people, both in the groups that we study and in the class, are always doing the best that they can. In other words, the guidelines ask that we assume that everyone and every group does their best to live and to live well and that if they are not living well, are sick or die, just as with the miner's canary, we need to examine the social context in which they are striving, not to blame them for failing to live. When we give each other human respect, learning can take place across the most diverse of groups.

Lani Guinier notes that discussions that move people toward deep understanding can also take place in "intermediate public spaces"—civic associations, churches, and neighborhood associations—in addition to the classroom. In *Lift Every Voice: Turning a Civil Rights Setback into a New Vision of Social Justice*, Guinier (1998a) shares the lessons she has learned about justice from her life as a civil rights attorney and through the political maelstrom that occurred in 1993 after President Clinton nominated and then withdrew her nomination as Assistant Attorney General for Civil Rights. She argues that knowledge to promote effective action for social justice is gained in collaborative environments that become safe spaces because differences are respected and trust develops. In these spaces, people can be empowered to solve problems, not just to win arguments.

Guinier contends that these spaces for serious committed conversation should at a minimum involve:

- A willingness to include a range of people (as individuals and as members of organized, interested groups such as neighborhood associations and organizations such as the NAACP and La Raza)
- Continued interaction with concrete local challenges, informed by an understanding of the way race links issues of gender, power, and class
- The capacity to deliberate and collaborate again and again because the process of public education, brainstorming, sharing solutions and experimenting in the field is never totally finished (1998a, 310).

And although Guinier was focusing on racial justice, her suggestions are consistent with the kinds of processes envisioned by people working for social justice along different and intersecting dimensions of oppression. In *Community Activism and Feminist Politics: Organizing Across Race, Class, and Gender*, for example, Nancy Naples (1998) collected the stories of women working as community activists against the abuse of women, against corporate poisoning of their neighborhoods, against homophobia and racism and for people-centered economic development, immigrants' rights, educational equity, and adequate wages. Naples summarizes the process of change for justice that can be gleaned from the stories of these activists working at the intersections of multiple systems of oppression:

I remain convinced that progressive social change requires envisioning a "just society" as well as drawing upon contemporary political practices based on participatory democracy, antiracism, and deep understanding of as well as respect for our many differences. I believe that women community activists from diverse racial, ethnic, class, and regional backgrounds have much to teach us about achieving such a vision. (1998, 346)

From workplaces to neighborhood associations to AIDS activist groups to classrooms, the general contours of a process that generates knowledge to guide effective action for social justice are consistent.

ACTION

Developing a deep understanding of the forces of oppression and acting in pursuit of social justice are mutually reinforcing parts of the same process. The actions we choose to take in the pursuit of social justice both flow from and create the knowledge we have of the forces of oppression around us in specific times and places. The extent to which particular actions will be effective in bringing about a change in the distribution of power in a particular social context will depend on a variety of factors, including the depth of understanding of the forces of oppression, the nature of the coalitions involved, and the strength of the forces of dominance. And as the examples of reform efforts in education suggest, each of these forces is likely to come into play in any effort for social change.

Lani Guinier learned the value of coalitions when her nomination in the first year of Bill Clinton's presidency to head the Civil Rights Division of the Justice Department was withdrawn. At her nomination, right-wing groups immediately labeled her "quota queen"—making a blatant connection with the popular image of Black women as "welfare queens." Within weeks, Guinier and her ideas were pilloried in the media, and Clinton rescinded her nomination—before she could have a hearing to defend her writings and strategies for including African Americans in the electoral process.

What Guinier concluded was that when she had traveled the country, particularly rural areas of the South, as a voting rights attorney, she had been integrated into communities. She was connected to a constituency. By the time of her nomination, she was a professor at the University of Pennsylvania, far removed from the people she had worked with to make change:

I eventually understood why the strategy my friends, supporters and defenders undertook ultimately could not succeed. An inside-the-beltway operation that failed to connect to our real clients, those people who formed the body of the civil rights movement, could never generate the kind of political pressure that would force the powers in Washington to act. In our intense focus on getting *me* this job, we had turned our backs on the more important constituency of people outside of Washington, many of whom had no job at all. (1998)

From his years of experience as a community organizer, Barak Obama certainly understands the importance of strong coalitions and constituencies. Some already call the 2008 election a "critical election," the label that political scientists give to those elections that tend to come around only once in a generation and shift the balance of power for years to come (e.g., 1980, Ronald Reagan; 1960, John F. Kennedy; 1932, Franklin Delano Roosevelt). President Obama's election was surely an unpredictable event in 2006 when Obama started his campaign, and there will be retrospective analyses of this election for years to come. But it is clear already that each of the factors that we know can shape change were at work in his election:

- Dominant groups were in a weakened state unprecedented in the previous thirty years—under the weight of two prolonged wars, impending economic collapse, declining economic power relative to other powerful nations, and a grossly unpopular president.
- Obama knew the value of coalition building and worked hard to mobilize millions of new voters, using a combination of new (high tech) and old (personal canvassing) methods of reaching and engaging supporters.
- His own life experiences across class, race, ethnicity, and nation, along with his education and involvement in grass-roots efforts for change, gave him the knowledge of injustice and of effective change strategies that dominant group members rarely have.
- He carefully and consistently showed respect not only to his supporters but also to his opponents.

His "big tent" vision of collaboration and inclusion resonated with a wide swath of the American public. How successful Obama can be now that he is in the office will in large part depend on how engaged people remain in the causes of justice and how he follows through on his promise of inclusion.

It is by collaborating and cooperating across our differences in respectful environments that meaning accrues and empowerment occurs. This theme appears in the writings of many different groups struggling for change. Awiatka, a Cherokee poet, teaches about justice, wisdom, and native values through telling the story of the Corn-Mother:

> the Corn-Mother teaches many wisdoms, one of which is cooperation. Just as a single plant cannot bear fruit and it requires a field of corn to bring in a harvest, neither can a person be as strong alone as in connection with one's family and one's people. In developing a new model for American life, each of us alone can do very little. But if we fuse our energies, if we plant together, we can do much. Let us do so. And look for signs of the harvest....(1993:166).

The pursuit of social justice gives meaning to people's lives. To derive meaning from the struggle for justice, we do not have to bring about a revolution. We can plant together. By preparing the fields and planting the seeds together, we can live fulfilling lives even as we wait for the harvest.

✦◯

Case Studies: Applying The Framework

To understand the complex and dynamic relationships of race, class, gender, and sexuality systems of inequality, our analyses must be grounded in real-life experience. And, as most anthologies on these systems demonstrate, beginning with personal experience is perhaps the best way to engage readers in an analysis of these complex intersections.

QUESTIONS FOR ANALYSIS

Accompanying each of the four case studies presented here is a set of specific questions associated with each of the five themes in the framework, as well as questions about the implications of the case for social action and social justice. These questions guide rather than prescribe. They are not intended to be comprehensive and to touch on every possible avenue to pursue in attempting to understand each thematic aspect of race, class, gender, and sexuality systems. And the questions are not organized in a linear progression. Instead, they are intended to spur critical thought about the multiple dimensions of each of these systems, as well as of their intersecting dynamics. Because each of us brings to an analysis the knowledge and perspectives that have been shaped by our own social location in race, class, gender, and sexuality hierarchies, our analyses will likely take many directions, as people situated differently in these hierarchies see the dynamics of inequality in different aspects of stories or situations. These various points of view illustrate the value of bringing multiple angles of vision to bear on the analysis of any case.

Although the questions are organized by conceptual theme, you will also find that some of the questions might fit into several of the themes. For just as race, class, gender, and sexuality systems intersect, so too do the conceptual themes that undergird these systems connect and overlap:

- That the meanings of race, class, gender, and sexuality are historically and geographically contextual implies that they are socially constructed and thus can and do change over time and space.
- That they are power relationships merely specifies that the relationships are of dominance and subordination, yet these relationships take place at both the macro institutional and micro individual levels.
- The simultaneous expression of race, class, gender, and sexuality inequalities is manifest as we explore all of the other themes.

So use the questions to generate complex, dynamic, and useful analyses of the intersections of race, class, gender, and sexuality in specific social situations and in specific lives—and, in so doing, to find deeper understanding of how social structures both privilege and oppress all of us.

ABOUT THE CASES

In presenting a range of different experiences across multiple social locations, these four cases represent considerable diversity of race, class, gender, and sexuality. But they are not intended to be comprehensive or exhaustive; they are intended to provide further opportunities for learning how to develop complex analyses of different types of situations and experiences.

Case Study 1, "Steinem and Walker: Clinton and Obama," juxtaposes the endorsements of two well known feminists for the two leading candidates for the Democratic nomination in the 2008 Presidential election—Gloria Steinem's for Hillary Clinton and Alice Walker's for Barack Obama.

Case Study 2, "The Valenzuela Family," describes the experiences of an undocumented Mexican American family: their reasons for coming to the United States, their difficulties and stresses in their work and family life, and their efforts to become citizens.

Case Study 3, "It's Like We Never Been Born," is largely a first-person account of one woman's experiences in trying to rebuild her life and community after Hurricane Katrina.

Case Study 4, "Getting Off on Feminism," recounts a young man's efforts to have a nonsexist bachelor party.

✐

Steinem and Walker: Clinton and Obama

In "Women Are Never Front-Runners," Gloria Steinem endorsed the candidacy of Hillary Clinton for President of the United States, and Alice Walker, in "Lest We Forget: An Open Letter to My Sisters Who Are Brave," endorsed Barack Obama. Walker and Steinem's essays enable us to interrogate how the systems of privilege and oppression in the United States have shaped not only the personal experiences and opinions of these two feminist icons but also the ways in which the hierarchies of inequality manifested themselves in the presidential election of 2008.

Steinem, Gloria. 2008. "Women are never front-runners." *The New York Times* January, 8.

Walker, Alice. 2008. "Lest we forget: An open letter to my sisters who are brave." *The Root* March, 27. Available from http://www.theroot.com/views/lest-we-forget-open-letter-my-sisters-who-are-brave accessed on April 4, 2009.

WOMEN ARE NEVER FRONT-RUNNERS
By Gloria Steinem

The woman in question became a lawyer after some years as a community organizer, married a corporate lawyer and is the mother of two little girls, ages 9 and 6. Herself the daughter of a white American mother and a black African father—in this race-conscious country, she is considered black—she served as a state legislator for eight years, and became an inspirational voice for national unity.

Be honest: Do you think this is the biography of someone who could be elected to the United States Senate? After less than one term there, do you believe she could be a viable candidate to head the most powerful nation on earth?

If you answered no to either question, you're not alone. Gender is probably the most restricting force in American life, whether the question is who must be in the kitchen or who could be in the White House. This country is way down the list of countries electing women and, according to one study, it polarizes gender roles more than the average democracy.

Sexism kind worst of oppression

That's why the Iowa primary was following our historical pattern of making change. Black men were given the vote a half-century before women of any race were allowed to mark a ballot, and generally have ascended to positions of power, from the military to the boardroom, before any women (with the possible exception of obedient family members in the latter).

If the lawyer described above had been just as charismatic but named, say, Achola Obama instead of Barack Obama, her goose would have been cooked long ago. Indeed, neither she nor Hillary Clinton could have used Mr. Obama's public style—or Bill Clinton's either—without being considered too emotional by Washington pundits.

So why is the sex barrier not taken as seriously as the racial one? The reasons are as pervasive as the air we breathe: because sexism is still confused with nature as racism once was; because anything that affects males is seen as more serious than anything that affects "only" the female half of the human race; because children are still raised mostly by women (to put it mildly) so men especially tend to feel they are regressing to childhood when dealing with a powerful woman; because racism stereotyped black men as more "masculine" for so long that some white men find their presence to be masculinity-affirming (as long as there aren't too many of them); and because there is still no "right" way to be a woman in public power without being considered a you-know-what.

I'm not advocating a competition for who has it toughest. The caste systems of sex and race are interdependent and can only be uprooted together. That's why Senators Clinton and Obama have to be careful not to let a healthy debate turn into the kind of hostility that the news media love. Both will need a coalition of outsiders to win a general election. The abolition and suffrage movements progressed when united and were damaged by division; we should remember that.

I'm supporting Senator Clinton because like Senator Obama she has community organizing experience, but she also has more years in the Senate, an unprecedented eight years of on-the-job training in the White House, no masculinity to prove, the potential to tap a huge reservoir of this country's talent by her example, and now even the courage to break the no-tears rule. I'm not opposing Mr. Obama; if he's the nominee, I'll volunteer. Indeed, if you look at votes during their two-year overlap in the Senate, they were the same more than 90 percent of the time. Besides, to clean up the mess left by President Bush, we may need two terms of President Clinton and two of President Obama.

But what worries me is that he is seen as unifying by his race while she is seen as divisive by her sex.

What worries me is that she is accused of "playing the gender card" when citing the old boys' club, while he is seen as unifying by citing civil rights confrontations.

What worries me is that male Iowa voters were seen as gender-free when supporting their own, while female voters were seen as biased if they did and disloyal if they didn't.

What worries me is that reporters ignore Mr. Obama's dependence on the old—for instance, the frequent campaign comparisons to John F. Kennedy—while not challenging the slander that her progressive policies are part of the Washington status quo.

What worries me is that some women, perhaps especially younger ones, hope to deny or escape the sexual caste system; thus Iowa women over 50 and 60, who disproportionately supported Senator Clinton, proved once again that women are the one group that grows more radical with age.

This country can no longer afford to choose our leaders from a talent pool limited by sex, race, money, powerful fathers and paper degrees. It's time to take equal pride in breaking all the barriers. We have to be able to say: "I'm supporting her because she'll be a great president and because she's a woman."

LEST WE FORGET: AN OPEN LETTER TO MY SISTERS WHO ARE BRAVE
By Alice Walker

(handwritten: (Obama) addressing remarks to colored women)

I have come home from a long stay in Mexico to find—because of the presidential campaign, and especially because of the Obama/Clinton race for the Democratic nomination—a new country existing alongside the old. On any given day we, collectively, become the Goddess of the Three Directions and can look back into the past, look at ourselves just where we are, and take a glance, as well, into the future. It is a space with which I am familiar.

When I was born in 1944 my parents lived on a middle Georgia plantation that was owned by a white distant relative, Miss May Montgomery. (During my childhood it was necessary to address all white girls as "Miss" when they reached the age of twelve.) She would never admit to this relationship, of course, except to mock it. Told by my parents that several of their children would not eat chicken skin she responded that of course they would not. No Montgomerys would.

My parents and older siblings did everything imaginable for Miss May. They planted and raised her cotton and corn, fed and killed and processed her cattle and hogs, painted her house, patched her roof, ran her dairy, and, among countless other duties and responsibilities, my father was her chauffeur, taking her anywhere she wanted to go at any hour of the day or night. She lived in a large white house with green shutters and a green, luxuriant lawn: not quite as large as Tara of *Gone with the Wind* fame, but in the same style.

We lived in a shack without electricity or running water, under a rusty tin roof that let in wind and rain. Miss May went to school as a girl. The school my parents and their neighbors built for us was burned to the ground by local racists who wanted to keep ignorant their competitors in tenant farming. During the Depression, desperate to feed his hardworking family, my father asked for a raise from ten dollars a month to twelve. Miss May responded that she would not pay that amount to a white man and she certainly wouldn't pay it to a nigger. That before she'd pay a nigger that much money she'd milk the dairy cows herself.

When I look back, this is part of what I see. I see the school bus carrying white children, boys and girls, right past me, and my brothers, as we trudge on foot five miles to school. Later, I see my parents struggling to build a school out of discarded army barracks while white students, girls and boys, enjoy a building made of brick. We had no books; we inherited the cast-off books that "Jane" and "Dick" had previously used in the all-white school that we were not, as black children, permitted to enter.

The year I turned fifty, one of my relatives told me she had started reading my books for children in the library in my home town. I had had no idea—so kept from black people it had been—that such a place existed. To this day knowing my presence was not wanted in the public library when I was a child I am highly uncomfortable in libraries and will rarely, unless I am there to help build, repair, refurbish or raise money to keep them open, enter their doors.

When I joined the freedom movement in Mississippi in my early twenties it was to come to the aid of sharecroppers, like my parents, who had been thrown off the land they'd always known, the plantations, because they attempted to exercise their "democratic" right to vote. I wish I could say white women treated me and other black people a lot better than the men did, but I cannot. It seemed to me then and it seems to me now that white women have copied, all too often, the behavior of their fathers and their brothers, and in the South, especially in Mississippi, and before that, when I worked to register voters in Georgia, the broken bottles thrown at my head were gender free.

I made my first white women friends in college; they were women who loved me and were loyal to our friendship, but I understood, as they did, that they were white women and that whiteness mattered. That, for instance, at Sarah Lawrence, where I was speedily inducted into the Board of Trustees practically as soon as I graduated, I made my way to the campus for meetings by train, subway and foot, while the other trustees, women and men, all white, made their way by limo. Because, in our country, with its painful history of unspeakable inequality, this is part of what whiteness means. I loved my school for trying to make me feel I mattered to it, but because of my relative poverty I knew I could not.

I am a supporter of Obama because I believe he is the right person to lead the country at this time. He offers a rare opportunity for the country and the world to start over, and to do better. It is a deep sadness to me that many of my feminist white women friends cannot see him. Cannot see what he carries in his being. Cannot hear the fresh choices toward Movement he offers. That they can believe that millions of Americans—black, white, yellow, red and brown—choose Obama over Clinton only because he is a man, and black, feels tragic to me.

When I have supported white people, men and women, it was because I thought them the best possible people to do whatever the job required. Nothing else would have occurred to me. If Obama were in any sense mediocre, he would be forgotten by now. He is, in fact, a remarkable human being, not perfect but humanly stunning, like King was and like Mandela is. We look at him, as we looked at them, and are glad to be of our species. He is the change America has been trying desperately and for centuries to hide, ignore, kill. The change America must have if we are to convince the rest of the world that we care about people other than our (white) selves.

True to my inner Goddess of the Three Directions, however, this does not mean I agree with everything Obama stands for. We differ on important points probably because I am older than he is, I am a woman and person of three colors (African, Native

American, European), I was born and raised in the American South, and when I look at the earth's people, after sixty-four years of life, there is not one person I wish to see suffer, no matter what they have done to me or to anyone else; though I understand quite well the place of suffering, often, in human growth.

I want a grown-up attitude toward Cuba, for instance, a country and a people I love; I want an end to the embargo that has harmed my friends and their children, children who, when I visit Cuba, trustingly turn their faces up for me to kiss. I agree with a teacher of mine, Howard Zinn, that war is as objectionable as cannibalism and slavery; it is beyond obsolete as a means of improving life. I want an end to the ongoing war immediately and I want the soldiers to be encouraged to destroy their weapons and to drive themselves out of Iraq.

I want the Israeli government to be made accountable for its behavior towards the Palestinians, and I want the people of the United States to cease acting like they don't understand what is going on. All colonization, all occupation, all repression basically looks the same, whoever is doing it. Here our heads cannot remain stuck in the sand; our future depends of our ability to study, to learn, to understand what is in the records and what is before our eyes. But most of all I want someone with the self-confidence to talk to anyone, "enemy" or "friend," and this Obama has shown he can do. It is difficult to understand how one could vote for a person who is afraid to sit and talk to another human being. When you vote you are making someone a proxy for yourself; they are to speak when, and in places, you cannot. But if they find talking to someone else, who looks just like them, human, impossible, then what good is your vote?

It is hard to relate what it feels like to see Mrs. Clinton (I wish she felt self-assured enough to use her own name) referred to as "a woman" while Barack Obama is always referred to as "a black man." One would think she is just any woman, colorless, race-less, past-less, but she is not. She carries all the history of white womanhood in America in her person; it would be a miracle if we, and the world, did not react to this fact. How dishonest it is, to attempt to make her innocent of her racial inheritance.

I can easily imagine Obama sitting down and talking, person to person, with any leader, woman, man, child or common person, in the world, with no baggage of past servitude or race supremacy to mar their talks. I cannot see the same scenario with Mrs. Clinton who would drag into twenty-first century American leadership the same image of white privilege and distance from the reality of others' lives that has so marred our country's contacts with the rest of the world.

And yes, I would adore having a woman president of the United States. My choice would be Representative Barbara Lee, who alone voted in Congress five years ago not to make war on Iraq. That to me is leadership, morality, and courage; if she had been white I would have cheered just as hard. But she is not running for the highest office in the land, Mrs. Clinton is. And because Mrs. Clinton is a woman and because she may be very good at what she does, many people, including some younger women in my own family, originally favored her over Obama. I understand this, almost. It is because, in my own nieces' case, there is little memory, apparently, of the foundational inequities that still plague people of color and poor whites in this country. Why, even though our family has been here longer than most North American families—and only partly due to the fact that we have Native American genes—we very recently, in my lifetime, secured the right to vote, and only after numbers of people suffered and died for it.

When I offered the word "Womanism" many years ago, it was to give us a tool to use, as feminist women of color, in times like these. These are the moments we can see clearly, and must honor devotedly, our singular path as women of color in the United States. We are not white women and this truth has been ground into us for centuries, often in brutal ways. But neither are we inclined to follow a black person, man or woman, unless they demonstrate considerable courage, intelligence, compassion and substance. I am delighted that so many women of color support Barack Obama—and genuinely proud of the many young and old white women and men who do.

Imagine, if he wins the presidency we will have not one but three black women in the White House; one tall, two somewhat shorter; none of them carrying the washing in and out of the back door. The bottom line for most of us is: With whom do we have a better chance of surviving the madness and fear we are presently enduring, and with whom do we wish to set off on a journey of new possibility? In other words, as the Hopi elders would say: Who do we want in the boat with us as we head for the rapids? Who is likely to know how best to share the meager garden produce and water? We are advised by the Hopi elders to celebrate this time, whatever its adversities.

We have come a long way, Sisters, and we are up to the challenges of our time. One of which is to build alliances based not on race, ethnicity, color, nationality, sexual preference or gender, but on Truth. Celebrate our journey. Enjoy the miracle we are witnessing. Do not stress over its outcome. Even if Obama becomes president, our country is in such ruin it may well be beyond his power to lead us toward rehabilitation. If he is elected, however, we must, individually and collectively, as citizens of the planet, insist on helping him do the best job that can be done; more, we must insist that he demand this of us. It is a blessing that our mothers taught us not to fear hard work. Know, as the Hopi elders declare: The river has its destination. And remember, as poet June Jordan and Sweet Honey in the Rock never tired of telling us: We are the ones we have been waiting for.

Namaste;
And with all my love,
Alice Walker
Cazul
Northern California
First Day of Spring

QUESTIONS FOR ANALYSIS

Historically and Geographically/Globally Contextual

1. What are Gloria Steinem's (born in 1934 in Toledo, Ohio) and Alice Walker's (born in 1944 in Eatonton, Georgia) backgrounds? How might the difference in their ages or places of birth have shaped their earliest understanding of systems of privilege and oppression in the United States? What path has each woman

taken as an adult? What kinds of causes has each woman been involved in and in what ways?

2. What were the major strengths and weaknesses of the Second Wave of the feminist movement in America? How much has the Second Wave influenced Steinem? Does she seem to have moved beyond the Second Wave in any significant way in this essay? If so, how?

3. In 1984, Alice Walker published *In Search of Our Mothers' Gardens*, in which she coined the term *womanism*. What is womanism? What is its relationship to the tenets of Second Wave feminism? How does Walker's assertion in this essay that this is a moment when "we…must honor devotedly our singular path of women of color in the United States" elucidate her understanding of womanism?

4. What historical evidence would you use to support Steinem's claim that "[g]ender is probably the most restricting force in American life"? In what ways does Walker seek to complicate Steinem's claim? What evidence would you use to support Walker's position?

Socially Constructed

1. Why, as Walker points out, is Hillary Clinton referred to only as a "woman," whereas Barack Obama is called a "black man"? What purpose does this distinction serve in maintaining the hierarchy of social inequality in the United States?

2. These two essays focus on Clinton and Obama in terms of their races and genders. How do sexuality and class also play a role in their lives?

3. How did the socially constructed nature of Barack Obama's racial identity in the United States shape his life experiences? Why, to some, was his "blackness" never questioned, whereas others accused him of not being "black enough"? Does Walker mention this issue? Why or why not?

4. How has society's perception of Hillary Clinton's "womanhood" changed over time? In what ways has she tried to align herself with more traditional notions of white femininity (especially during her husband's political career) and how, in her role as New York senator, was she able to diminish those concerns? By the time she ran for president, to what extent was Clinton able to minimize society's focus on her gender? Was this a positive or negative development? From what perspective? Does Steinem mention this issue? Why or why not?

Power Relationships

1. Gloria Steinem's piece was published in *The New York Times*, and Alice Walker's essay appeared online at www.theroot.com. What explanation(s) might you offer for the mainstream press's paying attention only to Steinem?

2. Steinem opens her piece with a fictional portrait of a female version of Barack Obama, in which everything about his life remains constant except for the change in gender, and asks readers to consider whether "she" could have been a viable candidate for president. Steinem argues, "[H]er goose would have been

cooked long ago." What if we imagine, under the same circumstances, instead, an African American version of Hillary Clinton? Could she have been a viable candidate for president? What, if anything, would have made her candidacy different from that of the female version of Barack Obama?

3. Steinem argues that the Iowa primary, which provided Obama with a key early victory over Clinton, followed our country's "historical pattern of making change" in giving access to institutional power in the form of the vote to African American men long before it gave it to women. What historical realities for African Americans attempting to vote temper Steinem's claim? Did women have access to some forms of institutional power before African American men did? Which women?

4. If we had to draw a dividing line between the choices for action made by Steinem and Walker, we might argue that Steinem chose the path of seeking change through the political structure while Walker heeded Audre Lorde's call that "poetry is not a luxury." What evidence of these emphases do you find in their essays? Does one approach have a better chance of shifting power relationships between the privileged and oppressed in this country? Why or why not?

Macro/Social Structural and Micro/Social Psychological Levels

1. Walker and Steinem have a history of friendship going back many years to *Ms. Magazine*. Is that history evident here? How? What kind of reply do you imagine Steinem might make to Walker's essay? What points might she agree with? Disagree with?

2. To what extent do you think that changes in the macroeconomic conditions of the society at the time of the campaign (e.g., declining employment opportunities and the rising gap between the rich and the poor) contributed to Obama's popularity? What groups (race, class, gender, sexuality) ultimately voted for Obama?

3. When considering the changing demographics of the country, what might you project for the future opportunities of people of color in American political life?

4. The 2008 presidential election has been argued by many to be a time of significant generational change. Obama was able to connect with younger voters because he challenged the traditional structure of political strategy in the United States. What does that traditional structure look like, and in what ways was Obama able to move beyond it to engage so many young people in the electoral process, both in the primaries and in the general election? What kept Clinton from making these connections with younger voters?

Simultaneously Expressed

1. Although Steinem seeks to address the oppression of women in this country, Walker complicates her analysis by reminding readers that White women also

occupy a position of privilege in the United States. Why might Steinem not acknowledge this privilege?

2. In his inaugural address, President Obama spoke of America's "patchwork heritage" as a source of our nation's strength. What did he mean by that statement, both in terms of the history of the United States and in his own life? In what ways is this patchwork a source of strength?

3. What collective and individual dreams for the future of our country are evident in Walker's, Steinem's, Clinton's, and Obama's stories and lives? What similarities and differences do you find in how they speak about their hopes for the future? How do race, class, gender, and sexuality influence the scope of their dreams?

Implications for Social Action and Social Justice

1. The title of Walker's essay addresses "my sisters who are brave," a reference to the title of the first anthology in Black women's studies, *All the Women Are White, All the Blacks Are Men, But Some of Us Are Brave: Black Women's Studies.* At that time, the title referred only to Black women, but who is Walker addressing in this essay?

2. President Obama appointed Hillary Clinton as secretary of state. She is the third woman (two White, one African American) to hold this position. What is the significance of this appointment? How well do Obama's cabinet members represent the patchwork heritage of America?

3. What signs of progressing beyond the question of whether race or gender is the prime site for oppression in this country can you find in these essays? How well do the authors recognize that race, class, gender, and sexuality are simultaneously expressed? What do your findings suggest about the rate and path of progress in dismantling systems of hierarchy in the United States? What does Obama's election (and Clinton's candidacy) suggest about the rate and path of progress?

REFERENCES

Clinton, Hillary. 2004. *Living History.* New York: Scribner.

Farrell, Amy Erdman. 1998. *Yours in Sisterhood: Ms. Magazine and the Pormise of Popular Feminism.* Chapel Hill: University of North Carolina Press. *New York Times,* "Election 2008." Available athttp://elections.nytimes.com/2008/index.html?scp=3&sq=election%25202008&st=cse.

Obama, Barack. 2004. *Dreams from My Father. A Story of Race and Inheritance.* New York: Crown.

Rosen, Ruth. 2006. *The World Split Open: How the Modern Women's Movement Changed America.* New York: Penguin Books.

Steinem, Gloria. 2008. "Women are never front-runners." *The New York Times* January, 8.

Walker, Alice. 2008. "Lest we forget: An open letter to my sisters who are brave." *The Root* March, 27. Available from http://www.theroot.com/views/lest-we-forget-open-letter-my-sister-who-are-brave accessed April 4, 2009.

——. 2003. *In Search of Our Mothers' Gardens: Womanist Prose.* New York: Harcourt Books.

CASE STUDY 2

✦

The Valenzuela Family[1]

Leo R. Chavez

B eatriz and Enrique Valenzuela live southeast of downtown San Diego. Their two-
bedroom house is on a street lined with other modest, single-family homes in
an older, relatively low-income neighborhood. A block away runs a major avenue,
along which the walls of some buildings are covered with graffiti. As we sat in their
living room sipping on sodas, they talked about their lives as undocumented immigrants. They were very open about their experiences. It had been more than fifteen
years since each had left Mexico for San Diego, having made the journey separately
before meeting, and marrying, here. As we talked, Beatriz slowly began to cry. "I was
afraid because I had never left home before," she said. "So when I was on my way
here, I was very afraid. All the way from Manzanillo to Tijuana I cried—the whole
way."

For Beatriz and others I talked with, leaving home was an important event. They
separated themselves from family, friends, and community in Mexico to live in the United
States as undocumented immigrants. The fundamental reason was work. A laborer can
earn seven to ten times as much working on the U.S. side of the border as on the Mexican side. But there is more to the story than this. Personal histories of undocumented
immigrants reveal a complex array of motives for migration. They provide insight into
why Mexicans view migration to the United States as something within the realm of
their possibilities....

Editor's Note: This case study was excerpted from *Shadowed Lives: Undocumented Immigrants in
American Society* by Leo R. Chavez. In his study, Leo Chavez provides a description and analysis of the
lives of undocumented workers in Southern California, particularly in San Diego County. Chavez has
conducted research among legal and undocumented Mexican immigrants since 1980. Although there
are many personal stories in *Shadowed Lives*, we have excerpted the stories of Beatriz and Enrique
Valenzuela here.

[1]Leo R. Chavez, "The Valenzuela Family" from *Shadowed Lives: Undocumented-Immigrants in
American Society.* Copyright © 1992 by Holt, Rinehart and Winston. Reprinted with the permission
of the publishers.

MIGRATION AS A PART OF FAMILY HISTORY [ENRIQUE][2]

As we sat and talked in his living room, Enrique Valenzuela told his story of coming to the United States. He was raised on a *rancho*—a very small agricultural community, usually consisting of only a few families, in the state of Puebla....His family's land depended upon rainfall to grow corn and beans. "If it rains, there is work for six months. If it doesn't rain, there is no work." During periods of little or no work, his father migrated elsewhere, including the United States, to earn money.

His father worked in the United States under the contract labor program known as the "Bracero Program." The term *bracero* is derived from *brazos*, or "arms," and refers to laborers, especially agricultural workers. In 1942, the U.S. government instituted the Bracero Program as a short-term solution to the agricultural labor shortage created by the influx of American men into the armed services during World War II. The program allowed American employers to hire, under contract, Mexican laborers for specific periods of time, usually a few months. Although it was originally a short-term program, the benefits of bracero labor resulted in the program's extension well beyond the war years. It was finally phased out in 1964. Over this twenty-two-year period, hundreds of thousands of Mexicans were hired to work temporarily in the United States (Craig 1971).

Enrique's father worked as a bracero for twelve years. "Sometimes he'd get a contract for three months, six months, and then he would return to the rancho, to Mexico. And then the next year he would return [to the United States] again. He did that until the Bracero Program ended." During this time, Enrique worked on the rancho. He was the oldest child and as such, he said, "[from the time] I was very young, I had to work to help feed my brothers and sisters and mother."

In 1963, when he was sixteen, Enrique decided to leave the rancho because "there was no work there. We were very hungry. We earned enough to barely get by. But I wanted to do better, to get out of poverty, to do something with my life." And so Enrique migrated to Mexico City, where he found a job in the market selling tomatoes and chiles for 50 pesos (about $4 U.S.) a week. After two months, he found a better job in a small factory, making car accessories such as antennas and mirrors. When he left that job, in 1970, he was earning about 275 pesos a week (about $22 U.S.).

After working in Mexico City for the same employer for nearly seven years, Enrique felt he needed a change. "I only earned enough to eat with and pay rent." He remembered his father talking about work in the United States. "My father would say that when it was good, you could get ahead. And that's how later I thought that someday I would come to this country." After the Bracero Program ended in 1964, Enrique's father continued to migrate to the United States as an undocumented worker, relying on contacts made with employers during his years as a bracero. His father always tried, however, both in person and in his letters to Enrique, to discourage Enrique's interest in migrating to the United States, "My father had told me that it was very hard and that he suffered a lot. 'When you first come to this country you suffer,' he would tell me. He tried not to have me come here."

---

[2]Text in brackets was added for clarification.

In 1970, his father was working on a ranch in northern San Diego County. Enrique decided to take advantage of the situation, and convinced his father to help him migrate. Before leaving, Enrique had to inform his employer, who tried to dissuade him from pursuing his plans.

> I told my boss that I was going to come and try my luck here. He didn't like that. He told me Mexicans were not wanted here [in the United States] and that I would be treated very poorly. He said that with him I would have work for a lifetime, that it would not work out for me here and that I would never progress. So I told him that I wanted to try my luck because I had been with him for seven years and could not do anything more. So he got mad at me.

Despite his employer's objections and warnings, Enrique migrated to San Diego. He was 23 years old....

MIGRATION AS A PART OF FAMILY HISTORY [BEATRIZ]

Beatriz was in her mid-forties and had the tired look of someone who regularly worked long days. She showed a sly sense of humor when she spoke. She was born and raised in Manzanillo, Colima, where her family owned a large bakery. Because of the family business, Beatriz was able to study through high school. But in 1964, when Beatriz was twenty years old, her father died, setting off a period of bitter conflict between her and her two older brothers, who believed they alone were entitled to their father's inheritance. Beatriz believed that her brothers, especially the oldest one, were taking advantage of her since she was the youngest child. She believed that she, too, deserved some of the inheritance. This led to a period of intense conflict, which eventually caused her to leave for the United States.

> We were feuding, especially with my oldest brother. I didn't fight with my sisters because they were already married. But it was with the two boys that I fought every day. My oldest brother kicked me out of the house. He would kick me out just like that, saying "Leave my house," because the house was left in his name. We lived in a very large house.

During this time, Beatriz had friends whose married sisters lived in the United States but often returned to Manzanillo. "They would tell me about the United States and invite me to go back with them." Beatriz declined their invitations until finally the pressure of feuding with her brothers became too much to bear.

> I tolerated them [her brothers] for five years, but only for my mother, only for her. I would tell her that I wanted to go to another place or come here [the United States], and she would start to cry. When I couldn't stand it anymore, that's when I asked her for permission to come here.

Beatriz did not migrate to the United States for economic reasons. Family conflict drove her out of her home. "If it hadn't been for the problems with my brothers I wouldn't have to come here because I worked in our own business." She received advice and encouragement from her friends, who arranged for a place in the United States for Beatriz to stay and told her their relatives would assist her in finding work. She accepted their help but "they didn't know about my family problems because I didn't talk about that with anyone." Beatriz's memory of her trip from Manzanillo to Tijuana recalls the loneliness and fear felt by someone who had never left home before. "I was afraid and I would think of my mother. So the whole way I cried." When I heard her story, it had been about seventeen years since Beatriz had last seen her mother.

. . .

Crossing over the hills and through the canyons presents risks that some individuals and families attempt to avoid. Various strategies attempt to blend illegal border crossers in with the thousands of people who daily cross legally at the official port of entry. Many apply for a temporary visiting permit, or shopping card, and use it as a pass across the border, staying beyond the time limitations. Beatriz, Enrique Valenzuela's wife, entered with such a card. As she remembered,

> I applied for a permit to cross. I went to Guadalajara and…they gave me a permit. So I came with a friend of mine. We got to Tijuana and…a sister of hers picked us up. My friend also had a permit. So there in San Ysidro they stamped our permits and we crossed. I came here on August 2, 1969.

Beatriz has returned to Mexico only once, for a few days in Tijuana in 1972 to have her first child. She has not been back since. As we sat on her sofa talking, Beatriz cried as she spoke of her longing to see her mother.

> During all these years I wanted to go but I am afraid of crossing the border and won't risk it. You know how they say that they assault people, murder women. I'm scared of crossing and that's why I don't go to Mexico. That's my problem.

Like Beatriz, many undocumented immigrants fear recrossing the border. This puts pressure on them to stay in the United States until they are sure they want, or are forced, to return home. This seems especially true for women, who very often immigrate on their first and only trip to the United States.

Perhaps realizing the desire to avoid the dangers associated with crossing the border, coyotes [border guides] also offer relatively safe passage by providing shopping cards that have been lost or stolen. Or, they make arrangements for women and children to pass through with other persons, particularly Americans, who make unlikely suspects for transporting illegal border crossers.

Beatriz found herself in need of such services in 1972, when she was ready to return to the U.S. after having her baby in a Tijuana hotel.

> I was in Tijuana and because I couldn't stay there my friend found someone to cross us. She sent a very young American guy. One of those guys who doesn't work, but wants money. He came after me and brought us. I didn't have any problems. They just asked him where we were headed. He said San Diego and they let us through without problems. That was the only time I left here [San Diego], but it was out of necessity.

...

[When] Beatriz arrived in San Diego, she stayed with the sister of a friend she had come with. After finding a job as a live-in maid, Beatriz would visit her friend on weekends. Her friend worked for an older American woman in a large house with a swimming pool. "This woman would drink a lot, night and day. On the weekends, those of us who didn't have a place to stay would get together there and the lady didn't mind."

Beatriz's friend would sometimes invite male friends over to go swimming. On one of these occasions, Beatriz met Daniel. "Later, on the beach in downtown La Jolla, it's called The Cove, Daniel introduced Enrique to us. From there, we started to go out together. He would invite me to go out to eat, and to just be out because we didn't have money. He didn't and I didn't. I sent my $27 a week [all her earnings] to my mother." Enrique and Beatriz did not have much time to spend together. She worked as a live-in maid during the week and on some Sundays cleaned another house in order to earn an additional ten dollars, which she would keep for spending money.

Their relationship grew despite having little time to actually be together. As Beatriz tells it: "When I met him I didn't live with him. I only went to see him on weekends because I lived at my job and he with his friends, until I got pregnant with Carolina. That's when we looked for our own place, apart from our friends." They married in 1977, a year after their son was born.

...

THE STEADY WORKER

Enrique typically is the first one to arrive at the Chinese restaurant where he works. He unlocks the kitchen door, straightens up a bit, and begins preparing the vegetables and meats to be used in the day's Cantonese and Mandarin dishes. It is a routine he knows well. He has worked for the same employer since he arrived in the United States in 1970, some sixteen years by the time I met him in 1986. "For fifteen, sixteen years, it is the same schedule. I go in at 10:30 A.M., and leave [the restaurant] at 9:45 or 10 at night. I return home and I arrive at 10:10 or 10:15 P.M. I am away from home for almost twelve hours."

Although Enrique had come to join his father, the owner of the farm where his father worked did not need more employees. And so he had the coyote drive him to La Jolla, where his father had heard that there was restaurant work available. He walked into the first restaurant he saw and asked for work. He was hired as a dishwasher part-time, which was enough for Enrique to survive, but barely. "When I began sixteen years ago, it went very bad for me. I only worked three hours per day. I earned $1.50 per hour. The money was only enough to eat and pay the rent. There was no money for anything else. One year, exactly, I earned that salary. After one year, I earned $300 per month. For me, it was much better."

Full-time employment also meant Enrique had to experience a great American tradition: taxes. At this time it was easy for anyone to obtain a social security card, a practice that would change in later years. "My boss told me that in this country one had to pay the government. So I went to apply for my social security card. I began to pay taxes in 1971 and I have done so ever since."

Enrique gradually learned to prepare Chinese food. "When I first began, I washed dishes. They graduated me to cut vegetables. Next to cut meats. Later to a position to fry foods. Then another position to prepare and cook. To date, I am at that same position." The evolution of his skills improved his position at work. He now works on a salary rather than by the hour, earning between $900 and $1,000 a month, depending on tips.

Enrique's acquisition of skills in the kitchen has helped him weather changes at the restaurant. In 1974, his employer opened a new Chinese restaurant east of downtown and eventually closed the La Jolla restaurant. Enrique continued to work at the new restaurant. Enrique has also managed to continue working despite personnel shifts at the restaurant. Once, the majority of kitchen help were Mexican. According to Enrique, "The Chinese bring their families little by little. So, they begin to employ their relatives and cut down on the number of Mexicans. Right now there are very few of us Mexicans, four or five." Enrique attributes his continued employment to hard work. "In all these years, I've never failed to go to work because of a stomachache or headache. They notice that and so they give me a chance. I'm the only Mexican there who gets a paid vacation. They give me a week a year."

Enrique realizes that he has little economic mobility left at his job. He is earning about the best he could possibly earn at the restaurant. He also realizes that despite having worked for so many years at this job, his job is not necessarily permanent. He also does not receive any other benefits, although he is able to buy medical insurance at a reduced rate through his work. And over the years, he has experienced many personal slights and often has had to reduce his expectations. But he has endured all of this because at least the work was steady. He also believed he had only limited opportunities elsewhere due to his undocumented status.

> Without papers you have to tolerate everything at a job: humiliations, low wages, long hours. But if you leave that job and go to another, it's the same thing because you don't have papers. So for us, our papers are the most important thing in order to get ahead in this country. We want to progress. With papers we can open a cafeteria, for example, or a taco stand, where we can earn more, because we are not educated enough to find a good job. But we do like to work a lot.

A few months after Enrique arrived in San Diego, he met Beatriz, who was working as a live-in maid. They soon married, and began a family. Beatriz's pregnancy presented Enrique and Beatriz with some important economic problems, especially as to where Beatriz would deliver the baby. As Enrique said, "I had very little money saved. You know how it is when you arrive here without knowing anyone. They don't trust you without having credit or anything. So we thought that she should have the baby in Tijuana because it was more affordable. She went to Tijuana to give birth and she returned about ten days later with her [daughter]."

With the return of his wife and daughter, Enrique now had a family of three in San Diego. He became concerned with his family's future. Faced with limited economic mobility at their jobs, Enrique and Beatriz embarked on a strategy of saving what they could from their earnings. According to Enrique, "It was around that time that we started to save, not enough because we were now three. But because we were ambitious to accomplish something, we tried very hard." The concern with providing for a growing family and saving for a better future put added pressure on both Enrique and Beatriz to stay at their jobs, work hard, and not take the unnecessary risks associated with frequent job changes.

Beatriz's work history in San Diego did not begin when she met Enrique. After her tearful bus ride from her mother's home and the family bakery she had worked in, she too had to find work in San Diego. Undocumented Mexican women in San Diego work in many types of jobs, including manufacturing, the garment industry, and restaurants. Many, however, are engaged in domestic work, as live-in babysitters, live-in housekeepers or maids, and housekeepers who service a number of houses a week. Beatriz's story, and that of other Mexican women, suggests that this type of work is not "natural" in the sense that women may not have had any particular training for it. On the contrary, their past work experiences may have been as varied as that of men. But faced with limited opportunities in the San Diego job market, immigrant women turn to domestic work. And at times, they view it as having strategic advantages for them in comparison to other types of jobs they might find.

WOMEN AND DOMESTIC WORK

Beatriz arrived in San Diego on August 2, 1969, a day she remembers well. She arrived at the house of her traveling companion's sister. After a couple of days' rest, her friend's sister helped her find work as a live-in maid in La Jolla. The job paid little, the work load was heavy, and she had little time off. "I started working for a family that had three girls and two adults. But I was overworked there. All day, until 1 A.M., I would be ironing for only 27 dollars a week. I got half a day on Sundays off. On Sundays, after feeding them breakfast, I would go out and then I would have to be back that same day because if I came back the next morning they would reduce my pay."

Beatriz left that job after six months. She found another that paid slightly better, 30 dollars a week, but the lady she worked for moved to Colorado. Without work, she stayed with a friend until she found work again. She continued to work as a live-in maid until her daughter was born in 1972, after which Beatriz decided being away from home all week would be too difficult. Her friend, who also worked as a housekeeper, had already been in the United States about thirteen years at that point and helped her find day work through her employer's friends. In this way she found her first daytime housecleaning job. This led to additional jobs.

> After I had Carolina, I went to work with [that family]. The lady liked the way I worked. I first started to work only one day a week with her because I had just gotten out of the hospital. She liked the way I worked so much that she gave me another day. I told her that I only had these two days of work and that I needed more. She got me work with an architect. That architect gave me two days, too. The lady next door to my first employer also asked me if I could work for her, and I said "Yes." She gave me one day, so I worked the five days.

After five years, Beatriz stopped working for the architect and the neighbor, and found two new employers to fill out her week. By 1986, she had worked for these two new employers for ten years and in her original household for fifteen years. Over this time she has seen her pay for a five and a half to six hour day go from ten to twelve to fourteen dollars a day, until finally she was earning about twenty-seven dollars a day in 1986 and 1987.

Over the years Beatriz has developed what she considers to be a personal relationship with her employers. Indeed, she has exchanged formal benefits and a contractual work relationship for this informal arrangement based upon personal relationships. Beatriz acknowledges that the lack of formal benefits, particularly medical insurance, is difficult. Although Enrique has medical insurance, it does not cover Beatriz and their children. "The day I get sick, it's expensive." She has come to depend upon an informal agreement for limited benefits.

> When I get sick and don't work, I get paid. Holidays I get paid. If I have a school meeting for the kids, I still get paid. Lots of times I've been sick and they've given me half the money so I can go to the doctor. And they treat me well. They don't give me too much work.

The fact that Beatriz has worked so many years for the same employers has allowed her to develop a personal relationship in which the informal benefits are understood and abided by. Other women do not develop such a relationship with an employer. Women who clean various houses a week typically get paid only on the days they work. They are, in essence, independent contractors. Their relationships with employers are more limited, and they often have many employers, some long-term but many on a short-term basis.

...

As Beatriz noted,

> When my kids are sick, I tell the lady that my youngest child is sick and she'll tell me to leave right away, even if I've worked for only an hour. She'll say that it's more important to be with your son than work. So, that's why I'm happy working there. They never check when I get there or when I leave...If I worked in a factory or laundromat, my hours would be controlled. I would have to be there at a certain hour and leave at a certain hour. Work the eight hours. I like working in homes...I can go whenever I want and leave when my kids need me. In a factory I wouldn't have that advantage. If my kids were sick I'd still have to go to work.

...

LEARNING TO LIVE AS AN "ILLEGAL ALIEN"

... Enrique Valenzuela describes his many years in San Diego as similar to being in jail.

> In all these sixteen years I feel like I've been in jail. I don't feel free. I came to this country to work, not to do things on the street that you shouldn't do. That's not what I mean by freedom. I'm referring to the feeling of being in a prison because if you go out, like when we go out for fun, it's always in the back of your mind, will immigration show up? Or when you go to work you think all the time, from

the moment you walk out of your home, you think, "Will the immigration stop me on the way or when I'm at work?" So I do feel like I'm in jail.

As Enrique and I talked about his feeling of being in jail, a song popular at the time, "Jaula de Oro" ("The Gilded Cage"),[3] came up in our conversation. He felt the song echoed his situation, and that of many undocumented immigrants who have been in the United States for many years. Two of the verses are particularly apt here:

Aquí estoy establecido en los Estados Unidos. Diez años pasaron ya en que cruzé de mojado. Papeles no me he arreglado sigo siendo ilegal.	Here I am established in the United States. It's been ten years since I crossed as a wetback. I never applied for papers, I'm still illegal.
¿De qué me sirve el dinero si yo soy como prisionero dentro de esta gran nación? Cuando me acuerdo hasta lloro aunque la jaula sea de oro, no deja de ser prisión.	What good is money if I am like a prisoner in this great nation? When I think about it, I cry. Even if the cage is made of gold, it doesn't make it less a prison.

Enrique believed that the song described his situation to a degree. But he wanted to make it clear that when the singer speaks of "gold," it does not mean that he is rich. It merely means that he has a job and an income. "I don't feel free, but we don't have a lot of money, either."

All these statements have in common the idea of being encapsulated within a larger social system. Describing themselves as being in jail, living within in a circle or a chicken coop, and feeling confined within San Diego's borders are all ways of relating how their undocumented status places limits on their incorporation into society. Although they work and live in San Diego, their movements are ultimately constrained. Their agreement on a lack of freedom of movement emphasizes that even though they are inside a larger social system, they are not fully part of that social system. Their incorporation has not been complete.

HOME AS A REFUGE

To allay some of the constant fear of apprehension and deportation, undocumented immigrants attempt to create some security through a network of friends and relatives. They tend to live near relatives and friends who had previously migrated, or people who they themselves helped to migrate and become established in the area. But at the heart of this attempt to create some sense of security is their home, which becomes a retreat, a place of refuge, a sanctuary in which they are less visible than on the streets or at work.

For Beatriz and Enrique Valenzuela, being home offers some relief from their daily fears. Beatriz leaves home as the sun rises and walks about ten blocks to the bus stop.

---

[3]"Jaula de Oro," performed by Los Tigres del Norte, produced by Profono Internacional Inc. 1985.

She has been robbed of her bus money twice while walking along the road. She then rides a series of buses to arrive in La Jolla, a trip that takes about an hour and a half. She returns late in the afternoon. Enrique leaves for work at about 10 A.M. and returns home at about 10:30 at night. During the week, Enrique rarely is able to talk with his family. His daughter and son both attend school during the day. On Sundays, the Valuenzuela family finally has the opportunity to interact with one another.

With their family outside of the home most of time, Enrique and Beatriz constantly worry about one of the family being apprehended. Only when they are all at home do they feel a sense of security. As Beatriz said, "When one is at home, one feels secure. We are always concerned with the danger of the immigration [agents] on the bus. I'm always in danger. When I arrive home, it's then that I can rest and feel content. Because there is always fear of walking the streets." Enrique agreed:

> When we are all at home [Sunday] is the only day that we are all happy, because it is that day that we all feel very secure, secure no matter what the danger. My wife is the first to leave. When she leaves the fear begins. Then, when my children leave, the same fear. Finally, when I leave, well all day long while I am at work, it is all I think about, that something could happen to us, because of the status that we have in this country.

Enrique and Beatriz carry these fears around with them during the day. Although Enrique has never been apprehended, he still becomes full of fear when he spots an immigration officer. Enrique and Beatriz believe that everything they have managed to acquire over almost two decades in the United States could easily be lost. In 1979, they purchased a modest two-bedroom home in a low-income area. They have appliances, a television, a car. And yet they realize that they live in a house of cards that could easily come tumbling down. As Enrique said, "At night I dream about it, that they catch me. That everything caves in." Beatriz added, "It's true. You're terrorized. I have nightmares!"

Once again, the song "Jaula de Oro" speaks to the fears held by undocumented immigrants and the security they often seek in seclusion:

De mi trabajo a mi casa. Yo no sé lo que me pasa aunque soy hombre de hogar. Casi no salgo a la calle pues tengo miedo que me hallen y me puedan deportar.	From my job to my home. I don't know what is happening to me. I am a home-body. I almost never go out to the street. I am afraid I will be found and could be deported.

For many undocumented immigrants who have formed a family in the United States, such as Enrique and Beatriz, one of their greatest fears is that a family member might be apprehended. When a spouse or child is late coming home, the fear quickly sets in that the person has been apprehended. Wives who do not work, and who do not have a great deal of experience interacting with the larger society, are particularly fearful of their husbands' sudden apprehension.

...

When undocumented immigrants are apprehended, they often experience a great deal of pressure to sign a voluntary departure form. When a person becomes defiant, as did Beatriz Valenzuela, the pressure can mount. Beatriz's experience reveals both the tragedy and the comedy of the situation.

Beatriz's greatest fear, for almost eighteen years, had been that she would be apprehended while riding the bus to work in La Jolla. On July 9, 1986, that fear became a reality. During that week, the immigration authorities were boarding most of the buses entering La Jolla in search of "illegal aliens" who worked in the beach community's restaurants, hotels, and private homes. On that day, Beatriz's bus arrived on La Jolla Boulevard at about 6:40 A.M. With officers stationed at the doors in front and back of the bus to ensure no one could jump off, officers asked the occupants for their documents. Not having any, Beatriz was asked to get off the bus. Because they were interested in legalizing their status, Beatriz and Enrique had consulted a lawyer whose advice was not to sign a voluntary departure, but to ask for a court hearing. Armed with this knowledge, Beatriz was ready when the immigration agent suggested signing a voluntary departure.

> He took out a piece of paper and told me that we were going to fill it out right now, so you can sign it, so that you can go to Tijuana. I told him that I was not going to sign anything. Why should I? He said, "You aren't going to sign?" I said, "No." He said, "Do you know how many years await you in jail?" I said, "No." He said. "You can expect two or three years in jail." I said, "Really." He said, "Yes, really, and all because you don't want to sign this document. If you sign it right now, you'll be taken to Tijuana. But if you don't sign it, it will go real bad for you," I said, "Well, too bad. If you're going to feed me in jail and I don't have to work, then that's a vacation for me!"

The immigration agents took Beatriz to a detention center near the border, where she stayed for three days. Beatriz remembers it well, since one of those days was her birthday. Three days later Beatriz was released, after Enrique posted a $2,000 bond to guarantee that she would appear at a court hearing.

Carolina, Beatriz's oldest child, was thirteen when her mother was pulled off the bus and detained. Carolina's reactions to the news of her mother's arrest reflects the confused fears of a young child, and her lack of experience with life in Mexico, the country of her birth. She said,

> I was worried that we were going to be sent back to Mexico, that we had to go back and live like those people, without any homes. They have to sleep in the streets, sell anything, like gum. There was going to be no food. Maybe I couldn't go to school because my parents needed money.... We were going to lose everything we had here.... I was afraid that maybe my brother [age eleven] had to stay here, and we had to go, because he's an American citizen. And maybe the government would send him to some kind of shelter for kids that don't have homes or anything. Maybe he was going to miss his parents and me.

Carolina's fears pictured the worst-case scenario, much of which was based on stereotypes of the poverty which exists in Tijuana. But even given that her depiction of possible events may not have been realistic, it was a very vivid image in her mind. She suddenly found the future security of her home and family in doubt. She was caught up in events over which she had no control and little understanding. The only thing she knew at the time was that her life had the possibility of being turned upside-down, changing from one of hope to one of despair. Carolina's fears of her brother's separation from the family because of his different status—born in the United States and therefore a U.S. citizen—reflects the types of stress found in binational families.

. . .

Because of their desire to legalize their status, undocumented immigrants seek out lawyers and immigration consultants, sometimes with disastrous consequences, as with Enrique and Beatriz Valenzuela.

In 1976, after their son José was born in San Diego, Enrique and Beatriz sought legal advice on legalizing their status. They had heard that a U.S. citizen child could apply to have his or her parents enter the country as legal immigrants. Unfortunately, the law had changed so that a child must be 21 years old before being able to assist his or her parents to immigrate legally.

The "lawyer" they sought out had been recommended by a friend. As Enrique said, since the law had changed, "The lawyer, who said he was a lawyer, said he couldn't do anything more. The only thing was to wait for amnesty." For amnesty for Enrique, Beatriz, and their daughter Carolina, the "lawyer" charged them $700, with half due immediately, and the rest after the case was completed. According to Enrique, "From 1977 to 1980–81, he couldn't do anything. Amnesty wasn't getting here."

Enrique then asked him if there was any other way to legalize his family's status. "He said that there was another way, but it was expensive. He said that it came to about $5,000. I asked if it was a sure way. He said that in 90 percent of the cases it was. He said that we had been here a long time and it would be possible. I told him that we had some money saved, but it was all that we had."

Enrique gave the "lawyer" $1,000 that day. He then arranged to pay $200 a month until he paid $2,500. The other half would be due when the case was over. However, there arose additional expenses in the case for which the "lawyer" needed more money. "He said if you don't pay more then that's the end of everything, and you lose all you've put into it [the case]." Enrique and Beatriz believed that something was wrong, since the initial agreement was to only pay half of the total cost before the case was settled. But they paid nonetheless. The reason: fear. As Enrique noted,

> The man didn't threaten me, but we were afraid. When he required the second half from me, after I had paid him the first, we were very afraid. So we continued paying. Not so much for ourselves, because we knew he was cheating us, but because if we didn't finish paying he would denounce us [to the immigration authorities].

Two years later, Enrique confronted the "lawyer." Enrique was angry because nothing had been done and he had paid everything requested of him. The man's response, according to Enrique, was that "It was a matter for the courts, they should be calling us."

As it turned out, Enrique soon found out that the "lawyer" had a partner, another lawyer, who was also involved in the case. When this second lawyer died shortly after Enrique's confrontation with his original "lawyer," he found his case had been taken over by yet another lawyer. At this point the original "lawyer" directed Enrique to see the new lawyer about his case. "He now didn't have any more to do with my case."

Enrique went to the new lawyer and found out something surprising and disturbing. Virtually nothing had been done on his case. There were no legal papers filed (so the court would not be "calling"). Moreover, "We thought he was a lawyer, but later when he told us that he couldn't continue our case any longer and sent us to another lawyer, it was the other lawyer who told us that he wasn't a lawyer. He was a notary public." The real lawyer, who had died, was actually the lawyer of record on the case.

As we sat in his living room, the center of the only island of security he had in San Diego, Enrique just shook his head in disbelief. He had sought to increase his security, and instead became a victim of those who prey on the misfortunes of others. As he said, "It's not fair that they steal from us in this way without doing anything. We earn our money as quickly as we can and it is not much that we can save. It's easy for them to take it away quickly." Beatriz was clearly angry when she reflected on the years they were involved with this person and the money they spent:

> In order to meet his installments we had to cut back and deny ourselves other things that we needed, for us and our children. We had to pay $200 every month, every month. It made me sick to think that over here we had to limit ourselves a lot because of him, and it's not fair.

Unfortunately, Enrique and Beatriz's experience is not uncommon. Undocumented immigrants who have lived in the United States for many years, have families, and fear that detection and apprehension will destroy everything they have worked for, provide easy targets for schemers who dangle the dream of security that comes with documentation. Enrique and Beatriz's experience was just one of the many, sometimes bitter, lessons undocumented immigrants encounter as they learn to live in the United States.

. . .

IMMIGRANT CHILDREN

Carolina Valenzuela had been born in Tijuana but was raised in San Diego since a few days after birth. Although she and her friends, some of them recently arrived from Mexico, rarely discuss their immigration status openly, she is certain that all her friends believe she is a U.S. citizen.

> I've told everybody I'm an American citizen, that I was born here. On applications, I just put I was born in the U.S.A. So all my friends know I'm a U.S. citizen. But I just lie.... And I think I have friends that lie just like me.... I'd rather say I'm American born because I feel I have more rights.... I feel more comfortable saying I'm an American citizen, like I could go to any college.... I have more opportunities.

Carolina participates as a citizen in various school activities. When I first met her in 1986, she was in her first year of high school and a member of the campus Reserve Officer Training Corps (ROTC). The year before that, she had been one of four students (out of about 300) chosen to speak at her eighth-grade graduation ceremony. She was the only Latina so chosen, an honor she believes she would not have received had it been known she was an "illegal alien." Through their children's activities, such as Carolina's, undocumented parents are drawn into the larger society.

. . .

[Carolina] had been raised in San Diego since infancy and her [Beatriz's] ten-year-old son had been born in the city. When considering taking her children back to Mexico to live, she said, "You can only imagine the brutal change they would face. First of all, our children would lose their friendships, school, customs, food, manner of dress. For them, it would be terrible." Beatriz likened such an experience to a plant being pulled out of the ground by its roots. "The roots are here and it's like ripping a tree out of the ground and taking it over there. Can you imagine those roots? By the time they got there, they would be practically dead."

. . .

Enrique and Beatriz Valenzuela also see more opportunities for their children in the United States. They view education as an important key to mobility, as Beatriz noted:

> I think that our children do have more opportunities here for an education, to study, to have what I didn't have. I didn't get an education in Mexico, but we worked and worked so that they would have more opportunities than we had. And that's why I want them to study and study hard so that they won't have to work as hard as we did.

Unfortunately, life does not always proceed as desired. Three years after this interview, the Valenzuela's daughter, Carolina, became pregnant, dropped out of high school and moved in with her boyfriend. Given that she was a very good student, her parents hold onto the hope that she will eventually finish her education.

QUESTIONS FOR DISCUSSION AND ANALYSIS

Historically and Geographically/Contextual

1. What historical policies in the twentieth-century United States have been directed toward Mexican immigrants?

2. How are these policies reflected across the generations of this family? How is Enrique's life different from and similar to his father's life? How is Beatriz's life different from and similar to Carolina's life? How would Beatriz's and Enrique's lives be different if they were legal immigrants in California? Would Beatriz and Enrique have made different choices for themselves and their family if the Bracero Program still existed?

3. What new political debates, policies, and assistance programs for legal and illegal immigrants have most likely affected the Valenzuelas in the years since Chavez interviewed them?

4. What negative ideologies or controlling images do Enrique, Beatriz, or their children confront? Trace the historical development of these ideologies.

Socially Constructed

5. Do we know anything about Enrique, Beatriz, or Carolina in terms of their sexuality? If so, what do we know? What don't we know?

6. Why does Carolina deny to her friends that she is Mexican by birth? What are the consequences for her? If her response is a common survival strategy among the children of Mexican immigrants, how might that strategy shape future group identity and political actions?

7. Why did some of Beatriz's early employers dock her pay if she came to work in the morning, rather than spending the night in their household?

8. What is Enrique's conception of work? How does it fit with the ideology of the "American Dream"?

9. Does the Valenzuelas' success in this country challenge structures of race, class, gender, and sexuality? Does their success reinforce dominant assumptions? How?

10. Are Enrique and Beatriz likely candidates to join a union? Why?

11. How might the meaning of race, class, gender, and sexuality in their lives be different if they were working-class residents of California? How does immigration construct these inequalities differently?

Power Relationships

12. Beatriz's working so many years for the same employers has allowed her to develop a personal relationship in which informal benefits are understood and abided by. What are some of these informal benefits? How does Beatriz's position compare with those other of women employed in domestic service? What are some of the reasons that Beatriz is *still* in a precarious position at work?

13. Why is fear a central part of the Valenzuelas' lives? What are some of the things they fear? How are their fears related to their social locations?

14. Discuss the power relationships between employers, Beatriz, and Enrique. In what ways do Beatriz and Enrique have power over their work experiences? Do Beatriz or Enrique desire to resist exploitation of their labor by their employers? Do they resist unfavorable conditions at work? How?

15. We hear nothing about the sexuality of the Valenzuelas until the discussion of Beatriz's and Carolina's accidental pregnancies. What kinds of birth control might have been available to Beatriz and Carolina? What barriers to effective use of birth control might they have experienced? How might their social location put them at greater risk for accidental pregnancy?

Macro Social-Structural and
Micro Social-Psychological Levels

16. Describe how macro structures (i.e., economic institutions, government, educational systems, etc.) have influenced the Valenzuelas' lives in the United

States. How have they both benefited and suffered from macro structural influences? What are some of the ways they have learned to negotiate these structures?

17. Technically it is illegal for individuals such as Beatriz or Enrique to live in California, yet what social groups benefit the most from having undocumented immigrants in the United States? Why?

18. Language is never mentioned as a structural constraint for either Enrique or Beatriz. Discuss how language could have affected the Valenzuelas' lives.

19. What are the "multiple truths" that surface around the Valenzuelas' situation? How might a wealthy employer view Beatriz's family situation or illegal immigrant status? How might teachers view Carolina's unintended pregnancy? How might the Valenzuela children view their parents?

20. Why is it so common for undocumented immigrants such as Beatriz and Enrique to work in restaurants and hotels, within private homes, or on farms? Discuss the macro forces that make this the case, as well as the individual reasons people such as Beatriz or Enrique might have for taking these kinds of jobs.

21. How has Carolina's success in the education system privileged her? How might her life have been different if she had never lied about her immigrant status?

Simultaneously Expressed

22. What social characteristics or dimensions of inequality seem more prominent in the Valenzuelas' situation? Which seem less apparent? Why?

23. How do race, class, gender, and sexuality shape Beatriz's, Enrique's, and Carolina's lives differently?

24. How does race affect Beatriz's, Enrique's, and Carolina's lives? Does it affect them in the same ways? Different ways?

25. What impact do sexuality and gender have on the Valenzuelas' life experiences? (For example, if Carolina had been a lesbian or male, how might her life have been different? If Enrique had been caught by the immigration services rather than Beatriz, would he have been treated differently?)

26. If Beatriz had been Puerto Rican, how might her life have been different?

Implications for Social Action and Social Justice

27. Where does this story lead us? What can we learn from it about the experiences of illegal immigrants? What will it take to improve life for families like the Valenzuelas?

28. If we could take this vignette and create one policy that might improve the Valenzuelas' current situation, what would it be and how would we implement it?

29. What kinds of resistance benefited Beatriz, Enrique, or Carolina? What can we learn from their actions?

REFERENCES

Bean, Frank D., Rodolfo O. de la Garza, Bryan R. Roberts, and Sidney Weintraub, eds. 1997. *At the Crossroads: Mexican Migration and U.S. Policy.* Lanham, MD: Rowman and Littlefield.

Brebenner, Candice Lewis. 1998. *A Nationality of Her Own: Women, Marriage, and the Law of Citizenship.* Berkeley, CA: University of California Press.

Chavez, Leo R. 1992. *Shadowed Lives: Undocumented Immigrants in American Society.* Fort Worth, TX: Harcourt Brace.

—— 1998. *Shadowed Lives: Undocumented Immigrants in American Society.* 2nd ed. Fort Worth, TX. Harcourt Brace.

Craig, Richard B. 1971. The Bracero Program: Interest Groups and Foreign Policy. Austin, TX: University of Texas Press.

Del Castillo, Richard G., and Arnoldo de León. 1996. *North to Aztlán: A History of Mexican Americans in the United States.* New York: Twayne.

Hondagneu-Sotelo, Pierrette. 1994. *Gendered Transitions: Mexican Experiences of Immigration.* Berkeley, CA: University of California Press.

Jacobsen, David. 1998. *The Immigration Reader: America in a Multidisciplinary Perspective.* Malden, MA: Blackwell.

Maciel, David R., and María Herrera-Sobek, eds. 1998. *Culture Across Borders: Mexican Immigration and Popular Culture.* Tucson, AZ: University of Arizona Press.

Romero, Mary, Pierrette Hondagneu-Sotelo and Vilma Ortiz, eds. 1997. *Challenging Fronteras: Structuring Latina and Latino Lives in the U.S.* New York: Routledge.

Ruiz, Vicki L. 1998. *From Out of the Shadows: Mexican Women in Twentieth-Century America.* New York: Oxford University Press.

Torre, Adela de la and Beatríz M. Pesquera, eds. 1993. *Building with Our Hands: New Directions in Chicana Studies.* Berkeley, CA: University of California Press.

CASE STUDY 3

⤝◯

"It's Like We Never Been Born:" Rebirth on the Mississippi Gulf Coast After Hurricane Katrina

Sharon Hanshaw, a middle-aged African American woman, is a native of Biloxi, Mississippi. A cosmetologist, she owned and operated a beauty salon for twenty-one years, while raising her three daughters. When three of her five siblings died from heart conditions, Sharon, who is single, also helped to care for her nieces and nephew. On August 29, 2005, Hurricane Katrina swept away her home, her business, and her livelihood.

Sharon's home, one of nearly eighty thousand homes in Mississippi's coastal counties destroyed by the storm, was in East Biloxi, which sits on a peninsula separating Biloxi's Back Bay from the Gulf of Mexico. Before the storm, East Biloxi was a racially mixed (Black, Vietnamese, and White), low- to middle-income community. Many of the residents worked in the resorts and casinos, as well as in shrimping. Since the storm, a Latino presence has increased across the coast as migrants have come to work in the rebuilding effort. At the same time, a lack of affordable housing—especially for those who had previously rented or lived in subsidized housing—has inhibited the return of the poor, elderly, and working-class populations.

Although Hurricane Katrina made a more direct hit on Mississippi than on Louisiana, New Orleans sustained greater housing losses and casualties (McCarthy and Hanson 2007). For that reason and because Katrina destroyed one of America's great cities, New Orleans received significantly more media coverage than any of the other places destroyed by the storm. Despite New Orleans' losses and the media coverage, however, Mississippi received disproportionately more federal aid than Louisiana. Many attribute this imbalance in funding to the politicization of the federal aid process and the connections between the Bush administration and Mississippi's Republican leadership: Governor Haley Barbour (former chairman of the Republican National Committee), Senator Trent Lott (former Senate majority leader), Senator Thad Cochran (chairman of the Senate Appropriations Committee). And yet despite a greater share of federal aid flowing into the state, as of May 2008, Mississippi had spent only 38 percent of its $1.75 billion in community development block grant allocation, much of which was approved by Congress for reconstructing affordable housing. In contrast, Louisiana had spent 53 percent (Steps Coalition 2008).

Activist groups on the Mississippi coast continue to struggle for increased funding for affordable housing and to resist state government plans to divert it to other uses, including the expansion of the port in Gulfport (Steps Coalition, 2008). Contention surrounding the use of these funds drags on, but media attention and public pressure for action have long since waned, donations have dwindled, and volunteers have become increasingly scarce.

From the beginning, some longtime residents like Sharon Hanshaw took on the challenge of reviving their communities, reconstructing their families, and rebuilding their own lives in the wake of the storm. And Sharon's life has taken an entirely new path as a consequence.

SHARON'S STORY

Before Hurricane Katrina, "everybody owned little Mom and Pop businesses. We had beauty shops, restaurants, computer shops, car dealerships, all these things that were owned before. Everybody had a business; everybody was paying—we had, let's see, maybe 30 percent ownership of homes, and the rest were renters …but renters are people, too."

That scene changed rapidly following the storm. "When Katrina hit land, I happened to be in Aberdeen, Mississippi, where my girlfriend's sister passed. And it must have been—I know it was God and still is God—God's working for me to be in Aberdeen, Mississippi, because they [Sharon's daughters] wanted me to come back, and I said, 'I'm not coming back'.… They said, 'Mama, we've been through storms; it's no big deal.' I said, 'This is a little different, and I have to have you all here, and please get your nieces and my nephew'—because my sister passed, so I was responsible for them, too. [My daughters] kept saying, 'No, no, no.' I was like having a heart attack. Finally, they got in the car; it was my brother's car. He's passed also—and they're young; my siblings were young. I was taking care of both of my siblings in Jackson, Mississippi, and they died within a year and a half of each other."

A few days after the storm, Sharon returned to Biloxi to find that her home and business had been destroyed, along with much of coastal Mississippi. "So we finally got here [to Biloxi], and when I saw that—no house 'cause I was on the Back Bay where the casinos are, the Imperial Palace." Her house had stood on what later became the casino parking lot. "I was like 'Oh my god.' So it's really nothing I can do—'cause I was a renter. Yes, I was a renter. I just left the house, and I was renting. I called it my layaway house for two years, and then I was going to buy my house. I had furniture from Hurricane Camille from my parents. The whole house was antique, everything, so I tried to retrieve things, and gas was escaping, and I'm just in this pile of rubble.…I was trying to get my siblings' journals and the Bible that was 160 years old that my father owned. It was two of them, and I couldn't get those things.…

"And then my niece came from Killen, Texas, and she saw me, and she said, 'Oh, my god, what are you doing?' I said, 'I'm trying to save my stuff.' She said, 'It's gone; it's poison.' And then during the process, we got these pictures and this album. The pictures were totally gone. It was like a silhouette, but I kept them anyway…it took me 16 hours just to clean the gook off these pictures. And all you saw was a silhouette of our past like we'd never had a past." Her youngest daughter, who lived with her and was a writer and photographer, lost her materials and photographs. "When she lost that stuff, she just…stopped functioning. She was like, 'Mama, we don't have nothing. We really don't have nothing.' I asked my daughter to list the things she lost so we can start the FEMA dilemma. She said, 'Mama, can we say nothing? We have nothing.' And I said, 'Well, we have each other.' You know? But she said, 'But it's like we never been born.' She was so devastated as a young woman just starting her life from college. Can you imagine a young woman lost and didn't know what her next step would be?"

After a brief displacement to Houston, where Sharon tried to come to terms with her situation while fighting a dangerous eye infection "from the poisonous mud on the ground from Katrina's devastation," she returned again to Biloxi, working as an administrator for the Army Corps of Engineers and moving between her daughter's homes. "The job was in Gautier, Mississippi—Corps of Engineers…for three months, twelve hours a day. You know I had no car; I had to come from Gulfport with my middle daughter to catch my baby daughter to take me to Gautier. Had to be at work at seven and off at seven. Come from there at like seven-something at night, call somebody half way for three months, three months. So that meant I didn't sleep because I was working. I was up fifteen hours."

Shortly after this job ended, Sharon attended a meeting hosted by Oxfam America to bring together nearly fifty women to discuss their needs in the reconstruction of the coast: "affordable housing, child . care, the female elevation, and historical landmarks." Hanshaw quickly became involved: "I was all fired up.…We started having local government forums. So I had to get information and contact the mayor and tell him, 'We want to meet; we want to meet.' He was like, 'Who are ya'll?' I said, 'We gotta get a name.'" And so Coastal Women for Change (CWC) was born. Despite her lack of experience in community activism, Sharon was determined to save her community: "I wasn't used to doing this. I had no choice but to do it; otherwise, we have no voice. And we have to have a voice. I don't think it's fair for us to sit here like we're just puppets. We're human beings with flesh and blood, and this is our home."

For eight months, Sharon worked "pro bono," attending meetings with Oxfam and taking notes. "All these different entities were having meetings to rebuild Biloxi without the grassroots people.…I knew if we were going to recover that we women had to get to work, and that we did. So the first thing we did was put women from the organization on these committees: the finance committee, the education and the mixed-use committee, the rebuild committee—every committee that they had we put women on the committee so they could see what's going on 'cause if we didn't put people on the committee, we would not know. So that was good. And through those committees, we were able to go to D.C. We were able to go to Jackson, tell people, 'Why are we being left out of the community?' Why was nobody on the ground saying, 'Let's rebuild these people's community'?

"Why are there people on the ground saying, 'Let's redevelop and do condos and casinos?'.…They're like, 'You believe in redevelopment?' I said, 'Oh, yes, I do. Yeah, we had Mom-and-Pop businesses, we had beauty salons, we had gyms.…There's no community center, there's no library—is that not investment for our future?' 'Yeah, but we want to put casinos up to give people jobs.' I said, 'But that kind of reminds me of slavery because you're not thinking about us being entrepreneurs and on our own.' The empowerment piece was left out. You don't want to empower the people?

"It was going on all around me like we're going back to slavery. These people [developers] actually had these plans before Katrina....Katrina came, and they said, 'Let's go for it. Everybody's devastated; everybody's miserably challenged. Let's just'....I said, 'Wait a minute ya'll. We gonna have to get some medicine or something...'cause they're trying to take over our stuff 'cause we're like in a daze because while this is happening, people are dying every day from depression....So the whole time I'm saying, 'Come to City Council.' They're [people in the community] saying, 'What for if they don't listen to us anyway?' If you keep going, they will have to listen. If you stay away, you won't get anything accomplished. So they said, 'Okay.' So I made sure when we had meetings that people were delegated—you go this week, you go next week because at the beginning, remember, no one had jobs, so it was awesome because the people had time to put into their community."

But as she worked for the empowerment of her community, Sharon encountered resistance: "So the people that helped me are people that are secure with themselves. Then you have people that were—internalized racism, they did not want to help you.... 'Why you got this position?' You know, all this stuff was going on. I said, 'I'm working for free....' They were happy then. 'As long as she's not getting any money, she's working for free.' That's a sick mentality right there."

Sharon also found herself deprived of the social networks that she had relied on in the past: "People are saying, 'Well, how are you making it, Sharon, if you've lost three siblings?' I lost two before Katrina and one after....I still cannot wrap my head around the fact that I'm the only one here in my family. That support system is not there anymore. The issues are the same as displaced persons because of no support. The support system is displaced. This is what Hurricane Katrina has done, separate families, separate your resource system so you can't do what you need to do, and that's scary to think about."

Nearly a year after Katrina hit, Sharon was appointed to a paid position, as the executive director of CWC: "So eventually eight months down the line, it was like, we need to hire somebody to do this work, so all these women in this meeting are pointing at me." Most of the people working with CWC and the Steps Coalition, another community activist group, are women. "In my office, it's all women. One man....Steps, I would say 60 percent....And that's what I mean about women and how much power that women didn't know that they had, because we've already been oppressed by the men's world....Mind you, I'm a cosmetologist. Now I'm in a whole different world. I'm learning as I go. I'm like, 'Okay, what am I going to do?'"

As Sharon helps guide CWC as it expands and adapts to the issues of recovery on the coast, she confronts a number of problems—developing affordable housing, labor equality, community empowerment, simply making the Mississippi coast livable for low- and middle-income people. "The CTA, the bus system, the bus starts at seven, ends at seven—the casinos are open twenty-four hours. People have lost their jobs because the bus system shut down. What? Why is there not a bus system in place for twenty-four hours, can you tell me that? Why? To make it impossible for you to work, to keep your job. It's like it's just made to keep us down.

"We have been involved with so many meetings, so many forums…developers come from out of town [have a plan for] how they want the city to look. Well, we have a plan, too…affordable housing. I'm talkin' about a home you can afford with the income that you receive.…Now we're in here fighting for houses.…Why are we still doing this year three? Because 'We don't want the people of color to live.' You really just want them to come to the casino…and just deplete them and not have a productive area, a productive community.…

"It's like you could see the government going around you, and you're sitting here, and they're leaving the people of color out of everything. It's like, 'Put them in the middle.' Eight hundred feet inland is where the casinos could go that was put in the community right here.…The first thing we did was get all the information from the displaced persons and let them know the status. They were like, 'I really wanna come home, Sharon, but there's no place.'

"You go to the community, you see one house, no neighbor, one house, no neighbor. And people can't live without people. It makes you weak. Like a house can't live without people in it because it dies, and that's what's happening to our people. They're dying because they're tired of fighting. And then they say, 'Well, the people not coming to the council meeting.' I said, 'People are tired, and guess what else? You purposely had this council meeting during the daytime.' We're having an open discussion of trying to put an evening council meeting in place once a month. People are tired. So they have the biggest voting turnout now because people are seeing that through voting, they do change…that it does make a difference when you go to the legislature and talk to them about a bill."

In addition to housing, she is fighting for community schools. "These people that are in these meetings are saying, 'Why would you wanna build back schools in the people of color community?' Because we owned the school…it was owned by Black people. It was an Afro-American school, and the kids made the top scores in Mississippi. That's a good reason right there." Through a lawsuit, the community got one school rebuilt, which mostly African Americans and Vietnamese attend. It sits three blocks from a predominantly White school. Because both schools have low enrollments, the local government wants to shut one of them—the African American/Vietnamese school. "I said, 'Uhn, uhn.' We fought for that. That [closing the school] didn't happen, but they're still working on closing the school now.…."

If the community is ever to come back, community day care and health care are also critical issues. And Sharon and CWC are fighting for both. They are seeking approval for licensed in-home day care, rather than off-site day care, which is more expensive and requires transportation. The health of the population is being damaged by all the toxic waste left in Katrina's wake and by lack of medical care and health insurance. "Doctors have left. Nurses have left. I'm over in nonprofit, but do you think I have health insurance? No, I don't have insurance. How do you exist without insurance? But you're helping the community…When you're in it too [not having insurance], you can tell the story better because you can say…'I recovered from Katrina because I will not be a victim anymore.'"

CWC is also a "resource center of everything." The mission statement of CWC is "to adequately give the community the information so they can make adequate, informed decisions in the future, now and in the future." "If they call me and say domestic violence situation, okay, I know where you can go for that. We did a presentation two weeks ago on domestic violence. It's big here now.…We have the women's shelter; they've connected with us.…It's worse since Katrina.…It's worse. I mean you have women that left their husbands from Lucedale, Mississippi, to come here because there's nothing in Lucedale. Then you have women have left their husbands, but since there's no home here, no apartments here, they will say they'll be abused just to get some covered shelter or temporary shelter to stay somewhere. So it's a lot that's going on, and we need, we need shelters.…

"But the only downfall is you have a certain amount of time to stay in the shelter, and then you have to find somewhere to live, and it's just nothin' affordable for these women to go to—and that's scary because then you have to stay in the shelter more time with your children. It's very difficult.…And that's why some of 'em stray back…because of the housing situation and the job situation and transportation situation, the child care.…We have a rape crisis center, too, because, oh my god, it's a lot of homeless women now. And they end up stayin' with—under the bridge or with somebody, and all of a sudden they bein' raped.…When I say women, you have to put housing, child care, transportation in one lump sum…because it goes together.…"

To preserve community history, CWC is collecting oral histories: "I don't believe I'm here by mistake. I don't believe that these women that are staying in it for the long haul are here by mistake. It's gonna be something that they bring to their children, and the bigger picture is oral history. We're collecting elderly's stories of how they want their community to look. From these stories, I want a book. I want a book for the children and the future so they can hear the real left-behind community stories."

In fighting for the community, Sharon is also trying to hold various factions together so they present a united front. "I wanted to make sure that everybody wanted to fit in, but as you grow, you will see the separation starting to happen. Latinos like this—this is where the Latino group goes over here. This is the Vietnamese group over here. But in the end, it separates us, and we don't get the bigger picture then. And then the governor be like, 'See that's what I'm sayin': they can't pull together.'…I think it comes from the greed of money. 'Let's save our community, forget about theirs….'Why can't we just stick this together and be subcommittees under one, like, big coalition?…We're not elevating.…I'm still seeing the separation."

In spite of all the difficulties, though, Sharon has had a number of uplifting experiences outside the community—meeting Naomi Klein, author of *The Shock Doctrine: The Rise of Disaster Capitalism*, and being credentialed to attend the Democratic National Convention to see Barack Obama officially nominated. She also organized a group of community activist women from Biloxi to attend Superdome Super Love. Marking the tenth anniversary of V-Day, an international movement founded by Eve Ensler to raise money for programs to end violence against women and girls, the two-day event in

New Orleans brought together celebrities and ordinary women and offered everything from massage to consciousness raising sessions. "I'm so excited about it because I'm hoping that all the people...the stars and everybody really have a dialogue with the women and let them know that we need each other. Do not hurt each other. And we're all different, but we're all the same. We're caring, we're nurturing, we're caregivers. Don't hurt each other, respect—you don't have to agree with each other, but just respect each other."

Traveling to India with ActionAid, an agency that works with poor and excluded people to eradicate poverty and injustice in the United States and across the globe, Sharon met other poor people who were struggling to better their own lives and their communities. "I met these women, and what it did was give me a second boost....I said, 'Oh my god, these people are living in hellacious conditions, and they're still marching. I dare you to stop.' And that in itself brought us to a calmness. I said, 'Okay, I can fight.'...We went to several villages, and we met all these women and these men that are fighting together. And you found out that you're still blessed, Sharon. You're still not off the side like they are.... Their buildings are built out of asbestos. Our FEMA trailers are built out of formaldehyde. Demographics, same thing. So I brought that back, and I did a presentation when they came here."

Although she is often burned out—"I'm numb about the brain"—Sharon sees her task continuing beyond recovery from Katrina into the indefinite future: "My goal for them [funders] is to really listen to grassroots community people and to really get it and to don't keep thinking Katrina. Think future empowerment, 'cause that piece in itself will save the communities. If you think Katrina survivors, the funders can say, 'We've done four years. We done with them [community people].' And then you drop them. What are they supposed to do? "So if you're here just to up level yourself, that's not gonna help the future of the communities....The funders are like, 'They [the community] gonna have to figure out something.' Well, the Lord has—this storm came about to let people know that people still live like this, people not even being fairly compensated for their work well done....

"So I really want the funders, and I want the schools, anybody that's studying Katrina survivors or victims or displacements needs to know that we need the volunteers to keep coming. We need the volunteers to know that...maybe 26 percent are coming back. We need to go ahead and let's be 75, let's at least be 75 percent because you do wanna create a better world, not a lesser world....That's what we need....The infrastructure stuff is not in line. That's where the sadness lies, and that's why I say we have to really stay prayed up and stay faithful and believe that it will change if you keep fighting." And she is.

QUESTIONS FOR ANALYSIS

Historically and Geographically Contextual

1. What kinds of historical factors need to be considered to fully understand an event such as Hurricane Katrina?

2. What role did politics play in determining how federal and state governments responded to Hurricane Katrina? How were political decisions shaped by race, class, gender, and sexuality hierarchies?
3. How does the history of slavery inform how Sharon understands her present situation?
4. How was Sharon's life affected by the civil rights movement and the women's rights movement?

Socially Constructed

1. How do definitions of *family* and *community* overlap in Sharon's life? In what ways does Sharon's understanding of the responsibilities that accompany her family and community relationships provide a model for creating a social network that strengthens and enriches life?
2. How does Sharon's gender shape the choices she has made and how she understands her situation?
3. How can we understand the absence of men in Sharon's story? How might her life have been different (in positive and negative ways) if men were at the center of her and her extended family's life story? In her community? Can social change happen if men are not present?

Power Relationships

1. How does an event such as Hurricane Katrina reveal the systems of privilege and oppression that in normal situations remain largely hidden from view? How might the aftermath of an event such as this be a time when social change can be enacted? How might it also be a time when inequalities are reseeded, deepened?
2. What kinds of power has Sharon had over her own decisions throughout her life? What kind of power does Sharon believe that she possesses? That she lacks?
3. What institutional structures does Sharon describe that keep people in Biloxi from becoming financially secure? Why do city and state governments resist making changes that would enable people to become politically involved and to find and keep jobs and housing?

Macro Social-Structural and Micro Social-Psychological Levels

1. How did the federal government respond in the aftermath of Hurricane Katrina? What does Sharon mean when she refers to the "FEMA dilemma"? What has been the balance between governmental and volunteer relief efforts? Is this an appropriate division of responsibility? Why or why not?
2. How cut off from full participation in American society does Sharon feel (for herself and for others in her situation) because she doesn't own a home? What

does her sense of alienation suggest about the centrality of home ownership in achieving the American Dream?

3. Is religion a force of oppression or liberation in Sharon's life?
4. What is Sharon's perspective on the significance of segregated vs. integrated educational opportunities? What does a historical perspective suggest about the viability of Sharon's desire to keep the African American/Vietnamese school operating?

Simultaneously Expressed

1. What structures of oppression or privilege seem least important in Sharon's life? Why? If we focused on only one site of oppression or privilege, what would we be missing from Sharon's narrative?
2. To what extent does Sharon understood the story of her community in terms of race? Does this limit her vision for social change? Why or why not?
3. Lani Guinier and Gerald Torres (2002) argue that progressive political change strategies in America today are most effective if racial minorities and racial projects lead the way and other groups join the effort, as was the case in the civil rights movement. Might Sharon agree with that argument? Does her story support or refute that argument? Can social movements centered in an intersectional vision be effective?

Implications for Social Action and Social Justice

1. In what ways does the story reveal both the possibilities and the limitations of grassroots community organizing?
2. What implications does Sharon's story have for federal, state, and local governments dealing with catastrophic events in the future?
3. What can we learn from Sharon's story about models of effective leadership? Does Sharon's understanding of gender limit or expand the possibilities she sees for herself as a leader? What should the role of gender be in establishing models of leadership?
4. To whom does Sharon address this story? How important is the telling of this very personal story in the quest for social justice for her community? For the nation? What other stories like Sharon's are you aware of that need to be told? To whom could you tell those stories?

REFERENCES

Brunsma, D. L., D. Overfelt, and J. S. Picou. 2007. The Sociology of Katrina: Perspectives on a Modern Catastrophe. Lanham, MD: Rowman & Littlefield.

Cutter, Susan. 2006. The Geography of Social Vulnerability: Race, Class, and Catastrophe. http://understandingkatrina.ssrc.org/Cutter (accessed February 4, 2009).

Erickson, Kai and Lori Peek. 2009. Hurricane Katrina Research Bibliography. New York: Social Science Research Bibliography. http://katrinaresearchhub.ssrc.org/KatrinaBibliography.pdf (accessed February 4, 2009).

Gault, Barbara, Heidi Hartmann, Avis Jones-DeWeever, Misha Werschkul, and Erica Williams. 2005. The Women of New Orleans and the Gulf Coast: Multiple Disadvantages and Key Assets for Recovery: Part 1. Poverty, Race, Gender, and Class. Washington, DC: Institute for Women's Policy Research. Available online at http://tanyatelfairsharpe.com/societal_pdfs/women_poverty_new_orleans_1.pdf (accessed February 4, 2009).

Jones-DeWeever, Avis. 2008. Women in the Wake of the Storm: Examining the Post-Katrina Realities of the Women of New Orleans and the Gulf Coast. Washington, DC: Institute for Women's Policy Research. http://www.iwpr.org/pdf/D481.pdf (accessed February 4, 2009).

McCarthy, Kevin F. and Mark Hanson. 2007. Post-Katrina recovery of the housing market along the Mississippi Gulf Coast. Santa Monica, CA: Rand Corporation.

Oxfam America. 2008. "Sharon's Story." http://www.oxfamamerica.org/whatwedo/campaigns/climate_change/sisters-on-the-planet/sharon Accessed April 4, 2009.

Steps Coalition. 2008. Is Mississippi Building Back Better Than Before? Problems and Solutions Regarding Mississippi's Use of CDBG Recovery Funds. http://www.stepscoalition.org, (accessed April 4, 2009).

Squires, C., and G. Hartman, eds. 2006. There is No Such Thing As a Natural Disaster. New York: Routledge.

Williams, Erica, Olga Sorokina, Avis Jones-DeWeever, and Heidi Hartmann. 2006. The Women of New Orleans and the Gulf Coast: Multiple Disadvantages and Key Assets for Recovery. Part 2. Gender, Race, and Class in the Labor Market. Washington, DC: Institute for Women's Policy Research. http://www.iwpr.org/pdf/D465.pdf (accessed February 4, 2009).

CASE STUDY 4

⤚◯

Getting Off on Feminism[1]

Jason Schultz

When it comes to smashing a paradigm, pleasure is not the most important thing. It is the only thing.

—GARY WOLF, *Wired Magazine*

Minutes after my best friend told me he was getting married, I casually offered to throw a bachelor party in his honor. Even though such parties are notorious for their degradation of women, I didn't think this party would be much of a problem. Both the bride and groom considered themselves feminists, and I figured that most of the men attending would agree that sexism had no place in the celebration of this union. In fact, I thought the bachelor party would be a great opportunity to get a group of men together for a social event that didn't degenerate into the typical antiwomen, homophobic male-bonding thing. Still, ending one of the most sexist traditions in history—even for one night—was a lot tougher than I envisioned.

I have to admit that I'm not a *complete* iconoclast: I wanted to make the party a success by including at least some of the usual elements, such as good food and drink, great music, and cool things to do. At the same time, I was determined not to fall prey to traditional sexist party gimmicks such as prostitutes, strippers jumping out of cakes, or straight porn. But after nixing all the traditional lore, even *I* thought it sounded boring. What were we going to do except sit around and think about women?

"What about a belly dancer?" one of the ushers suggested when I confided my concerns to him. "That's not as bad as a stripper." I sighed. This was supposed to be an occasion for the groom and his male friends to get together, celebrate the upcoming marriage, and affirm their friendship and connection with each other as men. "What the fuck does hiring a female sex worker have to do with any of that?" I shouted into the

[1]Jason Schultz, "Getting Off on Feminism" from Rebecca Edby Walker, ed., *To Be Real: Telling the Truth and Changing the Face of Feminism* (New York: Anchor Books, 1995). Copyright © 1995 by Jason Schultz. Reprinted with the permission of the author. The author can be contacted at jschultz@ alumni.Duke.edu.

phone. I quickly regained my calm, but his suggestion still stung. We had to find some other way.

I wanted my party to be as "sexy" as the rest of them, but I had no idea how to do that in the absence of female sex workers. There was no powerful alternative image in our culture from which I could draw. I thought about renting some gay porn, or making it a cross-dressing party, but many of the guests were conservative, and I didn't want to scare anyone off. Besides, what would it say about a bunch of straight men if all we could do to be sexy was act queer for a night?

Over coffee on a Sunday morning, I asked some of the other guys what they thought was so "sexy" about having a stripper at a bachelor party.

"Well," David said, "it's just a gag. It's something kinda funny and sexy at the same time."

"Yeah," A.J. agreed. "It's not all that serious, but it's something special to do that makes the party cool."

"But *why* is it sexy and funny?" I asked. "Why can't we, as a bunch of guys, be sexy and funny ourselves?"

"'Cause it's easier to be a guy with other guys when there's a chick around. It gives you all something in common to relate to."

"Hmm. I think I know what you mean," I said. "When I see a stripper, I get turned on, but not in the same way I would if I was with a lover. It's more like going to a show or watching a flick together. It's enjoyable, stimulating, but it's not overwhelming or intimate in the same way that sex is. Having the stripper provides a common emotional context for us to feel turned on. But we don't have to do anything about it like we would if we were with a girlfriend, right?"

"Well, my girlfriend would kill me if she saw me checking out this stripper," Greg replied. "But because it's kind of a male-bonding thing, it's not as threatening to our relationship. It's not because it's the stripper over her, it's because it's just us guys hanging out. It doesn't go past that."

Others agreed. "Yeah. You get turned on, but not in a serious way. It makes you feel sexy and sexual, and you can enjoy feeling that way with your friends. Otherwise, a lot of times, just hanging out with the guys is pretty boring. Especially at a bachelor party. I mean, that's the whole point, isn't it—to celebrate the fact that we're bachelors, and he"—referring to Robert, the groom—"isn't!"

Through these conversations, I realized that having a female sex worker at the party would give the men permission to connect with one another without becoming vulnerable. When men discuss sex in terms of actions—who they "did," and how and where they did it—they can gain recognition and validation of their sexuality from other men without having to expose their *feelings* about sex.

"What other kinds of things make you feel sexy like the stripper does?" I asked several of the guys.

"Watching porn sometimes, or a sexy movie."

A.J. said, "Just getting a look from a girl at a club. I mean, she doesn't even have to talk to you, but you still feel sexy and you can still hang out with your friends."

Greg added, "Sometimes just knowing that my girlfriend thinks I'm sexy, and then talking about her with friends, makes me feel like I'm the man. Or I'll hear some other guy talk about his girlfriend in a way that reminds me of mine, and I'll still get that same feeling. But that doesn't happen very often, and usually only when talking with one other guy."

This gave me an idea. "I've noticed that same thing, both here and at school with my other close guy friends. Why doesn't it happen with a bunch of guys, say at a party?"

"I don't know. It's hard to share a lot of personal stuff with guys," said Adam, "especially about someone you're seeing, if you don't feel comfortable. Well, not comfortable, because I know most of the guys who'll be at the party, but it's more like I don't want them to hassle me, or I might say something that freaks them out."

"Or you're just used to guys talking shit about girls," someone else added. "Like at a party or hanging out together. They rag on them, or pick out who's the cutest or who wants to do who. That's not the same thing as really talking about what makes you feel sexy."

"Hmm," I said. "So it's kind of like if I were to say that I liked to be tied down to the bed, no one would take me seriously. You guys would probably crack up laughing, make a joke or two, but I'd never expect you to actually join in and talk about being tied up in a serious way. It certainly wouldn't feel 'sexy,' would it? At least not as much as the stripper."

"Exactly. You talking about being tied down here is fine, 'cause we're into the subject of sex on a serious kick and all. But at a party, people are bullshitting each other and gabbing, and horsing around. The last thing most of us want is to trip over someone's personal taste or start thinking someone's a little queer."

"You mean queer as in homosexual?" I asked.

"Well, not really, 'cause I think everyone here is straight. But more of queer in the sense of perverted or different. I mean, you grow up in high school thinking that all guys are basically the same. You all want the same thing from girls in the same way. And when someone like you says you like to be tied down, it's kinda weird—almost like a challenge. It makes me have to respond in a way that either shows me agreeing that I also like to be tied down or not. And if someone's a typical guy and he says that, it makes you think he's different—not the same guy you knew in high school. And if he's not the same guy, then it challenges you to relate to him on a different level."

"Yeah, I guess in some ways it's like relating to someone who's gay," Greg said. "He can be cool and all, and you can get along totally great. But there's this barrier that's hard to cross over. It kinda keeps you apart. And that's not what you want to feel toward your friends, especially at a party like this one, where you're all coming together to chill."

As the bachelor party approached, I found myself wondering whether my friends and I could "come together to chill"—and affirm our status as sexual straight men— without buying into homophobic or sexist expressions. At the same time, I was doing a lot of soul-searching on how we could challenge the dominant culture's vision of male heterosexuality, not only by deciding against having a stripper at our party, but also by examining and redefining our own relationships with women.

...

Not becoming a sitting target to have *my manhood shot down was high* on my mind when the evening of my best friend's bachelor party finally arrived. But I was determined not to be silent about how I felt about the party and about new visions for straight men within our society.

We decided to throw the party two nights before the wedding. We all gathered at my house, each of us bringing a present to add to the night's activities. After all the men had arrived, we began cooking dinner, breaking open beer and champagne, and catching up on where we had left off since we last saw each other.

During the evening, we continued to talk off and on about why we didn't have a stripper or prostitute for the party. After several rounds of margaritas and a few hands of poker, tension started to build around the direction I was pushing the conversation.

"So what don't you like about strippers?" David asked me.

This was an interesting question. I was surprised not only by the guts of David to ask it, but also by my own mixed feelings in coming up with an answer. "It's not that I don't like being excited, or turned on, per se," I responded. "In fact, to be honest, watching a female stripper is an exciting and erotic experience for me. But at the same time, it's a very uncomfortable one. I get a sense when I watch her that I'm participating in a misuse of pleasure, if that makes sense."

I looked around at my friends. I couldn't tell whether the confused looks on their faces were due to the alcohol, the poker game, or my answer, so I continued. "Ideally, I would love to sit back and enjoy watching someone express herself sexually through dance, seduction, flirtation—all the positive elements I associate with stripping," I said. "But at the same time, because so many strippers are poor and forced to perform in order to survive economically, I feel like the turn-on I get is false. I feel like I get off easy, sitting back as the man, paying for the show. No one ever expects me to get up on stage.

"And in that way, it's selling myself short sexually. It's not only saying very little about the sexual worth of the woman on stage, but the sexual worth of me as the viewer as well. By *only* being a viewer—just getting off as a member of the audience—the strip-tease becomes a very limiting thing, an imbalanced dynamic. If the purpose is for me to feel sexy and excited, but not to act on those feelings, I'd rather find a more honest and direct way to do it. So personally, while I would enjoy watching a stripper on one level, the real issues of economics, the treatment of women, and the limitation of my own sexual personae push me to reject the whole stripper thing in favor of something else."

"But what else do you do to feel sexy?" A.J. asked.

"That's a tough question," I said. "Feeling sexy often depends on the way other people act toward you. For me, right now, you guys are a huge way for me to feel sexy. [Some of the men cringe.] I'm not saying that we have to challenge our sexual identities, although that's one way. But we can cut through a lot of this locker-room macho crap and start talking with each other about how we feel sexually, what we think, what we like, etc. Watching the stripper makes us feel sexy because we get turned on through the dynamic between her performance and our voyeurism. We can find that same erotic connection with each other by re-creating that context between us. In such a case, we're still heterosexual—we're no more having sex with each other than we are with the stripper. But we're not relying on the imbalanced dynamic of sex work to feel pleasure as straight men."

…

The guys were silent for a few seconds, but soon afterwards, the ice seemed to break.

…

They agreed that, as heterosexual men, we should be able to share with each other what we find exciting and shouldn't *need* a female stripper to feel sexy. In some ways it may have been the desire to define their own sexuality that changed their minds; in others it may have been a traditionally masculine desire to reject any dependency on women. In any case, other men began to speak of their own experiences with pleasure and desire, and we continued to talk throughout the night, exploring the joys of hot sex, one-night stands, and even our preferences for certain brands of condoms. We discussed the ups and downs of monogamy versus "open" dating and the pains of long-distance relationships.

Some men continued to talk openly about their desire for straight pornography or women who fit the traditional stereotype of femininity. But others contradicted this, expressing their wish to move beyond that image of women in their lives. The wedding, which started out as the circumstance for our gathering, soon fell into the background of our thoughts as we focused away from institutional ideas of breeder sexuality and began to find common ground through our real-life experiences and feelings as straight men. In the end, we all toasted the groom, sharing stories, jokes, and parts of our lives that many of us had never told. Most importantly, we were able to express ourselves sexually without hiding who we were from each other.

Thinking back on the party, I realized that the hard part was figuring out what we all wanted and how to construct a different way of finding that experience. The other men there wanted it just as much as I did. The problem was that we had no ideas of what a different kind of bachelor party might look like. Merely eliminating the old ways of relating (i.e., the female sex workers) left a gap, an empty space which in many ways *felt* worse than the sexist connection that existed there before; we felt passive and powerless. Yet we found a new way of interacting—one that embraced new ideas and shared the risk of experiencing them.

Was the party sexy? Did we challenge the dominance of oppressive male sexuality? Not completely, but it was a start. I doubt anyone found my party as "sexy" as traditional ones might be, but the dialogue has to start somewhere. It's going to take a while to generate the language and collective tension to balance the cultural image of heterosexual male sexuality with true sexual diversity. Still, one of my friends from high school—who's generally on the conservative end of most issues—told me as he was leaving that of all the bachelor parties he had been to, this was by far the best one. "I had a great time," he said. "Even without the stripper."

…

QUESTIONS FOR DISCUSSION AND ANALYSIS

Historically and Geographically/Contextual

1. Jason writes of his experiences coming of age as a man in the 1990s. How might Jason's situation be different if he lived in a different time period? Could Jason have pulled off this type of bachelor party in the 1950s? Why or why not?

2. Historically, how has White, middle-class, heterosexual masculinity been socially constructed? For whom is this construction beneficial, according to Jason? Whom does it harm?

3. Jason discusses how the bride and groom self-identified as feminists and clearly espouses his own version of feminism. In this context, how would Jason define feminism? Is this definition positive or negative or both? Would Jason, the bride, and the groom have defined themselves as feminists a decade ago? In the 1970s? In the 1950s? Discuss the historically contextual nature of feminism.

4. Where did the notion of a bachelor party originate in U.S. society? What groups of men tend to participate in this ritual?

Socially Constructed

5. Despite Jason's attempts to challenge current definitions of class, gender, and sexuality, which structures of oppression are left intact and why? Does Jason challenge the institutions of heterosexuality or marriage?

6. Jason believes that men must be able to feel "sexy" at bachelor parties. What does he mean by sexy? Why do men expect to feel sexy in these situations? How does Jason challenge those expectations?

7. Much of Jason's story deals with the idea that men cannot relate to each other in a social group and that many need to have a diversion that will reduce tension in all-male gatherings. Why?

8. Do Jason and his friends show that men can be feminists, too? Is their feminism different from that of their women friends?

9. In what ways does acting out their privileged position as White, hetero-sexual, middle-class males restrict the range of behavior available and acceptable for them? Why? How is privilege (race, class, gender, and sexuality) constructed in this story?

Power Relationships

10. What power relations do Jason and his friends reinforce in the story? In the end, do they seriously challenge the sex and gender system of inequality?

11. What does Jason mean when he suggests that the use of a stripper limits male sexuality? What does this have to do with power?

12. Do strippers have power as they work? If so, what types of power do they have? In what ways are strippers oppressed?

Macro Social-Structural and Micro Social-Psychological Levels

13. What are the institutional arrangements that allow Jason and/or the groom to begin pondering what a feminist bachelor party would look like?
14. What reasons does Jason give for not wanting to have a stripper at his best friend's bachelor party? How do these reasons relate to larger structures of oppression and privilege?
15. While it seems that this new type of bachelor party has the potential to challenge certain social hierarchies, is this new version of a bachelor party enough? How significant are Jason's efforts in the larger picture?
16. Since men ultimately have power over women in our society, what does Jason mean when he implies that men also face gender and sexuality oppression?
17. What are some of the personal consequences Jason may face when he resists gender and sexuality oppression?
18. Who are the men who seem most likely to identify as feminists today? Why?

Simultaneously Expressed

19. How does the atmosphere of a bachelor party constrain or define men's reactions to the strippers/porn movies? Is it socially acceptable for men to get aroused at a bachelor party?
20. Why are race and class never mentioned in this story? What is the significance of Jason's ignoring race and class at the same time he is discussing gender and sexuality?
21. When the night of the bachelor party arrived, why was Jason worried about having his own manhood challenged? What did he fear?
22. Why did this "new" kind of bachelor party still exclude women? What are the implications for gender relations?
23. Are bachelor parties common among African American, Latino, Asian, and non-Christian communities? How is hegemonic White, middle-class masculinity being constructed in this story?

Implications for Social Action and Social Justice

24. In creating a new kind of bachelor party, what is Jason's goal? Does he achieve it? Who benefits from this new type of bachelor party? All men? Certain groups of men? All women? Certain groups of women?
25. If Jason's bachelor party challenges male forms of sexism, how could women challenge structures of oppression at bridal showers or bachelorette parties? What would you do if you were a maid of honor for a wedding and had the assignment of challenging gender and sexuality hierarchies when planning

one of these events? How could you resist societal definitions of women, men, marriage, and heterosexuality? What would feminist wedding rituals encompass?

26. For whom does Jason write? Who is his audience? Who can relate to this story? All men? All women? Feminists? Only certain groups of men or women?

REFERENCES

Brod, Harry and Michael Kimmel, eds. 1994. *Theorizing Masculinities.* Thousand Oaks, CA: Sage.

Digby, Tom, ed. 1998. *Men Doing Feminism.* New York: Routledge.

Kimmel, Michael and Michael Messner. 2001. *Men's Lives.* 3rd ed. Boston: Allyn and Bacon.

Levit, Nancy. 1998. *The Gender Line: Men, Women, and the Law.* New York: New York University Press.

Schact, Steven P. and Doris W. Ewing, eds. 1998. *Feminism and Men: Reconstructing Gender Relations.* New York: New York University Press.

Tobias, Sheila. 1997. *Faces of Feminism: An Activist's Reflections on the Women's Movement.* Boulder, CO: Westview Press.

Walker, Rebecca, ed. 1995. *To Be Real: Telling the Truth and Changing the Face of Feminism.* New York: Anchor Books.

Web Sites

General
Advancement Project
www.advancementproject.org
American Civil Liberties Union
www.aclu.org
Center for American Progress
www.americanprogress.org
Human Rights First
www.humanrightsfirst.org
Media Matters
www.mediamatters.org
National Center for Health Statistics
www.cdc.gov/nchs
National Urban League
www.nul.org
Out History
www.OutHistory.org
Oxfam International
www.oxfam.org
People for the American Way
www.pfaw.org
Southern Poverty Law Center
www.splcenter.org
The Justice Project
www.thejusticeproject.org
U.S. Bureau of Labor Statistics
www.bls.gov
U.S. Census Bureau
www.census.gov

Focus on Women
Catalyst Women
www.catalystwomen.org

Center for Women Policy Studies
www.centerwomenpolicy.org

Black Women's Health Imperative
www.blackwomenshealth.org

Indigenous Women's Network
www.indigenouswomen.org

Institute for Women's Policy Research
www.iwpr.org

League of Women Voters
www.lwv.org

MANA: A National Latina Organization
www.hermana.org

National Association of Colored Women's Clubs
www.nacwc.org

National Coalition of 100 Black Women
www.ncbw.org

National Collaborative of Women's Historic Sites
www.ncwhs.oah.org/mission.htm

National Conference of Puerto Rican Women
www.nacoprw.net

National Council for Research on Women
www.ncrw.org

National Council of Negro Women
www.ncnw.org

National Organization for Women
www.now.org

National Partnership for Women and Families
www.nationalpartnership.org

National Women's Law Center
www.nwlc.org

National Women's Studies Association
www.nwsa.org

Schlesinger Library, Radcliffe College
www.radcliffe.edu/schles/index.php

General Education
Alliance for Excellent Education
www.all4ed.org

American Council on Education
www.acenet.edu

Center on Education Policy
www.cep-dc.org

Childstats.gov
www.childstats.gov

Interagency Education Research Initiative (IERI)
drdc.uchicago.edu/community/main.php

Learning First Alliance
www.learningfirst.org

National Assessment of Education Progress (NAEP)
www.nces.ed.gov/nationsreportcard

National Center for Education Statistics
www.nces.ed.gov

National Center for Fair and Open Testing
www.fairtest.org

National Education Association (NEA)
www.nea.org

National PTA (Parent-Teacher Association)
www.pta.org

Public Education Network
www.publiceducation.org

Teach for America
www.teachforamerica.org

Teaching Tolerance: A Project of the Southern Poverty Law Center
www.tolerance.org

The Education Trust
www2.edtrust.org

United States Students Association
www.usstudents.org

Early Education

Center on the Social and Emotional Foundations of Early Learning (CSEFEL)
www.vanderbilt.edu/csefel

Child Care and Early Education Research Connections
www.childcareresearch.org

Division for Early Childhood (DEC)
www.dec-sped.org

Edward Zigler Center in Child Development and Social Policy
ziglercenter.yale.edu

Foundation for Child Development
www.fcd-us.org

National Association for the Education of Young Children
www.naeyc.org

National Center for Early Development and Learning
www.fpg.unc.edu

National Head Start Association
www.nhsa.org

National Institute for Early Education Research
www.nieer.org

Orelena Hawks Puckett Institute
www.puckett.org

Society for Research in Child Development
www.srcd.org

Southern Early Childhood Association
www.southernearlychildhood.org

Tools of the Mind
www.mscd.edu/extendedcampus/toolsofthemind

Voices for America's Children
www.voices.org

Zero to Three
www.zerotothree.org

Higher Education

Institute for Higher Education Policy
www.ihep.org

National Association for Equal Opportunity in Higher Education
www.nafeo.org

The Institute for College Access and Success
www.ticas.org

Race and Education

African Americans
National Urban League
www.nul.org

National Association for the Advancement of Colored People (NAACP)
www.naacp.org

NAACP Legal Defense and Education Fund
www.naacpldf.org

National Alliance of Black School Educators
www.nabse.org

Frederick D. Patterson Research Institute
www.patterson-uncf.orghome.htm

United Negro College Fund
www.uncf.org

Asian American and Pacific Islanders
The National Korean American Services and Education Consortium
www.nakasec.org

CARE: National Commission on Asian American and Pacific Islander Research
in Education
www.nyu.edu/projects/care/index.html

Asian and Pacific Islander American Scholarship Fund
www.apiasf.org

National Association for the Education and Advancement of Cambodian, Laotian,
and Vietnamese Americans (NAFEA)
www.searac.orgnafea.html

National Association for Asian and Pacific American Education
www.naapae.net

National Pacific Islander Education Network
www.npien.com

Native Hawaiian Education Association (NHEA)
www.nhea.net

Hispanic/Latinos
ASPIRA
www.aspira.org

Hispanic Association of Colleges and Universities
www.hacu.net

Hispanic Scholarship Fund
www.hsf.net

National Latino Children's Institute
www.nlci.org

Mexican American Legal Defense and Educational Fund
www.maldef.org

American Indians
National Indian Education Association
www.niea.org

American Indian Higher Education Consortium
www.aihec.org

American Indian Science and Engineering Society
www.aises.org

American Indian College Fund
www.collegefund.org

American Indian Higher Education Consortium
www.aihec.org

Office of Indian Education
www.indianeducation.org

National Indian Child Welfare Association
www.nicwa.org

American Indian Graduate Center
www.aigc.com

Gender and Education

National Coalition for Women and Girls in Education
www.ncwge.org

American Association of University Women
www.aauw.org

National Women's Law Center
www.nwlc.org

Women's College Coalition
www.womenscolleges.org

Women's Sports Foundation
www.womenssportsfoundation.org

Sexuality and Education

ACLU Lesbian Gay Bisexual Transgender Project
www.gbge.aclu.org

California Safe Schools Coalition
www.casafeschools.org

Children of Lesbians and Gays Everywhere (COLAGE)
www.colage.org

Family Equality Council
www.familyequality.org

Gay, Lesbian and Straight Education Network (GLSEN)
www.glsen.org

Gay/Straight Alliance Network
www.gsanetwork.org

Gender Public Advocacy Coalition
www.gpac.orgcata/catamaterials.html

Gender Spectrum
www.genderspectrum.org

Human Rights Campaign
www.hrc.org/issues/youth_and_campus_activism

National Youth Advocacy Coalition
www.nyacyouth.org

Parents, Families and Friends of Lesbians and Gays (PFLAG)
www.community.pflag.org

Sexuality Information and Education Council of the United States
www.siecus.org

The Safe Schools Coalitiion
www.safeschoolscoalition.org

The Trevor Project
www.thetrevorproject.org

Transgender Law Center
www.transgenderlawcenter.org

Disability and Education

Advocacy Institute
www.advocacyinstitute.org

American Association of Adapted Sports Programs
www.adaptedsports.org

Building the Legacy: IDEA 2004
idea.ed.gov

Center for Special Education Finances
csef.air.org

Council for Exceptional Children
www.cec.sped.org

Disability Statistic Center
www.dsc.ucsf.edu

ERIC Clearinghouse on Disabilities and Gifted Education
eric.hoagiesgifted.org

Families and Advocates Partnership for Education (FAPE)
www.fape.org

Individuals with Disabilities Education Act (IDEA) Data
www.ideadata.org

National Center for Learning Disabilities
www.ncld.org

National Association of State Directors of Special Education
www.nasdse.org

National Center on Educational Outcomes
www.cehd.umn.edu/NCEO

National Dissemination Center for Children with Disabilities
www.nichcy.org

National Early Childhood Technical Assistance Center
www.nectac.org

Appendix:
Historical Time Line References

Education

1896 Jack Salzman, David Lionel Smith, and David West, eds., *Encyclopedia of African American Culture and History*, vol. 4 (New York: Simon & Schuster, 1996), p. 2162.

1944 Victor Bondi, ed., *American Decades: 1940–1949*, vol. 5 (Detroit: Gale Research, 1994), p. 143.

1948 Bondi, *American Decades: 1940–1949*, p. 133.

1954 Jack Salzman, David Lionel Smith, and David West, eds., *Encyclopedia of African American Culture and History*, vol. 2 (New York: Simon & Schuster, 1996), p. 859.

1955 David O'Brien, *Constitutional Law and Politics: Struggles for Power and Government Accountability*, vol. 1 (New York: W.W. Norton, 1997), p. 172.

1964 O'Brien, *Constitutional Law and Politics*, p. 176.

1965 Richard Layman, ed., *American Decades: 1960–1969*, vol. 7 (Detroit: Gale Research, 1994), p. 215.

1966 Layman, *American Decades: 1960–1969*, p. 215.

1968 Layman, *American Decades: 1960–1969*, p. 124.

1969 Judy Galens, Anna J. Sheets, and Robyn V. Young, eds., *Gale Encyclopedia of Multicultural America*, vol. 2 (Detroit: Gale Research, 1995), p. 959.

1970 Layman, *American Decades: 1960–1969*, p. 117.

1971 Victor Bondi, ed., *American Decades: 1970–1979*, vol. 8 (Detroit: Gale Research, 1994), p. 149.

1972 Irene Franck and David Brownstone, *Women's World: A Timeline of Women in History* (New York: HarperCollins, 1995), p. 509; National Women's History Project (NWHP), "A timeline of the women's rights movement, 1848–1998," available from http://www.Legacy98.org/timeline.html, accessed March 19, 2000.

1973 Bondi, *American Decades: 1970–1979*, p. 158.

1975 Bondi, *American Decades: 1970–1979*, p. 158.

1978 NWHP, "A timeline of the women's rights movement, 1848–1998."

— Bondi, *American Decades: 1970–1979*, p. 166.

1979 Bondi, *American Decades: 1970–1979*, p. 152.

1983 National Women's History Project (NWHP), *Living the Legacy: A National Women's History Project Gazette* (Santa Rosa, CA: NWHP, 1998), pp. 13–15.

1988 Franck and Brownstone, *Women's World*, p. 578.

1994 NWHP, "A timeline of the women's rights movement, 1848–1998."

1996 California Secretary of State, "Proposition 209: Prohibition against discrimination or preferential treatment by state and other public entities," available from http://Vote96.ss.ca.gov/Vote96/html/BP/209.htm, accessed March 19, 2000.

— Tarlton Law Library–University of Texas Law School, "Hopwood v. State of Texas Materials," available from http://www.law.utexas.edu/hopwood/hopwood.htm, accessed March 19, 2000.

— NWHP, "A timeline of the women's rights movement, 1848–1998."

1997 Ethan Bronner, "Black and Hispanic admissions off sharply at U. of California," *New York Times*, April 1, 1998.

— Susan Richardson, "Texas educators seek clarification of Hopwood decision: Minority admissions to Texas elite public college in free-fall," *Black Issues in Higher Education* 14, no. 5 (May 1, 1997), pp. 18–22.

— NWHP, "A timeline of the women's rights movement, 1848–1998."

1997 Lani Guinier and Gerald Torres, *The Miner's Canary: Enlisting Race, Resisting Power, Transforming Democracy* (Cambridge: Harvard University Press, 2002), 66–74; Rose Gutfeld, "Ten Percent in Texas," *Ford Foundation Report* 33, no. 4 (2002): 16–19, available at http://www.texastop10.princeton.edu/inthenews.html, accessed 25 January 2009.

1999 Lynn Weber, e-mail to Suzanne Ozment, Dean of Women Students, The Citadel, February 10, 2000.

— Tim Simmons and Irwin Speizer, "Busing for balance halted," *Raleigh News and Observer* (North Carolina), September 11, 1999; Irwin Speizer, "Charlotte schools face the future," *Raleigh News and Observer* (North Carolina), November 26, 1999.

— American Civil Liberties Union, "Utah school discriminated against lesbian high school teacher, court rules," available from http://www.aclu.org/news/n113098a.html, accessed March 19, 2000.

2001 National Education Association, "NCLB—The Basics," available at http://www.nea.org/home/1248.htm, accessed 12 January, 2009.

2002 R. Kenneth Godwin, Suzanne M. Leland, Andrew D. Baxter, and Stephanie Southworth, "Sinking *Swann*: Public School Choice and the Resegregation of Charlotte's Public Schools," *Review of Policy Research* 23, no. 5 (September 2006): 963–1118.

2003 Oyez: U.S. Supreme Court Media, "Grutter v. Bollinger," available at http://www.oyez.org/cases/2000-2009/2002/2002_02_241/, and "Gratz v. Bolliner," available at http://www.oyez.org/cases/2000-2009/2002/2002_02_516/, accessed 12 January 2009.

— National Education Association, "The History of NCLB," available at https://sites.nea.org/neatoday/0604/nclbtimeline.html, accessed 12 January 2009.

2005 Institute of Education Sciences, *Digest of Education Statistics 2006*, Tables 174 and 232, available at http://nces.ed.gov/pubSearch/pubsinfo. asp?pubid=2007017, accessed 12 January 2009.

— National Education Association, "The History of NCLB," available at https://sites.nea.org/neatoday/0604/nclbtimeline.html, accessed 12 January 2009.

2006 The Citadel, "Values and Respect Survey," available at http://pao.citadel. edu/respect-fact-sheet, accessed 12 January 2009.

2007 The Citadel, "The Citadel Quick Facts," available at http://pao.citadel.edu/ debate07 quickfacts, accessed 12 January 2009; The Citadel, "Coeducation: A Timeline," available at http://www.citadel.edu/pao/women/coeducation timeline.html, accessed 12 January 2009; The Citadel, "Admissions and Enrollment Data," available at http://www.citadel.edu/pao/women/enroll- ment data.html, accessed 12 January 2009.

— On the Docket: U.S. Supreme Court News, "Parents Involved in Commu- nity Schools v. Seattle School District #1, et al.," available at http:// otd.oyez.org/cases/2006/parents-involved-community-schools-v-seattle- school-district-1-et-al-06282007, accessed 12 January 2009.

2008 The National Center for Public Policy and Higher Education, "Mea- suring Up 2008: The National Report Card on Higher Education," available at http://measuringup2008.highereducation.org/, accessed 29 January 2009.

Citizenship

1778 James Q. Wilson, *American Government: Institutions and Policies* (Lexing- ton, MA: D.C. Heath, 1986), p. 167.

1790 Ronald Takaki, ed., *From Different Shores: Perspective on Race and Ethnicity in America* (New York: Oxford University Press, 1994), p. 26.

1830 Institute for Learning Technologies, "Native American Navigator Project Pages," available from http://www.ilt.columbia.edu/k12/naha/1800s.html, accessed March 19, 2000.

1848 Nicolas Kanellos, ed., *The Hispanic American Almanac: A Reference Work on Hispanics in the United States* (Detroit: Gale Research, 1993), p. 230.

1857 Harold W. Chase, Thomas C. Cochran, Jacob E. Cooke, Robert W. Daly, Wendall Garrett, and Robert P. Multhauf, eds., *Dictionary of American History*, vol. 2 (New York: Scribner, 1976), p. 370; *Encyclopedia of African American Culture and History*, vol. 4, p. 1788.

1866 Franck and Brownstone, *Women's World*, p. 161.

1870 *Encyclopedia of African American Culture and History*, vol. 5 (New York: Simon & Schuster, 1996), p. 2589.

1875 'Kathryn Cullen-DuPont, ed., *The Encyclopedia of Women's History in America* (New York: Facts On File, 1996), 77; Franck and Brownstone, *Women's World*, p. 173; Robert J. Dinkin, *Before Equal Suffrage: Women In Partisan Politics from Colonial Times to 1920* (Westport, Conn.: Greenwood Press, 1995).

1882 *Dictionary of American History*, vol. 2, p. 29; Takaki, *From Different Shores*, p. 30.

1887 Institute for Learning Technologies, "Native American Navigator Project Pages"; Britannica Online, "Native American," available from http://www.britannica.com/bcom/eb/article/0/0,5716,127680+2,00.html, accessed March 20, 2000.

1902 Kanellos, *Hispanic American Almanac*, p. 230.

1920 Sheila Ruth, ed., *Issues in Feminism: An Introduction to Women's Studies* (London: Mayfield, 1990), p. 435.

1924 Kanellos, *Hispanic American Almanac*, p. 232.

— Judith S. Baughman, ed., *American Decades: 1920–1929*, vol. 3 (Detroit: Gale Research, 1994), p. 234; Britannica Online, "Native American," available from http://www.britannica.com/bcom/eb/article/0/0,5716,127680+3,00.html, accessed March 20, 2000.

1926 Britannica Online, "Eugenics," available from http://www.britannica.com/bcom/eb/article/5/0,5716,33785+1,00.html, accessed March 19, 2000.

1934 Britannica Online, "Native American."

1942 Wilma P. Mankiller, *Mankiller: A Chief and Her People* (New York: St. Martin's Press, 1993), p. 64; Britannica Online, "Nisei," available from http://www.britannica.com/bcom/eb/article/2/0,5716,57322+1,00.html, accessed March 19, 2000; The Japanese American Network, "A short chronology of Japanese American history," available from http://www.janet.org/janet_history/niiya_chron.html, accessed March 19, 2000.

— Mankiller, *Mankiller*, p. 63.

1945 Mankiller, *Mankiller*, p. 65.

1948 Galens, Sheets, and Young, *Gale Encyclopedia of Multicultural America*, vol. 2, p. 963.

1952 Takaki, *From Different Shores*, p. 26; Kanellos, *The Hispanic American Almanac*, p. 262.

1957 Galens, Sheets, and Yonng, *Gale Encyclopedia of Multicultural America*, vol. 2, p. 963.

1965 Kanellos, *The Hispanic American Almanac*, pp. 232–33.

— Layman, *American Decades: 1960–1969*, pp. 291–92.

1975 *Encyclopedia of African American Culture and History*, vol. 5, pp. 2753–54; U.S. Code, "Voting Rights Act Amendment (1975)," available from http://www4.law.cornell.edu/uscode/42/1973b.text.html, accessed March 20, 2000; Kanellos, *The Hispanic American Almanac*, p. 236.

1983 Galens, Sheets, and Young, *Gale Encyclopedia of Multicultural America*, vol. 2, p. 917.

1985 NWHP, "A timeline of the women's rights movement 1848–1998."

1988   The Japanese American Network, "A short chronology of Japanese American history,"; Britannica Online, "Nisei."

1990   Kanellos, *The Hispanic American Almanac*, p. 233.

1990   Peacework Magazine (October 2004), "American Voting Rights Timeline," available at http://www.peaceworkmagazine.org/pwork/0410/041005.htm, accessed 12 January 2009.

1992   Nicolas Kanellos, *Hispanic Firsts: 500 Years of Extraordinary Achievement* (Detroit: Gale Research, 1997), p. 131.

1993   Avoice: African American Voices in Congress, "Voting Rights Act: Timeline," available at http://www.avoiceonline.org/voting/timeline.html, accessed 12 January 2009.

2000   Northern California Citizenship Project, "U.S. Voting Rights Timeline," available at www.kqed.org/assets/pdf/education/digitalmedia/us-voting-rights-timeline.pdf, accessed 12 January 2009.

—   FairVote, "Voting Rights Timeline," available at http://www.fairvote.org/righttovote/timeline.htm, accessed 12 January 2009; Stefan Lovgren, "Are

—   Electronic Voting Machines Reliable?" *National Geographic*, available at http://news.nationalgeographic.com/news/2004/11/1101_041101_election_voting.html, accessed 12 January 2009.

2001   Northern California Citizenship Project, "U.S. Voting Rights Timeline," available at www.kqed.org/assets/pdf/education/digitalmedia/us-voting-rights-timeline.pdf, accessed 12 January 2009.

2002   Northern California Citizenship Project, "U.S. Voting Rights Timeline," available at www.kqed.org/assets/pdf/education/digitalmedia/us-voting-rights-timeline.pdf, accessed 12 January 2009.

2008   *New York Times*, "Election 2008," available at http://elections.nytimes.com/2008/index.html?scp=3&sq=election%25202008&st=cse, accessed 25 January 2009.

Government Offices

1822   Kanellos, *The Hispanic American Almanac*, p. 257.

1870   Joseph Nathan Kane, *Famous First Facts* (New York: H.W. Wilson, 1981), p. 543, 569.

1892   Sharon Malinowski, *Notable Native Americans* (New York: Gale Research, 1995), pp. 105–07.

1917   Ruth, *Issues in Feminism*, p. 435.

1958   Susan Gall and Irene Natividad, eds., *The Asian American Almanac: A Reference Work on Asians in the United States* (Detroit: Gale Research, 1993), p. 650.

1969   Ruth, *Issues in Feminism*, p. 438.

1970   NWHP, *Living the Legacy*, p. 13.

1974   NWHP, "A timeline of the women's rights movement, 1848–1998."

1976   Gall and Natividad, *Asian American Almanac*, pp. 617–18.

1981   NWHP, "A timeline of the women's rights movement, 1848–1998."

1986   Malinowski, *Notable Native Americans*, pp. 64–65.

—   NWHP, "A timeline of the women's rights movement, 1848–1998."

1988 "Our Brightest and Best Advocates," *The Advocate*, available from http://www.advocate.com/html/stories/792/792 frank.html, accessed March 20, 2000; U.S. House of Representatives "Congressman Barney Frank," available from http://www.house.gov/frank/, accessed March 20, 2000.

1989 U.S. House of Representatives, "Representative Ileana Ros-Lehtinen," available from http://www.house.gov/ros-lehtinen/, accessed March 20, 2000.

1992 Gall and Natividad, *Asian American Almanac*, p. 655; U.S. House of Representatives "Congresswoman Lucille Roybal-Allard," available from http://www.house.gov/roybal-allard, accessed March 20, 2000; United States Senate, "Senator Ben Nighthorse Campbell," available from www.senate.gov/campbell/bio.htm, accessed March 20, 2000. U.S. House of Representatives "Congresswoman Nydia M. Velázquez," available from http://www.house.gov/velazquez, accessed March 20, 2000; NWHP, "A timeline of the women's rights movement, 1848–1998."

1997 Gale Group, "Madeleine Korbel Albright," available from http://www.gale.com/freresrc/womenhst/albrighm.htm, accessed March 20, 2000.

1998 Tammy Baldwin for Congress, "About Tammy," available from http://www.tammy baldwin.com/about/index.html, accessed October 4, 2000.

1999 CIS Congressional Universe 2000, "Member Profile Reports," available from Congressional Universe (Online Service), Bethesda, MD: Congressional Information Service.

2000 Center for American Women and Politics, "Women in State Legislatures 2000," available from http://www.cawp.rutgers.edu/pdf/stleg.pdf, accessed March 20, 2000.

2007 Congresswoman Nancy Pelosi Biography, available at http://www.house.gov/pelosi/biography/bio.html, accessed 12 January 2009.

2008 Center for American Women and Politics, Rutgers University, "Facts on Women Officeholders, Candidates and Voters," available at http://www.cawp.rutgers.edu/fast_facts/, accessed 12 January 2009.

2009 Congressional Research Service, "Membership of the 111th Congress: A Profile," available at http://opencrs.com/document/R40086, accessed 12 January 2009.

Military

1792 Salzman, Smith, and West, *Encyclopedia of African American Culture and History*, vol. 4, p. 1787.

1812 Salzman, Smith, and West, *Encyclopedia of African American Culture and History*, vol. 4, p. 1788.

1917 Vincent Tompkins, *American Decades: 1910–1919*, vol. 2 (Detroit: Gale Research, 1994), p. 259.

1948 Salzman, Smith, and West, *Encyclopedia of African American Culture and History*, vol. 4, p. 1793.

—   Franck and Brownstone, *Women's World*, p. 423.

1973   NWHP, "A timeline of the women's rights movement, 1848–1998."

1976   NWHP, "A timeline of the women's rights movement, 1848–1998."

1980   Ruth, *Issues in Feminism*, p. 442.

1991   American Women in Uniform, "Operations Desert Shield / Desert Storm," available from http://userpages.aug.com/captbarb/femvetsds.html, accessed March 20, 2000.

1993   U.S. Coast Guard, "Coast Guard Spars," available from http://www.uscg.mil/reserve/magazine/mag1997/nov1997/spars.html, accessed March 20, 2000; RAND, "New opportunities for military women: effects upon readiness, cohesion and morale," available from http://www.rand.org/publications/MR/MR896/, accessed March 20, 2000.

1994   Service Members Legal Defense Network, "The 'don't ask, don't tell' policy," available from http://www.sldn.org/scripts/sldn.ixe?page=article 0003, accessed March 20, 2000.

1994   Women's Research and Education Institute, "Chronology of Significant Legal and Policy Changes Affecting Women in the Military, 1947–2006," available at http://www.wrei.org/Women%20in%20th%20Military/Women%20in%20the%20Military%20Chronology%20of%20.Legal%20Policy.pdf, accessed 5 September 2008.

2001   Women's Research and Education Institute, "Chronology," available at http://www.wrei.org/Women%20in%20the%20Military/Women%20in%20the%20Military%20Chronology%20of%20Legal%20Policy.pdf, accessed 5 September 2008.

2002   Women's Research and Education Institute, "Positions and Occupations Currently Open to Active Duty Women by Branch of Service, 2002," available at http://www.wrei.org/Women%20in%20the%20Military/OccupationsCurrentlyOpen2002.pdf, accessed 5 September 2008.
         U.S. Department of Defense, "Table B-25. FY 2002 Active Component Enlisted Members by Race/Ethnicity, Service, and Gender with Civilian Comparison Group," available at http://www.defenselink.mil/prhome/poprep2002/appendixb/b 25.htm, accessed 5 September 2008.

2003   Women's Research and Education Institute, "Chronology," available at http://www.wrei.org/Women%20in%20the%20Military/Women%20in%20the%20Military%20Chronology%20of%20Legal%20Policy.pdf, accessed 5 September 2008.

2006   Servicemembers Legal Defense Network, "Total 'Don't Ask, Don't Tell' Discharges, 1994–2006," available at http://www.sldn.org/binary-data/SLDN ARTICLES/pdf file/3864.pdf and "Conduct Unbecoming (Tenth Annual Report on "Don't Ask, Don't Tell) available at http://www.sldn.org/binary-data/SLDN ARTICLES/pdf_file/1411.pdf, accessed 5 September 2008.

2007   Center for American Progress, "Beyond the Call of Duty," available at http://www.americanprogress.org/issues/2007/03/readiness   report.html, accessed 8 September 2008.

—   Women's Research and Education Institute, "Active Duty Service Personnel by Branch of Service, Officer/Enlisted Status & Sex as of 30 September 2007," available at http://www.wrei.org/Sept 2007 Active.pdf, accessed 5 September 2008.

2008   Department of Defense Personnel and Procurement Statistics, "Operation Iraqi Freedom Military Death (March 19, 2003 through August 2, 2008)," available at http://siadapp.dmdc.osd.mil/personnel/CASUALTY/oif-deaths-total.pdf, accessed 8 September 2008.

—   Department of Defense Personnel and Procurement Statistics, "Operation Iraqi Freedom Military Wounded in Action (March 19, 2003 through August 2, 2008)," available at http://siadapp.dmdc.osd.mil/personnel/CASUALTY/oif-wounded-total.pdf, accessed 8 September 2008.

—   Iraq Coalition Casualty Count, "Iraqi Security Forces and Civilian Deaths," available at http://icasualties.org/oif/Default.aspx, accessed 8 September 2008.

—   CNN Money.com, "Iraq war could cost taxpayers $2.7 trillion," (June 12, 2008) available at http://money.cnn.com/2008/06/11/news/economy/iraq_war_hearing/index.htm?cnn=yes, accessed 8 September 2008.

Work/Economy

1848   Cullen-DuPont, *Encyclopedia of Women's History in America*, pp. 125–26; Ruth, *Issues in Feminism*, p. 433.

1904   Vincent Tompkins, *American Decades: 1910–1919*, vol. 2. (Detroit: Gale Research, 1994), p. 87.

1910   Tompkins, *American Decades: 1910–1919*, p. 267.

1933   Victor Bondi, ed., *American Decades: 1930–1939*, vol. 4 (Detroit: Gale Research, 1994), p. 93.

1935   Bondi, *American Decades: 1930–1939*, p. 229.

—   Britannica Online, "Works Progress Administration," available from http://www.britannica.com/bcom/eb/article/9/0,5716,79559+1,00.html, accessed March 20, 2000.

1938   Bondi, *American Decades: 1930–1939*, p. 96; Tompkins, *American Decades 1910–1919*, p. 269.

1939   Bondi, *American Decades: 1930–1939*, p. 96.

1941   Bondi, *American Decades: 1940–1949*, p. 95; Worldbook, "A. Philip Randolph," available from http://www.worldbook.com/fun/aajourny/html/bh073.html, accessed July 19, 2000.

1947   Rick Fantasia, *Cultures of Solidarity: Consciousness, Action, and Contemporary American Workers*. (Berkeley: University of California Press, 1988).

1962   Ruth, *Issues in Feminism*, p. 436.

1963   Cullen-DuPont, *Encyclopedia of Women's History in America*, p. 65; Franck and Brownstone, *Women's World*, p. 475.

1964   Cullen-DuPont, *Encyclopedia of Women's History in America*, p. 37; Franck and Brownstone, *Women's World*, p. 478; NWHP, "A timeline of the women's rights movement, 1848–1898."

1968 Fair Housing Act, *Statutes at Large* 82, sec. 804–805 (1968); Ruth, *Issues in Feminism*, p. 440.

1969 Donald L. Barlett and James B. Steele, *America: Who Really Pays the Taxes?* (New York: Simon and Schuster, 1994), p. 44.

1970 Bondi, *American Decades: 1970–1979*, p. 132.

1972 Cullen-DuPont, *Encyclopedia of Women's History in America*, p. 65; Franck and Brownstone, *Women's World*, p. 475.

— Deb Price, "Gays make state-by-state progress" *Detroit News*, January 10, 2000.

1974 NWHP, "A timeline of the women's rights movement, 1848–1998"; Ruth, *Issues in Feminism*, p. 440.

1975 U.S. Census Bureau, "Historical income tables—People," available from http://www.census.gov/hhes/income/histinc/incperdet.html, accessed March 20, 2000.

1980 Institute for Policy Studies, "Executive Excess 2007." Available online at http://www.ips-dc.org/reports/070829-executiveexcess.pdf, accessed 12 October 2008.

1986 NWHP, "A timeline of the women's rights movement, 1848–1998."

1988 *Encyclopedia of American History*, (New York: HarperCollins, 1996), p. 545.

— Fair Housing Amendments Act of 1988, *Statutes at Large* 102, sec. 5 (1988); Ruth, *Issues in Feminism*, p. 440.

1994 *Encyclopedia of American History*, p. 545.

1995 U.S. Census Bureau, "Historical income tables—People."

1996 State of California Department of Consumer Affairs, "Implementing the Federal Personal Responsibility and Work Opportunity Reconciliation Act," available from http://www.dca.ca.gov/legal/wor_act.htm, accessed March 20, 2000; State of West Virginia, "Executive summary," available from http://www.legis.state.wv.us/joint/perd/workssum1.html, accessed March 20, 2000.

2000 U.S. Equal Employment Opportunity Committee, "Sexual Harassment Charges (1997–2007)," available at http://www.eeoc.gov/stats/harass.html, accessed 8 September 2008.

2005 U.S. Department of Health and Human Services, "About TANF," available at http://www.acf.hhs.gov/programs/ofa/tanf/about.html, accessed 8 September 2008.

2007 U.S Census, "Income, Poverty, and Health Insurance Coverage in the United States: 2007," available at http://www.census.gov/prod/2008pubs/p60-235.pdf, accessed 8 September 2008.

— International Labour Organization, "World of Work Report," available at http://www.ilo.org/public/english/bureau/inst/download/world08.pdf, accessed 12 October 2008.

Marriage/Reproduction

1873 Cullen-DuPont, *Encyclopedia of Women's History in America*, p. 41; NWHP, "A timeline of the women's rights movement, 1848–1998."

1921 Cullen-DuPont, *Encyclopedia of Women's History in America*, p. 43; Britannica Online, "Margaret Sanger," available from http://www.britannica.com/bcom/eb/article/7/0,5716,67197+1,00.html, accessed March 20, 2000.

1922 Franklin Ng, ed., *The Asian American Encyclopedia*, (New York: Marshall Cavendish, 1995), p. 156.

1931 Ruth, *Issues in Feminism*, p. 436.

1936 Ng, *Asian American Encyclopedia*, p. 156.

1965 Franck and Brownstone, *Women's World*, p. 482.

1966 Angela Evans, "What's color got to do with it?" available from http://cctr.umkc.edu/wicc/Inter1.html, accessed March 20, 2000.

1967 FindLaw, "U.S. Supreme Court Loving v. Virginia," available from http://laws.findlaw.com/US/388/1.html, accessed March 20, 2000.

1972 Cullen-DuPont, *Encyclopedia of Women's History in America*, p. 43.

1973 NWHP, "A timeline of the women's rights movement, 1848–1998"; Ruth, *Issues in Feminism*, p. 440.

1977 NWHP, "A timeline of the women's rights movement, 1848–1998."

1978 Franck and Brownstone, *Women's World*, p. 539; NWHP, "A timeline of the women's rights movement, 1848–1998."

1981 Britannica Online, "AIDS," available from http://www.britannica.com, accessed March 20, 2000.

1987 AEGIS, "So little time: An AIDS history," available from http://www.aegis.com, accessed March 20, 2000.

1988 AEGIS, "So little time: An AIDS history."

1990 Yggdrasil, "Statistics on interracial marriage," available from http://www.ddc.net/ygg/ms/ms-05.htm, accessed March 20, 2000.

—   Franck and Brownstone, *Women's World*, p. 583.

1992 Franck and Brownstone, *Women's World*, p. 590; Rock For Choice: A Project of the Feminist Majority and the Feminist Majority Foundation, "History of Abortion Rights in the U.S.: January 22, 1973 to Present," available from http://www.feminist.org./rock4c/book/hist.html, accessed March 20, 2000.

1993 Franck and Brownstone, *Women's World*, p. 595; NWHP, "A timeline of the women's rights movement, 1848–1998."

—   NWHP, "A timeline of the women's rights movement, 1848–1998."

1994 Rock for Choice, "History of Abortion Rights."

1996 American Civil Liberties Union (ACLU), "Gay marriage: Should lesbian and gay couples be allowed to marry?" available from http://www.aclu.org/library/aagay marriage.html, accessed March 20, 2000.

—   ACLU, "ACLU blasts senate passage of anti-gay marriage ban; Calls vote a 'deplorable act' and vows legal challenge," available from http://www.aclu.org/news/n091096a.html, accessed March 20, 2000.

1998   ACLU, "ACLU vows to continue fight as Hawaii, Alaska voters rejects same-sex marriage," available from www.aclu.org/news/n110498a.html, accessed March 20, 2000.

1999   Human Rights Campaign, "States denying equal marriage rights to lesbian and gay Americans," available from http://www.hrc.org/issues/marriage/marstate.html, accessed March 20, 2000.

—   National Freedom to Marry Coalition, "Baker v. State," available from http://www.qrd.org/usa/vermont/baker-v-state, accessed March 20, 2000.

—   U.S. Food and Drug Administration, "Plan B (Levonorgestrel) Tablets," available at http://www.fda.gov/cder/foi/nda/99/21-045_PlanB.htm, accessed 13 January 2009.

—   Britannica Online, "AIDS"; UNAIDS, "AIDS Epidemic Update: December 1999," available from http://www.unaids.org/publications/documents/epidemiology/index.html, accessed March 20, 2000.

2000   Carey Goldberg, "Vermont's house backs wide rights for gay couples," *New York Times*, March 17, 2000.

—   NARAL Pro-Choice America, "RU 486 (Non-Surgical/Medical Abortion)," available at http://www.prochoiceamerica.org/issues/abortion/medical-abortion/, accessed 13 January 2009.

2006   NARAL Pro-Choice America, "Emergency Contraception: The "Morning-After" Pill," available at http://www.prochoiceamerica.org/issues/birth_control/emergency-contraception/, accessed 13 January 2009.

2007   UNAIDS, "2008 Report on the global AIDS epidemic," available at http://www.unaids.org/en/KnowledgeCentre/HIVData/GlobalReport/2008/2008_Global_report.asp, accessed 13 January 2009.

—   NARAL Pro-Choice America, "Key Findings: Threats to Choice," available at http://www.prochoiceamerica.org/choice-action-center/in_your_state/who-decides/introduction/key-findings-threats.html, accessed 13 January 2009.

2008   Guttmacher Institute, "State Funding of Abortion Under Medicaid," available at www.guttmacher.org/statecenter/spibs/spib_SFAM.pdf, accessed 13 January 2009.
        Lambda Legal, "In Your State," available at http://www.lambdalegal.org/our-work/states/, accessed 13 January 2009; Human Rights Campaign (HRC), "Maps of State Laws and Policies," available at http://www.hrc.org/about_us/state_laws.asp, accessed 13 January 2009.

—   UNAIDS, "2008 Report on the global AIDS epidemic," available at http://www.unaids.org/en/KnowledgeCentre/HIVData/GlobalReport/2008/2008_Global_report.asp, accessed 13 January 2009.

—   NARAL Pro-Choice America, "Access to Abortion" available at http://www.prochoiceamerica.org/issues/abortion/access-to-abortion/, accessed 13 January 2009.

References

Abramovitz, Mimi. 1996. *Under Attack, Fighting Back: Women and Welfare in the United States*. New York: Monthly Review Press.

Abramovitz, Mimi, and Sandra Morgen. 2006. *Taxes Are a Woman's Issue: Reframing the Debate*. New York: Feminist Press at the City University of New York.

Alexander, Karl, Doris Entwisle, and Maxine Thompson. 1987. "School performance, status relations, and the structure of sentiment: Bringing the teacher back in." *American Sociological Review* 52 (October): 665–82.

Almaguer, Tomás. 1993. "Chicano men: A cartography of homosexual identity and behavior." In *The Lesbian and Gay Studies Reader*, ed. Henry Abelove, Michèle Aina Barale, and David M. Halperin. New York: Routledge.

American Association of University Women (AAUW). 1991. *Shortchanging Girls, Shortchanging America: Executive Summary*. Washington, DC: American Association of University Women Educational Foundation.

———. 1992. *How Schools Shortchange Girls: The AAUW Report: A Study of Major Findings on Girls and Education*. Washington, DC: American Association of University Women Educational Foundation.

———. 1999. *Gender Gaps: Where Our Schools Still Fail Our Children*. New York: Marlowe & Co.

———. 2004. *Under the Microscope: A Decade of Gender Equity Projects in the Sciences*. Available from http://www.aauw.org/research/upload/underthemicroscope.pdf, accessed January 31, 2009.

——— 2007. *Separated by Sex: Title IX and Single Sex Education*. Available from http://www.aauw.org/research/all.cfm, accessed December 2008.

American Sociological Association. 2003. *The Importance of Collecting Data and Doing Social Scientific Research on Race*. Washington, DC: American Sociological Association.

Amott, Teresa, and Julie Matthaei. 1996. *Race, Gender, and Work: A Multi-Cultural Economic History of Women in the United States*. Rev. ed. Boston: South End Press.

Anderson, Gerard F., Dennis G. Shea, Peter S. Hussey, Salometh Keyhani, and Laurie Zephyrin. 2004. "Donut holes and price controls." *Health Affairs*, July 1. Available from http://content.healthaffairs.org/cgi/content/short/hlthaff.w4.396, accessed January 2, 2009.

Anderson, Sarah, John Cavanagh, Chuck Collins, Sam Pizzigati. 2008. *Executive Excess 2008: How Average Taxpayers Subsidize Runaway Pay: 15th Annual CEO Compensation survey*. Washington, DC: Institute for Policy Studies and United for a Fair Economy. Available from www.ips-dc.org, accessed January 2, 2009.

Anyon, Jean. 1980. "Social class and the hidden curriculum of work." *Journal of Education* 162:67–92.

——. 1997. *Ghetto Schooling: A Political Economy of Urban Educational Reform*. New York: Teachers College Press, Columbia University.

Anzaldua, Gloria. 1987a. *Borderlands/La Frontera: The New Mestiza*. San Francisco: Aunt-Lute Books.

——, ed. 1987b. *Making Faces, Making Soul/Haciendo Caras: Creative and Critical Perspectives by Women of Color*. San Francisco: AuntLute Books.

Appell, Annette. 1998. "On fixing 'bad' mothers and saving their children." In *Bad Mothers: The Politics of Blame in Twentieth-Century America*, ed. Molly Ladd-Taylor and Lauri Umansky. New York: New York University Press.

Arnold, David H., and Greta L. Doctoroff. 2003. "The early education of socioeconomically disadvantaged children." *Annual Review of Psychology* 54:517–45.

Arroyo, Carmen G. 2008. *The Funding Gap*. Washington, DC: The Education Trust. Available from http://www2.edtrust.org/edtrust/product+catalog/main, accessed December 30, 2008.

Arthur Levitt Public Affairs Center. 2006. "The Hamilton College youth hot button issues Poll: Guns, gays, and abortion." Available from http://www.hamilton.edu/news/polls/HotButtonIssues/index.html, accessed January 4, 2009.

Awaiakta, Marilou. 1993. *Selu: Seeking the Corn Mother's Wisdom*. Golden, CO: Fulerum.

Baca Zinn, Maxine, Lynn Weber Cannon, Elizabeth Higginbotham, and Bonnie Thornton Dill. 1986. "The costs of exclusionary practices in women's studies." *SIGNS: Journal of Women in Culture and Society* 11 (Winter): 290–303.

Baca Zinn, Maxine, and Bonnie Thornton Dill, eds. 1994. *Women of Color in U.S. Society*. Philadelphia: Temple University Press.

——. 1996. "Theorizing difference from multiracial feminism." *Feminist Studies* 22(2): 321–31.

Badgett, M. V. Lee. 1995. "The wage effects of sexual orientation discrimination." *Industrial and Labor Relations Review* 48 (4): 726–39.

Badgett, M. V. Lee, Christopher Ramos, and Brad Sears. 2008. "Evidence of employment discrimination on the basis of sexual orientation and gender identity: Complaints filed with state enforcement agencies 1999–2007." Los Angeles, CA: Williams Institute, UCLA School of Law. Available from http://www.law.ucla.edu/williamsinstitute, accessed January 5, 2009.

Bailey, Stanley R. 2004. "Group dominance and the myth of racial democracy: Antiracism attitudes in Brazil." *American Sociological Review* 69 (5):728–47.

Baker, Therese, and William Velez. 1996. "Access to and opportunity in postsecondary education in the United States: A review." *Sociology of Education* [Extra Issue]: 82–101.

Barnes, Robert. 2007. "Divided court limits use of race by school districts." The Washington Post June, 29.

Basu, A., and M.J. Dutta. 2008. "The relationship between health information seeking and community participation: The roles of health information orientation and efficacy." *Health Communication* 23 (1):70–79.

Beckert, Jens. 2008. *Inherited Wealth*. Princeton, NJ: Princeton University Press.

Benkov, Laura. 1994. *Reinventing the Family: The Emerging Story of Lesbian and Gay Parents*. New York: Crown.

Berardelli, Phil. 2006. "Spying with a fly's eyes." *ScienceNOW Daily News* 281:2.

Berger, Michele. 2004. *Workable Sisterhood: The Political Journey of Stigmatized Women with HIV/AIDS*. Princeton, NJ: Princeton University Press.

Bernardi, Daniel. 2009. *Filming Difference: Actors, Directors, Producers and Writers on Gender, Race, and Sexuality in Film*. Austin, TX: University of Texas Press.

Bethard, Rebecca. 2004. "New York's Harvey Milk School: A viable alternative." *Journal of Law and Education* 33(3):417–23.

Bettie, Julie. 2003. *Women Without Class: Girls, Race, and Identity*. Berkeley, CA: University of California Press.

Bills, David B. 2003. "Credentials, signals, and screens: Explaining the relationship between schooling and job assignment." *Review of Educational Research* 73(4):441–69.

"Black colleges with white golfers." 2000–2001. *Journal of Blacks in Higher Education* 30(Winter):78–79.

Blank, R.K., R.A. Dentler, C.E. Baltzell, and K. Chabotar, 1983. *Survey of magnet schools: Analyzing a model for quality integrated education*. Final Report of a National Study for the U.S. Department of Education, No. 300-81-0420. Chicago, IL: Lowry Associates. (ERIC Document Reproduction Service No. ED 236–304).

Blasius, Mark, and Shane Phelan. 1997. *We Are Everywhere: A Historical Sourcebook of Gay and Lesbian Politics*. New York: Routledge.

Blee, Kathleen. 1991. *Women of the Klan: Racism and Gender in the 1920s*. Berkeley: University of California Press.

———, ed. 1998. *No Middle Ground: Women and Radical Protest*. New York: New York University Press.

Bloom, Allan. 1988. *The Closing of the American Mind*. New York: Touchstone Books.

Bonilla-Silva, E. 2003. "'New racism,' color-blind racism and the future of whiteness in America." In *White Out: The Continuing Significance of Racism*, ed. A. W. Doane and E. Bonilla-Silva, New York: Routledge.

Bookman, Ann, and Sandra Morgen, eds. 1988. *Women and the Politics of Empowerment: Perspectives, from the Workplace and the Community*. Philadelphia: Temple University Press.

Boozer, Michael, Alan Krueger, and Shari Wolkon. 1992. "Race and school quality since Brown v. Board of Education." *Brookings Papers on Economic Activity: Microeconomics:* 269–338.

Brantlinger, Ellen A. 1993. *The Politics of Social Class in Secondary School: Views of Affluent and Impoverished Youth*. New York: Teachers College Press, Columbia University.

Bravo, Ellen. 2007. *Taking on the Big Boys or Why Feminism is Good for Families, Business, and the Nation*. New York, NY: The Feminist Press.

Brobeck, Stephen, and Catherine Montalto. 2008. *The Financial Condition of Women on Their Own*. Consumer Federation of America. Available from http://www.consumerfed.org/pdfs/Women_on_Their_Own_Report_12-2-08.pdf, accessed January 17, 2009.

Brod, Harry, and Michael Kaufman, eds. 1994. *Theorizing Masculinities*. Thousand Oaks, CA: Sage.

Brodkin, Karen. 2004. "How Jews became White folks and what that says about race in America." In *Race, Class, and Gender in the United States*, ed. Paula S. Rothenberg, New York: Worth.

Brown, David. 1995. *Degrees of Control: A Sociology of Educational Expansion and Occupational Credentialism*. New York: Teachers College Press, Columbia University.

——— 2001. "The social sources of educational credentialism: Status cultures, labor markets, and organizations." *Sociology of Education* [Extra Issue]: 19–34.

Burkett, Elinor. 1998. "Don't tread on my tax rate." *New York Times Magazine*, April 26:42.

Burelli, David and Charles V. Dale. 2006. *Homosexuals and U.S. Military Policy: Current Issues*. Library of Congress, Congressional Research Service. Available from http://digital.library.unt.edu/govdocs/crs/permalink/meta-crs-8572:1tkl, accessed April 4, 2009.

Button, James W., Barbara A. Rienzo and Kenneth Wald. 1997. *Private Lives, Public Conflicts: Battles over Gay Rights in American Communities*. Washington, DC: Congressional Quarterly.

Callahan, Rebecca M. 2005. "Tracking and high school English learners: Limiting opportunity to learn." *American Educational Research Journal* 42 (2): 305–28.

Calefati, Jessica. 2008. "Gay high schools offer a haven from bullies." *U.S. News and World Report*, December 31.

Carbado, Devon W., and G. Mitu Gulati. 2001. "The fifth black woman: The future of intersectionality and critical race feminism." *Journal of Contemporary Legal Issues* 11 (2): 701–29.

CARE (National Commission on Asian American and Pacific Islander Research in Education). 2008. *Asian Americans and Pacific Islanders, Facts Not Fiction: Setting the Record Straight*. New York: College Board.

Carlson, Dennis. 1997. *Making Progress: Education and Culture in New Times*. New York: Teachers College Press, Columbia University.

Catalyst. 2009. "Women CEOs of the Fortune 1000." Available from http://www.catalyst.org/publication/271/women-ceos-of-the-fortune-1000, accessed February 2, 2009.

Centers for Disease Control and Prevention. "United States suicide deaths and rates per 100,000: 1997." Available from http://webapp.cdc.gov/sasweb/ncipc/mortrate.html, accessed March 20, 2000.

Chesler, Phyllis. 1986. *Mothers on Trial: The Battle for Children and Custody*. New York: McGraw-Hill.

Children's Defense Fund. 2003. *Prekindergarten Initiatives: Efforts to Help Children Enter School Ready to Succeed*. Available from http://www.childrensdefense.org//site/PageServer?pagename=research_early_childhood, accessed December 30, 2009.

——— 2005. *State of America's Children*. Available from http://www.childrensdefense.org/site/DocServer/Greenbook_2005.pdf?docID=174, accessed December 30, 2008.

Cho, Stephanie, Chris Daley, Courtney Joslin, Carolyn Laub, and Sean Saifa M. Wall. 2004. *Beyond the Binary: A Tool Kit for Gender Identity Activism in Schools*. Gay-Straight Alliance Network; Transgender Law Center; and National Center for Lesbian Rights. Available from http://www.gsanetwork.org/BeyondtheBinary/toolkit.html, accessed December 30, 2008.

Chou, Rosalind S., and Joe R. Feagin. 2008. *The Myth of the Model Minority: Asian Americans Facing Racism*. Boulder, CO: Paradigm.

Ciscel, David. 2002. "What is a living wage for Memphis?" Research paper. Center for Research on Women, University of Memphis.

Cloud, John. 1997. "Out, proud, and very young." *Time*, December 8.

Clark, Terry N. and Seymour M. Lipsett. 1991. "Are social classes dying? *International Sociology* 6(4): 397–411.

CNN.com. 2009. "Angry senator wants pay cap on Wall Street 'idiots.'" Available from http://www.cnn.com/2009/POLITICS/01/30/executive.pay/index.html, accessed February 2, 2009.

Collins, Chuck. 2008. *Talking Points: Economic Meltdown*. Institute for Policy Studies, Working Group on Extreme Inequality. Available from http://www.ips-dc.org/reports, accessed February 2, 2009.

Collins, Patricia Hill. 1986. "Learning from the outsider within: The sociological significance of Black feminist thought." *Social Problems* 33(6):14–32.

———. 1991a. *Black Feminist Thought: Knowledge, Consciousness and the Politics of Empowerment*. New York: Routledge.

———. 1991b. "Learning from the outsider within: The sociological significance of black feminist thought." In *Beyond Methodology: Feminist Scholarship as Lived Research*. Mary Margaret Fonow and Judith A. Cook, eds. Bloomington: Indiana University Press.

———. 1998. *Fighting Words: Black Women and the Search for Justice*. Minneapolis: University of Minnesota Press.

———. 2000. *Black Feminist Thought: Knowledge, Consciousness, and the Politics of Empowerment*. 2nd ed., New York: Routledge.

———. 2004. *Black Sexual Politics*. New York: Routledge.

Comas-Diaz, Lillian, and Beverly Greene. 1994. *Women of Color: Integrating Ethnic and Gender Identities in Psychotherapy*, New York: Guilford.

Commission on Professionals in Science and Technology. 2004. "Women in science and technology: The Sisyphean challenge of change." Report no. 2. *STEM Workforce Data Project*. Available from www.cpst.org, accessed January 28, 2009.

Condron, Dennis J., and Vincent J. Roscigno. 2003. "Disparities within: Unequal spending and achievement in an urban school district." *Sociology of Education* 76 (1): 18–36.

Congressional Budget Office. 2007. *Historical Effective Tax Rates 1979-2005, Table 1C*. Available from http://www.cbo.gov/ftpdocs/88xx/doc8885/12-11-HistoricalTaxRates.pdf, accessed on April 3, 2009.

Congressional Research Service. 2008. *Membership of the 111th Congress: A Profile*. Available from http://assets.opencrs.com/rpts/R40086_20081231.pdf, accessed January 2, 2009.

Connell, R. W. 1987. *Gender and Power: Society, the Person, and Sexual Politics*. Stanford, CA: Stanford University Press.

———. 1995. *Masculinities*. Berkeley: University of California Press.

Coontz, Stephanie. 1992. *The Way We Never Were: American Families and the Nostalgia Trap*. New York: Basic Books.

Corbett, Christianne, Catherine Hill, and Andresse St. Rose. 2008. *Where the Girls Are: The Facts About Gender Equity in Education*. Washington, DC: American Association of University Women. Available from http://www.aauw.org/research/upload/whereGirlsAre.pdf, accessed January 28, 2009.

Crenshaw, Kimberle. 1989. "Demarginalizing the intersection of race and sex: A Black feminist critique of antidiscrimination doctrine, feminist theory and antiracist politics." *University of Chicago Legal Forum* 1989: 139–67.

———. 1991. "Mapping the margins: Intersectionality, identity politics, and violence against women of color." *Stanford Law Review* 43(6):1241–79.

Crosby, Faye J., and Margaret Stockdale, eds. 2007. *Sex Discrimination in the Workplace: Multidisciplinary Perspectives*. Boston, MA: Blackwell.

Crosnoe, Robert. 2005. "Double disadvantage or signs of resilience? The elementary school contexts of children from Mexican immigrant families." *American Educational Research Journal* 42 (2):269–303

Crow Dog, Mary, and Richard Erdoes. 1996. "Civilize them with a stick: Education as an institution for social control." In *Mapping the Social Landscape: Readings in Sociology*, ed. Susan J. Ferguson. Mountain View, CA: Mayfield.

Dawkins, Marvin P., and Jomills Henry Braddock II. 1994. "The continuing significance of desegregation: School racial composition and African American inclusion in American society." *Journal of Negro Education* 63:394–405.

D'Emilio, John. 1983. *Sexual Politics, Sexual Communities: The Making of a Homosexual Minority in the United States, 1940–1970*. Chicago: University of Chicago Press.

———. 1993. "Capitalism and gay identity." In *The Lesbian and Gay Studies Reader*, ed. Henry Abelove, Michele Barale, and David M. Halperin. New York: Routledge.

———. 2002. *The World Turned: Essays on Gay History, Politics, and Culture*. Durham, NC: Duke University Press.

———. 2003. *Lost Prophet: Bayard Rustin and the Quest for Peace and Justice in America*. New York: Free Press.

———. 2006. "The marriage fight is setting us back." *Gay and Lesbian Review Worldwide* 13 (6):10–11.

D'Emilio, John, and Estelle Freedman. 1988. *Intimate Matters: A History of Sexuality in America*. New York: Harper and Row.

Degler, C. N. 1971. *Neither Black nor White: Slavery and Race Relations in Brazil and the United States*. New York: Macmillan.

Denverpost.com. 2008. "Full text of Obama's education speech." *The Denver Post*, December 12. Available from http://www.denverpost.com/news/ci_9405199, accessed April 18, 2009.

DeParle, Jason. 1998. "What welfare-to-work really means." *New York Times Magazine*, December 20.

De Welde, Kristine, Sandra Laursen, and Heather Thiry. 2007. *Women in Science, Technology, Engineering and Math (STEM)*. Kingston, RI: Sociologists for Women in Society. Available from http://www.socwomen.org/page.php?ss=25, accessed January 28, 2009.

Diamond, John B., Antonia Randolph, and James P. Spillane. 2004. "Teachers' expectations and sense of responsibility for student learning: The importance of race, class, and organizational habitus." *Anthropology and Education Quarterly* 35(1):75–98.

Dominus, Susan. 2008. "The color of love: Theirs was a marriage that broke the law—and then fixed it." *New York Times Magazine*, December 28.

Dougherty, Kevin. 1996. "Opportunity-to-learn standards: A sociological critique." *Sociology of Education* [Extra Issue]:40–65.

D'Souza, Dinesh. 1991. *Illiberal Education: The Politics of Race and Sex on Campus*. New York: Free Press.

Duberman, Martin, Martha Vicinus, and George Chauncey, Jr., eds. 1989. *Hidden from History: Reclaiming the Gay and Lesbian Past*. New York: New American Library.

Eaton, Susan E. 2001. *The Other Boston Busing Story: What's Won and Lost Across the Boundary Line*. New Haven, CT: Yale University Press.

Edin, Kathryn, and Laura Lein. 1997. *Making Ends Meet: How Single Mothers Survive Welfare and Low-Wage Work*. New York: Russell Sage Foundation.

Edwards, Jim. 2005. "Follow the money." *Brandweek*, February 7, 24–6.

Egan, Patrick J., and Kenneth Sherrill. 2005. "Marriage and the shifting priorities of a new generation of lesbians and gays." *PS: Political Science and Politics* 38(2):229–32.

Ehrenreich, Barbara. 1999. "Nickel-and-dimed: On (not) getting by in America." *Harpers Magazine*, January: 37–52.

Eisenmenger, Michelle. 2002. "Sexual orientation discrimination: Teachers as positive role models for tolerance." *Journal of Law and Education* 31(2):235–44.

Enloe, Cynthia. 1997. "The globetrotting sneaker." In *Women's Lives: Multicultural Perspectives*, eds. Gwyn Kirk and Margo Okazawa-Rey. Mountain View, CA: Mayfield.

———. 2007. *Globalization and Militarism*. Lanham, MD: Rowman & Littlefield.

Entwisle, Doris R., Karl L. Alexander, and Linda Steffel Olson. 1997. *Children, Schools, and Inequality*. Boulder, CO: Westview Press.

EPE Research Center. 2008. "School to college: Can state P-16 councils ease the transition?" *Education Week Special Supplement: Diplomas Count.* Available from www.edweek. org/go/dc08, accessed April 3, 2009.

Fair Labor Association. *2007 Annual Report.* Available from http://www.fairlabor.org/ images/WhatWeDo/2007_annualpublicreport.pdf, accessed January 2, 2009.

FairTest. 2007. *The Dangerous Consequences of High-Stakes Standardized Testing.* Boston, MA: National Center for Fair and Open Testing. Available from http://www.fairtest.org/ dangerous-consequences-highstakes-standardized-tes, accessed December 30, 2008.

Farley, Reynolds. 1996. *The New American Reality: Who We Are, How We Got Here, Where We Are Going.* New York: Russell Sage Foundation.

Fausto-Sterling, Anne. 2000. "Dueling dualisms." In *Sexing the Body: Gender Politics and the Construction of Sexuality,* ed. Anne Fausto-Sterling. New York: Basic Books.

Feinberg, Leslie. 1996. *Transgender Warriors: Making History from Joan of Arc to Dennis Rodman.* Boston: Beacon Press.

Ferber, Abigail L. 1998. *White Man Falling: Race, Gender and White Supremacy.* Lanham, MD: Rowman and Littlefield.

Ferree, Myra Marx, and Elaine J. Hall. 1990. "Visual images of American society; Gender and race in introductory sociology textbooks." *Gender and Society* 4(4):500–33.

Fields, Barbara. 1990. "Slavery, race, and ideology in the United States of America." *New Left Review* (181):95–118.

Fountain, John W. 2003. "Mamie Mobley, 81, dies; Son, Emmett Till, slain in 1955." *New York Times,* January 7.

Frankenberg, Erica. 2006. *The Segregation of American Teachers.* Cambridge, MA: The Civil Rights Project at Harvard University. Available from http://www.civilrightsproject.ucla. edu/research/deseg/segregation_american_teachers12-06.pdf, accessed January 26, 2009.

Frankenberg, Erica, Chungmei Lee, and Gary Orfield. 2003. "A multiracial society with segregated schools: Are we losing the dream?" Cambridge, MA: The Civil Rights Project at Harvard University.

Frankenberg, Erica, and Genevieve Siegel-Hawley. 2008. *The Forgotten Choice? Rethinking Magnet Schools in a Changing Landscape: A Report to Magnet Schools of America.* Los Angeles, CA: Civil Rights Project, at The University of California, Los Angeles.

Freedman, Estelle B. 2006. *Feminism, Sexuality, and Politics: Essays by Estelle B. Freedman.* Chapel Hill NC,: University of North Carolina Press.

Freeman, Richard, ed. 1994. *Working Under Different Rules.* New York: Russell Sage Foundation.

Fugh-Berman, Adriane. 2008. "The physician-pharma relationship." Available from http:// www.pharmedout.org/type.htm#slideshows, accessed January 3, 2009.

Gallagher, Charles A. 2007. "White." In *Handbook of the Sociology of Racial and Ethnic Relations,* ed. Hernan Vera and Joe R. Feagin. New York: Springer Science and Business Media, LLC.

Gamson, Joshua, and Dawne Moon. 2004. "The sociology of sexualities: Queer and beyond." *Annual Review of Sociology* 30:47–64.

Gantz, Julie. 2004. "Fifty years after Brown: Tarnished gold, broken promises." *History Teacher* 38 (1):66–113.

Gay and Lesbian Alliance Against Defamation. 2009. Available from http://www.glaad.org/ eye/ontv/2008/index.php, accessed February 4, 2009.

Gay, Lesbian and Straight Education Network (GLSEN). 2008. "Facts about gay–straight alliances." Available from http://www.glsen.org, accessed December 30, 2008.

Gaylin, Willard. 1992. *The Male Ego.* New York: Viking.

Gay-Straight Alliance Network, 2004. *Beyond the Binary: A Tool Kit for Gender Identity Activism in Schools.* Available from http://www.gsanetwork.org/BeyondtheBinary/toolkit.html, accessed December 30, 2008.

Gilkes, Cheryl. 1994. "'If it wasn't for the women ...': African American women, community work, and social change." In *Women of Color in U.S. Society*, ed. Maxine Baca Zinn and Bonnie Thornton Dill. Philadelphia: Temple University Press.

Gilligan, Carol; Nona Lyons; and Trudy Hanmer, eds. 1990. *Making Connections: The Relational Worlds of Adolescent Girls at Emma Willard School.* Cambridge: Harvard University Press.

Gitlin, Andrew, Edward Buendía, Kristen Crosland, and Fode Doumbia. 2003. "The production of margin and center: Welcoming-unwelcoming of immigrant students." *American Educational Research Journal* 40(1):91–122.

Glenn, Evelyn Nakano. 1992. "From servitude to service work: Historical continuities in the racial division of paid reproductive labor." *Signs* 18 (Autumn):1–43.

Global Exchange. 2008. "Understanding Fair Trade." Available from http://www.globalexchange.org/campaigns/fairtrade, accessed January 4, 2009.

Goings, Ken. 1994. *Mammy and Uncle Mose: Black Collectibles and American Stereotyping.* Bloomington: Indiana University Press.

Goldthorpe, John, and Michelle Jackson. 2008. "Education-based meritocracy: The barriers to its realization." In *Social Class: How Does it Work?* Eds. Annette Lareau and Dalton Conley. New York: Russell Sage Foundation.

Goodbyeminimallyadequate.com. 2009. Available from http://goodbyeminimallyadequate.com, accessed January 31, 2009.

Gramsci, Antonio. 1971. *Selections from the Prison Notebooks.* New York: International.

Granfield, Robert, and Thomas Koenig. 1992. "Pathways into elite law firms: Professional stratification and social networks." *Research in Politics and Society* 4:325–51.

Grant, Linda. 1994. "Helpers, enforcers, and go-betweens: Black females in elementary school classrooms." In *Women of Color in U.S. Society*, ed. Maxine Baca Zinn and Bonnie Thornton Dill. Philadelphia: Temple University Press.

Guinier, Lani. 1998a. *Lift Every Voice: Turning a Civil Rights Setback into a New Vision of Social Justice.* New York: Simon & Schuster.

———. 1998b. "Reframing the affirmative action debate." Speech, University of South Carolina, February 26.

Guinier, Lani, Michelle Fine, and Jane Balin. 1997. *Becoming Gentlemen: Women, Law School, and Institutional Change.* Boston: Beacon Press.

Guinier, Lani, and Gerald Torres. 2002. *The Miner's Canary: Enlisting Race; Resisting Power, Transforming Democracy.* Cambridge, MA: Harvard University Press.

Gutfeld, Rose. 2002. "Ten percent in Texas." *Ford Foundation Report* 33(4):16–19.

Hacker, Andrew. 1997. *Money: Who Has How Much and Why.* New York: Scribner.

Hallinan, Maureen. 1995. "Tracking and detracking practices." In *Transforming Schools.* eds. Peter Cookson and Barbara Schneider. New York: Garland.

Hancock, Ange-Marie. 2004. *The Politics of Disgust: The Public Identity of the Welfare Queen.* New York: New York University Press.

———. 2007. "When multiplication doesn't equal quick addition: Examining intersectionality as a research paradigm." *Perspectives on Politics* 5 (1):63–79.

Harlem Children's Zone. 2009. Available online from http://www.hcz.org, accessed January 28, 2009.

HarrisInteractive. 2009. "Gay, Lesbian, Bisexual & Transgender." Available from http://www.harrisinteractive.com/services/glbt.asp, accessed January 5, 2009.

Harrison, Roderick, and Claudette Bennett. 1995. "Racial and ethnic diversity." In *State of the Union in the 1990s*, Vol. 2: *Social Trends*, ed. Reynolds Farley. New York: Russell Sage Foundation.

Hartmann, Heidi. 1997. "The unhappy marriage of Marxism and feminism." In *The Second Wave: A Reader in Feminist Theory*, ed. Linda Nicholson. New York: Routledge.

Harvard Law Review, eds. 1990. *Sexual Orientation and the Law*. Cambridge: Harvard University Press.

Herek, Gregory. 1987. "On heterosexual masculinity." In *Changing Men: New Directions in Research on Men and Masculinity*. Michael Kimmel, ed. Newbury Park, CA. Sage.

Heck, Ronald H., Carol L. Price, and Scott. L. Thomas. 2004. "Tracks as emergent structures: A network analysis of student differentiation in a high school." *American Journal of Education* 110 (August):321–53.

Hecker, Daniel E. 2001. "Occupational employment projections to 2010." *Monthly Labor Review*, 124(11):57–84.

Herrnstein, Richard J., and Charles A. Murray. 1994. *The Bell Curve: Intelligence and Class Structure in American Life*. New York: Free Press.

Higginbotham, Elizabeth, and Lynn Weber. 1992. "Moving up with kin and community: Upward social mobility for black and white women," *Gender & Society* 6 (September): 416–40.

Hochschild, Jennifer. 1995. *Facing Up to the American Dream: Race, Class, and the Soul of the Nation*. Princeton, NJ: Princeton University Press.

Hughes, Langston. 2000. "Dream Variations." In *The Compact Bedford Introduction to Literature: Reading, Thinking, Writing*, ed. Michael, Meyer. Boston: Bedford/St. Martins.

Hull, Gloria, Patricia Bell Scott, and Barbara Smith, eds. 1982. *All the Women Are White, All the Blacks Are Men, But Some of Us Are Brave: Black Women's Studies*. Old Westbury, NY: Feminist Press.

Human Rights Watch. 2008. "China: Olympic sponsors ignore human rights abuses." Available from http://hrw.org/english/docs/2008/18/china19646_txt.htm, accessed January 6, 2009.

Hunt, Darnell M. 2008. "UCLA's new admission policy rights a wrong." *Los Angeles Times*, September 7.

Ignatiev, N. 1995. *How the Irish Became White*. New York: Routledge.

Ihejirika, Maudlyne. 2008. "Still 'separate and unequal.'" *Chicago Sun-Times*, August 21.

Internal Revenue Service. 2008. *Data Book, 2007*. Publication 55B (March). Washington DC. Available from http://www.irs.gov/pub/irs-soi/07databk.pdf, accessed January 18, 2009.

Institute for Women's Policy Research. 2008. "The Gender Wage Gap: 2007." Fact Sheet, IWPR No. C350. Available from http://www.iwpr.org/pdf/C350.pdf, accessed January 22, 2009.

Jackson, Shirley. 1998. "Something about the word: African American women and feminism." In *No Middle Ground: Women and Radical Protest*, ed. Kathleen Blee. New York: New York University Press.

Jackson, Steve. 2005. *Thinking Straight: New Work in Critical Heterosexuality Studies*. New York: Routledge.

Jacobs, Lawrence. 2005. "Health disparities in the land of equality." In *Healthy, Wealthy, and Fair: Health Care and the Good Society*, ed. James A. Morone and Lawrence Jacobs. New York: Oxford University Press.

Jaschik, Scott. 2008. "The SAT's Growing Gaps" *Inside Higher Ed* August 28. Available from http://www.insidehighered.com/news/2008/08/27/sat, accessed October 12, 2008.

Johnston, David Cay. 2004. "The very rich, it now appears, give their share and even more." *New York Times*. January 1.

Jones, James, Beth Vanfossen, and Margaret Ensminger. 1995. "Individual and organizational predictors of high school track placement." *Sociology of Education* 68 (October):287–300.

Karabel, Jerome. 2005. *The Chosen: The Hidden History of Admissions and Exclusion at Harvard, Yale, and Princeton.* Boston: Houghton Mifflin.

Katznelson, Ira, and Margaret Weir. 1985. *Schooling for All: Class, Race, and the Decline of the Democratic Ideal.* New York: Basic Books.

Kawachi, Ichiro. 2005. "Why the United States is not number one in health." In *Healthy, Wealthy, and Fair: Health Care and the Good Society,* ed. James A. Morone and Lawrence Jacobs. New York: Oxford University Press.

Kennickell, Arthur B. 2006. "Currents and undercurrents: Changes in the distribution of wealth, 1989–2004." Washington, DC: Federal Reserve Board. Available from http://www.federalreserve.gov/pubs/oss/oss2/scfindex.html, accessed January 3, 2009.

Kerekhoff, Alan. 1995. "Institutional arrangements and stratification process in industrial societies." *Annual Review of Sociology* 21:323–47.

KewalRamani, Angelina, Lauren Gilbertson, Mary Ann Fox, and Stephen Provasnik. 2007. *Status and Trends in the Education of Racial and Ethnic Minorities.* Washington, DC: National Center for Education Statistics. Available from http://nces.ed.gov/pubs2007/2007039.pdf, accessed January 28, 2009.

Kim, Seung-Kyung. 1997. *Class Struggle or Family Struggle: The Lives of Women Factory Workers in South Korea.* London: Cambridge University Press.

Kimmel, Michael S. 2009. "Masculinity as homophobia: Fear, shame, and silence in the construction of gender identity." In *Rethinking Foundations: Theorizing Sex, Gender, and Sexuality,* eds. Abby L. Ferber, Kimberly Holcomb, and Tre Wentling. New York: Oxford University Press.

Kine Phelim. 2008. "Censorship isn't good for China's health." *Wall Street Journal,* October 11.

King, James. 1981. *The Biology of Race.* Berkeley: University of California Press.

Kingston, Paul. 2001. *The Classless Society.* Palo Alto, CA: Stanford University Press.

Kivisto, Peter. 2007. "What would a racial democracy look like?" In *Handbook of the Sociology of Racial and Ethnic Relations,* ed. Hernan Vera and Joe R. Feagin. New York: Springer Science and Business Media, LLC.

Klein, Julia. 2005. "Merit's Demerits." *The Chronicle Review* 52(11):B12.

Klein, Naomi. 2007. *The Shock Doctrine: The Rise of Disaster Capitalism.* New York: Metropolitan Books, Henry Holt.

Kohn, Alfie. 2004. "NCLB and the effort to privatize public education." In *Many Children Left Behind: How the No Child Left Behind Act Is Damaging Our Children and Our Schools* eds. Deborah Meier and George Wood. Boston, MA: Beacon Press.

Kosciw, Joseph G., Elizabeth M. Diaz, and Emily A. Greytak. 2008. *The 2007 National School Climate Survey: The Experiences of Lesbian, Gay, Bisexual and Transgender Youth in Our Nation's Schools.* New York: Gay, Lesbian and Straight Education Network. Available from http://www.glsen.org, accessed December 30, 2008.

Kotlowitz, Alex. 1991. *There Are No Children Here.* New York: Doubleday.

Kozol, Jonathan. 2005. *The Shame of the Nation: The Restoration of Apartheid Schooling in America.* New York: Crown.

Kroll, Luisa, ed. 2008. "The World's Billionaires." *Forbes,* March 5. Available from http://www.forbes.com/2008/03/05/buffett-worlds-richest-cx_mm_0229buffetrichest.html, accessed December 30, 2008.

Kung, H.C., D.L. Hoyert, J.Q. Xu, and S.L. Murphy. 2008. "Deaths: Final data for 2005." *National Vital Statistics Reports* 56(10). Hyattsville, MD: National Center for Health

Statistics. Available from http://www.cdc.gov/nchs/data/nvsr/nvsr56/nvsr56_10.pdf, accessed January 3, 2009.

Ladner, Joyce. 1972. *Tomorrow's Tomorrow*. Garden City, New York: Doubleday.

Laird, Jennifer, Matthew DeBell, Gregory Kienzl, and Chris Chapman. 2007. *Dropout Rates in the United States: 2005*. Washington, DC: National Center for Education Statistics. Available from http://nces.ed.gov/pubs2007/2007059.pdf, accessed January 28, 2009.

Lambda Legal Defense and Education Fund. 2000. *Cases: Nabozny v. Podlesny*. Available from http://lambdalegal.org/cgi-bin/pages/cases/record?record=54, accessed March 20, 2000.

Lapidus, June. 2004. "All the lesbian mothers are coupled, all the single mothers are straight, and all of us are tired: Reflections on being a single lesbian mom." *Feminist Economics* 10 (2):227–36.

Larabee, David. 1995. Foreword, *Degrees of Control: A Sociology of Educational Expansion and Occupational Credentialism*, by David Brown. New York: Teachers College Press, Columbia University.

Lareau, Annette, 2008. "Introduction: Taking stock of social class." In *Social Class: How Does It Work?* Eds. Annette Lareau and Dalton Conley. New York: Russell Sage Foundation.

Lareau, Annette, and Dalton Conley, eds. 2008. *Social Class: How Does It Work?* New York: Russell Sage Foundation.

LaVeist, Thomas A. 1992. "The political empowerment and health status of African-Americans: Mapping a new territory." *American Journal of Sociology* 97 (January):1080–95.

Lee, Jaekyung. 2006. *Tracking Achievement Gaps and Assessing the Impact of NCLB on the Gaps: An In-depth Look into National and State Reading and Math Outcome Trends*. Cambridge, MA: The Civil Rights Project at Harvard University. Available from http://www.civilrightsproject.ucla.edu/research/esea/nclb_naep_lee.pdf, accessed January 28, 2009.

Lee, Jennifer, and Frank D. Bean. 2004. "America's changing color lines: Immigration, race/ethnicity, and multiracial identification." *Annual Review of Sociology* 30:221–42.

Leibowitz, Fran. 1997. "Fran Leibowitz on race." *Vanity Fair*, October, 220–23.

Lein, Laura, and Deanna T. Schexnayder. 2007. *Life After Welfare: Reform and the Persistence of Poverty*. Austin: University of Texas Press.

Lemann, Nicholas. 1999. *The Big Test: The Secret History of the American Meritocracy*. New York: Farrar, Strauss, and Giroux.

Lerner, Gerda. 1976. "Placing women in history: A 1975 perspective." In *Liberating Women's History: Theoretical and Critical Essays*, ed. Bernice Caroll. Urbana: University of Illinois Press.

Levine, Samantha. 2007. "Taking action to admit." *U.S. News and World Report*, June 4.

Lewis, Tyler. 2006. "Race categories to change on 2010 census form." Leadership Conference on Civil Rights/Leadership Conference on Civil Rights Education Fund. Available from http://www.civilrights.org/library/features/race-categories-to-change-on-2010-census-form.html, accessed February 3, 2009.

Lorber, Judith. 1994. *Paradoxes of Gender*. New Haven: Yale University Press.

Lorde, Audre. 1995. "Age, race, class, and sex: Women redefining difference." In *Words of Fire: An Anthology of African-American Feminist Thought*, ed. Beverly Guy-Sheftall. New York: New Press.

Lovell, Vicky, Heidi Hartman, and Claudia Williams. 2008. *Women at Greater Risk of Economic Insecurity: A Gender Analysis of the Rockefeller Foundation's American Worker Survey*. Washington, D.C.: Institute for Women's Policy Research.

Lubiano, Wahneema. 1992. "Black ladies, welfare queens, and state minstrels: Ideological war by narrative means." In *Race-ing Justice, En-gendering Power: Essays on Anita Hill, Clarence Thomas and the Construction of Social Identity,* ed. Toni Morrison. New York: Pantheon Books.

Lucal, Betsy. 1994. "Class stratification in introductory textbooks: Relational or distributional models?" *Teaching Sociology* 22 (April):139–50.

Lucas, Samuel R., and Mark Berends. 2002. "Sociodemographic diversity, correlated achievement, and de facto tracking." *Sociology of Education* 75(4):328–48.

Ma, J., R.S. Stafford, I.M. Cockburn, and S.N. Finkelstein. 2003. "A statistical analysis of the magnitude and composition of drug promotion in the United States in 1998." *Clinical Therapeutics* 25 (5):1503–17.

Maccoby, Eleanor. 1988. "Gender as a social category." *Developmental Psychology* 24:755–65.

———. 2000. "Perspectives on gender development." *International Journal of Behavioral Development* 24(4):398–406.

MacDorman, Marian F., and T. J. Mathews. 2008. "Recent trends in infant mortality in the United States." Data Brief. *National Center for Health Statistics* 9 (October). Available from http://http://www.cdc.gov/nchs/data/databriefs/db09.htm, accessed January 2, 2009.

Manalansan, Martin IV. 1995. "In the shadows of Stonewall: Examining gay transnational politics and the diasporic dilemma." *Gay and Lesbian Quarterly* 2:425–38.

Margolis, Eric, and Mary Romero. 1998. "'The department is very male, very white, very old, and very conservative': The functioning of the hidden curriculum in graduate sociology departments." *Harvard Educational Review* 68(1):1–32.

Marshall, Susan. 1998. "Rattle on the right: Bridge labor in antifeminist organizations." In *No Middle Ground: Women and Radical Protest,* ed. Kathleen Blee. New York: New York University Press.

Massey, Douglas, and Nancy Denton. 1993. *American Apartheid: Segregation and the Making of the Underclass.* Cambridge: Harvard University Press.

Mayer, Susan E. 2001. "How economic segregation affects children's educational attainment." *Working Paper Series 01.18.* Chicago: Harris School of Public Policy, University of Chicago. Available from http://harrisschool.uchicago.edu/About/publications/working-papers/pdf/wp_01_18.pdf, accessed January 26, 2009.

McCall, Leslie. 2005. "The complexity of intersectionality." *Signs: A Journal of Women in Culture and Society* 30(3):1771–1800.

McDermott, Monica, and Frank L. Samson. 2005. "White racial identity in the United States." *Annual Review of Sociology* 31:245–61.

McGuire, Gail M., and Barbara Reskin. 1993. "Authority hierarchies at work: The impacts of race and sex." *Gender and Society* 7:487–506.

McIntire, Mike. 2009. "Bailout is a windfall to banks, if not to borrowers." *New York Times,* January 18.

McIntosh, Peggy. 1998. "White privilege and male privilege: A personal account of coming to see correspondences through work in women's studies." In *Race, Class, and Gender: An Anthology,* Margaret Andersen and Patricia Hill Collins, 3rd ed. Belmont, CA: Wadsworth.

McNamee, Stephen J., and Robert K. Miller, Jr. 2004. *The Meritocracy Myth.* New York: Rowman and Littlefield.

McNeil, Michele. 2008. "Single-sex schooling gets new showcase." *Education Week* 27 (36):20–2.

Media Matters for America. 2009. Available from http://mediamatters.org/items/print-able/200810290010, accessed January 9, 2009.

Meier, Deborah and George Wood, eds. 2004. *Many Children Left Behind*. Boston, MA: Beacon.

Meier, Kenneth J., Joseph Stewart, Jr., and Robert England. 1989. *Race, Class, and Education: The Politics of Second-Generation Discrimination*. Madison: University of Wisconsin Press.

Messner, Michael. 1992. *Power at Play. Sports and the Problem of Masculinity*. Boston: Beacon.

———. 2002. *Taking the Field: Women, Men, and Sports*. Minneapolis: University of Minnesota Press.

———. 2007. *Out of Play: Critical Essays on Gender and Sport*. Albany: State University of New York Press.

Metz, Mary Haywood. 1986. *Different by Design: The Context and Character of Three Magnet Schools*. New York: Routledge & Kegan Paul.

Mezey, Nancy. 2008. *New Choices, New Families: How Lesbians Decide About Motherhood*. Baltimore: Johns Hopkins University Press.

Millbank, Jenni. 2008. "Unlikely fissures and uneasy resonances: Lesbian co-mothers, surrogate parenthood and fathers' rights." *Feminist Legal Studies* 16 (2):141–67.

Mink, Gwendolyn. 2001. "Violating women: Rights in the welfare police state." *Annals of the American Academy of Political and Social Science* 577 (1):79–93.

Minnich, Elizabeth Kamarck, Jean O'Barr, and Rachel Rosenfeld, eds. 1988. *Reconstructing the Academy: Women's Education and Women's Studies*. Chicago: University of Chicago Press.

Mishel, Lawrence, and Jared Bernstein, eds. 1994. *The State of Working America 1994–95*. Economic Policy Institute Series, 1994–1995. Armonk, NY: M. E. Sharpe.

Mishel, Lawrence, Jared Bernstein, and Sylvia Allegretto. 2007. *The State of Working America 2006/2007*. Ithaca, NY: ILR Press.

Moore, Megan, Mardie Townsend, and John Oldroyd. 2006. "Linking human and ecosystem health: The benefits of community involvement in conservation groups." *Eco Health*, 3 (4):255–61.

Morgen, Sandra, and Ann Bookman. 1988. "Rethinking women and politics: An introductory essay." In *Women and the Politics of Empowerment*, eds. Sandra Morgen and Ann Bookman. Philadelphia: Temple University Press.

Morris, Edward W. 2005. "'Tuck in that shirt!' Race, class, gender, and discipline in an urban school." *Sociological Perspectives* 48(1):25–48.

Mullings, Leith. 1994. "Images, ideology, and women of color." In *Women of Color in U.S. Society*, ed. Maxine Baca Zinn and Bonnie Thornton Dill. Philadelphia: Temple University Press.

Mullings, Leith, and Alaka Wali. 2001. *Stress and Resilience: The Social Context of Reproduction in Central Harlem*. New York: Kluwer/Plenum.

Naples, Nancy. 1998. *Community Activism and Feminist Politics: Organizing Across Race, Class and Gender*. New York: Routledge.

National Center for Education Statistics. 2007. *Digest of Education Statistics: 2007 Tables and Figures*. U.S. Department of Education. Available from http://nces.ed.gov/programs/digest/d07/tables/dt07_105.asp, accessed April 3, 2009.

National Center for Health Statistics. *Health, United States, 2007 with Chartbook on Trends in the Health of Americans*. Hyattsville, MD: U.S. Government Printing Office. Available from http://http://www.cdc.gov/nchs/hus.htm, accessed January 2, 2009.

National Center for Public Policy and Higher Education. 2008. *Measuring up 2008: The National Report Card on Higher Education*. San Jose, CA: Available from www.higher-education.org. accessed April 18, 2009.

National Research Council. 1993. *National Science Education Standards Working Papers: An Enhanced Sampler (Progress Report)*. National Committee on Science Education Standards and Assessments. Washington, DC: National Research Council: February and July.

———. 1996. *National Science Education Standards*. Washington, DC: National Academy Press.

Navarette, Ruben, Jr. 1997. "A darker shade of crimson: Odyssey of a Harvard Chicano." In *Race, Class, and Gender in a Diverse Society*. Diana Kendall, ed. Boston: Allyn and Bacon.

National Science Foundation. 2007. *Women, Minorities, and Persons with Disabilities in Science and Engineering*. Division of Science Resources Statistics, Arlington, VA.

——— 2009. *ADVANCE: Increasing the Participation and Advancement of Women in Academic Science and Engineering Careers (ADVANCE)*. Available from http://www.nsf.gov/pubs/2007/nsf07582/nsf07582.htm, accessed January 31, 2009.

National Women's Law Center. 2007. *When Girls Don't Graduate We All Fail: A Call to Improve High School Graduation Rates for Girls*. Available from http://www.nwlc.org/details.cfm?id=3367&section=education, accessed December 30, 2008.

Neill, Monti. 2004. "Leaving no child behind: Overhauling NCLB." In Deborah Meier and George Wood, eds. 2004. *Many Children Left Behind*. Boston, MA: Beacon.

Newman, Katherine S. 1993. *Declining Fortunes: The Withering of the American Dream*. New York: Basic Books.

Nicholson, Barbara. 2003. "Beyond Jefferson: The rhetoric of meritocracy and the funding of public education." *Educational Foundations* 17 (1):21–40.

Nobles, Melissa. 2000. *Shades of Citizenship: Race and the Census in Modern Politics*. Palo Alto, CA: Stanford University Press.

Oakes, Jeannie. 1985. *Keeping Track: How Schools Structure Inequality*. New Haven: Yale University Press.

Oakes, Jeannie, and Amy Stuart Wells. 1998. "Detracking for high student achievement." *Educational Leadership* 55(6): 38–41.

Oakes, Jeannie, Amy Stuart Wells, Makeba Jones, and Amanda Datnow. 1997. "Detracking: The social construction of ability, cultural politics, and resistance to reform." *Teachers College Record* 98(3):482–510.

Obama, Barack. 1995. *Dreams from My Father: A Story of Race and Inheritance*. New York: Times Books.

——— 2006. *The Audacity of Hope*. New York: Three Rivers Press.

——— 2008. "A more perfect union." *The Black Scholar* 38(1):17–23.

Office of the Under Secretary of Defense. 1998. "Review of the effectiveness of the application and enforcement of the Department's policy on homosexual conduct in the military." Washington, DC: Available online from http://www.defenselink.mil/pubs/rpt040798.html, accessed March 19, 2000.

O'Hare, William P. 1992. "America's minorities: The demographics of diversity." *Population Bulletin* 47(4): S2(44).

Oliver, Melvin, and Thomas Shapiro. 1995. *Black Wealth/White Wealth: A New Perspective on Racial Inequality*. New York: Routledge.

Omi, Michael, and Howard Winant. 1994. *Racial Formation in the United States from the 1960s to the 1990s*. New York: Routledge.

Orfield, Gary, and Chungmei Lee. 2007. *Historic Reversals, Accelerating Resegregation, and the Need for New Integration Strategies.* Cambridge, MA: The Civil Rights Project at Harvard University. Available from http://www.civilrightsproject.ucla.edu, accessed April 18, 2009.

Ortiz, Flora Ida. 1988. "Hispanic-American children's experiences in classrooms. A comparison between Hispanic and non-Hispanic children." In *Class, Race, and Gender in American Education.* Lois Weis, ed. Albany. State University of New York Press.

Ortiz, Vilma. 1994. "Women of color: A demographic overview." In *Women of Color in U.S. Society,* eds. Maxine Baca Zinn and Bonnie Thornton Dill. Philadelphia: Temple University Press.

Ostrander, Susan. 1984. *Women of the Upper Class.* Philadelphia: Temple University Press.

Oxfam Australia. 2008. *Nike Watch.* Available from www.oxfam.org.au/campaigns/labour-rights/nikewatch, accessed January 4, 2009.

Padilla, Amado M., and Rosemary Gonzalez. 2001. "Academic performance of immigrant and U.S.-born Mexican heritage students: Effects of schooling in Mexico and bilingual/ English language instruction." *American Educational Research Journal* 38(3): 727–42.

Page, Reba. 1991. *Lower-Track Classrooms: A Curricula and Cultural Perspective.* New York: Teachers College Press, Columbia University.

Panagopoulos, Costas, and Pete L. Francia. 2008 "The polls—trends: Labor unions in the United States." *Public Opinion Quarterly* 72 (1) 134–59.

Pascoe, C. J. 2007. *Dude, You're a Fag: Masculinity and Sexuality in High School.* Berkeley: University of California Press.

Patillo, Mary. 2008. "Race, class and neighborhoods." In *Social Class: How Does It Work?* Eds. Annette Lareau and Dalton Conley. New York: Russell Sage Foundation.

Pegula, Stephen M. 2004. "An analysis of workplace suicides, 1992–2001." Bureau of Labor Statistics. U.S. Department of Labor. Available from http://www.bls.gov/opub/cws/sh20040126ar01pl.htm, accessed January 10, 2009.

Perlman, Joel. 2005. *Italians Then, Mexicans Now: Imimigrant Origins and Second-Generation Progress 1890–2000.* New York: Russell Sage Foundation.

Persell, Caroline. 1977. *Education and Inequality: A Theoretical and Empirical Synthesis.* New York: Free Press.

Peterson, Bob. 2008. "Whitewashing the past: A proposal for a national campaign to rethink textbooks." *Rethinking Schools,* 23 (1):34–37.

Phillips, Lynn, and Michelle Fine. 1992. "What's 'left' in sexuality education?" In *Sexuality and the Curriculum: The Politics and Practices of Sexuality Education,* ed. James Sears. New York: Teachers College Press, Columbia University.

Phyllis Schlafly Report. 1993. "NEA steps up anti-parent policies." September.

Pipher, Mary. 1994. *Reviving Ophelia: Saving the Selves of Adolescent Girls.* New York: Putnam.

Planty, Michael, William Hussar, Thomas Snyder, Stephen Provasnik, Grace Kena, Rachel Dinkes, Angelina KewelRamani, and Jana Kemp. 2008. *The Condition of Education.* Washington, DC: National Center for Education Statistics. Available from http://nces.ed.gov/pubs2008/2008031.pdf, accessed January 28, 2009.

Poirier, Jeffrey M., Karen B. Francis, Sylvia K. Fisher, Kristin Williams-Washington, Tawara D. Goode, and Vivian H. Jackson. 2008. *Practice Brief 1: Providing Services and Supports for Youth Who Are Lesbian, Gay, Bisexual, Transgender, Questioning, Intersex, or Two-Spirit.* Washington, DC: National Center for Cultural Competence, Georgetown University Center for Child and Human Development. Available from http://www11.georgetown.edu/research/gucchd/NCCC/documents/lgbtqi2s.pdf, accessed April 18, 2009.

Polakow, Valerie. 1993. *Lives on the Edge: Single Mothers and Their Children in the Other America.* Chicago: University of Chicago Press.

Pollock, Mica. 2004. "Race bending: "Mixed" youth practicing strategic racialization in California." *Anthropology and Education Quarterly* 351(1):30–52.

Poulantzas, Nicos. 1974. *Classes in Contemporary Capitalism*. London: New Left Books.

Powell, John A., Hasan Kwame Jeffries, Daniel W. Newhart, and Eric Stiens. 2006. "Towards a transformative view of race: The crisis and opportunity in Katrina." In *There Is No Such Thing As a Natural Disaster*, eds. Chester Hartman and Gregory D. Squires. New York: Routledge.

Preves, Sharon E. 2009. "Intersex narratives: Gender, medicine, and identity." In *Sex, Gender, and Sexuality*, ed. Abby L. Ferber, Dimberly Holcomb, and Tre Wentling. New York: Oxford University Press.

Reskin, Barbara F. 1998. *The Realities of Affirmative Action in Employment*. Washington, DC: American Sociological Association.

Reyhner, J., and J. Eder. 2004. *American Indian Education: A History*. Norman, OK: University of Oklahoma Press.

Rich, Adrienne. 1993. "Compulsory heterosexuality and lesbian existence." In *The Lesbian and Gay Studies Reader*, ed. Henry Abelove, Michèle Aina Barale, and David M. Halperin. New York: Routledge.

Roberts, Sam. 1995. *Who We Are: A Portrait of America Based on the Latest U.S. Census*. Rev. ed. New York: Times Books.

Robinson, Bill. 1999. "S.C. house endorses First Steps: Hodges, lawmakers share power in plan." *The State* (Columbia, S.C.), April 29.

Robnett, Belinda. 1997. *How Long? How Long? African–American Women in the Struggle for Civil Rights*. New York: Oxford University Press.

Root, Maria P. 1992. *Racially Mixed People in America*. Newbury Park, CA: Sage.

Rosen, James. 2009. "Sanford bypass in bill: Clyburn addition to stimulus bill is aimed at ensuring S.C. gets its share." *The State* (Columbia, S.C.), January 30.

Rothstein, Richard. 2002. "LESSONS: Schools, accountability and a sheaf of fuzzy math," *New York Times*, April 10. Available from http://query.nytimes.com/gst/fullpage.html?res=9D01E1D9113DF933A25757C0A9649C8B63&scp=1&sq=Richard%20Rothstein%20april%2010,%202002&ast=cse, accessed February 1, 2009.

Sacks, Peter. 2007. *Tearing Down the Gates: Confronting the Class Divide in American Education*. Berkeley: University of California Press.

Saenz, Rogelio, Karen M. Douglas, David G. Embrick, and Gideon Sjoberg. 2007. "Pathways to downward mobility: The impact of schools, welfare, and prisons on people of color." In *Handbook of the Sociology of Racial and Ethnic Relations*, eds. Hernan Vera and Joe R. Feagin. New York: Springer Science and Business Media, LLC.

Saltman, Kenneth J. 2007. "Schooling in disaster capitalism: How the political right is using disaster to privatize public schooling." *Teacher Education Quarterly* 34(2): 131–156.

Schemo, Diana Jean. 2006a. "Republicans propose national school voucher program." *New York Times*, July 19.

——— 2006b. "More small women's colleges opening doors to men." *New York Times*, September 21.

Schneider, Barbara L., and Venessa A. Keesler. 2007. "School reform 2007: Transforming education into a scientific enterprise." *Annual Review of Sociology* 33:197–217.

Schultz, Brian. 2008. *Spectacular Things Happen Along the Way: Lessons from an Urban Classroom*. New York: Teachers College Press, Columbia University.

Schuster, Marilyn, and Susan Van Dyne. 1984. "Placing women in the liberal arts: Stages of curriculum transformation." *Harvard Educational Review* 54(4):413–28.

Sears, James, ed. 1992. *Sexuality and the Curriculum: The Politics and Practices of Sexuality Education*. New York: Teachers College Press, Columbia University.

Seccombe, Karen, and Kim A. Hoffman. 2007. *Just Don't Get Sick: Access to Health Care in the Aftermath of Welfare Reform*. New Brunswick, NJ: Rutgers University Press.

Sellers, R. M., M.A. Smith, N. J. Shelton, S. J. Rowley, and T. M. Chavous. 1998. "Multidimensional model of racial identity: A reconceptualization of African American racial identity." *Personality and Social Psychology Review* 2 (1):18–39.

Sered, Susan Starr, and Rushika Fernandopulle. 2007. *Uninsured in America: Life and Death in the Land of Opportunity*. Berkeley, CA: University of California Press.

Severson, Kim. 2005. "Harlem school introduces children to Swiss Chard." *The New York Times* September 9.

Smith, Lillian. 1949. *Killers of the Dream*. New York: Norton.

Sobel, Stacey L., Kathi S. Westcott, Michelle M. Benecke, and C. Dixon Osburn (with Jeffrey M. Cleghorn). 2000. "Conduct unbecoming: Sixth annual report on 'don't ask, don't tell, don't pursue.'" Washington, DC: Servicemembers Legal Defense Network. Available from http://www.sldn.org/reports/sixth.htm, accessed March 19, 2000.

Solinger, Rickie. 1992. *Wake up Little Susie: Single Pregnancy and Race Before Roe v. Wade*. New York: Routledge.

———. 1998. "Poisonous Choice." In *Bad Mothers: The Politics of Blame in Twentieth-Century America*, ed. Molly Ladd-Taylor and Lauri Umansky. New York: New York University Press.

Sorokin, Pitirim. 1927. *Social Mobility*. New York: Harper.

Spade, Joan, Lynn Columba, and Beth Vanfossen. 1997. "Tracking in mathematics and science: Courses and course-selection procedures." *Sociology of Education* 70 (April):108–27.

Spector, Mike. 2009. "Bear market for charities: A Harlem education project that won big corporate backing now faces cutbacks as donors close their wallets." *Wall Street Journal*, January 24.

Spickard, Paul R. 1992. "The illogic of American racial categories." In *Racially Mixed People in America*, ed. Maria Root. Newbury Park, CA: Sage.

Stewart, Abigail, and Christa McDermott. 2004. "Gender in psychology." *Annual Review of Psychology* 55:519–44.

Streitmatter, Janice. 1999. *For Girls Only: Making the Case for Single-Sex Schooling*. Albany: State University of New York Press.

Stroud, Joseph. 1999a. "Education policy draws fire: Hodges, GOP split over budget plans." *The State* (Columbia, SC), February 28.

———. 1999b. "First Steps proposal 'welfare' in disguise, Republicans charge." *The State* (Columbia, SC), March 3.

Sturm, Susan, and Lani Guinier. 1996. "The future of affirmative action: Reclaiming the innovative ideal." *California Law Review* 84(4): 953–1036.

Takagi, Dana. 1993. *The Retreat from Race: Asian-American Admissions and Racial Politics*. New Brunswick, NJ: Rutgers University Press.

Tavris, Carol. 1992. *The Mismeasure of Woman*. New York: Touchstone.

Terkel, Studs. 1992. *Race: How Blacks and Whites Think and Feel about the American Obsession*. New York: New Press.

Thompson-Miller, Ruth, and Joe R. Feagin. 2007. "The reality and impact of legal segregation in the United States." In *Handbook of the Sociology of Racial and Ethnic Relations*, eds. Hernan Vera and Joe R. Feagin. New York: Springer Science and Business Media, LLC.

Thorne, Barrie. 1993. *Gender Play: Girls and Boys in School*. New Brunswick, NJ: Rutgers University Press.

Tienda, Marta, and Sunny Niu. 2004. "Texas' 10-percent plan: The truth behind the numbers." *Chronicle of Higher Education*, January 23.

Timmer, Doug, Stanley Eitzen, and Kathryn Talley. 1994. *Paths to Homelessness: Extreme Poverty and the Urban Housing Crisis*. Boulder, CO: Westview Press.

Twine, France Winddance. 1998. *Racism in a Racial Democracy: The Maintenance of White Supremacy in Brazil*. New Brunswick, NJ: Rutgers University Press.

Tyack, David, and Larry Cuban. 1995. *Tinkering Toward Utopia: A Century of Public School Reform*. Cambridge: Harvard University Press.

Tyson, Laura D'Andrea. 2005. "Land of unequal opportunity: New Orleans graphically showed what the Census report could not." *Business Week*, September 26. Available from http://www.businessweek.com/magazine/content/05_39/b3952139.htm, accessed February 2, 2009.

U.S. Bureau of Labor Statistics. 2008a. *Employment and Earnings*, 55(12). Washington, DC: U.S. Government Printing Office. Available from http://www.bls.gov/opub/ee/empearn200812.pdf, accessed January 18, 2009.

———. 2008b. *Economic News Release: Union Members Summary*. Available from http://www.bls.gov/news.release/union2.nr0.htm, accessed January 12, 2009.

———. 2008c. *Economic News Release: Employment Situation Summary*. Available online from http://www.bls.gov/news.release/empsit.nr0.htm, accessed January 22, 2009.

———. 1999. *Statistical Abstract of the United States*. 120th ed. Washington, DC. U.S. Government Printing Office. Available from http://www.census.gov/prod/2004pubs/censr-17.pdf, accessed January 15, 2009.

———. 2001. *Profile of the Foreign Born Population in the United States: 2000*. Available from http://www.census.gov/prod/2002pubs/p23-206.pdf, accessed January 15, 2009.

———. *Married-Couple and Unmarried-Partner Households: 2000*. Available from http://www.census.gov/prod/2003pubs/censr-5.pdf, accessed on February 2, 2009.

———. *We the People: Hispanics in the United States*. Available from http://www.census.gov/prod/2004pubs/censr-18.pdf, accessed January 15, 2009.

———. *We the People: Asians in the United States*. Available from http://www.census.gov/prod/2004pubs/censr-17.pdf, accessed January 15, 2009.

———. 2008a. *Current Population Survey, Annual Social and Economic Supplement*. Available from http://www.census.gov/hhes/www/cpstc/cps_table_creator.html, accessed January 26, 2009.

———. 2008b. *Historical Income Tables-People*. Available from http://www.census.gov/hhes/www/income/histinc/p24.html, accessed, January 2, 2009.

———. 2008c. *Historical Income Tables-People*. Available from http://www.census.gov/hhes/www/income/histinc/p38AR.html, accessed, January 2, 2009.

———. 2008d. "Labor force, employment, and earnings." *Statistical Abstract of the United States*. Available from http://www.census.gov/prod/2007pubs/08abstract/labor.pdf accessed April 3, 2009.

———. 2008e. *National Population Projections: Table 6. Percent of the Projected Population by Race and Hispanic Origin for the United States: 2010 to 2050*. Available from http://www.census.gov/population/www/projections/summarytables.html, accessed January 7, 2009.

———. 2009. *Statistical Abstract of the United States: 2009*. Available from www.census.gov/prod/2008pubs/09statab/pop.pdf, accessed January 2, 2009.

U.S. Department of Education. 1994a. "Distribution of college-bound senior and average verbal and mathematics SAT scores by selected characteristics." In *The Condition of Education*. Washington, DC: U. S. Government Printing Office: Table 19–4:227.

——— . 1994b. "Percent of high school seniors who plan to go to college after graduation by student characteristics: 1982 and 1992." *Digest of Education Statistics*. Washington, DC: National Center for Educational Statistics: Table 144:138.

U.S. Department of Labor. 2007. *Employment Status of Women and Men in 2007*. Available from http://www.dol.gov/wb/factsheets/Qf-ESWM07.htm, accessed January 26, 2009.

Valdes, Guadalupe. 1996. *Con Respeto: Bridging the Distances Between Culturally Diverse Families and Schools: An Ethnographic Portrait*. New York: Teachers College Press, Columbia University.

Van Ausdale, Debra, and Joe Feagin. 1996. "Using racial and ethnic concepts: The critical case of very young children." *American Sociological Review* 61(October):779–93

Van den Berg, Axel. 1993. "Creeping embourgeoisement? Some comments on the Marxist discovery of the new middle class." In *Research in Social Stratification and Mobility*, 12, eds. Robert Althauser and Michael Wallace. Greenwich, CT: JAI Press.

Van de Werfhorst, Herman G., and Robert Andersen. 2005. "Social background, credential inflation and educational strategies." *Acta Sociologica* 48 (4):321–40.

Vanneman, Reeve, and Lynn Weber Cannon. 1987. *The American Perception of Class*. Philadelphia: Temple University Press.

Weber, Lynn. 1990. "Fostering positive race, class, and gender dynamics in the classroom." *Women's Studies Quarterly* 18 (Spring/Summer, 1990):126–134.

Weber, Lynn, Tina Hancock, and Elizabeth Higginbotham. 1997. "Women, power, and mental Health." In *Women's Health: Complexities and Differences*, ed. Sheryl Ruzek, Virginia Olesen, and Adele Clark. Columbus: Ohio State University Press.

Weber, Lynn. 2001. *Understanding Race, Class, Gender, and Sexuality: A Conceptual Framework*. New York: McGraw-Hill.

——— . 2005. "Classroom discussion guidelines: Promoting understanding across race, class, gender, and sexuality." In *Teaching Sociological Concepts and the Sociology of Gender*, Marybeth C. Stalp and Julie Childers, eds. 2nd ed. Washington, DC: American Sociological Association Teaching Resources Center.

Weber, Lynn, and Elizabeth Fore. 2007. "Race, ethnicity, and health: An intersectional perspective." In *Handbook of the Sociology of Racial and Ethnic Relations*, ed. Hernan Vera and Joe R. Feagin. New York: Springer Science and Business Media, LLC.

Weber, Lynn, and Elizabeth Higginbotham. 1992. "Moving up with kin and community: Upward social mobility for black and white women," *Gender Society* 6 (September):416–40.

Websdale, Neil. 2001. *Policing the Poor: From Slave Plantation to Public Housing*. Boston: Northeastern University Press.

Weil, Elizabeth. 2008. "Teaching boys and girls separately." *New York Times Magazine*, March 2.

Wells, Amy Stuart, Jennifer Jellison Holme, Anita Tijerina Revilla, and Awo Korantemaa Atanda. 2004. "How society failed school desegregation policy: Looking past the schools to understand them." *Review of Research in Education* 28:47–99.

West, Candace, and Sarah Fenstermaker. 1995. "Doing difference." *Gender Society* 9(1):8–37.

Western, Mark, and Erik Olin Wright. 1994. "The permeability of class boundaries to intergenerational mobility among men in the United States, Canada, Norway, Sweden." *American Sociological Review* 59(August):606–29.

Wilkinson, John. 2007. "Fair Trade: Dynamics and Dilemmas of a Market Oriented Global Social Movement." *Journal of Consumer Policy* 30 (3): 219–39.

Wilke, Mike, and Michael Applebaum. 2001. "Peering out of the closet." *Brandweek* 42 (41): 26–32.

Winant, Howard. 2000. "Race and race theory." *Annual Review of Sociology* 26: 169–85.

———. 2001. *The World is a Ghetto: Race and Democracy Since World War II.* New York: Basic Books.

Woliver, Laura. 2002. *The Political Geographies of Pregnancy.* Urbana: University of Illinois Press.

Women's Sports Foundation. 2008. *2008 Statistics-Gender Equity in High School and College Athletics: Most Recent Participation and Budget Statistics.* Available from http://www. womenssportsfoundation.org/Content/Articles/Issues/General/123/2008-Statistics-- Gender-Equity-in-High-School-and-College-Athletics-Most-Recent-Participation– Budge.aspx, accessed April 4, 2009.

Wright, Erik Olin. 1989. *The Debate on Classes.* New York: Verso.

———. 1997. *Class Counts: Comparative Studies in Class Analysis.* New York: Cambridge University Press.

———. 2008. "Logics of class analysis." In *Social Class: How Does it Work?* Eds. Annette Lareau and Dalton Conley. New York: Russell Sage Foundation.

Wrigley, Julia, ed. 1992. *Education and Gender Equality.* Washington, DC: Falmer Press.

Wyche, Karen Fraser, and Sherryl Browne Graves. 1992. "Minority women in academia: Access and barriers to professional participation." *Psychology of Women Quarterly* 16(4):429–37.

Wyner, Joshua S., John M. Bridgeland, and John J. Diiulio, Jr. 2007. *Achievement trap: How America Is Failing Millions of High-Achieving Students from Lower-Income Families.* Washington, DC: Jack Kent Cooke Foundation. Available from http://www.jkcf.org/ news-knowledge/publications, accessed December 30, 2008.

Yonezawa, Susan, Amy Stuart Wells, and Irene Serna. 2002. "Choosing tracks: 'Freedom of Choice' in detracking schools." *American Educational Research Journal* 39 (1): 37–67.

Young, Susan. 1999. "School funding fails to close gap." *Bangor Daily News.* 20 February.

Zajac, Brian, ed. 2008. "Global high performers: Household and personal products." *Forbes,* April 2. Available from http://www.forbes.com/2008/04/02/global-high-perform- ers-biz-2000global08-cz_bj_0402highperformers_slide_16.html?thisSpeed=30000, accessed January 4, 2009.

Zuberi, Tukufu. 2001. *Thicker than Blood: An Essay on How Racial Statistics Lie.* Minneapo- lis: University of Minnesota Press.]

Permissions Acknowledgments

CHAPTER 2

Figure 2.5: "Share of U.S. median income received by low- and high-income OECD households;" Figure 2.7 "Distribution of wealth by wealth class, 1983-2004." Reprinted from Lawrence Mishel, Jared Bernstein and Sylvia Allegretto, *The State of Working America, 2006-2007*, Copyright © 2007 by Cornell University. Used by permission of the publisher, Cornell University Press.

CHAPTER 3

Studs Terkel, except from "Margaret Welch," *Race: How Blacks and Whites Think and Feel About the American Obsession*, Copyright © 1992. Reprinted by permission of The New Press. www.thenewpress.com.

CASE STUDY 1

Gloria Steinem, "Women are never front-runners," From *The New York Times*, January 8 © 2008. Reprinted by permission of The New York Times. All rights reserved www.nytimes.com.
Alice Walker, "An open letter to Barack Obama" First published by TheRoot.com, Copyright © 2008 by Alice Walker. Reprinted by permission of The Wendy Weil Agency, Inc.

CASE STUDY 2

"The Valenzuela Family," From Chavez, *Shadowed Lives*, 2E © 1998 Wadsworth, a part of Cengage Learning, Inc. Reproduced by permission, www.cengage.com/permissions.

CASE STUDY 4

Michael Kimmel, "Getting off on Feminism," *Men's Lives*, © Reproduced by permission of Pearson Education, Inc.

Indexes

Name Index

Subject Index